D1792321

To Smitha & Sailesh

with God's

Blessings

on her birthday

today

18-7-2015

from Amma (Radha Ramakrishnan)

Praise for My questions and God's Answers

Satya Karla's beautiful book, "My Questions and God's Answers," thrilled my very being as I read her enlighten text.

— Janet Bray Attwood, New York Times Bestseller Author
"The Passion Test-The Effortless Path to Living your life purpose"

Ever since I was a teenager, I wanted to learn about my religion and culture, but couldn't find the right sources of knowledge. I bought several translations of the Gita, but could not understand or relate to these. They were either too esoteric or biased. What Satya has produced is a gem. The book "My questions and God's Answer's" preserves the original concepts and presents these in a way that anyone can understand.

— Vivek Wadhwa, Director of Research, Pratt School of Engineering, Duke University and Senior Research Associate, Harvard Law School

I had the privilege to go through "*My questions and God's Answers*" work on Bhagvad Gita, written by Satya Kalra. Though several commentaries on Gita are available but the work by Satya has impressed me the most, because it is for the first time someone has taken the character of Arjuna as oneself and has put the questions on ones behalf. In no doubt Krishna is the Lord Himself, so the answers have come from God within oneself. The work is successful in exposing the spirit of Gita, "Absolute devotion to the cause oneself without any thought of personal reward or appreciation." I am sure the work will enlighten the life of many seekers in the modern world and will bring physical, mental and spiritual love, peace and bliss.

— Shankaracharyaji Swami Divyanand Teerthji

"Satya Kalra's annotations of the verses of the Bhagavad-gita, in an easy-to-understand question and answer form, are simple expositions of her realizations and experiences in living out the message of Bhagavad Gita. She has brilliantly threaded the entire exposition around the personality of limitlessly brilliant and loving Lord Krishna Himself without merely impersonally extracting the secret message of peace and eternal happiness by leaving behind the very source, the centerpin, of Gita. She has succeeded in churning out from Gita a blueprint, to a great extent practical, for a peaceful, happy and united global community through self-transformation. Satya Kalra has earned the valuable divine credit of being an instrument in this by her intelligent work of devotion to Godhead, Krishna. May Lord Krishna open higher and higher divine doors of secrets of existence to her."

— Madhu Pandit Dasa, Chairman, The Akshaya Patra Foundation and President, ISKCON-Bangalore

Satya Karla's book "My questions and God's Answer's" on the Gita demonstrates solid scholarship, with fresh translations and apparent well-honed attention to the Sanskrit originals. Her graphics and colors make it an attractive work, which illuminates Krishna's message and captivates the reader.

— Hal W. French, Distinguished Professor (Emeritus), Dept. of Religious Studies, University of South Carolina

This book, "*My questions and God's Answers*" on Bhagwad Gita is an attempt from a novice to an ultimate devotee of the Lord who understood the problems of today's man-kind and attempted to find answers. Satya Kalra has presented her work in an easily understood and interesting format with colorful graphics. A very deep scripture has been presented in a very lucid form. Satya has given a superb gift to fellow seekers of modern times. A great work to seek the "Path of Anandam (bliss)" and to understand "Self". Congratulations!

— B.L. Joshi, Senior Vice President, Gita Dham Trust,
Vice Chairman, Gita Ashram of America

Satya Karla's book, "*My questions and God's Answers*" highlights the significance and relevance of the teachings of the Bhagavad Gita to the problems of life. The way she has framed vital questions and her lucid translations of the verses of the Gita are very helpful to the reader. Her comments on and explanations of Gita's teachings are not theoretical or speculative; they have come from her heart, from her spiritual experience. She has emphasized that suffering is the result of forgetting one's spiritual nature and that happiness consists in Self/God-Realization. She desires to share her experience with others and work for human good. Accordingly, the wisdom of the Gita is presented in simple and clear terms as practical guidance for a happy, balanced and peaceful life.

— K.L. Seshagiri Rao, Professor (Emeritus), Department of Religious Studies, University of Virginia, and Chief Editor of the Encyclopedia of Hinduism project

Wow! What a simple and practical approach Satya Kalra has taken to present the secular teachings of Gita in her book, 'My questions and God's Answers, Guide to Eternal happiness, Peace, Anandam.' Reading this spiritual guide, gave me the complete picture of secular teachings and philosophy of the Gita where I had bits and pieces before. I feel the hunger of my soul has been satiated. The book clarifies the basic doubts and questions of life. I would recommend the book to everyone, who wants to live happily, peacefully and enjoy their life the fullest, specially the young, modern and busy people of today.

— Romesh K. Japra, M.D., Chairman, F.I.A.,
Chairman, Hindu Temple, Fremont California,
CEO/President, India Post, USA

Satya Kalra explains the essence of Gita in a logical and simple fashion in her book "My questions and God's Answers". There have been several scholarly works done on Gita. However, the real value of Gita is in being able to practice it. Congratulations to Satya in breaking down the practice of Gita into simple steps.

— Desh Deshpande, Chairman, Sparta Group LLC.

One of the hardest tasks that we face, as we embark on a spiritual journey, is letting go of ingrained thought processes and dogmatic beliefs. After reading Satya Kalra's various books on spiritual enlightenment, I had learned to appreciate the practical values that can be deemed from the *Bhagavad Gita*, since it imparts guidance on how each of us can tune into our inner wisdom, in order to attain natural calm and happiness. Ms. Kalra in her book "My questions and God's Answer's" was able to deconstruct a highly complex Eastern spiritual dogma, and apply this into a 21st century perspective, thus providing pragmatic approaches that all of us can integrate into our daily existence.

— Philipp Novales-Li, DMedSc, PhD, DPhil (Oxford),
Livermore, California, USA

"Gita", The Divine Way of Life. The book "*My questions and God's Answers*" of Satya Kalra is not intended to satisfy intellectual curiosity of its readers. It is not an exercise in intellectual gymnastics. It expounds the philosophy of life as taught by the great spiritual teacher, Lord Krishna. Their form of expression is by way of question and answers which is most suitable for showing the spiritual path of life to common man. I am feeling delighted while recommending the book to every one who is experiencing spiritual disquiet within himself.

— Prof. Chandmal Sharma (Retd.), Dept. of Philosophy,
University of Jaipur, Jaipur India

Satya Kalra's writing is very simple, straight forward and seasoned. It is highly provocative and can inspire us to start thinking beyond our accustomed patterns. Diverse are the ways, but the goal is one and the same. Peace, happiness and bliss are the prerequisites for attaining the ULTIMATE TRUTH. Devotees who are seeking and are still unfulfilled, they can re-evaluate their thinking process and the way they intellectualize by understanding the two separate methods systematically described within; the meditative way of having intuitive knowledge and the way of contemplation for attaining the Supreme State of Consciousness. and enlightenment, free from all pains, miseries and ignorance.

Blessings and good wishes for your spiritual writing may you write more for path seekers.

— Guru Jitendra Maharaj, Kathak Nrityaacharya,
Varanasi Gharana, New Delhi

I had a chance to glance through the manuscript of Smt. Satya Karla's work on Srimad Bhagavad Gita in a format of question and answers, "My questions and God's answer's". It was evident that she had put a lot of efforts and long time in writing this book. She is the person most benefitted by this labor of love and I believe it will benefit its readers as well.
Prem & Om

— Swami Tejomayananda, Chairman,
Chinmaya International Foundation (CIF)

"My Questions and God's Answers," a guide for eternal happiness, peace, and Ananda. Such commentaries on the Bhagavad Gita are always helpful to spiritual seekers who have to fight in the battle of life. May Lord Krishna shower His blessings on you and also the readers of your book is my prayer.

— Swami Prabuddhananda, Vedanta Society of Northern California

Her book is a beautiful bridge between Preya (materialistic happiness) and Shreya (spiritual welfare) . It is a complete ocean of bliss in itself. Whosoever would dive into it would find pricelss jewels of Anandam.

Satya Kalra has done self-study and spiritual practice for many years. Thus, she has attained divine knowledge. This knowledge is meant for the entire humanity. This knowledge is for all countries. It is valid for all Ages. It is equally useful to all types of men. Sat Chit Ananate

— Swami Brahmanand Ji
Supreme Spiritual Head of Geeta Ashram and Geeta Dham

About the Author

Satya Kalra, the founder of *Path to Anandam*, is a seeker, teacher and international lecturer, popularly known for Anandam Lifestyle (*Blissful Living*). Satya's personal mission is to live in love, peace, and *Anandam*—leading, practicing, and propagating blissful living and helping others become more self-dependent and self-reliant—especially destitute women and children.

For more than 15 years she has taught and promoted the awareness of spirituality and the effulgent wisdom of the Gita and its applications in daily life, family, business, and community matters to various groups and organizations.

Satya has been unfolding herself through meditation for over 32 years and the study of Bhagavad Gita for over 18 years.

Satya went to the USA from India in 1969. She has Biochemistry degrees from Gwalior, India and University of Illinois, Chicago, and business management education from University of Berkeley, CA.

She worked in the biotech industry for 35 years as a visionary, founder, CEO, and chairperson. Few years ago, a divine call came to her and she quit her job as a CEO and become a fulltime seeker to discover her True Self.

Today, Satya spends most of her time in the company of saints and seers, she motivates and uplits others and propagates spirituality. She is a chief coordinator in the USA for Divine Shakti Foundation. She is the author of Path to *Anandam* book series—*Enjoy Worry-Free Life in 30 Days* and *Lasting Forever...Birth, Death and Beyond.*

My questions & God's Answers

Guide to Eternal Happiness Peace Anandam

email : info@pathtoanandam.org

ISBN: 978-81-288-2551-4

Published 2010 by
DIAMOND POCKET BOOKS PVT. LTD.
X-30, Okhla Industrial Area, Phase-II
New Delhi-20 (INDIA)
Tel : 011-40712100, 40716600 Fax : 011-41611866
e-mail : sales@dpb.in   website : ww.dpb.in

Typesetting and Layout Design by
Techastra Solutions (P) Ltd., Hyderabad, INDIA.

Graphic Design by
Deepak Gupta, Oceanic Studio, New Delhi, INDIA.

My questions & God's Answers

Guide to Eternal Happiness Peace Anandam

Satya Kalra

www.pathtoanandam.org

H.H. Swami Hariharji Maharaj

Dedicated

to

His Holiness Swami Hariharji Maharaj

All the gurus, sages and Lord Krishna whose guidance
and blessings led me on the Path to Anandam

May this be a light for all the spiritual seekers.

About our Logo

'ॐ Aum' is the cosmic sound that transforms humans to Divinity-Immortality

'ॐ *AUM/Om*'—the symbol of divinity and primeval sound of infinity. It is the Supreme mantra, the most sacred of holy words in the Yoga tradition. It has neither beginning nor end. *Aum* is also called Pranava means both life-giver (infuser of Prana) and controller of life force (Prana). *AUM is another name of God/Self.*

In our Path to Anandam logo, ॐ *AUM* is placed in the heart; Anandam, Love and Peace are on three sides of the heart and divine light is emitting from the center of the heart.

When the seed of divinity – ॐ *AUM* is put in the heart, it will gradually start cultivating and emitting the LIGHT of divinity. The individual will start transforming gradually. His miseries and pain, sorrows and stress, worries and feares and his emotional attachments, will start diminishing little by little. He or she will slowly yet surely start feeling enriched with Love, Peace and Joy—*Anandam.* (All the three—Love, Peace and *Anandam* are triplets, and if one comes others will automatically follow) He will start enjoying his life more and more and feel:

- Happy and Joyful
- Loving and Compassionate
- Caring and sharing
- Contentment and Patient
- Free from fear, stress, worry
- Self-confident
- Positive
- Respectful
- Forgiving
- Less argumentative
- Calm & creative
- Anandam

The aura around the person will change and it will be reflected through the glow on his face. He will be transformed into Ananadmayi, Premamayi, and Shantimayi and will finally be connected to the Self and eventually attain the purpose of his life which is '*Sat Chit Anandam.*'

Universal Prayer

ॐ

Asato Maa Sat Gamaya
Tamso Maa Jyotir Gamaya
Mrityor Maa Amritam Gamaya.
Aum Shanti, Shanti, Shantihi
"God lead me from untruth to truth
From darkness to light
From death to immortality"

Aum, Peace, Peace, Peace

"Gita leads to Inner Peace,
Inner Peace leads to Global Peace"

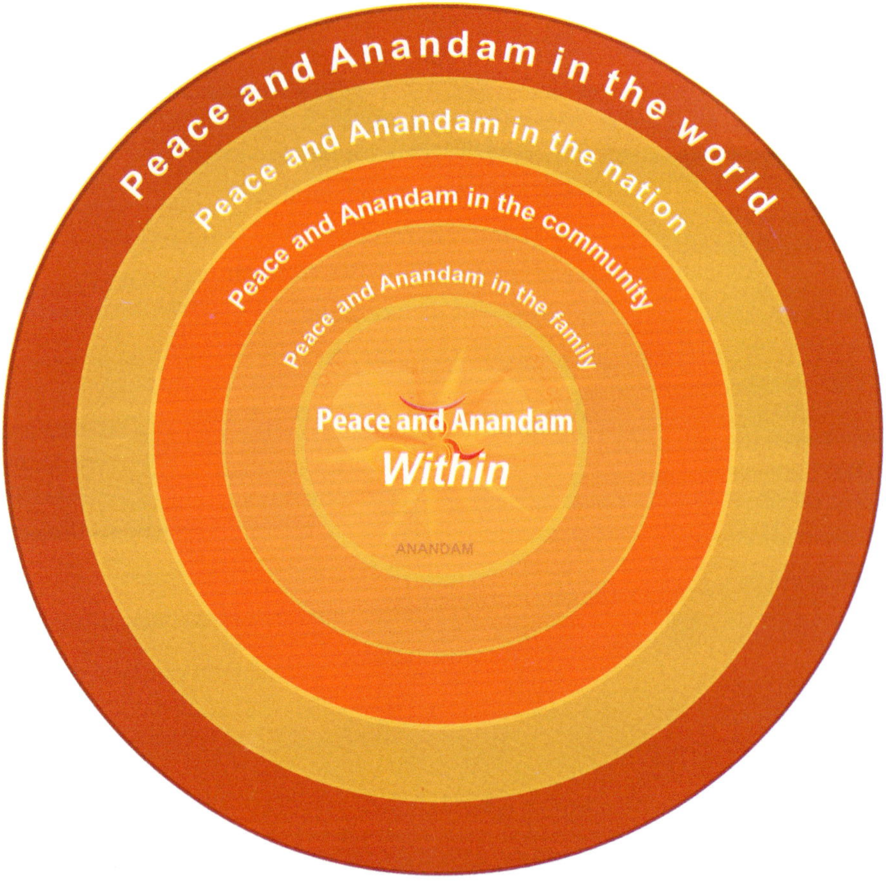

Contents

Foreword ... *xix*

Preface ... *xxi*

Acknowledgements ... *xxv*

Opinions of Bhagavad Gita by others ... *xxvii*

List of Pictures, Flow Charts and Poems ... *xxix*

Introduction ... 1

1. Arjuna Vishad Yoga—*Arjuna Despondency and Dilemma* ... 19
   - Main message ... 23
   - Chapter overview and verses 1–47 ... 24
   - Lesson to learn and practice in daily life ... 35
2. Sankhya Yoga—*The Path of Self-Knowledge* ... 37
   - Main message ... 40
   - Chapter overview and verses 1–72 ... 42
   - Lesson to learn and practice in daily life ... 64
3. Karma Yoga—*The Path of Right Action* ... 67
   - Main message ... 71
   - Chapter overview and verses 1–43 ... 72
   - Lesson to learn and practice in daily life ... 85
4. Jnana-Karma-Sanyasa Yoga—*The Path of Knowledge, Action and Renunciation* ... 87
   - Main message ... 91
   - Chapter overview and verses 1–42 ... 92
   - Lesson to learn and practice in daily life ... 104
5. Karma-Sanyasa Yoga—*The Path of Action and Renunciation* ... 107
   - Main message ... 110
   - Chapter overview and verses 1–29 ... 111
   - Lesson to learn and practice in daily life ... 120
6. Dhyana Yoga—*The Path of Self-discipline and Meditation* ... 121
   - Main message ... 124
   - Chapter overview and verses 1–47 ... 125
   - Lesson to learn and practice in daily life ... 138

7. Jnana-Vijnana Yoga—*The Path of Knowing and Experiencing God* 141
- Main message 144
- Chapter overview and verses 1–30 145
- Lesson to learn and practice in daily life 154

8. Aksara-Brahma Yoga—*The Path of the Eternal Brahman* 155
- Main message 158
- Chapter overview and verses 1–28 159
- Lesson to learn and practice in daily life 167

9. Rajavidya-Rajaguhya Yoga—*The Path of the Most Secret and Sacred Knowledge* 169
- Main message 172
- Chapter overview and verses 1–34 173
- Lesson to learn and practice in daily life 184

10. Vibhuti Yoga—*The Path of Divine Glories and Manifestations* 187
- Main message 190
- Chapter overview and verses 1–42 191
- Lesson to learn and practice in daily life 202

11. Visvarupa-Darsana Yoga—*The Path of the Divine Vision of the Cosmic Form* 205
- Main message 208
- Chapter overview and verses 1–55 209
- Lesson to learn and practice in daily life 226

12. Bhakti Yoga—*The Path of Love and Devotion* 227
- Main message 230
- Chapter overview and verses 1–20 231
- Lesson to learn and practice in daily life 237

13. Ksetra-Ksetrajna Vibhaga Yoga—*The Path of knowing the Field and the Knower of the Field* 239
- Main message 242
- Chapter overview and verses 1–34 243
- Lesson to learn and practice in daily life 252

14. Guna-Traya Vibhaga Yoga—*The Path of the Division of the Three Gunas* 255
- Main message 257
- Chapter overview and verses 1–27 259
- Lesson to learn and practice in daily life 267

15. Purushottama Yoga—*The Path of the Supreme Person* 269
- Main message 271
- Chapter overview and verses 1–20 273
- Lesson to learn and practice in daily life 279

16. Deva-Asura Sampad Vibhaga Yoga—*The Path of Divine vs. Demonic Qualities*......281
- Main message......283
- Chapter overview and verses 1–24......285
- Lesson to learn and practice in daily life......292

17. Sraddhatriya-Vibhag Yoga—*The Path of Threefold Division of Faith*......293
- Main message......296
- Chapter overview and verses 1–28......297
- Lesson to learn and practice in daily life......305

18. Moksha-Sanyasa Yoga—*The Path of Liberation through Renunciation*......307
- Main message......309
- Chapter overview and verses 1–78......311
- Lesson to learn and practice in daily life......334

Summary of Gita's Teachings......337

Summary of Karma Yoga, Bhakti Yoga and Jnana Yoga......345

Summary of Gunas: Tamasic, Rajasic and Sattvic......349

Assessment Guide......355

Glossary......357

Index......373

Anandam

O divine being! have–
Anandam in thoughts
speech
seeing
Anandam in action
listening
communication
Anandam in relationship
seva
studying
Anandam in eating
sleeping
brushing teeth
Anandam in working
crying and
singing!
Live in Anandam Consciousness
Anandam in everything and every activity of life
Spread the Anandam, Anandam, Anandam everywhere…

Foreword

H.H. PUJYA SWAMI CHIDANAND SARASWATIJI
Parmarth Niketan, Rishikesh, India

As Paramhansa Yoganandaji said, "*The Bhagavad Gita is the most beloved scripture of India, a scripture of scriptures. It is the Hindu's Holy Testament, the one book that all masters depend upon as a supreme source of scriptural authority.*" The Gita provides wisdom and upliftment, comfort and solace to people of all ages, from all walks of life, from all corners of the Earth.

The Gita is a "Map of Life" for it clearly shows us not only the destination but also the clearest and best path to reach there. However, like any good map, the Gita does not give us only one path. Rather, throughout the Divine Song, Bhagwan Krishna explains how – through devotion, through wisdom, and through action—one can reach the ultimate destination of union with God. For different temperaments He lays out different paths, all the while reminding us that true, earnest yearning and pure, surrendered love for God are the surest and simplest way to attain liberation. The lessons of the Gita do not require one to be a great scholar or a great philosopher. Nor do they demand decades of exacting penance to earn God's favor. Rather, Bhagwan Krishna offers infinite and eternal comfort by His words, "whoever comes to me with devotion will attain me."

Bhagwan Shri Krishna says, "Stand up! Do divine! Be divine! Don't expect, but accept!" Life is about the journey, not about the destination. If the reins of your life-chariot are in His hands, you will be ever happy, ever peaceful. This is the lesson of ultimate surrender that we must take to heart.

The Bhagavad Gita shows us the way to live with God, to live with each other and to live with Mother Earth in peace and harmony. This wisdom and insight is as changing as the River Ganga, able to address the concerns of each generation, and yet as stable and everlasting as the Himalayas themselves.

I am very proud of Smt. Satya Kalra for having brought forth this divine wisdom into a format which is easy, accessible, understandable and most importantly implementable. The question-answer and bullet-point format is sure to appeal to busy, pragmatic and practical people of today's world who are looking to bring spirituality into their lives.

This special interpretation and rendering of the message of the Bhagavad Gita is sure to be very useful to those who, due to their busy lifestyles, are looking for quick, simple and easily-implementable steps they can take to bring the teachings of the Gita into their daily lives. The way that Satyaji has prepared and presented the book is geared toward those looking not for an in-depth, esoteric and complex rendering, but rather for the basic, distilled version of Bhagawan Shri Krishna's message.

The message of the Gita is as relevant for people living in India and the West today as it was for the people of India more than 5000 years ago. It is as relevant for Hindus as for people of all other religions. It teaches Hindus how to be better Hindus, but it also teaches Muslims to be better Muslims, Christians to be better Christians, and Jews to be better Jews. For, if something is really "truth," it must be universal. Truth is not limited to a religious framework. If it is truth, it must pertain to all. Such is the profound truth of Bhagwan Shri Krishna's words.

I am sure that those who read and truly implement the teachings in this "Song of God" will be touched, taught and transformed, and they will find that deep peace to which Bhagawan Krishna's message leads.

With love and blessings,
In the service of God and humanity,

Swami Chidanand Saraswati

Preface

"My questions and God's Answers" is not just another commentary on Gita

Some of you may be wondering why I decided to write another translation and commentary on the *Bhagavad Gita* when this has already been done hundreds of times before. First, let me assure you that the book, "My questions and God's Answers" is not another philosophical commentary on Gita. However, it presents the secular teachings of the Gita in a simple, reader friendly fashion with tips on how to practice and apply every day. Hence one can **overcome predicaments of daily life and live happily and peacefully in a material world** and also attain eternal happiness and peace—the very purpose of life.

My Search for Truth

In 1990, I was facing many challenges in every area of my life, business, family, and health. I felt my life was falling apart. I felt totally lost, depressed and confused until I met Swami Hariharji Maharaj (Founder of International Gita Ashram) who advised me to read the Gita.

I had already tried reading many times and had always given up because I could not understand its message. The words were too deep and too complicated for me. I told Swamiji the same. He suggested that I start by reading just three verses per day, *the advice that changed my life.*

While following his advice, I also read some of the commentaries on Gita. For a greater grasp of Gita's verses I also learned Sanskrit.

To understand Gita's teachings more thoroughly, I developed my own graphics and flow charts. This made my understanding of Gita's teachings easier and I started applying them in my daily life. It has a profound effect on my life. It has brought self-awareness and self-transformation in me. It has completely changed my thinking process and the direction of my life. Now, I have become calmer, happier, more self-confident and focused. It has not only helped me cope with difficult situations but to learn from each situation and move forward in life. The greatest reward I got, I must confess, is that I started feelings self-satisfied, feelings that I had never experienced before, even after achieving all the goals which I had set myself in the past.

Since 1969, when I came to the USA, I had set many goals for myself in different arenas of life, education, family, corporate world, and society, and I believe that I had reached most of them. However, I had always felt some sought of dissatisfaction; I was searching for meaning and validation in my surroundings. Truthfully, I was not happy within.

The Wisdom of Gita has not only answered my questions but it has also guided me on how to overcome sorrows and pain; handle difficult situations, enjoy my day to day life, live happily and peacefully; and still strive towards the higher purpose. *The Gita offers me all!*

The teachings of Gita gave me a meaning and purpose to my life "Live in Anandam (Bliss) and spread the same to others."

I am still continuing my spiritual journey and focusing on discovering my true nature (Sat Chit Ananda). At the same time, I also enjoy my life to the fullest. The complexity of studying the Gita brought me to a standstill several times, but the beauty and the power of its teachings always had brought me back.

Birth of My questions and God's Answers

Although I had never dreamt about writing a book, I remember the exact time and location when divine inspiration came to me to write this book. It was June 2, 2007 and I was in Washington D.C. celebrating our son Amit's 25th birthday. He looked at me while I was sitting in a chair and remarked that I should retire for the night as I looked half asleep. It was 10:30 P.M. and as I made my way to the bedroom, the thought of writing a book on Gita hit me, so instead of going to sleep, I started writing and spent the entire night doing so. This was the beginning of what has been an arduous but also an exciting and uplifting journey.

During this journey I felt, I was Arjuna myself and Lord Krishna was answering me through many channels, inner voice, dreams, contemplation, meditation, prayers, sages, etc. Whenever, I got stuck with my computer, thoughts, writing, He came to rescue me in a short period of time. I followed a very disciplined life as He recommended in Gita, eating *Sattvic* food (light and fresh vegetarian), doing a lot of yoga asanas, pranayam, and meditating, walking in the lap of nature, practicing silence, staying with the company of light minded people and staying fully focused on the project.

With the help of the Divine Power and based upon my marketing experiences, I have written the teachings of the Gita in a simple and practical manner so that who wishes to unlock his unlimited power and enjoy his life with the unlimited transforming power of the Gita will not have to struggle as I did. I believe, the book is written by Lord Krishna Himself and He assigned me to deliver His message in a simple and applicable format because His teachings are needed in the world today more than ever.

Spiritual Guide for a Fast-paced Lifestyle

Keeping in mind today's challenging and fast-paced life style, I have attempted to simplify the Gita's teachings but still keeping true to its spirit and form, so that it becomes suitable for a mainstream reader even if he or she has just a few minutes to spare. I have translated its verses into simple English without losing the actual meaning of the Sanskrit translation and the essence of Gita. Each verse has been written in the original Sanskrit along with Roman English.

In today's world, man is very inquisitive and he needs quick answers to his questions. Therefore I have also written this book in a question and answer format, with graphics, flow charts and poems. Hence, one can easily understand, follow and apply its teachings everyday and enhance the quality of one's life, attain happiness, bliss and Anandam in this lifetime and beyond.

Spiritual Guide Only a Road Map

Each chapter begins with a link to the previous chapter along with the main message and overview of the chapter. At the end of each chapter there is a lesson to learn along with an action plan to practice for daily use.

You will notice that several similar words have been put in parenthesis. I have done this purposely to give a broader meaning to the word and at the same time, maintain consistency and simplicity. Sanskrit words have been italicized.

Certain words, equations and graphics have been repeated. This has been done intentionally to register important points in the reader's mind. Here, I have followed Lord Krishna's approach as He used with Arjuna to clarify His points again and again in different contexts.

In this simple and practical spiritual guide, I hope that the message of the Gita reaches as many people as possible so they too can lead happier and blissful lives.

I hope it answers your questions and helps you as it has helped me, to understand the purpose of life. I also hope it gives you enough strength to face life's difficult situations and brings eternal happiness and peace in your daily life and beyond.

The Gita says that it is never too late to make a fresh start. Even a sinner can become a saint if it is his true desire.

Even the sinner can cross over the ocean of miseries and sins by the boat of Self-Knowledge. (9.30)

Again, the only purpose of "My questions and God's Answers" is to reap the benefit of the divine teachings of Gita "Universal Truth." Apply these teachings in daily life, and receive the priceless reward—the best quality of your life you could ever imagine and also the purpose of your existence, Self-Realization.

While the Gita teaches everything we need to know about self-transformation, we have to admit that true change is not an easy road. First, we must want it, and then work every day to achieve lasting results. However, do not be discouraged because self-transformation is slow and steady process. To that end, this book has been written not to be read once and forgotten, but as a reference that can be read over and over again whenever the need may arise.

If you sincerely contemplate and practice the tips given in this Anandam guide, you will gradually experience a self-development and self-transformation, and feel emotionally stronger.

This spiritual guide is only a road map; you must drive yourself to reach your destination.

If you want to avail the maximum benefit from this spiritual guide, follow the suggestions appended below:

> Read any page, chapter or 1–3 verses as you wish each day (preferably in the mornings). Contemplate on it and practice it during the day.
>
> With each contemplation and practice, you will not only come closer and closer to liberation from pain and sorrow but you will also live more happily and peacefully and enjoy your life to the fullest.

Lord Krishna tells his dear friend Arjuna, "Reflect upon My teachings and guidance, but do as you wish."

Similarly, the choice is ours, to suffer or free ourselves from suffering.

Satya Kalra
Author

Acknowledgements

"My questions and God's Answer's" is not just a combination of words and letters, but the collective love of many radiant souls who helped give shape and form to my vision of creating a spiritual road map to blissful life (*Anandam*) through the teachings of *Srimad Bhagavad Gita*.

First and foremost I would like to offer my deepest gratitude to Lord Krishna who has assigned me to deliver His message through this book, "My questions and God's Answers."

I want to pay my homage to H.H. Swami Hariharji Maharaj, founder of the Gita Ashram, who personally guided me to read the Gita. Guruma for her unwavering support and encouragement.

My heartfelt appreciation goes to my husband Krishan Kalra. Your encouragement and quiet confidence rejuvenated me before I even knew I needed an energy boost to complete this noble work.

My loving thanks to our children Monika, Mintee, Amit, Anurag, and Ambika, first of the next generation and treasured family members and friends for their love and support. To my late parents Sahib Ram and Jamuna Bai for giving me the teachings and values I live upon.

My sincere thanks to Bhanwar L. Joshi from Gita Ashram, Chicago, who, through his courage and sacrifice, helped to create the vision of this book and made it his personal mission to ensure it reached readers in its essence.

To great friends, T.S. and Jogi Khanna (Alamo, Ca), for their assistance for making sure that the true meaning of the message is not lost, and at the same time the significance of the message for the modern world is not diluted.

To all the people who come to me seeking spiritual counseling. You have helped me to refine and discover new dimensions of the Gita's message.

To Sujata C and K.K. Gaul (retired Chicago journalist) for editorial advice and help.

Satya Sai Baba I thank you for your grace.

May Lord Krishna accept this humble offering.

Aum Shanti, Shanti, Shantihi

Opinions of Bhagavad Gita by Others

The *Bhagavad Gita* is considered to be among the greatest spiritual books the world has ever known by Eastern and Western scholars. Because of its universal appeal, it has been translated into almost all languages in the world. It has been held in reverence by many saints and scholars. The following are some of quotes from many well-known, great souls throughout the world who have read the Bhagavad Gita and have extolled its universal message:

Gita stands as a beacon light for the salvation of mankind which is being swept by the violent storm of materialism. Scientific and technological advancement alone does not complete man's evolution. Spiritual awareness and awakening as imparted in the Gita, elevates man's perception, who then sees the existence as one whole, breaking the barriers of caste, creed and color, thereby doing away with racial and religious prejudice. Any embodied being who lives the Divine teachings of Gita gives up his mortal self and attains liberation.

—H.H. Swami Hariharji Maharaj

When reading the Bhagavad-Gita I think about how God created the universe and then everything else seemed so superfluous. —Albert Einstein

When doubts haunt me, when disappointments stare me in the face, and I see not one ray of hope on the horizon, I turn to Bhagavad-Gita and find a verse to comfort me; and I immediately begin to smile in the midst of overwhelming sorrow. Those who meditate on the Gita will derive fresh joy and new meanings from it every day. —Mahatma Gandhi

The Bhagavad-Gita deals essentially with the spiritual foundation of human existence. It is a call of action to meet the obligations and duties of life; yet keeping in view the spiritual nature and grander purpose of the universe. —Jawaharlal Nehru

Bhagavad-Gita has a profound influence on the spirit of mankind by its devotion to God which is manifested in all actions. —Dr. Albert Schweizer

In the morning I bathe my intellect in the stupendous and cosmogonal philosophy of the Bhagavad-Gita, in comparison with which our modern world and its literature seem puny and trivial. —Henry David Thoreau

From a clear knowledge of the Bhagavad-Gita, all the goals of human existence become fulfilled. Bhagavad-Gita is the manifest quintessence of all the teachings of the Vedic scriptures. —Adi Shankara

The Bhagavad-Gita reveals the goal of the all the Vedic scriptures. —Ramanujam

Bhagavad-Gita is the most comprehensive statement of perennial philosophy.
—Aldous Huxley

The Gita is a gate opening on the whole world of spiritual truth and experience; and the view it gives us embraces all the provinces of that supreme region. —Sri Aurobindo

For the mastery of Gita may lead one automatically to a comprehension of the spiritual truths contained in other scriptures and no separate study is required to obtain this knowledge. —Jayadyal Goyandka

The Mahabharata has all the essential ingredients necessary to evolve and protect humanity and that within it the Bhagavad-Gita is the epitome of the Mahabharata just as ghee is the essence of milk and pollen is the essence of flowers. —Madhvacharya

The marvel of the Bhagavad-Gita is its truly beautiful revelation of life's wisdom which enables philosophy to blossom into religion. —Herman Hesse

I owed a magnificent day to the Bhagavad-gita. It was the first of books; it was as if an empire spoke to us, nothing small or unworthy, but large, serene, consistent, the voice of an old intelligence which in another age and climate had pondered and thus disposed of the same questions which exercise us. —Ralph Waldo Emerson

Gita is universal mother
Gita is the life boat to cross the ocean of life
Gita is a casket of social mantra
Gita is a beautiful garden of flowers

It is Ganga that washes our sins and is more than Ganga because it teaches us how to help others to wash their sins as well. —Sathya Sai Baba

List of Pictures, Flow Charts and Poems

Fig. I.1 Yogas of Bhagavad Gita 4
Fig. I.2 Relationship of Karma Yoga, Jnana Yoga and Bhakti Yoga 5
Fig. 1.1 Vishad leads to negative thoughts which results in toxins, diseases and disruptions in the body 22
Fig. 1.2 Cycle of destruction of human values 34
Fig. 2.1 Obstacles on the path of Self-Realization (62–63) 41
Fig. 2.2 Journey of the soul from one body to the next 49
Fig. 2.3 Three modes of Gunas: Tamasic, Rajasic and Sattvic 55
Fig. 2.4 Attachment to confusion 61
Fig. 3.1 Five monkeys practicing Goodness 70
Fig. 3.2 Relationship of body, mind and Spirit 84
Fig. 3.3 Kamadhenu/milch cow (3.10) 86
Fig. 6.1 Balanced lifestyle is the prerequisite for meditation 130
Fig. 8.1 How to die? 163

Flow chart 1.1 Consequences of Vishad 22
Flow chart 3.1 Summary of Karma Yoga 70
Flow chart 6.1 Relationship of thoughts, action and destiny 124

Poem – Anandam xviii
Poem – Gita is the Song of God 2
Poem – Who is Arjuna, who is Lord Krishna and what is Gita? 38
Poem – What is My Duty (Svadharma)? 87
Poem – Meditation 122
Poem – AUM 156
Poem – The Ultimate Purpose of Life 186
Poem – My True Nature is Sat Chit Ananda 268
Poem – Ultimate 336

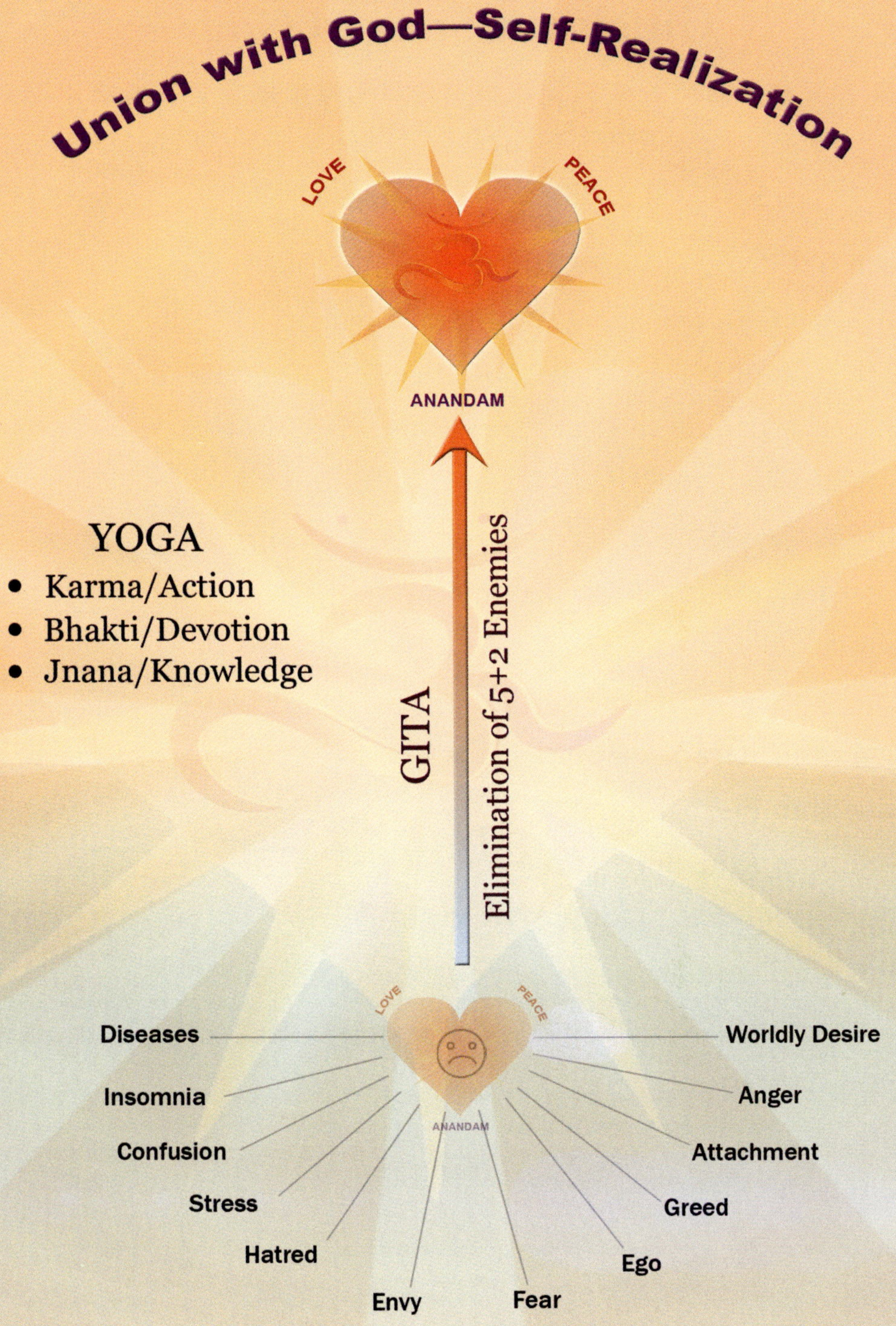

Self-Purification and Transformation through Gita

Gita is the Song of God

sung by Lord Krishna for us to sing every moment of our life*

Gita is a Royal Road to Liberation

Gita is a Guide to the Art of Right Living

Gita is a Spiritual Instruction Manual to Operate our Life

Gita is a Answer to Every Question

Gita is a Boat to Cross the Ocean of Life

Gita is the Ocean of Knowledge

Gita is a Sarathi (Divine company)

Gita is a Peace Ambassador

Gita is a Universal Mother

Gita is a Character Builder

Gita is an Eternal Mantra

Gita is an Atmadershani

Gita is a Spiritual Guide

Gita is a Transformer

Gita is a Jagad Guru

Gita is a Mirror

Gita is a Purifier

Gita is the Light Within

The word Gita means song and Bhagavad means God, hence, Bhagavad-Gita is called the 'Song of God'.

Inauguration
of
My questions and God's Answers
Guide to Eternal Happiness

On April 4, 2010, this spiritual book was inaugurated at the Maha Kumbh Mela at the Parmarth Niketan, Rishikesh (Uttarakhand). Shri Lal Krishan Advani, a prominent leader of India, inaugurated the book. Swami Chidanand Saraswati Ji, Swami Aginvesh Ji, Pujya Sant Rameshbhai Ojha Ji, and Swami Guru Sharananand Ji were present at the auspicious occasion. Several thousand people witness the divine occasion.

Shri Anoop Jalota sang *bhajans* on the occasion while Sonal Mansingh, the renowned danseuse, staged a dance to thrill the audience present on the occasion.

With this release, Mrs. Satya Kalra, an Indian-American spiritual thinker, seeker, and writer, has been catapulted into (spiritual) limelight.

The beautiful, colored book is a must-have for the readers of all genres.

Q Is it possible to live in today's world in peace and joy, free from the miseries of life: anxiety, stress, fear, and frustration?

Yes! The *Bhagavad Gita* 'The Song of God' blesses us with that possibility because:

The Gita is a vehicle that takes us from miseries and pains to Anandam—a happy and peaceful life

Q What is Srimad Bhagavad Gita?

Srimad Bhagavad Gita is timeless wisdom for the entire mankind

Srimad Bhagavad Gita is the eternal message of spiritual wisdom, a most sacred and well-known scripture of Self-Knowledge from the ancient India that emanated from the lips of Lord Krishna Himself. Therefore it is also know as 'The Song of God' (Gita means song and Bhagavan means God).

The Gita is the nectar, a summary of the four Vedas and Upanishads, the philosophical and psychological wisdom of the ancient Hindu scriptures.

It contains 700 Sanskrit *shlokas* (verses). Each verse is a mantra by itself that offers guidance and advice. There are theories to support each advice and also provide the know-how of applying it in our daily life.

The Gita is a book of God and Self-Knowledge that offers different paths to experience and realize God and also gives the nectar of enjoyment, happiness and peace during the journey of God-Realization and Self-Realization

The Gita has 18 chapters and each chapter is called Yoga. Yoga means the Unity with the Self, alignment of mind, body and soul that results in eternal happiness and peace (*Anandam*). Each Yoga or chapter represents a different spiritual path that teaches us how to self-transform, self-awaken and unite ourselves with the Supreme.

Therefore, the Gita is called *Yoga Sastra*, Scripture of Yogas. However, in a real sense, it is a *Moksha Sastra* (scripture of Liberation, *Moksha*), because it guides us how to liberate ourselves and convert our miseries (*Vishad*) into blessings (*Prasad*). It is also known as *Brahma-Vidya*, (Knowledge of God, Self, Soul, Spirit, *Atma*).

These 18 chapters have been further categorized into three main Yogas:

1. **Karma Yoga (Action Yoga):** How to perform action righteously and attain Union with God through selfless action
2. **Bhakti Yoga (Devotion Yoga):** How to become the best devotee and very dear to God
3. **Jnana Yoga (Knowledge Yoga):** What qualities to develop to qualify for Liberation

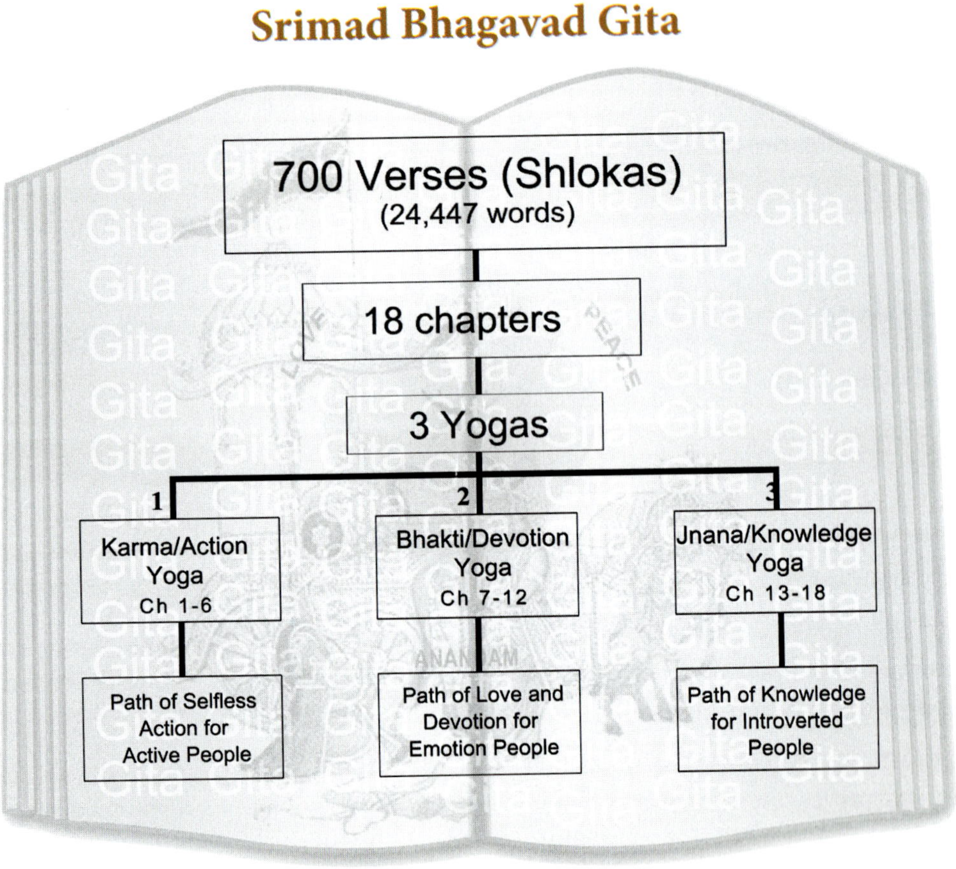

Fig. I.1 *Yogas of Bhagavad Gita*

The Gita can be compared to the human body, where *Jnana Yoga* is the head, *Bhakti Yoga* is the heart, and *Karma Yoga* is the arms and hands. In order to function properly and perform a proper action, all three (head, heart and hands) must be connected with each other. Therefore, all three paths of Yoga, *Karma Yoga*, *Bhakti Yoga* and *Jnana Yoga* are inter-connected and must be practiced together for self-purification and self-transformation that leads to Self-Realization.

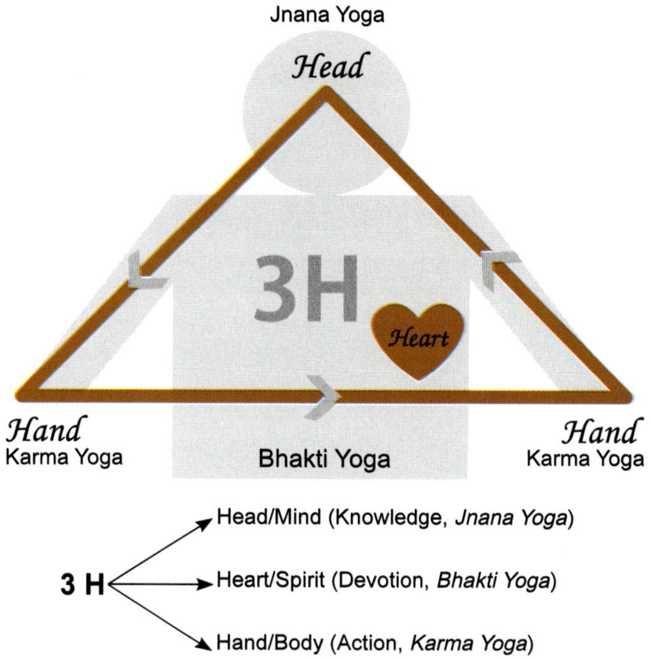

Fig. I.2 *Relationship of Karma Yoga, Jnana Yoga and Bhakti Yoga*

Karma Yoga + Bhakti Yoga + Jnana Yoga → Self-Purification → Self-Transformation → Self-Realization

All the three Yogas must be practiced together

Example: Driving a car – In order to drive and reach the destination safely one must know how to drive and know the rules of the road – knowledge. He must get behind the wheel and drive the car in order to reach his destination—Action. However he must do it willingly with a good attitude, if not he must get into an accident. The good attitude comes only from heart – love and devotion. So knowledge, action and love, are all needed to drive and reach safely. Similarly, all three Yogas are needed to attain Self-Realization.

Summary

The complete description of the glory of the Gita is impossible for a human being to describe; however, in summary, it represents the three Gs as below.

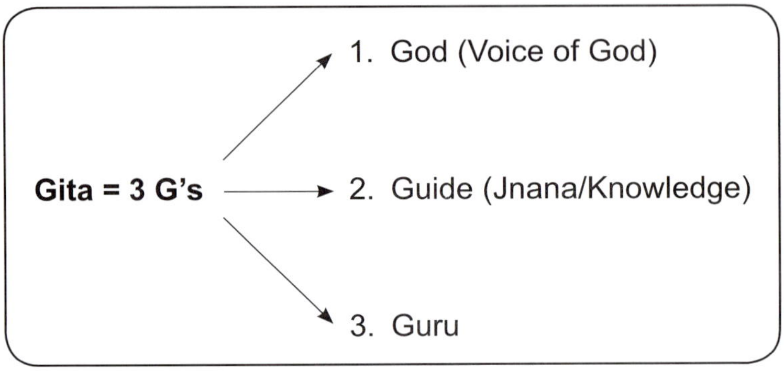

The Gita is an ocean of wisdom

It offers everything we could ever want:

- If we want to swim, we can swim. (Action)
- If we do not want to swim, we can just sit on the shore and enjoy the sound of waves. (Relax and enjoy)
- If we want to dive deep into the ocean, we can pick a pearl from an oyster. (Self-Knowledge and Self-Realization).

It is up to us what we want from the Gita. The Gita offers all. However, one thing is definite, the more we read and contemplate on the Gita's teachings, more we learn about God and Self, more we come closer and closer to God, and realize Self (God-Realization and Self-Realization).

Q When and where did the Gita come from?

More than 5,200 years ago, the divine dialogue between Lord Krishna (*Parmatma*, God) and Arjuna (individual soul), Srimad Bhagavad Gita, took place at a very critical moment on the battlefield of *Kurukshetra* (located in the northern part of India, see map at page 18).

The battle of Kurukshetra was narrated in chapters 23–40 of the historical epic of India—the Mahabharata, consisting of 100,000 verses in Sanskrit. It was chronicled by Veda Vyas, a divine incarnated soul.

An Epic War

The Mahabharata describes the story of two brothers fighting over a kingdom. Through the story of two kings, the Mahabharata imparts knowledge of codes of ethics, morality, social laws, metaphysics, philosophy and spirituality. It became a profound message of spiritual guidance, and solace for mankind.

The two brothers were named Dhritarashtra and Pandu. Dhritarashtra was born blind and had one hundred wicked sons called Kauravas. Pandu had five pious sons called Pandavas. Duryodhana was the eldest son of Dhritarashtra. He and his wicked brothers were very eager to take over the part of the kingdom that belonged to their cousins, the Pandavas. They tried every tactic, fair and foul, to achieve their objective. God's grace, however, rescued the Pandavas from many threats.

An Unlawful Exile

However, the Kauravas managed to unlawfully exile the Pandavas from the kingdom for thirteen years. After successfully completing the period of exile, Duryodhana refused to give them their rightful share of the kingdom without a war. Many attempts by well wishers of the family, as well as Lord Krishna were made to avert the armed conflict. But all failed. Thus the war of Mahabharata became inevitable and the Pandavas had no choice but to fight.

Lord Krishna, as an impartial well-wisher, offered to help both parties; they could choose either Him or His vast army. The Kauravs chose the army, and the Pandavas were happy that they could have Lord Krishna on their side. Lord Krishna served as the charioteer of Arjuna, one of the Pandavas.

Dhritrashtra, the blind king, was complacent knowing that his sons not only had the strength of the army behind them, but that Bhishma, a royal warrior, a warrior of unparalleled valor, and who could not be slain against his own will, would ensure their victory. On the tenth day of the battle, however, Bhishma was struck by Arjuna and disabled. Dhritrashtra's faith was shaken and he called upon his intuitive minister, Sanjaya to narrate the events of the war to him. The whole Bhagavad Gita was told by Sanjaya to King Dhritarashtra. (Sanjay was granted the power of clairvoyance and clairvision by Sage Vyasa, the author of Mahabharata therefore he could see and hear from distance).

Thus, the Bhagavad Gita begins with the statement of Dhritarashtra as a first verse and the complete sermon ends with 700 verses (Shlokas) as a holy dialogue between Lord Krishna and Arjuna.

The Moment of Reckoning

The great warrior, Arjuna, was the most skillful warrior of Pandu's sons and had been trained in the arts of war, and had won many previous battles. However, after seeing his friends and relatives arrayed on the battlefield of Kurukshetra and ready to fight, Arjuna, felt very confused and dejected and went into a state of despondency, *Vishad*. Arjuna's dejection and dilemma was due to his attachment to his family members, friends and respected gurus and the fear of losing them and also causing them injury.

Arjuna had two options; he could fight the war and kill his near and dear ones (violence) or he could run away from the war for the sake of preserving peace and non-violence (*Ahinsa*). He chose the second option, and refused to fight the righteous war and perform his duty as a warrior. He laid down his arms and said, "I will not fight." According to the Gita, confusion can lead to serious conflict and if the conflict is not resolved, one can fall into a state of depression and despondency.

When faced with a moral crisis and having no ray of hope, Arjuna surrendered himself and asked Lord Krishna for His advice and guidance (2.07). Lord Krishna revealed His Cosmic, Universal Form to Arjuna and taught him the great wisdom of life, death, and enlightenment.

Through Arjuna's questions and Lord Krishna's answers, a long dialogue of divine teachings, made Arjuna aware of his Dharma, righteous duty. (Here Arjuna represents a *jivatma*, individual soul, mind filled with *vishad* and Lord Krishna represents a divine teacher Supreme-Soul, Supreme Consciousness, God). Ultimately, Arjuna was transformed and surrendered to the wisdom of Lord Krishna. With His guidance, he fulfilled his duty by fighting the righteous war, became enlightened and attained a *Brahmic* state of Pure Super Consciousness, love, peace and *Anandam*. (2.72)

Thus, Arjuna's questions and Lord Krishna's answers, the divine teaching, led to the rebirth of Bhagavad Gita. (4.01–03)

Q Can the Gita's teachings be applied to life today?

The Gita is Eternal Wisdom for ancient man as well as for today's man with all types of different personalities.

The divine dialogue is between Lord Krishna, (Higher Self, Super-Soul, Supreme Consciousness) and Arjuna (lower self, individual soul) whose mind is filled with anguish. It is a conversation between intuitions (Inner voice) and the logical mind-Higher self and lower self.

Thus, Arjuna was transcended by Lord Krishna's teaching and guidance—The Gita.

The immortal message of the Gita (Universal Truth) was not only imparted to Arjuna for a specific condition and situation but also for all of mankind, based upon the eternal conditions of human nature. All people in this world face similar issues and go through similar confusions and emotions throughout their lives. Every individual processes information differently, according to his own perception, limitations and ego, which results in various problems. However, when one lives in God's Consciousness (Supreme Consciousness, Higher Self), he overcomes his limitations and realizes that he is more than just body, mind and ego. He gradually transcends from set beliefs, fears, and anxieties to a higher state of Freedom, Joy and Peace.

> *Gita is all about you and me*

Since the teachings of the Gita are based upon human psychology they have a very *SYMBOLIC* and profound meaning in our daily lives. Therefore, the secular teachings of Gita are not limited to any time, nation or religion but apply equally to everyone of us.

Here, Arjuna represents a typically confused mind. Every one of us goes through similar dilemmas in life and we need guidance to make proper decisions. The battlefield of Kurukshetra was not just the battlefield of Arjuna, it is also the battlefield of life, where one is faced many times with issues and problems and goes into a state of *Vishad*. The real *Kurukshetra* is within us.

Each of us is Arjuna facing the same war of right or wrong, fear and frustration, confusion and dejection. We all need help. Therefore, Lord Krishna, who is merciful, spoke the Gita for us, using Arjuna, His friend and student, as a DEMO MODEL, to convey His divine message for mankind. We too can achieve the same transformation of self by following His teachings in the form of the Gita.

The teaching of the Gita apply to today's man with a modern lifestyle (young and old, housewife to professional) and all types of people with different personalities, in every field and every situation of life from family to global and from personal to business. Since Gita is the voice of Lord Krishna, it has the miraculous ability to give readers the true meaning of what they are searching for. Gita's message is still as fresh today as it was when first given on the battlefield of *Kurukshetra*. As a matter of fact, in today's materialistic world, its teachings are needed more than ever.

> *The Gita is an answer to all those seeking enlightenment on the various problems of human life at all times.*
>
> —H.H. Swami Hariharji Maharaj

Q What is the central message of the Gita?

Do your work/duty with love and devotion, without any selfish motive, and leave the rest to God

The central message of the Gita is: "You have a right to perform your work (respective duty) only but no control or claim to its results. The fruits of work should not be your motive and you should never be inactive." (2.47)

"Your Duty (Righteousness) is Your *Dharma*." By doing your duty, you can attain freedom from miseries and Liberation , (*Moksha*, Self-Realization, Purpose of Life).

The Gita starts with the word '*Dharma*' and ends with the word 'Mama' (My duty—*svadharma*).

Dharma (Duty) + Mama (My) = My Duty (svadharma) → Eternal Happiness, Peace and Anandam/Bliss

By performing your own duty, you will develop self-confidence, self-contentment and divine qualities. You will purify and transform yourself, be enlightened as Arjuna and live in peace and *Anandam* in the material world as well.

Q What does the Gita offer?

The Gita is Brahma-Vidya—Knowledge of God/Self

The Gita offers accurate, fundamental knowledge about God and His creation (metaphysical science, matter and energy)—the Ultimate Truth, (birth and death), the results of actions, the eternal soul, Liberation and the purpose and the Supreme goal of human life. It describes in detail the science of Self-Realization and the step-by-step process of self-purification and self-transformation by which one can establish one's eternal relationship with God.

Gita offers the knowledge of science and spirituality

The Gita is the guru that awakens the guru within

The ultimate objective of the Gita is to remove darkness and ignorance of the human mind and awaken the guru within, who guides us to realize our true nature, *Sat Chit Ananda*. The Gita allows us to attain Self-Realization while living and performing our daily activities in the material world.

The Gita answers every question in our life as well as the most common and basic five universal questions:

1. Who am I?
2. Where did I come from?
3. Where will I go from here (after death)?
4. What is the purpose of my life?
5. How can I fulfill the purpose of my life (God/Self-Realization) and still lead a happy and peaceful life in this material world?

Arjuna asked many questions covering all the problems of mankind and Lord Krishna answered them all. Therefore, the Gita gives answers to every question in our life and a solution to all problems and issues that we face daily in our very fast-paced lifestyle.

Q What does the Gita teach?

The Gita is a step-by-step spiritual practical guide for our daily lives

The Gita is a spiritual instruction manual to operate our daily life skillfully. It teaches us how to convert every activity of life into Sadhana/Spiritual practices, and attain Self-Realization while living in a material world.

Gita teaches how to listen and communicate effectively

The Gita is a conversation or *Samvad* between two good friends and not an argument, *Vivad*. One person is talking and the other person is listening quietly. This is the very first teaching of the Gita, how to listen to and communicate with each other. Lord Krishna is not just Arjuna's friend, He is our friend too and He talks to us all the time though our intuitions. Our job is to just listen to Him as an obedient student and to follow His guidance.

The Gita teaches us how to apply its teaching in our lives, fulfill our daily responsibilities, remove our doubts and confusions and to attain everlasting Peace, Prosperity and *Anandam* (Ultimate bliss).

Lord Krishna openly declared to Arjuna that he who studies this scripture, follows and practices its teachings, and propagates its teachings to others, will not only free himself from the miseries of the world, but becomes extremely dear to Him.

The Gita is a boat that takes us from one shore of the external world, (Maya—attachment, miseries) to another shore of non-attachment, Love, Peace, Bliss-Anandam

The Gita guides us to realize:

- Divinity is within us
- Peace is within us
- Love is within us
- The fountain of *Anandam*—Bliss, Joy—is within us and we are *Sat Chit Ananda.*

The Gita teaches us:

- What to do and what not to do
- Where to do it
- When to do it
- Why do we do it
- And how to do

The Gita teaches the art of living and the art of dying

The Gita's teachings transformed Arjuna from, "I will not fight the battle" to, "I will do as you advise," (2.09, 18.73). It took Arjuna, very gradually, from Vishad, confusion and dejection to when he says, "my doubts are dispelled, I have regained the memory of Self-Knowledge and will do as you advised."

The Gita is a road map to attain the Supreme Goal of our lives, 'Sat Chit Ananda'

It also guides one to transform from an average human being to a Self-realized person (Enlightened), man to God by eliminating bad qualities (vices) and developing divine qualities (virtues).

(Jivatma → Dharmatma → Mahatma → Parmatma)

The Gita guides us very systematically how to develop self-awareness, do self-analysis, identify our own shortcomings, take action for self-correction, balance the State of Mind (Equanimity), and attain Liberation.

The Gita is a spiritual guide for self-awareness, self-purification, self-transformation and Self-Realization

Q What was the original language of Bhagavad Gita?

The original language of the Bhagavad Gita was Sanskrit, an ancient language that is very elegant and euphonious. All the Vedic mantras are recited in Sanskrit language.

Q Who first translated the Bhagavad Gita into English and when?

In 1785, in London, Charles Wilkins, translated the Bhagavad Gita into English.

Q Why did I choose the Q & A format?

Arjuna is a question, Lord Krishna is the Answer and so is the Gita

In today's world, man is very inquisitive and due to his busy lifestyle, he needs quick answers to his questions. Therefore, I have prepared this spiritual guide 'My questions and God's Answers, Guide to Eternal Happiness, Peace and Ananadam'.

The entire divine dialogue of the Gita is based upon Arjuna's questions and Lord Krishna's answers. Therefore it also encouraged me to prepare the Gita's message into a question and answer format so that readers can easily understand these teachings and get answers to their questions about different situations in daily life.

Unless we are awakened and question the suffering in our life, we cannot become a perfect human being. Humanity begins when this sort of inquiry is awakened in one's mind. Therefore, those who question why they are suffering, or where they came from or where they shall go after death are proper students for the understanding of Gita.

—Swami Prabhupada

Self-inquiry is the basic foundation for Spiritual Growth and self-development

Q When and where should the Gita be used as a reference guide?

The best way to start the day is to read the Gita in the morning

The sermon of the Gita was delivered not in a holy place such as a temple or ashram nor was it sung in a place of natural beauty, like a forest or the Himalayas. Instead the Gita was delivered in the middle of a battlefield, Kurukshetra. Arjuna was transformed by following the teachings of the Gita during the war.

Similarly, one does not need to leave home, change locations or run away from a situation in order to lead a peaceful and happy life and also attain Self-Realization (Bliss/*Anandam* within). The goal of life can be achieved anywhere (home, office, temple, etc), just by changing the status of mind, practicing the Gita's teachings and performing one's own duties and daily activities while remaining in the material world.

Therefore, we can practice Gita's teachings:

- Any time of the day as we like
- Whenever we have doubts, confusion or questions
- When we feel dejected, distressed or lonely
- When we are fearful or worried
- When we want to relax

In the modern era of science and technology, the mind is always asking for reason and analysis. The Gita offers all. It has advice, the theory underpinning each piece of advice, and a practical way of applying it.

The Gita has a scientific approach to solutions. Being a scientist myself, and having an analytical mind, it helps me to understand the theory, hypothesis, and practical approach to apply in daily life, especially for solving problems.

When disappointment stares me in the face and all alone I see not one ray of light, I go back to the Bhagavad Gita. I find a verse here and a verse there, and I immediately begin to smile in the midst of overwhelming tragedies—and my life has been full of external tragedies. If they have left no visible, no indelible scar on me, I owe it all to the teaching of the Bhagavad Gita.

—Mahatma Gandhi

Q How to study the Gita and practice its teachings in daily life?

The Gita is a practical Spiritual Guide to the Righteous Living

The purpose of the Gita's message is to live in this world peacefully and harmoniously and still attain Self-Realization. In order to do so, we must perform righteously our prescribed duty (*Svadharma*) without expecting the result or the fruit of our action. Cause and effect is the Law of Nature and we must take full responsibility for our actions.

We should always maintain a spiritual lifestyle and live in His consciousness. To do every action that leads to the Supreme goal of our life; every thought, every action must be directed toward attaining permanent peace and Self-Realization—*Sat Chit Ananda*.

Only reading the Gita may bring some awareness to one, but he will not get the full experience, transformation and the complete realization without applying it in daily life. As one can never learn to swim just by reading a book, one must dive into the pool. Therefore, one must read, listen, contemplate, follow and practice its teachings in daily life (*Pathan, Sravan, Manana, Abhyasa*) as Lord Krishna advised. (18.67–73)

The Gita's style is so simple and elegant that after a little study, man can easily follow the structure of its words; but the thought behind those words is so deep and abstruse that even a lifelong, constant study does not show one the end of it. Everyday the Gita exhibits a new facet to thought, hence the Gita remains eternally new. Deep reflection with reverence and faith will make it directly appear impregnated with deep meaning at every step.

—Jayadayal Goyandka

In order to attain Self-Realization and enjoy life to the fullest, one must do self-purification and self-transformation (re-write and re-program the software of the mind) (2.45). This can be achieved by always living in God's Consciousness (practicing *Karma Yoga, Jnana Yoga, Bhakti Yoga*, meditation and prayers) and practicing the following seven steps.

Seven Steps

1. Self-discipline (Focus on self and not on others).
2. Have divine company (*Guru, Gita, Gopal*).
3. *Karma*-Action Yoga (Perform every action as selflessly a service to God-yoga).
4. *Bhakti*-Devotion Yoga (Offer unconditional love for God and His creation without any expectations).
5. *Jnana*-Knowledge Yoga (Attain own realize knowledge of the Absolute, God, Self).
6. Do Meditation, Prayers, *Pranayam* (breathing discipline), *Asanas* (physical postures).
7. Surrender to God.

Action Plan to Practice Spirituality Daily

Right practice makes men perfect

1. Read at least 3 verses of the Gita daily or as many as you wish preferably first thing in the morning,. The number is not important but reading daily is important (as Gandhiji did whenever he neaded an answer, guidance and inspiration, he picked up his Gita and read)
2. Take one verse for a specific purpose, contemplate the meaning and apply it in your daily life by practicing it. (each verse can be chosen as a prescription for a specific problem or question, and for developing divine qualities.)
3. Evaluate your progress every night before going to bed. If you feel that you might have done better, do not feel guilty. Just keep practicing it and pray for His guidance and support. Continue to practice until you feel satisfied.
4. Take the next verse and follow Step 3. By the grace of God, you will receive guidance from within and understand spiritual truth, and gradually attain Eternal happiness, Peace and Anandam (Bliss).
5. Continue until you reach the Supreme goal of life, which is to attain everlasting Love, Peace and Anandam. This is your True Nature, your Real Self.

This is a lifelong process and journey so it requires lots of discipline, effort and patience.

Spirituality is not instant but a slow process

Spirituality is not just an activity but a life style

Summary

The Gita	An extraordinary scripture
Narration of the Gita	Extraordinary juncture, just before the war begins
Extraordinary Setting/Situation	Battlefield/War
Extraordinary Person	Shri Krishna (Supreme Godhead)
Extraordinary Warrior	Arjuna (Skillfull warrior but lost his will just befor the war)

Extraordinary Listener	Dhritrashtra (who is blind and not present at that moment)
Extraordinary Speaker	Sanjaya (having divine sight that enabled him to be eyewitness to the war that was taking place elsewhere.)

Extraordinary Conclusion

We should indeed perform our duties, but we should remain detached from the fruits of action (*Karmanye vadhi karaste ma phaleshu kadachan 2/47*). Peace of mind comes not through inaction, but through the renunciation of the fruit of action. (*Yogah karmeshu kaushlam 2/50*). By doing so, man will continue to do his worldly duties and at the same time attain eternal happiness, peace and bliss (*Anandam*). He will live in the world, but not be of the world.

The Gita is a spiritual guide for my daily life that teaches me how to live in this material world, do my duty with love, be cheerful, be happy, and be in peace and still enjoy my life. I practice it, I preach it, and I promote it

Ground Zero
Kurukshetra, the battle field of Mahabharata

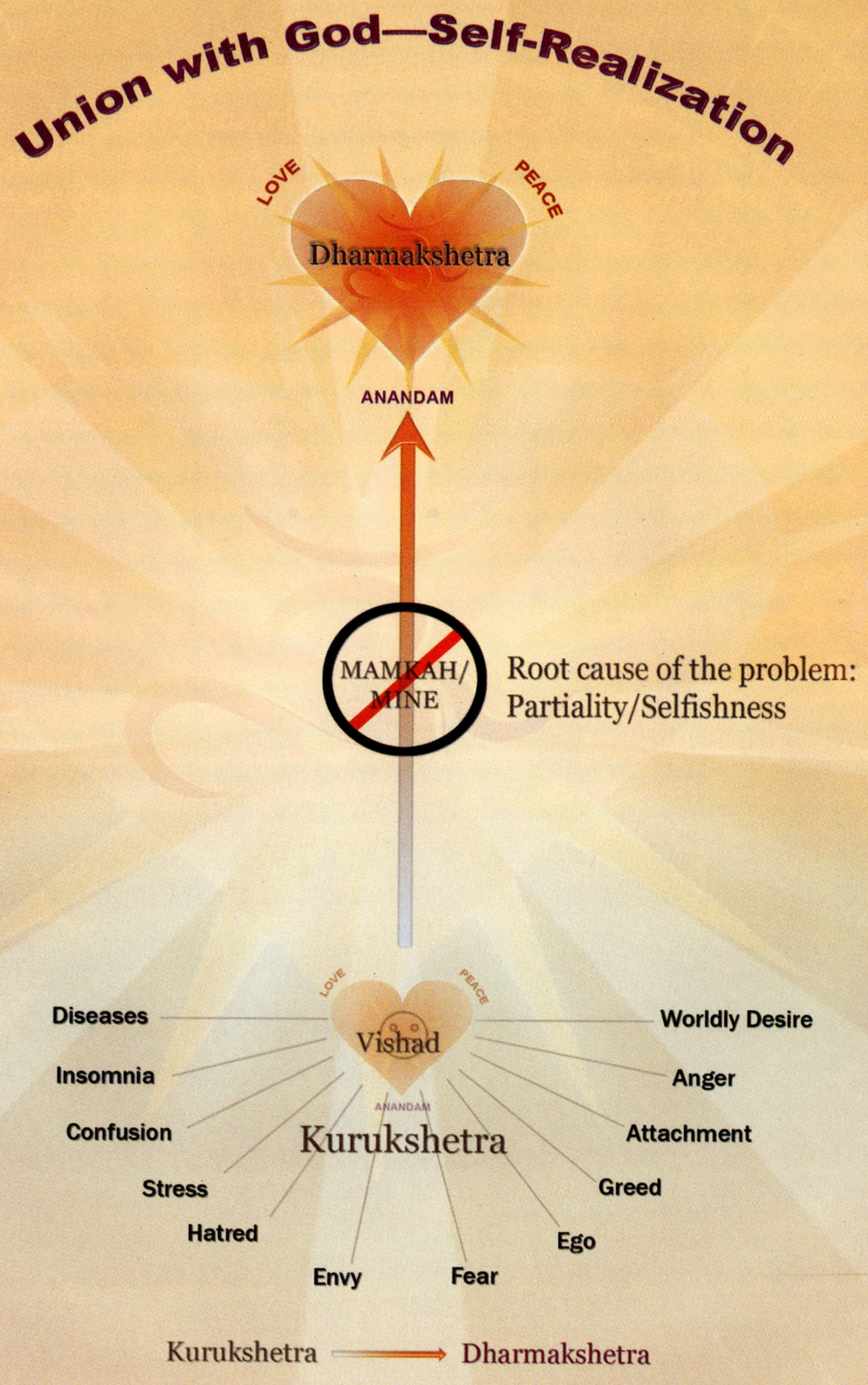

Self-Purification and Transformation through Vishad Yoga

ARJUNA VISHAD YOGA

Arjuna Despondency and Dilemma

Union with God (Self-Realization) through the path of despondency and dilemma

The Gita is a boat to cross the ocean of life

The first chapter of Srimad Bhagavad Gita is about Arjuna's *Vishad Yoga*, how he became very sad, confused and a detailed description of the battlefield.

When both the armies were arrayed in the battlefield of Kurukshetra, Arjuna asked to inspect the army to see who he was going to fight. After beholding his intimate relatives, gurus, teachers and friends on both sides of the army, ready to fight and sacrifice their lives, he was overcome by grief and pity, he felt very weak, confused and lost the will to fight. He went into deep sorrow, depression and despondency (*Vishad*). Arjuna was very sincere, but his mind was overwhelmed due to his attachment to family members and fear of having to kill them, which he thought would be a sin. He sat down on the back seat of the chariot silently and began to think. He had yet to learn the lesson of performing his own prescribed duty (*svadharma*) without expecting the fruit of action (selfless action).

Sick mind leads to sick body, sick society and disturbances in the world

Sick mind → sick body → Sick society → Disturbances in the world

Q What is *Vishad*?

Vishad means when one feels extremely distressed, dejected and one's mind is full of doubts, emotional conflicts, anger and fear These negative emotions generate toxins in the body and he feels very week both physically and emotionally and loses his capability of discrimination between rights and wrongs, thus can not make any proper decision. Arjuna, who was a great warrior, had been trained to fight skillfully, yet he became anguished, dejected and went into a state of confusion and dilemma, experienced deep sorrow (*Vishad*). He laid down his arms, refusing to fight and fulfill his duty.

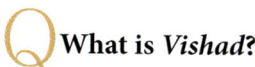

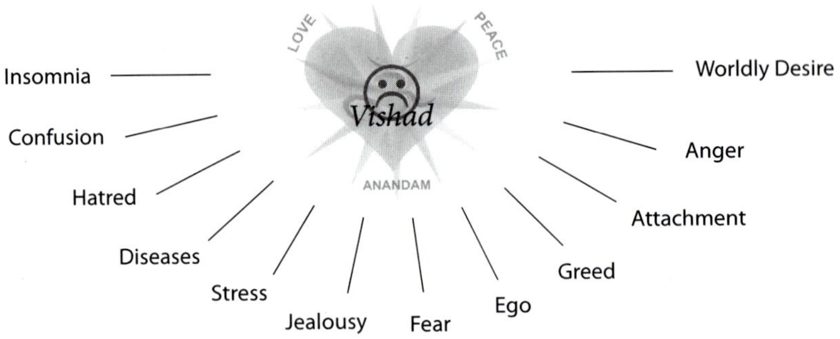

Fig. 1.1 *Vishad leads to negative thoughts which results in toxins, diseases and disruptions in the body*

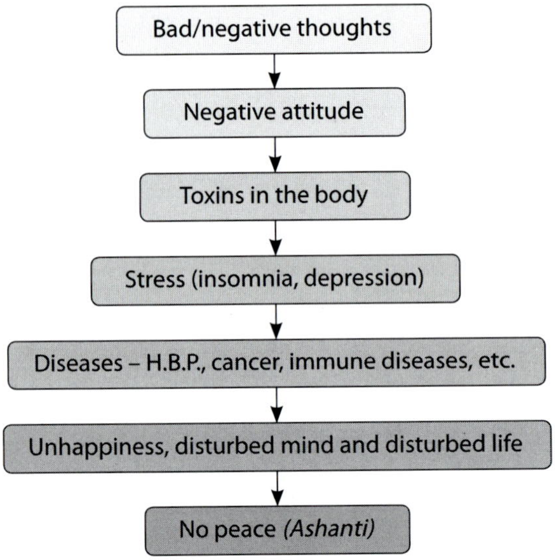

Flow chart 1.1 *Consequences of Vishad*

Q What is the cause of *Vishad*?

Mamakah (possessiveness)

Mamakah means mine/my-ness. King Dhritarashtra, who was the head of the family, should have treated everyone equally. However, he was partial between his children and his brother's children that became one of the main cause that led to the war. Possessiveness (my-ness) and partiality are the root cause of the problems in our lives. When we are not fair with others and take sides due to our own attachments, our vices start surfacing and bring a lot of miseries into our life.

The Gita starts with two words **Dharmakshetra** and **Kurukshetra** (first verse, chapter one). **Dharmakshetra** means the field of righteousness (*Dharma*). We should make *Dharma* the basis of our lives. *Dharma* means the welfare of all, it should override the dictates of *Mamakah* (my-ness)—personal interests of kith and kin. *Kuru* is the dynasty. *Kuru* also means to do. **Kurukshetra** is the field of activities (battlefield of life). What we do in our lives and how we conduct ourselves.

With these first two words, Dharmakshetra and Kurukshetra, Bhagavad Gita answers the fundamental question, "What is the Purpose and Supreme goal of life?"

The Gita says: Establish righteousness by converting Kurukshetra (battle field, action, confusion, turmoil, pains and miseries, etc.) into Dharmakshetra (Field of *Dharma*, Righteousness). Kurukshetra is within all of us. First we have to establish the Dharma within ourselves and then we can establish it externally by doing our duty lovingly.

Kurukshetra → Dharmakshetra

Field of action → Field of Righteousness (Dharma/Duty)

Thus we will be establishing Dharmakshetra and making this world a better place to live. First, we must develop harmony and peace within because the external world is only a reflection of our internal turmoil.

The real war of Kurukshetra is within us, each of us is Arjuna, struggling with right and wrong, temptations, fears and frustrations.

—H.H. Swami Chidanand Saraswatiji

Main Message

Attain Union with God/Self through the path of dejection, despondency, depression, deep sorrow and dilemma (Vishad)

The path of *Vishad Yoga* is the foundation and starting point to unite with God and to attain the Supreme Goal of life, Self-Realization. When we attain Union with God, we receive Everlasting Peace and *Anandam* (*Sat Chit Ananda*).

When we face calamities in life, we can turn towards alcohol and drugs or turn toward God, scriptures, and a divine friend for help. When we turn towards God, we are helped and also transformed from lower self to Higher Self.

- The description of the battlefield.
- Arjuna's dilemma to fight with his own family members and delusion due to his attachment to them.
- Arjuna's refusal to fight the battle due to fear of killing them.

Chapter Overview

01–11 Description of both armies and their main warriors on the battlefield of Kurukshetra

12–19 War cry

20–27 Arjuna's request

28–47 Arjuna's dilemma

Description of both armies and their main warriors on the battlefield of Kurukshetra

Q What did King Dhritarashtra want to know from his minister, Sanjaya?

धृतराष्ट्र उवाच
धर्मक्षेत्रे कुरुक्षेत्रे समवेता युयुत्सवः।
मामकाः पाण्डवाश्चैव किमकुर्वत संजय ॥1॥

dhṛtarāṣṭra uvāca
dharma-kṣetre kuru-kṣetre samavetā yuyutsavaḥ
māmakāḥ pāṇḍavāś caiva kim akurvata sañjaya

Dhritarashtra's one and only question in the entire Gita

Dhritarashtra said: O Sanjaya, please tell, having assembled in the holy field of Kurukshetra (battlefield of Righteousness), eager to fight, what did my sons, and the sons of Pandu (Pandavas) do? (1.01)

Q How did Prince Duryodhana describe the Pandava army to his guru, Drona, prior to the battle?

संजय उवाच
दृष्ट्वा तु पाण्डवानीकं व्यूढं दुर्योधनस्तदा।
आचार्यमुपसङ्गम्य राजा वचनमब्रवीत् ॥2॥

sañjaya uvāca
dṛṣṭvā tu pāṇḍavānīkaṁ vyūḍhaṁ duryodhanas tadā
ācāryam upasaṅgamya rājā vacanam abravīt

पश्यैतां पाण्डुपुत्राणामाचार्य महतीं चमूम्।
व्यूढां द्रुपदपुत्रेण तव शिष्येण धीमता ॥3॥

paśyaitāṁ pāṇḍu-putrāṇām ācārya mahatīṁ camūm
vyūḍhāṁ drupada-putreṇa tava śiṣyeṇa dhīmatā

अत्र शूरा महेष्वासा भीमार्जुनसमा युधि।
युयुधानो विराटश्च द्रुपदश्च महारथः ।।4।।

atra śūrā maheṣv-āsā bhīmārjuna-samā yudhi
yuyudhāno virāṭaś ca drupadaś ca mahā-rathaḥ

धृष्टकेतुश्चेकितानः काशिराजश्च वीर्यवान्।
पुरुजित्कुन्तिभोजश्च शैब्यश्च नरपुङ्गवः ।।5।।

dhṛṣṭaketuś cekitānaḥ kāśirājaś ca vīryavān
purujit kuntibhojaś ca śaibyaś ca nara-puṅgavaḥ

युधामन्युश्च विक्रान्त उत्तमौजाश्च वीर्यवान्।
सौभद्रो द्रौपदेयाश्च सर्व एव महारथाः ।।6।।

yudhāmanyuś ca vikrānta uttamaujāś ca vīryavān
saubhadro draupadeyāś ca sarva eva mahā-rathāḥ

Sanjaya said: O King, after seeing the army of the Pandavas gathered in the battle-field, King Duryodhana approached his guru Drona and spoke these words: (1.02)

Please see O Master, this well organized mighty army of the sons of Pandu gathered for battle by your talented disciple, the son of King Drupada (1.03)

There are many heroes and mighty archers in this army who are equal in warfare to Bhima and Arjuna such as Yuyudhana, Virata, and the great chariot-warrior Drupada (1.04), Dhrstaketu, Cekitana and the heroic King of Kashi, Purujit, Kuntibhoja, and Yaibya, the best among men and mighty Yudhamanyu, the valiant Uttamauja, Abhimanyu, son of Subhadra, and the five sons of Draupadi all of them are well known great warriors. (1.04–06)

Q How did King Duryodhana describe Kaurav's army?

अस्माकं तु विशिष्टा ये तान्निबोध द्विजोत्तम्।
नायका मम सैन्यस्य संज्ञार्थं तान्ब्रवीमि ते ।।7।।

asmākaṁ tu viśiṣṭā ye tān nibodha dvijottama
nāyakā mama sainyasya saṁjñārthaṁ tān bravīmi te

भवान्भीष्मश्च कर्णश्च कृपश्च समितिंजयः।
अश्वत्थामा विकर्णश्च सौमदत्तिस्तथैव च ।।8।।

bhavān bhīṣmaś ca karṇaś ca kṛpaś ca samitiṁ-jayaḥ
aśvatthāmā vikarṇaś ca saumadattis tathaiva ca

अन्ये च बहवः शूरा मदर्थे त्यक्तजीविताः।
नानाशस्त्रप्रहरणाः सर्वे युद्धविशारदाः ।।9।।

anye ca bahavaḥ śūrā mad-arthe tyakta-jīvitāḥ
nānā-śastra-praharaṇāḥ sarve yuddha-viśāradāḥ

O Best of the twice-born (*Brahmana*), for your information, I should also let you know who are the distinguished warriors on our side and name the commanders of my army for your information. (1.07)

Yourself, Bhisma, Karna and Krpa, who are ever victorious in battle, Asvattama, Vikarna, and Bhurisrava, the son of Somadatta. (1.08)

And there are many other heroes who have risked their lives for me, they are armed with various weapons and all are skilled in the strategy of warfare. (1.09)

Q What did King Duryodhana think about his army commander Bhisma and why did he ask others to protect him?

अपर्याप्तं तदस्माकं बलं भीष्माभिरक्षितम् ।
पर्याप्तं त्विदमेतेषां बलं भीमाभिरक्षितम् ।। 10 ।।

aparyāptaṁ tad asmākaṁ balaṁ bhīṣmābhirakṣitam
paryāptaṁ tv idam eteṣāṁ balaṁ bhīmābhirakṣitam

अयनेषु च सर्वेषु यथाभागमवस्थिताः ।
भीष्ममेवाभिरक्षन्तु भवन्तः सर्व एव हि ।। 11 ।।

ayaneṣu ca sarveṣu yathā-bhāgam avasthitāḥ
bhīṣmam evābhirakṣantu bhavantaḥ sarva eva hi

Very special instruction to protect the commander of the army

Our army, commanded by Bhisma, is unconquerable while their army, protected by Bhima, is easy to conquer. Therefore, all of you, stationed in your respective positions on all fronts must protect our commander Bhisma by all means. (1.10–11)

War Cry

Q Who blew the first conch on the battlefield and what happened after that?

तस्य संजनयन्हर्षं कुरुवृद्धः पितामहः ।
सिंहनादं विनद्योच्चैः शङ्खं दध्मौ प्रतापवान् ।। 12 ।।

tasya sañjanayan harṣaṁ kuru-vṛddhaḥ pitāmahaḥ
siṁha-nādaṁ vinadyoccaiḥ śaṅkhaṁ dadhmau pratāpavān

ततः शङ्खाश्च भेर्यश्च पणवानकगोमुखाः ।
सहसैवाभ्यहन्यन्त स शब्दस्तुमुलोऽभवत् ।। 13 ।।

tataḥ śaṅkhāś ca bheryaś ca paṇavānaka-gomukhāḥ
sahasaivābhyahanyanta sa śabdas tumulo 'bhavat

The mighty Bhishma, the eldest man of the Kuru dynasty, roaring like a lion, blew his conch loudly to cheer up Duryodhana. (1.12)

Then conches, kettledrums, cymbals, drums, and trumpets were sounded together and made tremendous noise. (1.13)

Q Who followed the blow of the first conch?

ततः श्वेतैर्हयैर्युक्ते महति स्यन्दने स्थितौ ।
माधवः पाण्डवश्चैव दिव्यौ शङ्खौ प्रदध्मतुः ॥ 14 ॥

tataḥ śvetair hayair yukte mahati syandane sthitau
mādhavaḥ pāṇḍavaś caiva divyau śaṅkhau pradadhmatuḥ

पाञ्चजन्यं हृषीकेशो देवदत्तं धनंजयः ।
पौण्ड्रं दध्मौ महाशङ्खं भीमकर्मा वृकोदरः ॥ 15 ॥

pāñcajanyaṁ hṛṣīkeśo devadattaṁ dhanañjayaḥ
pauṇḍraṁ dadhmau mahā-śaṅkhaṁ bhīma-karmā vṛkodaraḥ

अनन्तविजयं राजा कुन्तीपुत्रो युधिष्ठिरः ।
नकुलः सहदेवश्च सुघोषमणिपुष्पकौ ॥ 16 ॥

Pancanjaya—Lord Krishna's conch

anantavijayaṁ rājā kuntī-putro yudhiṣṭhiraḥ
nakulaḥ sahadevaś ca sughoṣa-maṇipuṣpakau

काश्यश्च परमेष्वासः शिखण्डी च महारथः ।
धृष्टद्युम्नो विराटश्च सात्यकिश्चापराजितः ॥ 17 ॥

kāśyaś ca parameṣv-āsaḥ śikhaṇḍī ca mahā-rathaḥ
dhṛṣṭadyumno virāṭaś ca sātyakiś cāparājitaḥ

द्रुपदो द्रौपदेयाश्च सर्वशः पृथिवीपते ।
सौभद्रश्च महाबाहुः शङ्खान्दध्मुः पृथक् पृथक् ॥ 18 ॥

drupado draupadeyāś ca sarvaśaḥ pṛthivī-pate
saubhadraś ca mahā-bāhuḥ śaṅkhān dadhmuḥ pṛthak pṛthak

Then Lord Krishna and Arjuna, seated in a grand chariot drawn by white horses, blew their celestial conches as well. (1.14)

Lord Krishna blew His conch, named Pancanjaya; Arjuna blew his conch called Devadatta; and Bhima, the doer of terrific deeds, blew his mighty conch, Paundra. (1.15)

The King Yudhisthira, son of Kunti, blew his conch named Anantavijaya and Nakula and Sahadeva blew Sughosa and Manipuspaka conches, respectively. (1.16)

And the King of Kasi, the chief of archers Sikhandi, the great warrior Dhrishtadyumna, Virata, the invincible Satyaki did likewise. (1.17)

King Drupada, as well as the five sons of Draupadi and the mighty armed Abhimanyu, the son of Subhadra, all of them blew their respective conches. (1.18)

Q What frightened the Kauravas?

स घोषो धार्तराष्ट्राणां हृदयानि व्यदारयत्।
नभश्च पृथिवीं चैव तुमुलो व्यनुनादयन्॥19॥

sa ghoṣo dhārtarāṣṭrāṇāṁ hṛdayāni vyadārayat
nabhaś ca pṛthivīṁ caiva tumulo 'bhyanunādayan

The tumultuous uproar, resounding through earth and sky, pierced the hearts of Dhritarashtra's sons (Kauravas). (1.19)

Arjuna's Request

Q After hearing the roaring noises, what did Arjuna ask Lord Krishna to do and why?

अथ व्यवस्थितान्दृष्ट्वा धार्तराष्ट्रान्कपिध्वजः।
प्रवृत्ते शस्त्रसंपाते धनुरुद्यम्य पाण्डवः॥20॥

atha vyavasthitān dṛṣṭvā dhārtarāṣṭrān kapi-dhvajaḥ
pravṛtte śastra-sampāte dhanur udyamya pāṇḍavaḥ

हृषीकेशं तदा वाक्यमिदमाह महीपते।
अर्जुन उवाच
सेनयोरुभयोर्मध्ये रथं स्थापय मेऽच्युत॥21॥

hṛṣīkeśaṁ tadā vākyam idam āha mahī-pate
arjuna uvāca
senayor ubhayor madhye rathaṁ sthāpaya me 'cyuta

Arjuna's desire to pre-evaluate the battlefield

यावदेतान्निरीक्षेऽहं योद्धुकामानवस्थितान्।
कैर्मया सह योद्धव्यमस्मिन् रणसमुद्यमे॥22॥

yāvad etān nirīkṣe 'haṁ yoddhu-kāmān avasthitān
kair mayā saha yoddhavyam asmin raṇa-samudyame

योत्स्यमानानवेक्षेऽहं य एतेऽत्र समागताः।
धार्तराष्ट्रस्य दुर्बुद्धेर्युद्धे प्रियचिकीर्षवः॥23॥

yotsyamānān avekṣe 'haṁ ya ete 'tra samāgatāḥ
dhārtarāṣṭrasya durbuddher yuddhe priya-cikīrṣavaḥ

Then looking at the sons of Dhritarashtra stationed in their army positions ready to operate their weapons, Arjuna, the son of Pandu whose banner bore the emblem of Lord Hanuman (Monkey god), raised his bow and spoke these words to Lord Krishna. (1.20)

Arjuna said: "O Lord, please place my chariot between the two armies." (1.21)

So I can carefully observe all the warriors who stand here desirous of war with whom I have to fight in this battle. (1.22)

I want to see those who are assembled here and ready to fight and wishing to please the evil-minded son of Dhritarashtra (Duryodhana). (1.23)

Q Where did Lord Krishna place the chariot in the battlefield?

संजय उवाच
एवमुक्तो हृषीकेशो गुडाकेशेन भारत।
सेनयोरुभयोर्मध्ये स्थापयित्वा रथोत्तमम् ।। 24 ।।

sañjaya uvāca
evam ukto hṛṣīkeśo guḍākeśena bhārata
senayor ubhayor madhye sthāpayitvā rathottamam

भीष्मद्रोणप्रमुखतः सर्वेषां च महीक्षिताम्।
उवाच पार्थ पश्यैतान् समवेतान् कुरूनिति ।। 25 ।।

bhīṣma-droṇa-pramukhataḥ sarveṣāṁ ca mahī-kṣitām
uvāca pārtha paśyaitān samavetān kurūn iti

Sanjaya said: O King, as requested by Arjuna , Lord Krishna placed the magnificent chariot between the two armies in front of Bhisma, Drona and all the other Kings, and said, "Arjuna, behold these Kurus assembled here." (1.24–25)

Q What did Arjuna see on the battlefield?

तत्रापश्यत्स्थितान्पार्थः पितृनथ पितामहान्।
आचार्यान् मातुलान् भ्रातृन्पुत्रान् पौत्रान्सखींस्तथा ।। 26 ।।

tatrāpaśyat sthitān pārthaḥ pitṝn atha pitāmahān
ācāryān mātulān bhrātṝn putrān pautrān sakhīṁs tathā

श्वशुरान् सुहृदश्चैव सेनयोरुभयोरपि।
तान्समीक्ष्य स कौन्तेयः सर्वान्बन्धूनवस्थितान् ।। 27 ।।

śvaśurān suhṛdaś caiva senayor ubhayor api
tān samīkṣya sa kaunteyaḥ sarvān bandhūn avasthitān

There, Arjuna saw his uncles, grandfathers, teachers, maternal uncles, brothers, cousins, sons, grandsons, friends, fathers-in-law, and other well wishers stationed between both the armies. (1.26–27)

Arjuna's Dilemma

Q Why did Arjuna go into *Vishad* (overwhelmed with grief, became nervous) and what kind of symptoms did he experience?

कृपयो परयाविष्टो विषीदन्निदमब्रवीत् ।
अर्जुन उवाच
दृष्ट्वेमं स्वजनं कृष्ण युयुत्सुं समुपस्थितम् ।। 28 ।।

kṛpayā parayāviṣṭo viṣīdann idam abravīt
arjuna uvāca
dṛṣṭvemaṁ sva-janaṁ kṛṣṇa yuyutsuṁ samupasthitam

सीदन्ति मम गात्राणि मुखं च परिशुष्यति ।
वेपथुश्च शरीरे मे रोमहर्षश्च जायते ।। 29 ।।

sīdanti mama gātrāṇi mukhaṁ ca pariśuṣyati
vepathuś ca śarīre me roma-harṣaś ca jāyate

The signs of anxiety

गाण्डीवं स्रंसते हस्तात्त्वक्चैव परिदह्यते ।
न च शक्नोम्यवस्थातुं भ्रमतीव च मे मनः ।। 30 ।।

gāṇḍīvaṁ sraṁsate hastāt tvak caiva paridahyate
na ca śaknomy avasthātuṁ bhramatīva ca me manaḥ

निमित्तानि च पश्यामि विपरीतानि केशव ।
न च श्रेयोऽनुपश्यामि हत्वा स्वजनमाहवे ।। 31 ।।

nimittāni ca paśyāmi viparītāni keśava
na ca śreyo 'nupaśyāmi hatvā sva-janam āhave

Seeing all his relatives standing in both armies, Arjuna was possessed with deep compassion and spoke these words in grief. (1.28)

Arjuna said: O Krishna, seeing my kinsmen assembled here eager to fight, my limbs have become weak and my mouth has become dry, my body shakes and my hair stands on end. (1.29)

The bow (Gandiva) is slipping from my hand and my skin is burning all over, my mind is reeling (shocked and confused) and I am not even able to stand firmly. (1.30)

And I see inauspicious omens, O Krishna; I do not perceive any good in killing my kith and kin in battle. (1.31)

Q Did Arjuna fight to add to his kingdom?

न काङ्क्षे विजयं कृष्ण न च राज्यं सुखानि च।
किं नो राज्येन गोविन्द किं भोगैर्जीवितेन वा ॥ 32 ॥

na kāṅkṣe vijayaṁ kṛṣṇa na ca rājyaṁ sukhāni ca
kiṁ no rājyena govinda kiṁ bhogair jīvitena vā

येषामर्थे काङ्क्षितं नो राज्यं भोगाः सुखानि च।
त इमेऽवस्थिता युद्धे प्राणांस्त्यक्त्वा धनानि च ॥ 33 ॥

yeṣām arthe kāṅkṣitaṁ no rājyaṁ bhogāḥ sukhāni ca
ta ime 'vasthitā yuddhe prāṇāṁs tyaktvā dhanāni ca

O Krishna, I do not desire any victory, or pleasure or kingdom. O Krishna, what is the use of the kingdom or enjoyment (luxuries) or even life itself to us? (1.32)

Because those for whom we desire kingdom, enjoyments, and pleasures are standing here for the battle and ready to give up their lives and wealth. (1.33)

Q Did Arjuna want to kill his relatives and his respected ones in the war?

आचार्याः पितरः पुत्रास्तथैव च पितामहाः।
मातुलाः श्वशुराः पौत्राः श्यालाः संबन्धिनस्तथा ॥ 34 ॥

ācāryāḥ pitaraḥ putrās tathaiva ca pitāmahāḥ
mātulāḥ śvaśurāḥ pautrāḥ śyālāḥ sambandhinas tathā

एतान्न हन्तुमिच्छामि घ्नतोऽपि मधुसूदन।
अपि त्रैलोक्यराज्यस्य हेतोः किं नु महीकृते ॥ 35 ॥

etān na hantum icchāmi ghnato 'pi madhusūdana
api trailokya-rājyasya hetoḥ kiṁ nu mahī-kṛte

निहत्य धार्तराष्ट्रान्नः का प्रीतिः स्याज्जनार्दन।
पापमेवाश्रयेदस्मान् हत्वैतानाततायिनः ॥ 36 ॥

nihatya dhārtarāṣṭrān naḥ kā prītiḥ syāj janārdana
pāpam evāśrayed asmān hatvaitān ātatāyinaḥ

तस्मान्नार्हा वयं हन्तुं धार्तराष्ट्रान्स्वबान्धवान्।
स्वजनं हि कथं हत्वा सुखिनः स्याम माधव ॥ 37 ॥

tasmān nārhā vayaṁ hantuṁ dhārtarāṣṭrān sa-bāndhavān
sva-janaṁ hi kathaṁ hatvā sukhinaḥ syāma mādhava

I do not wish to kill teachers, uncles, sons, grandfathers, maternal uncles, fathers-in-law, grandsons, brothers-in-law, and other relatives though they may kill me not even for the sovereignty of the three worlds, why then, for this earthly kingdom, O Krishna (1.34–35)

Lord Krishna, what pleasure can we derive by killing the sons of Dhritarashtra? We will only accrue sins as the result of killing these uncaring people. (1.36)

Therefore, O Krishna, we should not kill our relatives, the sons of Dhritarashtra. If we kill our relatives, how can we be happy? (1.37)

Q What does overpowering greed do to one's mind?

यद्यप्येते न पश्यन्ति लोभोपहतचेतसः।
कुलक्षयकृतं दोषं मित्रद्रोहे च पातकम् ॥ 38 ॥

yady apy ete na paśyanti lobhopahata-cetasaḥ
kula-kṣaya-kṛtaṁ doṣaṁ mitra-drohe ca pātakam

Greed is the biggest curse to human beings

Although these people, whose minds are overpowered and blinded by greed, do not see evil in the destruction of their own race and sin accruing from enmity towards friends. (1.38)

Q What kind of aftermath (due to the war) did Arjuna anticipate and what did he recommend Lord Krishna to do?

कथं न ज्ञेयमस्माभिः पापादस्मान्निवर्तितुम्।
कुलक्षयकृतं दोषं प्रपश्यद्भिर्जनार्दन ॥ 39 ॥

kathaṁ na jñeyam asmābhiḥ pāpād asmān nivartitum
kula-kṣaya-kṛtaṁ doṣaṁ prapaśyadbhir janārdana

O Krishna, why should we not, who clearly see evil in the destruction of the family, think of turning away from this crime? (1.39)

Q What is the result due to the destruction of the family?

कुलक्षये प्रणश्यन्ति कुलधर्माः सनातनाः।
धर्मे नष्टे कुलं कृत्स्नमधर्मोऽभिभवत्युत ॥ 40 ॥

kula-kṣaye praṇaśyanti kula-dharmāḥ sanātanāḥ
dharme naṣṭe kulaṁ kṛtsnam adharmo 'bhibhavaty uta

With the destruction of the family, the ancient family traditions and codes of conduct are destroyed. In the absence of virtues, immorality and unrighteousness (*adharma*) prevail in the family. (1.40)

Q What is the role of women in maintaining the family traditions and values?

अधर्माभिभवात्कृष्ण प्रदुष्यन्ति कुलस्त्रियः।
स्त्रीषु दुष्टासु वार्ष्णेय जायते वर्णसंकरः॥41॥

adharmābhibhavāt kṛṣṇa praduṣyanti kula-striyaḥ
strīṣu duṣṭāsu vārṣṇeya jāyate varṇa-saṅkaraḥ

Downfall of the social values and traditions starts at home

When immorality and unrighteousness prevails, O Krishna, the women of the family become corrupted; when women are corrupted, many intermixtures of castes (undesirable progeny) and social problems arise. (1.41)

Q Why is the intermixing of caste not recommended?

संकरो नरकायैव कुलघ्नानां कुलस्य च।
पतन्ति पितरो ह्येषां लुप्तपिण्डोदकक्रियाः॥42॥

saṅkaro narakāyaiva kula-ghnānāṁ kulasya ca
patanti pitaro hy eṣāṁ lupta-piṇḍodaka-kriyāḥ

दोषैरेतैः कुलघ्नानां वर्णसंकरकारकैः।
उत्साद्यन्ते जातिधर्माः कुलधर्माश्च शाश्वताः॥43॥

doṣair etaiḥ kula-ghnānāṁ varṇa-saṅkara-kārakaiḥ
utsādyante jāti-dharmāḥ kula-dharmāś ca śāśvatāḥ

Intermixing of castes leads to hell the destroyer of the family and also the entire race itself. The spirits of their ancestors are degraded by not performing the ceremonial offerings of food (rice-ball) and water to them. (This caste is not referred to caste by birth but by aptitude) (1.42)

By the misdeeds of those who destroy the family and create confusion of *Varnas*, the ancient laws of the caste and family traditions (everlasting qualities of social order) are destroyed. (1.43)

Q What happens when the family traditions and values are destroyed?

उत्सन्नकुलधर्माणां मनुष्याणां जनार्दन।
नरकेऽनियतं वासो भवतीत्यनुशुश्रुम॥44॥

utsanna-kula-dharmāṇāṁ manuṣyāṇāṁ janārdana
narake niyataṁ vāso bhavatīty anuśuśruma

O Krishna, we have heard that people whose family traditions are destroyed dwell in hell for an indefinite period of time. (1.44)

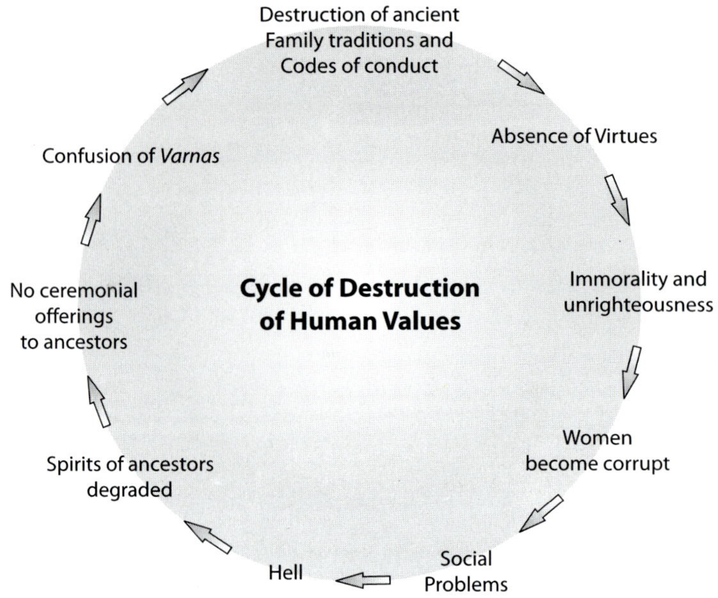

Fig. 1.2 *Cycle of destruction of human values*

Q According to Arjuna what was the reason for war?

अहो बत महत्पापं कर्तुं व्यवसिता वयम् ।
यद्राज्यसुखलोभेन हन्तुं स्वजनमुद्यताः ।। 45 ।।

aho bata mahat pāpaṁ kartuṁ vyavasitā vayam
yad rājya-sukha-lobhena hantuṁ sva-janam udyatāḥ

Alas! What a great sin we are ready to commit by killing our own kinsmen only for the sake of greed for kingdom and pleasures. (1.45)

Q How depressed did Arjuna feel?

यदि मामप्रतीकारमशस्त्रं शस्त्रपाणयः ।
धार्तराष्ट्रा रणे हन्युस्तन्मे क्षेमतरं भवेत् ।। 46 ।।

yadi mām apratīkāram aśastraṁ śastra-pāṇayaḥ
dhārtarāṣṭrā raṇe hanyus tan me kṣemataraṁ bhavet

It would be better for me if the well armed sons of Dhritarashtra kill me in the battle while I am unarmed and unresisting. (1.46)

Q What did Arjuna do when he was overwhelmed with grief and sorrow?

संजय उवाच
एवमुक्त्वार्जुनः संख्ये रथोपस्थ उपाविशत्।
विसृज्य सशरं चापं शोकसंविग्नमानसः ।।47।।

sañjaya uvāca
evam uktvārjunaḥ saṅkhye rathopastha upāviśat
visṛjya sa-śaraṁ cāpaṁ śoka-saṁvigna-mānasaḥ

Arjuna lost his heroism

Sanjaya said: Having spoken thus on the battle field and casting aside his bow and arrow, Arjuna sank down on the back seat of the chariot with his mind overwhelmed with sorrow. (1.47)

Lessons to learn and practice in daily life

The Gita is our Divine Company

Lord Krishna has not only guided and enlightened Arjuna by imparting Self-Knowledge and answering his questions, but He did it for the sake of all of mankind. Therefore, we must also learn from it and apply it in our daily lives to perform our duty and attain Inner Peace, Happiness and *Anandam*.

There are times in life when we all face difficult situations. At that time we have two options; let the situation take over us and we become sad, depressed and confused, or we get help from others such as a wise guru, wise family members, wise friends and divine counselors.

Arjuna had a friend like Lord Krishna so he was guided properly. Similarly we should have wise/divine company.

Lord Krishna has given us the Gita, the divine company (guru and guide, *Sarathi*). We should follow the Gita's teachings to connect within, communicate with Higher Self/Super Conscious, to get guidance and also build a relationship with God.

1. We should thoroughly evaluate the situation and its possible outcomes before taking any action, as Arjuna did.
2. Whenever we are in a difficult situation or deep sorrow, we must clarify all the doubts and ask for guidance from a divine company instead of wasting our energy by dwelling on it or just whining about it.
3. Study the Gita or any other scripture and practice its teachings in our daily life.
4. Develop Self-awareness, just like Arjuna did.

Gita is a guide to take us from dilemma to decision

ॐ तत्सदिति श्रीमद्भगवद्गीतासूपनिषत्सु ब्रह्मविद्यायां योगशास्त्रे
श्रीकृष्णार्जुनसंवादेऽर्जुनविषादयोगो नाम प्रथमोऽध्यायः ।।

AUM TAT SAT

Thus ends the first chapter named "*Arjuna Vishad Yoga*"
Arjuna Despondency and Dilemma
in the *Upanishad* of the glorious Bhagavad Gita, the scripture of Yoga,
the science of the Absolute (*Brahman*), in the form of the dialogue
between Lord Krishna and Arjuna.

Aum Shanti, Shanti, Shantihi

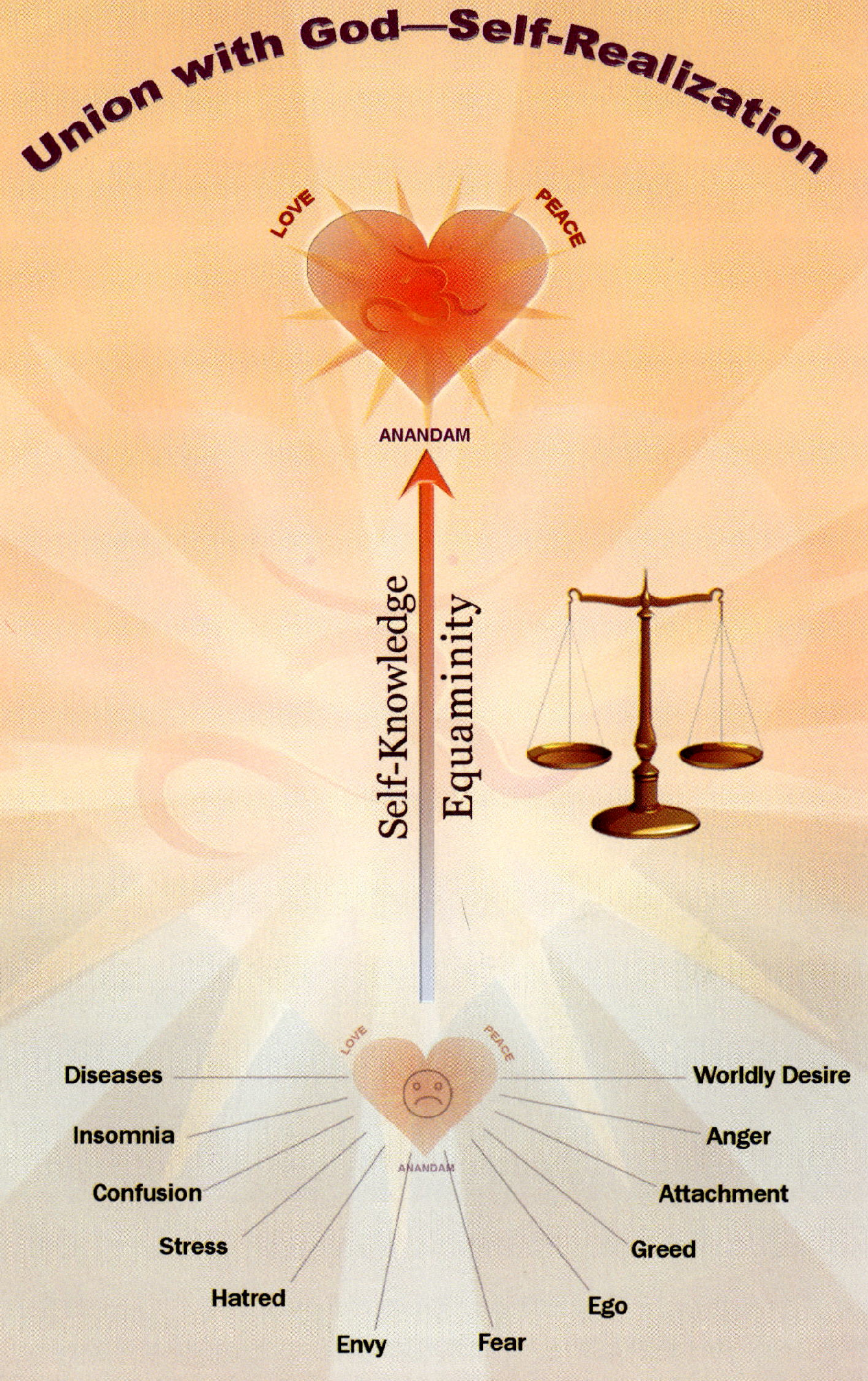

Self-Purification and Transformation through Self-Knowledge

Who is Arjuna, who is Lord Krishna and what is Gita

Arjuna is body, mind and Lord Krishna is Spirit
Arjuna is Jivatma and Lord Krishna is Parmatama
Arjuna is disciple and Lord Krishna is Guru
Arjuna is attachment and Lord Krishna is Detachment
Arjuna is dilemma and Lord Krishna is Decision
Arjuna is depression and Lord Krishna is JOY
Arjuna is imbalance and Lord Krishna is Equanimity
Arjuna is fear and Lord Krishna is Faith
Arjuna is grief and Lord Krishna is Grace
Arjuna is sorrow and Lord Krishna is Anandam
Arjuna is hurt and Lord Krishna is Healer
Arjuna is in pieces and Lord Krishna is Peace
Arjuna is problem and Lord Krishna is Solution
Arjuna is anxiety and Lord Krishna is Bliss
Arjuna is stress and Lord Krishna is Calmness
Arjuna is bondage and Lord Krishna is Liberation
Arjuna is Vishad and Lord Krishna is Prasad

"Arjuna is a question, Lord Krishna is an Answer and so is Gita"

SANKHYA YOGA

The Path of Self-Knowledge

> *Union with God (Self-Realization) through the path of Self-Knowledge*

The Gita is a Source of Self-Knowledge and Wisdom

Sankhya—Wisdom, Self-Knowledge

Yoga—Union with God, the Supreme-Soul, Self

Sankhya Yoga—Self-Knowledge (Transcendental Knowledge, Science) and Wisdom that unites one to God.

It is the science of Oneness of body, mind and Spirit.

- Knowledge of Spirit (*Atma*, Self) is called Self-Knowledge
- Knowledge that transcends one to his original nature, *Sat Chit Ananda*, is called Transcendental Knowledge

Sankhya Yoga is also known as Yoga of Wisdom. One who possesses the Wisdom is know as Wise.

In this chapter, the contents of the entire Gita have been summarized.

When Arjuna went into *Vishad* and became confused about his duty, he said to Lord Krishna, "I will not fight the war," however, he surrendered himself as His disciple and asked Him very humbly and sincerely for His guidance (2.07). Then Lord Krishna started His teachings with His very first verse (2.11) and enlightened Arjuna with two-fold path, the path of *Sankhya Yoga* and the path of *Karma Yoga*.

Main Message

Building Unity with God through the path of Self-Knowledge

- What is the fundamental distinction between the temporary material body and the eternal spiritual soul?
- What is the relationship of body, mind and spirit?
- What are the barriers to realizing one's true nature *Sat Chit Ananda*?
- What is the process of trans-migration and how does it occur?
- Characteristics of an enlightened person (*Sthita-Prajna*, Serene mind, Self-realized) and his glories
- How can one apply the teachings of Self-Knowledge and fulfill one's duty (*svadharma*) by performing Selfless action to make this world a better place to live and at the same time attain a *Brahmic state*, a state of *Anandam* and Ultimate Bliss.

The Gita is an Atmadarshini (Self-Realizer)

Lord Krishna not only enlightened Arjuna but also answered the basic universal questions of human beings such as:

- Who am I? (Super-Soul, Spirit, Self, *Atma*, God, Supreme Consciousness)
- How to realize one's true nature by applying His teachings of Self-Knowledge in daily life.
- How to fulfill his own duty/ responsibilities by performing Selfless action.
- How to overcome the obstacles of 5+2 Enemies* and negative behaviors during the process of Self-Realization.

***5 + 2 Enemies**

1. Selfish Desire
2. Anger
3. Greed
4. Attachments
5. Ego/Arrogance/Conceit
6. Envy
7. Hatred or Resentment

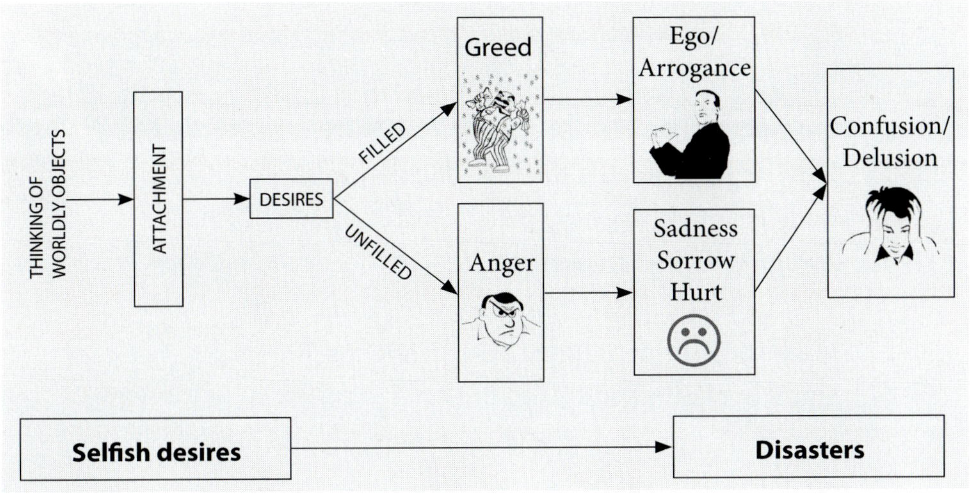

Fig. 2.1 *Obstacles on the path of Self-Realization (2.62–63)*

Lord Krishna as Counselor and Divine Teacher; Arjuna as a patient and student

The Bhagavad Gita is a unique spiritual dialogue between Lord Krishna and Arjuna that deals with all aspects of life. The Gita can be very useful to modern therapists, psychologists, and philosophers to understand how Lord Krishna counseled Arjuna. Arjuna was in a state of turmoil and felt incapable of coping with the situation. He was very honest and truthful about his feelings and his mental status, and did not try to hide it. Lord Krishna was an excellent counselor and a good listener. He would listen to Arjuna without any interruption. He continued to support, guide and advise Arjuna until he was uplifted and came out of confusion and dilemma, *Vishad*. However, He let Arjuna make the final decision.

Arjuna was very fortunate. He had a great teacher (Divine Company) and a true friend like Lord Krishna who acted as his counselor and guided him in the right direction. At the same time, Arjuna was a very good student who listened to Him very attentively, followed His advice and was self-transformed and finally said, "I will do as You advise." (*karisye vacanam tava*). (18.73)

Through Arjuna's honesty and sincerety, and with a true friend like Lord Krishna, Arjuna could fulfill his duty in the world as a warrior (kshatriya) and also attain Liberation

Chapter Overview

01–10 Arjuna's continuous dilemma and his unwillingness to fight the war

11–15 Lord Krishna started the teaching of Gita

16–30 Body is temporary but Spirit-Self is eternal

31–38 Arjuna's duty as a warrior

39–53 Theory, practice and importance of *Karma Yoga*

54–57 Marks of a stable-minded person and his glories

58–61 Stability of mind and Equanimity

62–63 Causes and process of falling from righteous path (committing sin)

64–72 Attaining Eternal Happiness and Peace-*Anandam* through Self-control and Self-Knowledge

Arjuna's continuous dilemma and his unwillingness to fight the war

Q How did Sanjay describe Arjuna's condition when he refused to fight the battle?

संजय उवाच
तं तथा कृपयाविष्टमश्रुपूर्णाकुलेक्षणम् ।
विषीदन्तमिदं वाक्यमुवाच मधुसूदनः ॥1॥

sañjaya uvāca
taṁ tathā kṛpayāviṣṭam aśru-pūrṇākulekṣaṇam
viṣīdantam idaṁ vākyam uvāca madhusūdanaḥ

Sanjaya said: Lord Krishna spoke these words to Arjuna who was overwhelmed with pity, very depressed and whose eyes were filled with tears of sorrow. (2.01)

Q What did Lord Krishna initially tell Arjuna to convince him to fight?

श्रीभगवानुवाच
कुतस्त्वा कश्मलमिदं विषमे समुपस्थितम् ।
अनार्यजुष्टमस्वर्ग्यमकीर्तिकरमर्जुन ॥2॥

śrī-bhagavān uvāca
kutas tvā kaśmalam idaṁ viṣame samupasthitam
anārya-juṣṭam asvargyam akīrti-karam arjuna

क्लैब्यं मा स्म गमः पार्थ नैतत्त्वय्युपपद्यते।
क्षुद्रं हृदयदौर्बल्य त्यक्त्वोत्तिष्ठ परंतप ।।3।।

klaibyaṁ mā sma gamaḥ pārtha naitat tvayy upapadyate
kṣudraṁ hṛdaya-daurbalyaṁ tyaktvottiṣṭha parantapa

The Supreme Lord said: O Arjuna, how has dejection come to you at this hour of crisis? This is unfit for a person of noble mind and deeds, and is indeed very disgraceful. It neither leads one to heaven nor to any worldly fame and glory. (2.02)

O Arjuna, do not become a coward because it does not befit you. Shake off this petty weakness of your heart and stand up for the battle, O Scorcher of enemies. (2.03)

Q How did Arjuna respond to Lord Krishna's initial advice?

अर्जुन उवाच
कथं भीष्ममहं संख्ये द्रोणं च मधुसूदन।
इषुभिः प्रति योत्स्यामि पूजार्हावरिसूदन ।।4।।

arjuna uvāca
kathaṁ bhīṣmam ahaṁ saṅkhye
droṇaṁ ca madhusūdana
iṣubhiḥ pratiyotsyāmi
pūjārhāv ari-sūdana

गुरूनहत्वा हि महानुभावान्
श्रेयो भोक्तुं भैक्ष्यमपीह लोके।
हत्वार्थकामांस्तु गुरूनिहैव
भुञ्जीय भोगान्रुधिरप्रदिग्धान् ।।5।।

gurūn ahatvā hi mahānubhāvān
śreyo bhoktuṁ bhaikṣyam apīha loke
hatvārtha-kāmāṁs tu gurūn ihaiva
bhuñjīya bhogān rudhira-pradigdhān

Dejection leads to delusion

न चैतद्विद्मः कतरन्नो गरीयो
यद्वा जयेम यदि वा नो जयेयुः।
यानेव हत्वा न जिजीविषाम-
स्तेऽवस्थिताः प्रमुखे धार्तराष्ट्राः ।।6।।

na caitad vidmaḥ kataran no garīyo
yad vā jayema yadi vā no jayeyuḥ
yān eva hatvā na jijīviṣāmas
te 'vasthitāḥ pramukhe dhārtarāṣṭrāḥ

Arjuna said: O Krisna, how can I fight against Bhisma (my grandfather) and Drona (my teacher) with arrows in the battle, who are worthy of my respect and worship? (2.04)

It is better, indeed, to live on alms in this world than to kill these noble gurus, because even after killing them, we will enjoy only bloodstained pleasures in the form of wealth and worldly enjoyments. (2.05)

We do not know which alternative is better for us (fight or leave). Further, we do not know whether we shall conquer them or they will conquer us. We should not even wish to live after killing the sons of Dhritarashtra, who are arrayed against us. (2.06)

Q How did Arjuna ask for advice?

कार्पण्यदोषोपहतस्वभावः
  पृच्छामि त्वां धर्मसंमूढचेताः।
यच्छ्रेयः स्यान्निश्चितं ब्रूहि तन्मे
  शिष्यस्तेऽहं शाधि मां त्वां प्रपन्नम् ॥7॥

kārpaṇya-doṣopahata-svabhāvaḥ
  pṛcchāmi tvāṁ dharma-sammūḍha-cetāḥ
yac chreyaḥ syān niścitaṁ brūhi tan me
  śiṣyas te 'haṁ śādhi māṁ tvāṁ prapannam

Arjuna became a disciple and surrenderd

Now my heart is overpowered by the weakness of pity and apprehension, I have lost all composure and my mind is confused about my duty (*Dharma*). I am requesting you to tell me, what is definitely good for me. I am your disciple, surrendered to you. Please instruct me. (2.07)

Q How did Arjuna express his dejection to Lord Krishna ?

न हि प्रपश्यामि ममापनुद्याद्
  यच्छोकमुच्छोषणमिन्द्रियाणाम्।
अवाप्य भूमावसपत्नमृद्धं
  राज्यं सुराणामपि चाधिपत्यम् ॥8॥

na hi prapaśyāmi mamāpanudyād
  yac chokam ucchoṣaṇam indriyāṇām
avāpya bhūmāv asapatnam ṛddhaṁ
  rājyaṁ surāṇām api cādhipatyam

"I will not fight the battle of life"

संजय उवाच
  एवमुक्तवा हृषीकेशं गुडाकेशः परंतप।
  न योत्स्य इति गोविन्दमुक्त्वा तूष्णीं बभूवह ॥9॥

sañjaya uvāca
  evam uktvā hṛṣīkeśaṁ guḍākeśaḥ parantapaḥ
  na yotsya iti govindam uktvā tūṣṇīṁ babhūva ha

I do not see any means that can remove this sorrow that is drying up my senses, not even if I gain undisputed sovereignty and a prosperous kingdom on this earth or even lordship over the celestial controllers (*devas*). (2.08)

Sanjaya said: after speaking like this to Lord Krishna, the mighty Arjuna said to Lord Krishna, "*I will not fight*" and he became silent. (2.09)

Q How did Lord Krishna respond to Arjuna's dejection and decision not to fight the battle?

तमुवाच हृषीकेशः प्रहसन्निव भारत ।
सेनयोरुभयोर्मध्ये विषीदन्तमिदं वचः ।। 10 ।।

tam uvāca hṛṣīkeśaḥ prahasann iva bhārata
senayor ubhayor madhye viṣīdantam idaṁ vacaḥ

O King (Dhritarashtra), Lord Krishna with a smile on his face spoke the following words to the distressed Arjuna in the midst of the two armies. (2.10)

Lord Krishna started the teaching of Gita

Q How does the wise man handle the calamities in life?

श्रीभगवानुवाच
अशोच्यानन्वशोचस्त्वं प्रज्ञावादांश्च भाषसे ।
गतासूनगतासूंश्च नानुशोचन्ति पण्डिताः ।। 11 ।।

Lord Krishna's very first advice, "Never grieve, always be happy."

śrī-bhagavān uvāca
aśocyān anvaśocas tvaṁ prajñā-vādāṁś ca bhāṣase
gatāsūn agatāsūṁś ca nānuśocanti paṇḍitāḥ

न त्वेवाहं जातु नासं न त्वं नेमे जनाधिपाः ।
न चैव न भविष्यामः सर्वे वयमतः परम् ।। 12 ।।

na tv evāhaṁ jātu nāsaṁ na tvaṁ neme janādhipāḥ
na caiva na bhaviṣyāmaḥ sarve vayam ataḥ param

Lord Krishna said, you grieve for those who are not worthy of grief, and yet you speak words of wisdom. The wise men do not grieve for the living or for the dead. (2.11)

There was never a time when I or you or these kings did not exist, nor there will ever be a time in the future when all of us ever cease to exist. (2.12)

Q Where does Soul (*Atma*) go after death?

देहिनोऽस्मिन्यथा देहे कौमारं यौवनं जरा ।
तथा देहान्तरप्राप्तिर्धीरस्तत्र न मुह्यति ॥ 13 ॥

dehino 'smin yathā dehe kaumāraṁ yauvanaṁ jarā
tathā dehāntara-prāptir dhīras tatra na muhyati

Just as the living entity (*jivatma*) continuously passes in this body from childhood to youth to old age during this life, similarly, *Atma* (Soul) passes into another body after death. The wise are not confused by this. (2.13)

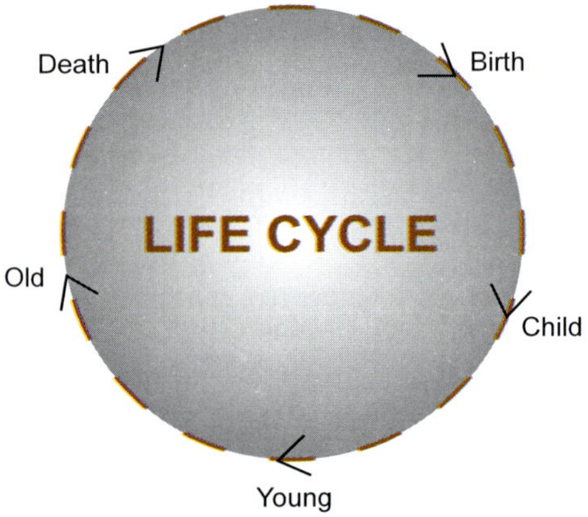

Q How to develop endurance and why?

मात्रास्पर्शास्तु कौन्तेय शीतोष्णसुखदुःखदाः ।
आगमापायिनोऽनित्यास्तांस्तितिक्षस्व भारत ॥ 14 ॥

mātrā-sparśās tu kaunteya śītoṣṇa-sukha-duḥkha-dāḥ
āgamāpāyino 'nityās tāṁs titikṣasva bhārata

Endurance helps to develop calmness

O Arjuna, the contacts between senses and sense objects give rise to the feelings of heat and cold, pain and pleasure. They are transitory and temporary, therefore, learn to endure these patiently. (2.14)

Q Who is qualified for immortality (Liberation from life cycle)?

यं हि न व्यथयन्त्येते पुरुषं पुरुषर्षभ ।
समदुःखसुखं धीरं सोऽमृतत्वाय कल्पते ॥ 15 ॥

yaṁ hi na vyathayanty ete puruṣaṁ puruṣarṣabha
sama-duḥkha-sukhaṁ dhīraṁ so 'mṛtatvāya kalpate

Calmness is the pre-requisite for Liberation

O Arjuna a calm person who is not afflicted by these sense objects and is steady in pain and pleasure becomes eligible for immortality. (2.15)

Body is temporary but Spirit-Self is eternal

Q What is Permanent (*Sat*, Truth, Real,) and what is Transitory (untruth, unreal, *asat*)?

नासतो विद्यते भावो नाभावो विद्यते सतः।
उभयोरपि दृष्टोऽन्तस्त्वनयोस्तत्त्वदर्शिभिः॥16॥

nāsato vidyate bhāvo nābhāvo vidyate sataḥ
ubhayor api dṛṣṭo 'ntas tv anayos tattva-darśibhiḥ

The visible world (including the physical body) is transitory and therefore has no existence. The invisible Spirit (*Sat, Atma*) is eternal and therefore it never ceases to be. The reality of these two is certainly seen by the seers of truth. (2.16)

Q Who pervades the universe and what is its nature?

अविनाशि तु तद्विद्धि येन सर्वमिदं ततम्।
विनाशमव्ययस्यास्य न कश्चित्कर्तुमर्हति॥17॥

avināśi tu tad viddhi yena sarvam idaṁ tatam
vināśam avyayasyāsya na kaścit kartum arhati

The Spirit (*Atma*) by which all this universe is pervaded, is indestructible (Real). No one can destroy the eternal Spirit. (2.17)

Q What is unreal and what is Real?

अन्तवन्त इमे देहा नित्यस्योक्ताः शरीरिणः।
अनाशिनोऽप्रमेयस्य तस्माद्युध्यस्व भारत॥18॥

antavanta ime dehā nityasyoktāḥ śarīriṇaḥ
anāśino 'prameyasya tasmād yudhyasva bhārata

Body is temporary but the Spirit is Eternal

These bodies of the embodied self are perishable, while the Self (*Atma*, Spirit) is Eternal, Imperishable, Indefinable and Incomprehensible. Therefore, O Arjuna, fight the battle. (2.18)

Q Who are the ignorant?

य एनं वेत्ति हन्तारं यश्चैनं मन्यते हतम्।
उभौ तौ न विजानीतो नायं हन्ति न हन्यते॥19॥

ya enaṁ vetti hantāraṁ yaś cainaṁ manyate hatam
ubhau tau na vijānīto nāyaṁ hanti na hanyate

One who thinks that *Atma* (Spirit) is a slayer (killer) and the one who thinks *Atma* is slain (killed), both of them fail to perceive the truth, because *Atma* neither kills nor is killed. (2.19)

Q How did Lord *Krishna* describe the Soul (*Atma*)?

न जायते म्रियते वा कदाचि-
न्नायं भूत्वाऽभविता वा न भूयः।
अजो नित्यः शाश्वतोऽयं पुराणो
न हन्यते हन्यमाने शरीरे ॥ 20 ॥

na jāyate mriyate vā kadācin
nāyaṁ bhūtvā bhavitā vā na bhūyaḥ
ajo nityaḥ śāśvato 'yaṁ purāṇo
na hanyate hanyamāne śarīre

The Spirit (*Atma*) is neither born nor it ever dies. It does not come into being or cease to exist. It is Unborn, Eternal, Permanent and Primeval. It is not killed even when the body is killed. (2.20)

Q What happens to a person who knows this?

वेदाविनाशिनं नित्यं य एनमजमव्ययम्।
कथं स पुरुषः पार्थ कं घातयति हन्ति कम् ॥ 21 ॥

vedāvināśinaṁ nityaṁ ya enam ajam avyayam
kathaṁ sa puruṣaḥ pārtha kaṁ ghātayati hanti kam

O Arjuna, how can a person who knows that the Spirit (*Atma*) is indestructible, eternal, unborn and immutable, kill anyone or cause anyone to be killed? (2.21)

Q Where does *Atma* (Soul) go after death?

वासांसि जीर्णानि यथा विहाय
नवानि गृह्णाति नरोऽपराणि।
तथा शरीराणि विहाय जीर्णा-
न्यन्यानि संयाति नवानि देही ॥ 22 ॥

vāsāṁsi jīrṇāni yathā vihāya
navāni gṛhṇāti naro 'parāṇi
tathā śarīrāṇi vihāya jīrṇāny
anyāni saṁyāti navāni dehī

Body is like an old garment for the Spirit/Soul

Just as a person takes off worn-out garments and puts on new ones, similarly the embodied soul casts off the worn out body and enters into a new physical body. (2.22)

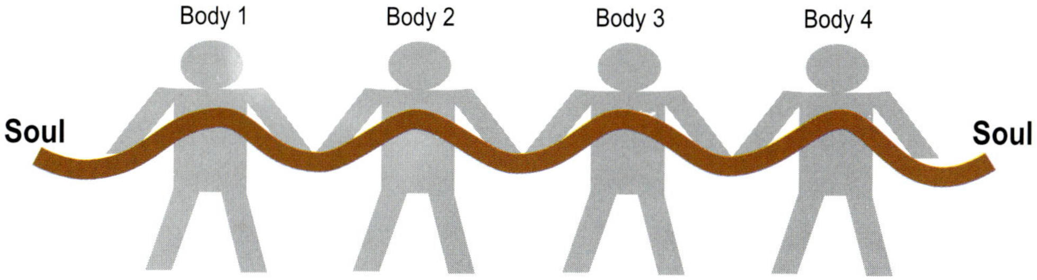

Fig. 2.2 *Journey of the soul from one body to the next*

Q What is the nature of Spirit (*Atma*) and why can It not be cut, burned, wet or dried?

नैनं छिन्दन्ति शस्त्राणि नैनं दहति पावकः।
न चैनं क्लेदयन्त्यापो न शोषयति मारुतः ॥23॥

nainaṁ chindanti śastrāṇi nainaṁ dahati pāvakaḥ
na cainaṁ kledayanty āpo na śoṣayati mārutaḥ

You are an Eternal Spirit

अच्छेद्योऽयमदाह्योऽयमक्लेद्योऽशोष्य एव च।
नित्यः सर्वगतः स्थाणुरचलोऽयं सनातनः ॥24॥

acchedyo 'yam adāhyo 'yam akledyo 'śoṣya eva ca
nityaḥ sarva-gataḥ sthāṇur acalo 'yaṁ sanātanaḥ

1. Weapons do not cut Self/Spirit (*Atma*)
2. Fire does not burn it (Fire-proof)
3. Water does not wet it (Water-proof)
4. Wind does not dry it (2.23)
5. *Atma* cannot be Cut, Burned, Wet, or Dried. It is Eternal, All-Pervading, Unchanging, Immovable, and Primeval. (2.24)

Q How does knowledge of Spirit (Self-Knowledge) help to console one in a difficult situation?

अव्यक्तोऽयमचिन्त्योऽयमविकार्योऽयमुच्यते।
तस्मादेवं विदित्वैनं नानुशोचितुमर्हसि ॥25॥

avyakto 'yam acintyo 'yam avikāryo 'yam ucyate
tasmād evaṁ viditvainaṁ nānuśocitum arhasi

The Spirit (*Atma*, Self) is said to be Unexplainable (Unmanifest), Incomprehensible, and Unchangeable. Therefore, knowing the Spirit as such you should not grieve. (2.25)

Q What is certain (unavoidable) in our life and why should one not grieve?

अथ चैनं नित्यजातं नित्यं वा मन्यसे मृतम्।
तथापि त्वं महाबाहो नैवं शोचितुमर्हसि ॥ 26 ॥

atha cainaṁ nitya-jātaṁ nityaṁ vā manyase mṛtam
tathāpi tvaṁ mahā-bāho nainaṁ śocitum arhasi

Death is certain for everyone

जातस्य हि ध्रुवो मृत्युर्ध्रुवं जन्म मृतस्य च।
तस्मादपरिहार्येऽर्थे न त्वं शोचितुमर्हसि ॥ 27 ॥

jātasya hi dhruvo mṛtyur dhruvaṁ janma mṛtasya ca
tasmād aparihārye 'rthe na tvaṁ śocitum arhasi

O Arjuna, even if you think that this living entity or body takes birth and dies perpetually, you should not grieve like this because death is certain for one who is born; birth too is certain for one who dies. Therefore, you should not grieve over this unavoidable matter. (2.26–27)

अव्यक्तादीनि भूतानि व्यक्तमध्यानि भारत।
अव्यक्तनिधनान्येव तत्र का परिदेवना ॥ 28 ॥

avyaktādīni bhūtāni vyakta-madhyāni bhārata
avyakta-nidhanāny eva tatra kā paridevanā

O Arjuna, all beings are unmanifest and invisible to our physical eyes before birth and after death. They manifest between the birth and the death only. So why grieve about it? (2.28)

Q What is the greatest wonder in the universe?

आश्चर्यवत्पश्यति कश्चिदेन-
माश्चर्यवद्वदति तथैव चान्यः।
आश्चर्यवच्चैनमन्यः शृणोति
श्रुत्वाप्येनं वेद न चैव कश्चित् ॥ 29 ॥

Death is the Number 1 wonder in the world

āścarya-vat paśyati kaścid enam
āścarya-vad vadati tathaiva cānyaḥ
āścarya-vac cainam anyaḥ śṛṇoti
śrutvāpy enaṁ veda na caiva kaścit

Some perceive the Spirit as a great wonder, another describes it as wonderful, and still another hear of it as a great wonder. Even after hearing about it hardly anyone understands it. (2.29)

Q How should one handle death?

देही नित्यमवध्योऽयं देहे सर्वस्य भारत।
तस्मात्सर्वाणि भूतानि न त्वं शोचितुमर्हसि ॥30॥

dehī nityam avadhyo 'yaṁ dehe sarvasya bhārata
tasmāt sarvāṇi bhūtāni na tvaṁ śocitum arhasi

O Arjuna, the Soul residing in the body of all beings is eternal and indestructible. Therefore, you should not grieve for any being. (2.30)

Arjuna's Duty as a Warrior

Q What role does one's own duty play in establishing righteousness?

स्वधर्ममपि चावेक्ष्य न विकम्पितुमर्हसि।
धर्म्याद्धि युद्धाच्छ्रेयोऽन्यत्क्षत्रियस्य न विद्यते ॥31॥

sva-dharmam api cā vekṣya
na vikampitum arhasi
dharmyād dhi yuddhāc chreyo 'nyat
kṣatriyasya na vidyate

Follow your svadharma

Besides, considering your own duty (*svadharma*) as a *Kshatriya* (warrior), you should also not waver, because there is nothing more beneficial to a warrior than a righteous war. (2.31)

Q What is the path to heaven?

यदृच्छया चोपपन्नं स्वर्गद्वारमपावृतम्।
सुखिनः क्षत्रियाः पार्थ लभन्ते युद्धमीदृशम् ॥32॥

yadṛcchayā copapannaṁ svarga-dvāram apāvṛtam
sukhinaḥ kṣatriyāḥ pārtha labhante yuddham īdṛśam

Doing own duty is the Path to Heaven

O Arjuna, only the fortunate warriors get such an opportunity to fight in a battle like this, which is an open door to heaven. (2.32)

Q What would have happened to Arjuna's reputation if he did not fight the righteous war and fulfill his duty?

अथ चेत्त्वमिमं धर्म्यं संग्रामं न करिष्यसि।
ततः स्वधर्मं कीर्तिं च हित्वा पापमवाप्स्यसि ॥33॥

atha cet tvam imaṁ dharmyaṁ saṅgrāmaṁ na kariṣyasi
tataḥ sva-dharmaṁ kīrtiṁ ca hitvā pāpam avāpsyasi

अकीर्तिं चापि भूतानि कथयिष्यन्ति तेऽव्ययाम् ।
संभावितस्य चाकीर्तिर्मरणादतिरिच्यते ।। 34 ।।

akīrtiṁ cāpi bhūtāni kathayiṣyanti te 'vyayām
sambhāvitasya cākīrtir maraṇād atiricyate

Disgrace is the most painful to individuals

भयाद्रणादुपरतं मंस्यन्ते त्वां महारथाः ।
येषां च त्वं बहुमतो भूत्वा यास्यसि लाघवम् ।। 35 ।।

bhayād raṇād uparataṁ maṁsyante tvāṁ mahā-rathāḥ
yeṣāṁ ca tvaṁ bahu-mato bhūtvā yāsyasi lāghavam

अवाच्यवादांश्च बहून्वदिष्यन्ति तवाहिताः ।
निन्दन्तस्तव सामर्थ्यं ततो दुःखतरं नु किम् ।। 36 ।।

avācya-vādāṁś ca bahūn vadiṣyanti tavāhitāḥ
nindantas tava sāmarthyaṁ tato duḥkhataraṁ nu kim

But, if you will not fight this righteous war (abondon your duty) then you will fail to fulfill your prescribed duty, lose your reputation, and incur sin. (2.33)

Besides, people will speak about your disgrace forever. For the one who has been always honored, dishonor is worse than death. (2.34)

And the great chariot warriors will think that you have withdrawn from the battle out of fear. Those who have greatly respected you in the past will now show disrespect to you. (2.35)

Your enemies will disparage your ability and speak many disgraceful words. What will be more distressing to you than this? (2.36)

Q What are two possible things could happen to Arjuna due to the war?

हतो वा प्राप्स्यसि स्वर्गं जित्वा वा भोक्ष्यसे महीम् ।
तस्मादुत्तिष्ठ कौन्तेय युद्धाय कृतनिश्चयः ।। 37 ।।

hato vā prāpsyasi svargaṁ
  jitvā vā bhokṣyase mahīm
tasmād uttiṣṭha kaunteya
  yuddhāya kṛta-niścayaḥ

Regardless of outcome, one must always perform his duty

If killed in battle (in the line of duty), you will attain heaven or if victorious, you will enjoy the kingdom on the earth. Therefore, get up with a determination to fight, O Arjuna. (2.37)

Q How does one avoid incurring bad karmas (sins)?

सुखदु:खे समे कृत्वा लाभालाभौ जयाजयौ।
ततो युद्धाय युज्यस्व नैवं पापमवाप्स्यसि ।। 38 ।।

sukha-duḥkhe same kṛtvā
lābhālābhau jayājayau
tato yuddhāya yujyasva
naivaṁ pāpam avāpsyasi

Performing our duty with a calm mind will not cause mistakes

Regarding pleasure and pain, gain and loss, a victory and defeat alike; get ready for the war and perform your duty, thus you will not incur sin. (2.38)

Theory, Practice and Importance of *Karma Yoga*

Q How can one free oneself from the bondage of action (*karma*) and fear of birth and death?

एषा तेऽभिहिता सांख्ये बुद्धिर्योगे त्विमां शृणु।
बुद्ध्या युक्तो यया पार्थ कर्मबन्धं प्रहास्यसि ।। 39 ।।

eṣā te 'bhihitā sāṅkhye buddhir yoge tv imāṁ śṛṇu
buddhyā yukto yayā pārtha karma-bandhaṁ prahāsyasi

The wisdom of Transcendental Knowledge has been presented to you. Now listen to the wisdom of *Karma Yoga* (the Yoga of selfless action/*Seva*). Endowed with this knowledge, O Arjuna, you will free yourself from the bondage of action (*karma*). (2.39)

Transcendental knowledge + Karma Yoga → Freedom from the bondage of action

Q Does *Karma Yoga* have any adverse effect and is any effort lost while doing it?

नेहाभिक्रमनाशोऽस्ति प्रत्यवायो न विद्यते।
स्वल्पमप्यस्य धर्मस्य त्रायते महतो भयात् ।। 40 ।।

nehābhikrama-nāśo 'sti pratyavāyo na vidyate
sv-alpam apy asya dharmasya trāyate mahato bhayāt

Spiritual effort is never wasted

In *Karma Yoga* (enlightened interest), no effort is ever lost and there is no adverse effect. Even a little practice of this discipline (righteous action) protects one from the great fear of birth and death. (2.40)

Q What is the difference between a ignorant person and a *Karma Yogi*?

व्यवसायात्मिका बुद्धिरेकेह कुरुनन्दन।
बहुशाखा ह्यनन्ताश्च बुद्धयोऽव्यवसायिनाम् ॥ 41 ॥

vyavasāyātmikā buddhir ekeha kuru-nandana
bahu-śākhā hy anantāś ca buddhayo 'vyavasāyinām

Secret of success and cause of failure

O Arjuna, on this blessed path a selfless worker has *one-pointed determination* for God-Realization whereas the ignorant (selfish) has endless desires to enjoy the fruits of work and is scattered in many directions. (2.41)

Q What is the real purpose of Vedas and how is it interpreted by misguided people?

यामिमां पुष्पितां वाचं प्रवदन्त्यविपश्चितः।
वेदवादरताः पार्थ नान्यदस्तीति वादिनः ॥ 42 ॥

yām imāṁ puṣpitāṁ vācaṁ
pravadanty avipaścitaḥ
veda-vāda-ratāḥ pārtha
nānyad astīti vādinaḥ

Vedas deal with both material and spiritual aspects of life

O Arjuna, the misguided (ignorant) ones who delight in the melodious chanting of the Veda without understanding the real purpose of the Vedas think that there is nothing else in the Vedas except the rituals for the sole purpose of attaining worldly pleasure and prosperity. (2.42)

Q Why do people usually perform rituals?

कामात्मानः स्वर्गपरा जन्मकर्मफलप्रदाम्।
क्रियाविशेषबहुलां भोगैश्वर्यगतिं प्रति ॥ 43 ॥

kāmātmānaḥ svarga-parā janma-karma-phala-pradām
kriyā-viśeṣa-bahulāṁ bhogaiśvarya-gatiṁ prati

They are obsessed with material desires and consider the attainment of heaven as the Supreme goal of their life. They perform many rituals for the sake of pleasure, power and prosperity and rebirth is the result of their action. (2.43)

Q What are the barriers to meditation?

भोगैश्वर्यप्रसक्तानां तयापहृतचेतसाम्।
व्यवसायात्मिका बुद्धिः समाधौ न विधीयते ॥ 44 ॥

bhogaiśvarya-prasaktānāṁ tayāpahṛta-cetasām
vyavasāyātmikā buddhiḥ samādhau na vidhīyate

Pleasure, Power and Pompousness are the road blocks for Oneness with God

Those who are deeply attached to pleasure, worldly prosperity and power and are carried away by such flowery speeches cannot develop firm determination of a concentrated mind that leads to meditation. (2.44)

Q How to overcome miseries, attain the Purpose of our life and live in Peace and *Anandam* (Blissful State)?

त्रैगुण्यविषया वेदा निस्त्रैगुण्यो भवार्जुन।
निर्द्वन्द्वो नित्यसत्त्वस्थो निर्योगक्षेम आत्मवान् ॥ 45 ॥

trai-guṇya-viṣayā vedā
nistrai-guṇyo bhavārjuna
nirdvandvo nitya-sattva-stho
niryoga-kṣema ātmavān

Formula for attaining Blissful State, "Rise above the three gunas"

The Vedas deal with the three modes of *Gunas* (attributes of *Prakriti*, Material Nature): *Sattva* (goodness), *Rajas* (passion), *Tamas* (ignorance). O Arjuna, transcend these *Gunas*, free yourself from duality (pairs of opposites), be unconcerned with acquisition and preservation and be established in purity (Supreme-Self) with your mind under full control. (2.45)

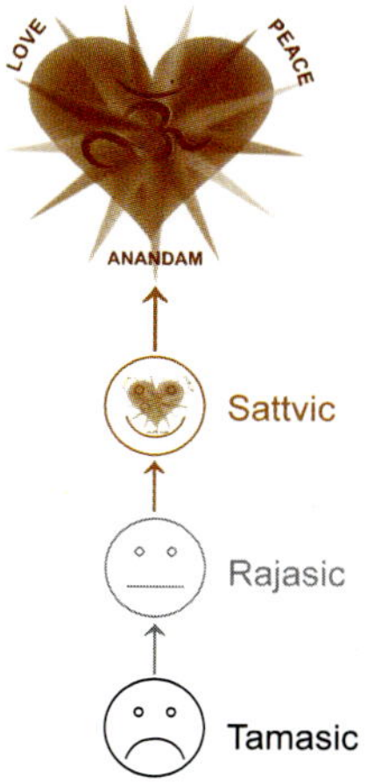

Fig. 2.3 *Three modes of Gunas: Tamasic, Rajasic and Sattvic*

Q What is the importance of Vedas for a Self-realized person?

यावानर्थ उदपाने सर्वतः संप्लुतोदके।
तावान्सर्वेषु वेदेषु ब्राह्मणस्य विजानतः ॥ 46 ॥

yāvān artha udapāne sarvataḥ samplutodake
tāvān sarveṣu vedeṣu brāhmaṇasya vijānataḥ

For a Self-realized person, the Vedas are as useful as a small reservoir of water in a place that is full of water on all sides. (2.46)

Q How should I work when I do not have control on the outcome of my efforts?

कर्मण्येवाधिकारस्ते मा फलेषु कदाचन।
मा कर्मफलहेतुर्भूर्मा ते सङ्गोऽस्त्वकर्मणि ।। 47 ।।

karmaṇy evādhikāras
te mā phaleṣu kadācana
mā karma-phala-hetur bhūr
mā te saṅgo 'stv akarmaṇi

Do selfless action and never be lazy

You have a right to perform your work (respective duty) only, but no control on or claim to its results. The fruits of work should not be your motive and you should never be inactive or lazy. (2.47)

Q What is the true meaning of Yoga and how to perform it?

योगस्थः कुरु कर्माणि सङ्गं त्यक्त्वा धनंजय।
सिद्ध्यसिद्ध्योः समो भूत्वा समत्वं योग उच्यते ।। 48 ।।

yoga-sthaḥ kuru karmāṇi
saṅgaṁ tyaktvā dhanañjaya
siddhy-asiddhyoḥ samo bhūtvā
samatvaṁ yoga ucyate

Equanimity of mind is called Yoga

O Arjuna, do your duty with the best of your ability, with mind attached to God, abandoning selfish attachments and be calm in both success and failure. Such Equanimity (stability) of mind is called Yoga. (2.48)

Q Who are very unhappy in their life?

दूरेण ह्यवरं कर्म बुद्धियोगाद्धनंजय।
बुद्धौ शरणमन्विच्छ कृपणाः फलहेतवः ।। 49 ।।

dūreṇa hy avaraṁ karma
buddhi-yogād dhanañjaya
buddhau śaraṇam anviccha
kṛpaṇāḥ phala-hetavaḥ

Unhappy are those, who are very selfish and want to control everything

O Arjuna, work done with selfish motives is far inferior to Yoga of wisdom-action performed with Equanimity of mind. Therefore, take refuge in evenness of mind, Equanimity. Those who work only for the fruits of their action are very unhappy because they cannot control the outcome of their actions. (2.49)

Q What is *Karma Yoga* (Service) and how does it help attain Liberation?

बुद्धियुक्तो जहातीह उभे सुकृतदुष्कृते।
तस्माद्योगाय युज्यस्व योगः कर्मसु कौशलम् ॥ 50 ॥
buddhi-yukto jahātīha ubhe sukṛta-duṣkṛte
tasmād yogāya yujyasva yogaḥ karmasu kauśalam

Karma Yoga is an Art of action

A person who is endowed with Equanimity (Wisdom-*Buddhi Yoga*) liberates himself in this lifetime from both vice (bad) and virtue (good). Therefore, strive for Yoga. Working to the best of one's abilities without being attached to the fruits of work is called *Karma Yoga* (an art of work). (2.50)

Q How does Equanimity and selflessness lead to Liberation?

कर्मजं बुद्धियुक्ता हि फलं त्यक्त्वा मनीषिणः।
जन्मबन्धविनिर्मुक्ताः पदं गच्छन्त्यनामयम् ॥ 51 ॥
karma-jaṁ buddhi-yuktā hi phalaṁ tyaktvā manīṣiṇaḥ
janma-bandha-vinirmuktāḥ padaṁ gacchanty anāmayam

Wise great sages or devotees who are endowed with Equanimity and give up the selfish attachment to the fruits of all work (*Karma Yogi*) are liberated from the bondage of rebirth (consequences of results from their action) and attain a Blissful Divine State. (2.51)

Q How would I know that I have become *Karma Yogi*?

यदा ते मोहकलिलं बुद्धिर्व्यतितरिष्यति।
तदा गन्तासि निर्वेदं श्रोतव्यस्य श्रुतस्य च ॥ 52 ॥
yadā te moha-kalilaṁ buddhir vyatitariṣyati
tadā gantāsi nirvedaṁ śrotavyasya śrutasya ca

Discrimination is the key

When your intellect completely past beyond the dense forest of confusion, then you will become indifferent to what has been heard and learned; and what is yet to be heard and learned from the scriptures. (2.52)

Q When do I attain Union with God (Yoga)?

श्रुतिविप्रतिपन्ना ते यदा स्थास्यति निश्चला।
समाधावचला बुद्धिस्तदा योगमवाप्स्यसि ॥ 53 ॥
śruti-vipratipannā te yadā sthāsyati niścalā
samādhāv acalā buddhis tadā yogam avāpsyasi

When your intellect that is confused by the conflicting opinions and the ritualistic doctrine of the Vedas is no longer confused, and remains steady and firm during meditation (*Samadhi*) on Supreme-Self, then you will attain union with God (Yoga). (2.53)

Marks of a stable-minded person and his glories

Q What are Arjuna's four questions to Lord Krishna regarding a stable minded person (*Sthita-Prajna*) and his lifestyle?

अर्जुन उवाच
स्थितप्रज्ञस्य का भाषा समाधिस्थस्य केशव।
स्थितधी: किं प्रभाषेत किमासीत व्रजेत किम्॥ 54॥

arjuna uvāca
sthita-prajñasya kā bhāṣā samādhi-sthasya keśava
sthita-dhīḥ kiṁ prabhāṣeta kim āsīta vrajeta kim

Arjuna asked: O Krishna:

1. What are the hallmarks of an enlightened person (*Sthita-Prajna*, God-realized) whose mind is stable and established in *Samadhi* (Transcendental meditation)?
2. How does the man of steady intellect speak?
3. How does he sit?
4. How does he walk? (2.54)

Q Who is the enlightened person (Peaceful and Blissful)?

Self-satisfaction leads to stability of mind

श्रीभगवानुवाच
प्रजहाति यदा कामान्सर्वान्पार्थ मनोगतान्।
आत्मन्येवात्मना तुष्ट: स्थितप्रज्ञस्तदोच्यते॥ 55॥

śrī-bhagavān uvāca
prajahāti yadā kāmān sarvān pārtha mano-gatān
ātmany evātmanā tuṣṭaḥ sthita-prajñas tadocyate

The Supreme Lord said: When one is completely free from all the desires of one's mind, feels satisfaction in the Self (Eternal-being, God, Supreme Consciousness) by self, then one is called an enlightened person, (Established in Pure Transcendental Consciousness *Sthita-Prajna*, Equanimous) O Arjuna. (2.55)

Q Who is called a *Muni* (Sage)?

दुःखेष्वनुद्विग्नमनाः सुखेषु विगतस्पृहः ।
वीतरागभयक्रोधः स्थितधीर्मुनिरुच्यते ।। 56 ।।

duḥkheṣv anudvigna-manāḥ
sukheṣu vigata-spṛhaḥ
vīta-rāga-bhaya-krodhaḥ
sthita-dhīr munir ucyate

Muni – who has full control on his mind/ emotions

यः सर्वत्रानभिस्नेहस्तत्तत्प्राप्य शुभाशुभम् ।
नाभिनन्दति न द्वेष्टि तस्य प्रज्ञा प्रतिष्ठिता ।। 57 ।।

yaḥ sarvatrānabhisnehas tat tat prāpya śubhāśubham
nābhinandati na dveṣṭi tasya prajñā pratiṣṭhitā

A person is called a sage of steadfast wisdom (*Sthita-Prajna*, *Muni*). Whose mind is:

1. Not disturbed by sorrow.
2. Not attracted toward pleasures and happiness.
3. Free from attachment.
4. Free from fear.
5. Free from anger. (2.56)

One who is not attached to anything, who is neither delighted nor troubled by meeting good and evil. His mind is steady and is established in Self-Knowledge. (2.57)

Stability of mind and Equanimity

Q How does one stabilize the mind and attain Equanimity?

यदा संहरते चायं कूर्मोऽङ्गानीव सर्वशः ।
इन्द्रियाणीन्द्रियार्थेभ्यस्तस्य प्रज्ञा प्रतिष्ठिता ।। 58 ।।

yadā saṁharate cāyaṁ kūrmo 'ṅgānīva sarvaśaḥ
indriyāṇīndriyārthebhyas tasya prajñā pratiṣṭhitā

विषया विनिवर्तन्ते निराहारस्य देहिनः ।
रसवर्जं रसोऽप्यस्य परं दृष्ट्वा निवर्तते ।। 59 ।।

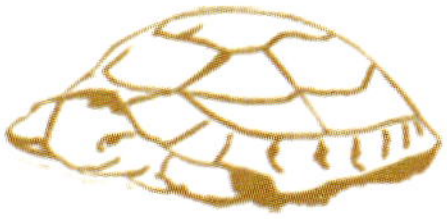

viṣayā vinivartante nirāhārasya dehinaḥ
rasa-varjaṁ raso 'py asya paraṁ dṛṣṭvā nivartate

When one can fully withdraw the senses from objects, like a tortoise that withdraws its limbs into the shell for protection, then one's intellect becomes steady (Equanimity). (2.58) (this answers the 3rd question of Arjuna. see 54).

If one abstains from sense enjoyment, then one's desire for sensual pleasures fades away, but the craving for them still remains in a very subtle form. This craving in subtle form also disappears from a person of steadfast mind, who has realized the Supreme Being. (2.59)

Q What disturbs the mind and how to control it?

यततो ह्यपि कौन्तेय पुरुषस्य विपश्चितः ।
इन्द्रियाणि प्रमाथीनि हरन्ति प्रसभं मनः ।। 60 ।।

yatato hy api kaunteya puruṣasya vipaścitaḥ
indriyāṇi pramāthīni haranti prasabhaṁ manaḥ

Uncontrolled senses will misguide the mind

तानि सर्वाणि संयम्य युक्त आसीत मत्परः ।
वशे हि यस्येन्द्रियाणि तस्य प्रज्ञा प्रतिष्ठिता ।। 61 ।।

tāni sarvāṇi saṁyamya yukta āsīta mat-paraḥ
vaśe hi yasyendriyāṇi tasya prajñā pratiṣṭhitā

Always live in God's Consciousness

Restless senses forcibly carry away the mind of even a wise person, who is practicing self-control and striving for Self-Realization, O Arjuna. (2.60)

Therefore, having controlled all the senses, one should *focus his mind on Me*, and *totally live in My Consciousness*. One, whose senses are mastered, certainly becomes steady intellect (Stable, Equanimous). (2.61)

Causes and process of falling from righteous path (committing sin)

Q How do attachment, desires and anger lead one to destruction and cause him fall from the spiritual path?

ध्यायतो विषयान्पुंसः सङ्गस्तेषूपजायते ।
सङ्गात्संजायते कामः कामात्क्रोधोऽभिजायते ।। 62 ।।

dhyāyato viṣayān puṁsaḥ saṅgas teṣūpajāyate
saṅgāt sañjāyate kāmaḥ kāmāt krodho 'bhijāyate

क्रोधाद्भवति संमोहः संमोहात्स्मृतिविभ्रमः ।
स्मृतिभ्रंशाद्बुद्धिनाशो बुद्धिनाशात्प्रणश्यति ।। 63 ।।

krodhād bhavati sammohaḥ sammohāt smṛti-vibhramaḥ
smṛti-bhraṁśād buddhi-nāśo buddhi-nāśāt praṇaśyati

One develops attachment to sense objects by thinking about them. From attachment arises desire for them. From unfulfilled desires comes anger. (2.62)

From anger comes delusion; from delusion comes confusion of memory; from disappearance of memory and bewildering mind, reasoning and discrimination is destroyed. When reasoning is destroyed, one falls from the right path (*adharma*). (2.63)

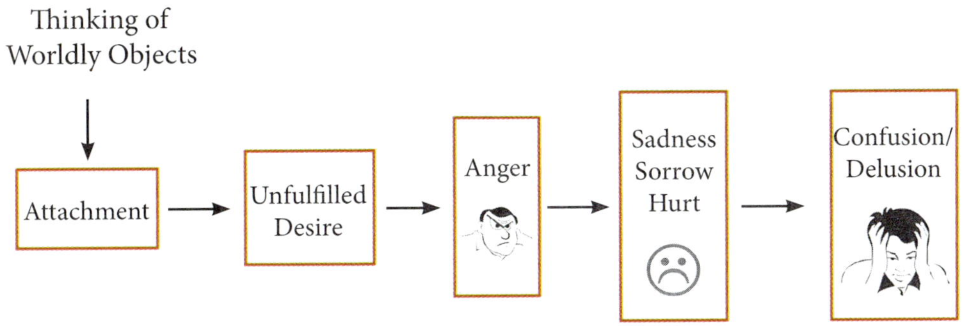

Fig. 2.4 *Attachment to confusion*

Attaining Eternal Happiness and Peace-*Anandam* through Self-control and Self-Knowledge

Q Who attains tranquility and serenity of mind and peace and lives in *Anandam*?

रागद्वेषवियुक्तैस्तु विषयानिन्द्रियैश्चरन् ।
आत्मवश्यैर्विधेयात्मा प्रसादमधिगच्छति ।। 64 ।।

rāga-dveṣa-vimuktais tu viṣayān indriyaiś caran
ātma-vaśyair vidheyātmā prasādam adhigacchati

प्रसादे सर्वदु:खानां हानिरस्योपजायते ।
प्रसन्नचेतसो ह्याशु बुद्धि: पर्यवतिष्ठते ।। 65 ।।

prasāde sarva-duḥkhānāṁ hānir asyopajāyate
prasanna-cetaso hy āśu buddhiḥ paryavatiṣṭhate

A person of a disciplined mind, who enjoys sense objects with his senses under control and free from likes and dislikes, attains serenity of mind. (2.64)

With the attainment of such serenity of mind, all his sufferings end and soon the intellect of such a person of tranquil mind attains Equanimity; and unites with the Eternal Being (God) - he is always in *Anandam*-Bliss and Peace. (2.65) (this answers the 4th question of Arjuna, see 54).

Healthy Mind and Healthy Body → Calmness/Equanimity → Unity with Divinity → Peace and Anandam

Q Who does not attain happiness and peace?

नास्ति बुद्धिरयुक्तस्य न चायुक्तस्य भावना।
न चाभावयतः शान्तिरशान्तस्य कुतः सुखम्॥66॥
nāsti buddhir ayuktasya na cāyuktasya bhāvanā
na cābhāvayataḥ śāntir aśāntasya kutaḥ sukham

Disturbed mind never attains Peace

There is neither Self-Knowledge nor a steady mind for those who are not united within. Without these, there is no peace and without inner peace how can there be any happiness? (2.66)

Q Why should one control the mind?

इन्द्रियाणां हि चरतां यन्मनोऽनु विधीयते।
तदस्य हरति प्रज्ञां वायुर्नावमिवाम्भसि॥67॥
indriyāṇāṁ hi caratāṁ yan mano 'nuvidhīyate
tad asya harati prajñāṁ vāyur nāvam ivāmbhasi

The mind, when controlled by the wandering senses, steals away the intellect and discrimination of a man just as the wind takes away a ship on the sea from its destination. (2.67)

Q Why should one control the senses?

तस्माद्यस्य महाबाहो निगृहीतानि सर्वशः।
इन्द्रियाणीन्द्रियार्थेभ्यस्तस्य प्रज्ञा प्रतिष्ठता॥68॥
tasmād yasya mahā-bāho nigṛhītāni sarvaśaḥ
indriyāṇīndriyārthebhyas tasya prajñā pratiṣṭhitā

Self-control leads to Self-Knowledge

Therefore, O Arjuna, one whose senses are completely controlled from sense objects becomes steady in Self-Knowledge. (2.68)

Q How do Yogis live differently?

Yogi always makes best use of his time

या निशा सर्वभूतानां तस्यां जागर्ति संयमी ।
यस्यां जाग्रति भूतानि सा निशा पश्यतो मुनेः ।। 69 ।।

yā niśā sarva-bhūtānāṁ tasyāṁ jāgarti saṁyamī
yasyāṁ jāgrati bhūtāni sā niśā paśyato muneḥ

A yogi is a self-controlled person, remains awake when it is night for an ordinary human beings. When ordinary human beings are awake, that is the night for the Muni, who sees. (2.69)

Q What role do desires play in making one happy or unhappy?

आपूर्यमाणमचलप्रतिष्ठं
समुद्रमापः प्रविशन्ति यद्वत् ।
तद्वत्कामा यं प्रविशन्ति सर्वे
स शान्तिमाप्नोति न कामकामी ।। 70 ।।

āpūryamāṇam acala-pratiṣṭhaṁ
samudram āpaḥ praviśanti yadvat
tadvat kāmā yaṁ praviśanti sarve
sa śāntim āpnoti na kāma-kāmī

One attains peace when all of one's desires dissipate within the mind and one is not disturbed by the increased flow of desires, just as the river waters enter into the ocean but the ocean is always unchanged and calm. However, the one who strives to fulfill every desire is always disturbed and never in peace. (2.70)

Q What is Super Conscious state (Supreme Blissful State) and how to attain it even at the time of death?

विहाय कामान्यः सर्वान्पुमांश्चरति निःस्पृहः ।
निर्ममो निरहङ्कारः स शान्तिमधिगच्छति ।। 71 ।।

vihāya kāmān yaḥ sarvān
pumāṁś carati niḥspṛhaḥ
nirmamo nirahaṅkāraḥ
sa śāntim adhigacchati

It is never too late to attain the Ultimate Liberation

एषा ब्राह्मी स्थितिः पार्थ नैनां प्राप्य विमुह्यति ।
स्थित्वास्यामन्तकालेऽपि ब्रह्मनिर्वाणमृच्छति ।। 72 ।।

eṣā brāhmī sthitiḥ pārtha
naināṁ prāpya vimuhyati
sthitvāsyām anta-kāle 'pi
brahma-nirvāṇam ṛcchati

One who abandons all his desires and becomes free from the feeling of "I" and "my" (Ego and attachment) attains Supreme Peace. (2.71)

Arjuna, this is the Super Conscious state (*Brahmisthiti, Brahmic state, Supreme Blissful state*), the state of transcendental unity with *Brahman* (God). Having attained this state, one overcomes delusion. Being established in this state, even at the moment of death, a person attains *Brahma-Nirvana* (Becomes one with the Absolute, Oneness with God). (2.72)

Self-control + Self-Knowledge → Eternal Happiness, Supreme Peace, Ultimate Bliss, Sat Chit Ananda (Brahma-Nirvana)

Lessons to learn and practice in daily life

Have a Divine company, build a strong relationship with Him and His Grace will pour on you

1. Develop self-awareness of your mental status, behaviour, responsibility and purpose of life
2. Be truthful to yourself and with others (especially to your own feelings, do not hide them or be embarrassed and egoistic/rigid about them)
3. Always have a Divine/good company/*guru*/Gita
4. Be a good company, an honest friend, a good listener and counselor to others (without a personal agenda)
5. Have a discussion (*Samvad*) and not arguments (*Vivad*) with others. "*Have Samvad not Vivad*"
6. Practice Equanimity (calmness)

The Gita is a path to connect with the Supreme Consciousness

The secret of action is to become established in Equanimity, renouncing all egocentric attachments, and forgetting to worry about our successes and failures.

—Swami Chinmayananda

ॐ तत्सदिति श्रीमद्भगवद्गीतासूपनिषत्सु ब्रह्मविद्यायां योगशास्त्रे
श्रीकृष्णार्जुनसंवादे सांख्ययोगो नाम द्वितीयोऽध्यायः ।।

AUM TAT SAT

Thus ends second chapter named "*Sankhya Yoga*"
The Path of Self-Knowledge
in the *Upanishad* of the glorious Bhagavad Gita, the scripture of Yoga, the science of the Absolute (*Brahman*), in the form of the dialogue between Lord Krishna and Arjuna.

Aum Shanti, Shanti, Shantihi

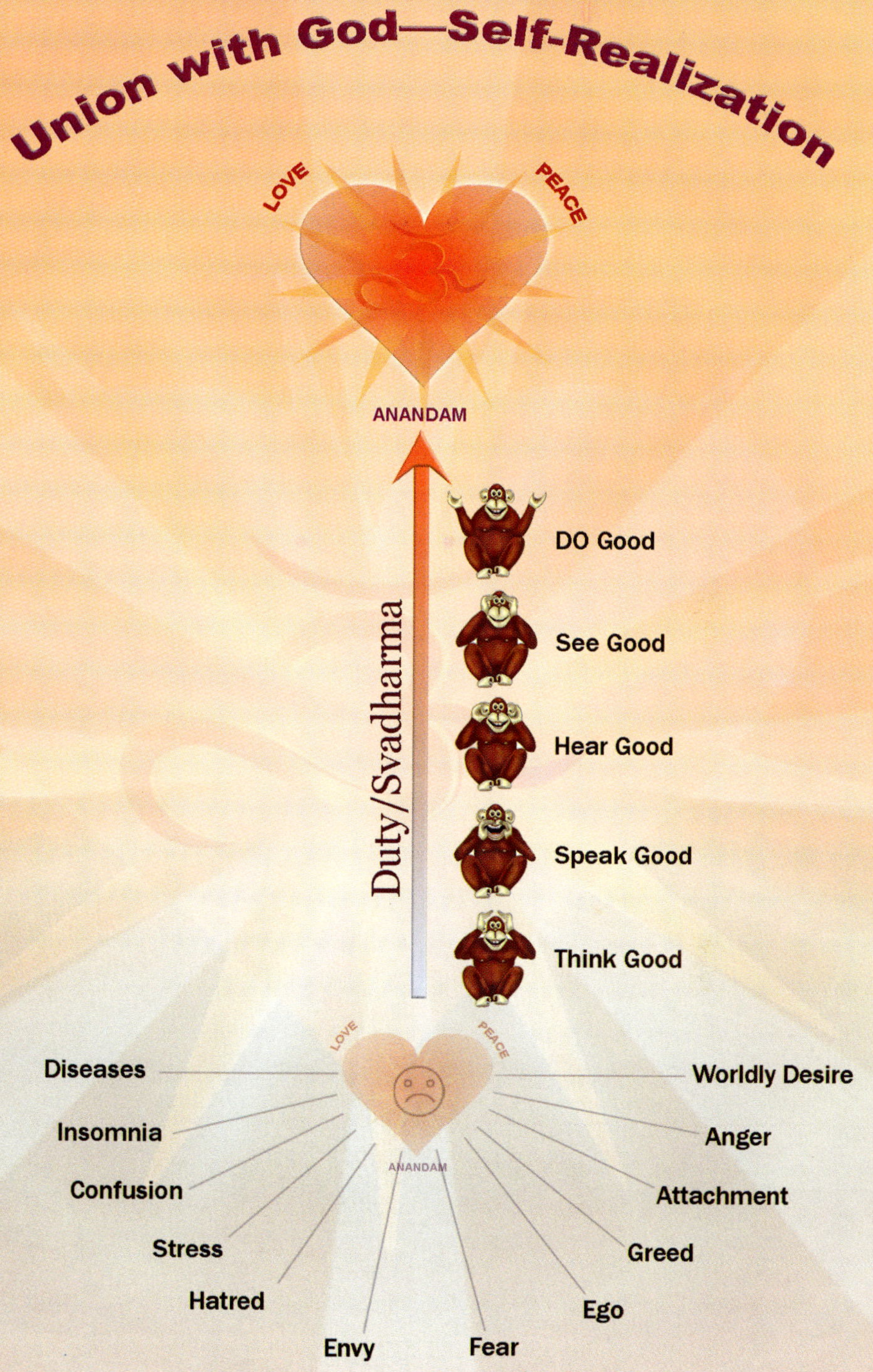

Self-Purification and Transformation through Duty/Dharma

KARMA YOGA

The Path of Right Action

Union with God (Self-Realization) through the path of selfless action

The Gita is a spiritual instruction manual to operate our lives righteously

In the previous chapter, Lord Krishna imparted the two-fold path; the path of *Sankhya Yoga* (Self-Knowledge) and the path of *Karma Yoga* (selfless action). Arjuna seemed confused so Lord Krishna blessed him with additional knowledge of *Karma Yoga* to remove his confusion.

Karma Yoga is one of the spiritual paths for self-transformation and self-purification and to attain Liberation from worldly miseries and fulfill the purpose of life. Therefore it answers one of the basic questions: *How to fulfill the Supreme goal of life* (Self-Realization) *through the path of action.*

Action that is done skillfully with knowledge (Wisdom, *Jnana*), love and devotion and to the best of one's ability without any expectation in return, for the benefit of others is called *Karma Yoga.*

Ingredients and Recipe for *Karma Yoga*:

1. Work/Action
2. Knowledge (know-how)
3. Best Efforts
4. Love and Devotion
5. Renunciation, *Tyaga* (no expectation of the fruit of action or personal gain), e.g. Mother Teresa, Mahatma Gandhi, etc.

Karma Yoga is an art of work. It is performed by controlling senses and practicing goodness.

Seva → Meva (Fruit of Self-Realization)

Action + Knowledge + Love and Devotion + Selfless Services → *Karma Yoga* (*Seva*)

***Karma Yoga* is the precursor for *Self-Knowledge* that leads to Liberation**

Karma Yoga ⟶ *Self-Knowledge* ⟶ *Liberation*

One who performs *Karma Yoga* develops Divine Qualities that leads to Liberation

Karma Yoga → Divine Qualities ↘

↑↓ *Liberation/Moksha/Nirvana/Self-Realization*

Karma Yoga → Self-Purification ↗

Selfless service → Purity → Unity → Divinity → Self-Realization (Union with God)

Flow chart 3.1 *Summary of Karma Yoga*

Goodness to Godliness:

Practicing goodness bring us closer to God and leads to Eternal Happiness and Peace—Anandam

Goodness → Godliness (Divinity)

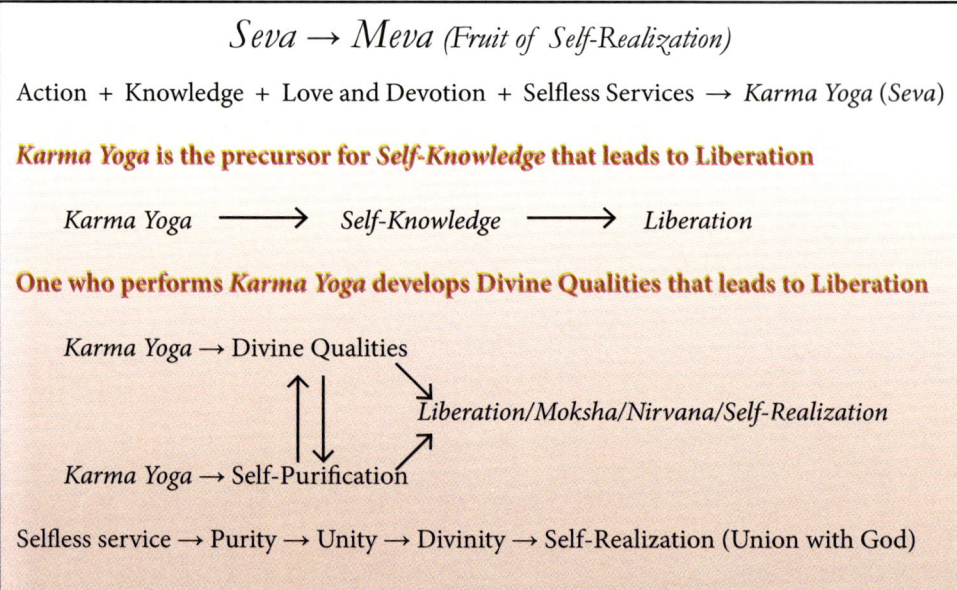

Think Good   See Good   Hear Good   Speak Good   Do Good

Fig. 3.1 *Five monkeys practicing Goodness*

Karma Yoga is an easier path to practice if one performs every action as an offering to God (with a pure heart). The person who practices *Karma Yoga* is called *Karma Yogi*; he lives in harmony and still attains everlasting Peace and Self-Realization.

Main Message

Union with God through sacrifices, selfless services and Seva

The Path of Selfless Action → Righteous Action = Karma Yoga (Art of work)

Everyone must engage in some sort of activity in this material world. No one can remain inactive due to his innate nature (*Gunas*). But actions can either bind one to this world or liberate him from it. By performing work without selfish motives, one can be liberated from the law of *karma* (action and reaction) and attain Transcendental Knowledge of the self and the Supreme.

Therefore, one must attempt to perform every action as seva, offering to God / *Yajna* (Sacrifice). However, action must be pure and free from 5 + 2 enemies (attachment, desires, anger, greed, ego, envy and hatred).

- One must perform one's own duty *svadharma* (*Kartavya*) toward his body, mind, spirit, family, society, nation and world.
- One must learn how to perform one's duty from a learned teacher.
- Lust, anger, and greed are triple gates to hell. They all lead to demonic characteristics and thus lead to bondage and hell.
- Overcome selfish desires (lust, *kama*) because they are the origin of sin.

The Path of *Karma Yoga* and selfless action helps to liberate one from worldly miseries, *karmic* bondage (law of *karma* - cause and effect) and attain *Self-Knowledge* (Self-Realization).

Chapter Overview

01–08 Should one follow the path of *Jnana Yoga* or *Karma Yoga*
09–17 Why perform the Services/Sacrifices/*Yajna*
18–26 Set an example for others
27–29 Play of *Gunas*
30–33 Perform your duty and free yourself from bondage of action
34–36 Major barriers to Self-Realization
36–43 How to get rid off selfish desires, the origin of sin

Should one follow the path of *Jnana Yoga* or *Karma Yoga*

Q Is the Path of Self-Knowledge better than the Path of Action to attain the Highest Good?

अर्जुन उवाच
ज्यायसी चेत्कर्मणस्ते मता बुद्धिर्जनार्दन।
तत्किं कर्मणि घोरे मां नियोजयसि केशव ॥ 1 ॥

arjuna uvāca
jyāyasī cet karmaṇas te matā buddhir janārdana
tat kiṁ karmaṇi ghore māṁ niyojayasi keśava

Knowledge path or Selfless action path?

व्यामिश्रेणेव वाक्येन बुद्धिं मोहयसीव मे।
तदेकं वद निश्चित्य येन श्रेयोऽहमाप्नुयाम् ॥ 2 ॥

vyāmiśreṇeva vākyena buddhiṁ mohayasīva me
tad ekaṁ vada niścitya yena śreyo 'ham āpnuyām

Arjuna said: O Krishna if You think that path of Self-Knowledge is better than path of Action, why are you urging me to do such a horrible act (war)? (3.01)

Certainly, you are confusing my mind by your perplexing words. Please tell me, decisively, only one path by which I may attain the highest good (Supreme). (3.02)

Q How many major paths of spiritual discipline are there and for whom?

श्रीभगवानुवाच
लोकेऽस्मिन्द्विविधा निष्ठा पुरा प्रोक्ता मयानघ।
ज्ञानयोगेन सांख्यानां कर्मयोगेन योगिनाम् ॥ 3 ॥

śrī-bhagavān uvāca
loke 'smin dvi-vidhā niṣṭhā purā proktā mayānagha
jñāna-yogena sāṅkhyānāṁ karma-yogena yoginām

The Supreme Lord said: O Arjuna, I have already explained earlier a twofold path of spiritual discipline (*Sadhana*) in this world. One is the path of Self-Knowledge (*Jnana-Yoga*) for the contemplative and the other is the path of selfless services, *Karma Yoga* for the active and analytical mind. (3.03)

Q Why should one work?

न कर्मणामनारम्भान्नैष्कर्म्यं पुरुषोऽश्नुते।
न च संन्यसनादेव सिद्धिं समाधिगच्छति ।।4।।

na karmaṇām anārambhān naiṣkarmyaṁ puruṣo 'śnute
na ca sannyasanād eva siddhiṁ samadhigacchati

No one attains freedom from the bondage of karma by merely abstaining from work nor does one attain perfection by merely giving up the work. (3.04)

Q What forces compel one to work?

Everyone is bound to act

न हि कश्चित्क्षणमपि जातु तिष्ठत्यकर्मकृत्।
कार्यते ह्यवशः कर्म सर्वः प्रकृतिजैर्गुणैः ।।5।।

na hi kaścit kṣaṇam api jātu tiṣṭhaty akarma-kṛt
kāryate hy avaśaḥ karma sarvaḥ prakṛti-jair guṇaiḥ

Certainly, no one can remain action-less even for a moment. Everyone is helplessly driven to action by his intrinsic qualities (natural-born, *Gunas*). (3.05)

Q Who is a hypocrite?

कर्मेन्द्रियाणि संयम्य य आस्ते मनसा स्मरन्।
इन्द्रियार्थान्विमूढात्मा मिथ्याचारः स उच्यते ।।6।।

karmendriyāṇi saṁyamya ya āste manasā smaran
indriyārthān vimūḍhātmā mithyācāraḥ sa ucyate

Those, who restrain their organs of action but mentally dwell upon the sense objects and their enjoyment, are called hypocrites. (3.06)

Q Who can excel on the spiritual path?

यस्त्विन्द्रियाणि मनसा नियम्यारभतेऽर्जुन।
कर्मेन्द्रियैः कर्मयोगमसक्तः स विशिष्यते ।।7।।

yas tv indriyāṇi manasā niyamyārabhate 'rjuna
karmendriyaiḥ karma-yogam asaktaḥ sa viśiṣyate

But one, who controls his senses and their functions by his will power (mind and intellect) and engages them to selfless service (*Karma Yoga*) without any attachment, is far superior and definitely excels, O Arjuna. (3.07)

Q Why should one perform one's prescribed duty?

नियतं कुरु कर्म त्वं कर्म ज्यायो ह्यकर्मणः।
शरीरयात्रापि च ते न प्रसिद्ध्येदकर्मणः॥8॥

niyataṁ kuru karma tvaṁ karma jyāyo hy akarmaṇaḥ
śarīra-yātrāpi ca te na prasiddhyed akarmaṇaḥ

Action is better than inaction

Perform your prescribed duty because working (action) is certainly better than not working (inaction). One cannot even maintain one's physical body without work. (3.08)

Why perform the Services/Sacrifices/*Yajna*

Q How to be free from the consequences of action (bondage, *karmas*)?

यज्ञार्थात्कर्मणोऽन्यत्र लोकोऽयं कर्मबन्धनः।
तदर्थं कर्म कौन्तेय मुक्तसङ्गः समाचर॥9॥

yajñārthāt karmaṇo 'nyatra
loko 'yaṁ karma-bandhanaḥ
tad-arthaṁ karma kaunteya
mukta-saṅgaḥ samācara

Serving selflessly is service to God

In this world, human beings are always bound by their action (*karma*) that is not performed for the sake of sacrifice (*Yajna*, selfless service, *Seva*). Therefore, O Arjuna, do your prescribed duty efficiently as a service to Me, with no selfish attachment to the fruits of action and this way you will always remain free from bondage. (3.09)

Q Why is *Yajna* (Sacrifice) known as a milch cow?

सहयज्ञाः प्रजाः सृष्ट्वा पुरोवाच प्रजापतिः।
अनेन प्रसविष्यध्वमेष वोऽस्त्विष्टकामधुक्॥10॥

saha-yajñāḥ prajāḥ sṛṣṭvā purovāca prajāpatiḥ
anena prasaviṣyadhvam eṣa vo 'stv iṣṭa-kāma-dhuk

Yajna is the milch cow of all the desires

In the beginning of creation, the Lord of all beings created human beings along with the spirit of sacrifice (*Yajna*) and said: "By this you may prosper and propagate. This shall be the milch cow, *Kamadhenu* of all your desires for both worldly needs and for Self-Realization. (3.10)

Q What is the benefit of nourishing a demi-god?

देवान्भावयतानेन ते देवा भावयन्तु वः।
परस्परं भावयन्तः श्रेयः परमवाप्स्यथ ॥ 11 ॥

devān bhāvayatānena te devā bhāvayantu vaḥ
parasparaṁ bhāvayantaḥ śreyaḥ param avāpsyatha

Nourish the demi-gods (*devas*) with this sacrifice (*Yajna*), and *devas* will nourish you and thus, mutually pleasing one another, you will attain the Supreme goal of your life, Self-Realization. (3.11)

Q Who is the real thief?

इष्टान्भोगान्हि वो देवा दास्यन्ते यज्ञभाविताः।
तैर्दत्तानप्रदायैभ्यो यो भुङ्क्ते स्तेन एव सः ॥ 12 ॥

iṣṭān bhogān hi vo devā dāsyante yajña-bhāvitāḥ
tair dattān apradāyaibhyo yo bhuṅkte stena eva saḥ

The demi-gods, *devas*, satisfied by sacrifice will surely reward you with all the necessities of life. But one who enjoys such a gift of the *devas* without offering them something in return is certainly a thief. (3.12)

Q Who is free from sins and who is not?

यज्ञशिष्टाशिनः सन्तो मुच्यन्ते सर्वकिल्बिषैः।
भुञ्जते ते त्वघं पापा ये पचन्त्यात्मकारणात् ॥ 13 ॥

yajña-śiṣṭāśinaḥ santo mucyante sarva-kilbiṣaiḥ
bhuñjate te tv aghaṁ pāpā ye pacanty ātma-kāraṇāt

The virtuous, who eat the remnants of sacrifice/*Yajna* are freed from all sins; but the selfish and wicked people who prepare food only for their own sense of enjoyment (without sharing with others or first offering to Me), in truth, eat only in sin. (3.13)

Q Does *Yajna* help to maintain Nature and what is its relationship with food and rain?

अन्नाद्भवन्ति भूतानि पर्जन्यादन्नसंभवः।
यज्ञाद्भवति पर्जन्यो यज्ञः कर्मसमुद्भवः ॥ 14 ॥

annād bhavanti bhūtāni
parjanyād anna-sambhavaḥ
yajñād bhavati parjanyo
yajñaḥ karma-samudbhavaḥ

Sacrifice is a noble act

All living beings are products of food grains. Grains are produced by rain; rain by performance of sacrifice as a prescribed duty and sacrifice is the noblest form of action. (3.14)

Q How could *Brahman*, The Supreme Being be in Sacrifice/*Yajna*?

कर्म ब्रह्मोद्भवं विद्धि ब्रह्माक्षरसमुद्भवम् ।
तस्मात्सर्वगतं ब्रह्म नित्यं यज्ञे प्रतिष्ठितम् ।। 15 ।।

karma brahmodbhavaṁ viddhi
brahmākṣara-samudbhavam
tasmāt sarva-gataṁ brahma
nityaṁ yajñe pratiṣṭhitam

Duty is prescribed in the Vedas and the Vedas come directly from the *Brahman* (Supreme Being, God). Therefore, all-pervading God is present in Selfless service. (3.15)

Q What happens to one who does not contribute to maintain the universe?

एवं प्रवर्तितं चक्रं नानुवर्तयतीह यः ।
अघायुरिन्द्रियारामो मोघं पार्थ स जीवति ।। 16 ।।

evaṁ pravartitaṁ cakraṁ
nānuvartayatīha yaḥ
aghāyur indriyārāmo
moghaṁ pārtha sa jīvati

Everyone's contribution is necessary to maintain a healthy world

In this world, one who does not help to keep the wheel of creation in motion by, selfless service, *seva*, sacrificial duty, but seeks instead mundane pleasures through sense-gratification, such a person certainly leads a useless life, full of sins and lives in vain, O Arjuna. (3.16)

Q Who is free from his duty and obligations?

यस्त्वात्मरतिरेव स्यादात्मतृप्तश्च मानवः ।
आत्मन्येव च संतुष्टस्तस्य कार्यं न विद्यते ।। 17 ।।

yas tv ātma-ratir eva syād ātma-tṛptaś ca mānavaḥ
ātmany eva ca santuṣṭas tasya kāryaṁ na vidyate

One who is delighted only in the Supreme-Self, one who is perfectly satisfied in the Consciousness of Self and who is contented in the Self alone has no duty and he is free from obligations. (3.17)

Set an example for others

Q Who does not depend on others?

नैव तस्य कृतेनार्थो नाकृतेनेह कश्चन।
न चास्य सर्वभूतेषु कश्चिदर्थव्यपाश्रय: ॥ 18 ॥

naiva tasya kṛtenārtho nākṛteneha kaścana
na cāsya sarva-bhūteṣu kaścid artha-vyapāśrayaḥ

Such a Self-realized person has no interest whatsoever is gaining or not gaining from his action, nor does he depend on any other living being (except on God) for anything. (3.18)

Q How does one attain the highest perfection?

तस्मादसक्त: सततं कार्यं कर्म समाचर।
असक्तो ह्याचरन् कर्म परमाप्नोति पूरुष: ॥ 19 ॥

tasmād asaktaḥ satataṁ kāryaṁ karma samācara
asakto hy ācaran karma param āpnoti pūruṣaḥ

One attains the Highest perfection, (Supreme Being) by performing his duty without attachment. Therefore, always fulfill your duty efficiently without any selfish attachment to the results. (3.19)

Q Has anyone attained perfection by performing his duty?

कर्मणैव हि संसिद्धिमास्थिता जनकादय:।
लोकसंग्रहमेवापि संपश्यन कर्तुमर्हसि ॥ 20 ॥

karmaṇaiva hi saṁsiddhim āsthitā janakādayaḥ
loka-saṅgraham evāpi sampaśyan kartum arhasi

King Janaka, famous for his righteous actions, and others attained Liberation only by performing their duty. You must also perform your duty with a view to maintaining the world in order and for welfare of the society. (3.20)

Q Why should one become a noble person and be a mentor to others?

Set an example and be a mentor

यद्यदाचरति श्रेष्ठस्तत्तदेवेतरो जन:।
स यत्प्रमाणं कुरुते लोकस्तदनुवर्तते ॥ 21 ॥

yad yad ācarati śreṣṭhas tat tad evetaro janaḥ
sa yat pramāṇaṁ kurute lokas tad anuvartate

Whatever a great man does, certainly common men follow. Whatever standards he sets up by exemplary conduct, the world follows. (3.21)

Q Who else is an example of doing selfless work for the welfare of others?

न मे पार्थास्ति कर्तव्यं त्रिषु लोकेषु किंचन।
नानवाप्तमवाप्तव्यं वर्त एव च कर्मणि ॥22॥

na me pārthāsti kartavyaṁ triṣu lokeṣu kiñcana
nānavāptam avāptavyaṁ varta eva ca karmaṇi

O Arjuna, in all the three worlds (heaven, earth, and the lower regions of hell) there is no duty whatsoever for Me to fulfill, nor is there anything for Me to attain and yet I am constantly engaged in work. (3.22)

Q Why does God always work?

यदि ह्यहं न वर्तेयं जातु कर्मण्यतन्द्रितः।
मम वर्त्मानुवर्तन्ते मनुष्याः पार्थ सर्वशः ॥23॥

yadi hy ahaṁ na varteyaṁ
jātu karmaṇy atandritaḥ
mama vartmānuvartante
manuṣyāḥ pārtha sarvaśaḥ

Consider God as your mentor and do as God does

उत्सीदेयुरिमे लोका न कुर्यां कर्म चेदहम्।
संकरस्य च कर्ता स्यामुपहन्यामिमाः प्रजाः ॥24॥

utsīdeyur ime lokā
na kuryāṁ karma ced aham
saṅkarasya ca kartā syām
upahanyām imāḥ prajāḥ

If I do not carefully engage myself in performing my prescribed duty, O Arjuna, certainly all men would follow my path in every respect. If I do not work, all these worlds would perish and I would be the cause of confusion and destruction of the people. (3.23–24)

Play of *Gunas*

Q How should one work to maintain the welfare of society?

सक्ताः कर्मण्यविद्वांसो यथा कुर्वन्ति भारत।
कुर्याद्विद्वांस्तथासक्तश्चिकीर्षुर्लोकसंग्रहम् ॥25॥

saktāḥ karmaṇy avidvāṁso yathā kurvanti bhārata
kuryād vidvāṁs tathāsaktaś cikīrṣur loka-saṅgraham

O Arjuna, as the ignorant work with attachment to the fruits of action, so the learned should also work without attachment for the sake of leading people on the right path and for the desire to maintain world order. (3.25)

Q How should one motivate others?

न बुद्धिभेदं जनयेदज्ञानां कर्मसङ्गिनाम् ।
जोषयेत्सर्वकर्माणि विद्वान्युक्तः समाचरन् ।। 26 ।।

na buddhi-bhedaṁ janayed
ajñānāṁ karma-saṅginām
joṣayet sarva-karmāṇi
vidvān yuktaḥ samācaran

One should motivate others to do their duty righteously

The wise person should not create any disturbance in the minds of the ignorant who are attached to the fruits of action. Instead, he should inspire them by performing his duty delightfully and efficiently without any selfish motives. (3.26)

Q Who thinks "I am the doer?"

प्रकृतेः क्रियमाणानि गुणैः कर्माणि सर्वशः ।
अहंकारविमूढात्मा कर्ताहमिति मन्यते ।। 27 ।।

prakṛteḥ kriyamāṇāni
guṇaiḥ karmāṇi sarvaśaḥ
ahaṅkāra-vimūḍhātmā
kartāham iti manyate

All action is done due to your attributes

All action is done by the energy and power of nature, the three modes of *Gunas*. However, due to the delusion of ignorance and egoism, the ignorant person thinks, "I am the doer." (3.27)

Q How does the knowledge of nature and *Gunas* and their respective functions help one to maintain his calmness?

तत्त्ववित्तु महाबाहो गुणकर्मविभागयोः ।
गुणा गुणेषु वर्तन्त इति मत्वा न सज्जते ।। 28 ।।

tattva-vit tu mahā-bāho guṇa-karma-vibhāgayoḥ
guṇā guṇeṣu vartanta iti matvā na sajjate

O Arjuna, one who knows the truth about the role of the forces of nature (*Prakriti* and *Gunas*) and their respective functions, does not engage himself in the senses and sense gratification, and does not become attached to action. (3.28)

Q How should the wise treat the ignorant and unsettled?

प्रकृतेर्गुणसंमूढाः सज्जन्ते गुणकर्मसु ।
तानकृत्स्नविदो मन्दान्कृत्स्नविन्न विचालयेत् ।। 29 ।।

prakṛter guṇa-sammūḍhāḥ sajjante guṇa-karmasu
tān akṛtsna-vido mandān kṛtsna-vin na vicālayet

Those who are deluded by the modes of nature (*Gunas*) and do not comprehend the play of the *Gunas* become attached to their action. Therefore they face the consequences of their actions. But the wise should not disturb the mind of those whose knowledge is imperfect. (3.29)

Perform Your Duty and Free Yourself from Bondage of Action

Q How should one deal with the battle of life?

मयि सर्वाणि कर्माणि संन्यस्याध्यात्मचेतसा ।
निराशीर्निर्ममो भूत्वा युध्यस्व विगतज्वरः ।। 30 ।।

mayi sarvāṇi karmāṇi sannyasyādhyātma-cetasā
nirāśīr nirmamo bhūtvā yudhyasva vigata-jvaraḥ

Do your duty and fight the battle of life

Surrendering all action to Me with your mind fully focused on Me, without selfishness and anticipation of any reward, no claims to proprietorship, attachment, and without any mental stress, do your duty and fight the battle without any hesitation. (3.30)

Q How does Lord Krishna's teachings help one liberate oneself from the bondage of action?

ये मे मतमिदं नित्यमनुतिष्ठन्ति मानवाः ।
श्रद्धावन्तोऽनसूयन्तो मुच्यन्ते तेऽपि कर्मभिः ।। 31 ।।

ye me matam idaṁ nityam
anutiṣṭhanti mānavāḥ
śraddhāvanto 'nasūyanto
mucyante te 'pi karmabhiḥ

Follow the teachings of the Gita and free yourself from the wheel of Karma

Those people who always follow and practice this teaching of Mine with full faith, sincerity and without envy also become free from the bondage of action/*karma*. (3.31)

Q Who are the losers in this universe?

ये त्वेतदभ्यसूयन्तो नानुतिष्ठन्ति मे मतम्।
सर्वज्ञानविमूढांस्तान् विद्धि नष्टानचेतसः ।। 32 ।।

ye tv etad abhyasūyanto
nānutiṣṭhanti me matam
sarva-jñāna-vimūḍhāṁs tān
viddhi naṣṭān acetasaḥ

Those who find faults out of envy and do not follow My teachings should be considered absolutely ignorant, devoid of all knowledge and lost. (3.32)

Q What is the most common question of today's man?

सदृशं चेष्टते स्वस्याः प्रकृतेर्ज्ञानवानपि।
प्रकृतिं यान्ति भूतानि निग्रहः किं करिष्यति ।। 33 ।।

sadṛśaṁ ceṣṭate svasyāḥ prakṛter jñānavān api
prakṛtiṁ yānti bhūtāni nigrahaḥ kiṁ kariṣyati

All living creatures including even a man of wisdom act in accordance with their natural tendencies and *Gunas*. 'If every one is so driven, then why bother restraining or controlling the senses?' (3.33)

Major barriers to Self-Realization

Q What are the major obstacles on the path of Self-Realization?

इन्द्रियस्येन्द्रियस्यार्थे रागद्वेषौ व्यवस्थितौ।
तयोर्न वशमागच्छेत्तौ ह्यस्य परिपन्थिनौ ।। 34 ।।

indriyasyendriyasyārthe
rāga-dveṣau vyavasthitau
tayor na vaśam āgacchet
tau hy asya paripanthinau

Attachment and envy are the two major stumbling blocks to spiritual growth

Attachment and Envy (*raga* and *dvesa*) for the objects of the senses are rooted in the senses. One must not come under the control of these two because they are major barriers on the Path of Self-Realization. (3.34)

Q How should one avoid stress?

श्रेयान्स्वधर्मो विगुणः परधर्मात्स्वनुष्ठितात्।
स्वधर्मे निधनं श्रेयः परधर्मो भयावह ॥35॥

śreyān sva-dharmo viguṇaḥ
para-dharmāt sv-anuṣṭhitāt
sva-dharme nidhanaṁ śreyaḥ
para-dharmo bhayāvahaḥ

Doing your own duty is better than mimicing others

It is far better to do one's own duty or natural work though it may be inferior to superior but unnatural work of others. Even death in the course of performing one's natural work is better than engaging in another's duties. The unnatural work of another's path is done with fear, therefore it produces too much stress. (3.35)

How to get rid off selfish desires, the origin of sin

Q What did Arjuna ask about committing wrong acts?

अर्जुन उवाच
अथ केन प्रयुक्तोऽयं पापं चरति पूरुषः।
अनिच्छन्नपि वार्ष्णेय बलादिव नियोजतः ॥36॥

arjuna uvāca
atha kena prayukto 'yaṁ pāpaṁ carati pūruṣaḥ
anicchann api vārṣṇeya balād iva niyojitaḥ

Arjuna said: O Krishna, but what compels one to commit sin, even against his will as though by force? (3.36)

Q What are the major barriers to and disturbances in our peace and why?

श्रीभगवानुवाच
काम एष क्रोध एष रजोगुणसमुद्भवः।
महाशनो महापाप्मा विद्ध्येनमिह वैरिणम् ॥37॥

śrī-bhagavān uvāca
kāma eṣa krodha eṣa
rajo-guṇa-samudbhavaḥ
mahāśano mahā-pāpmā
viddhy enam iha vairiṇam

Selfish desires are the root cause of all the miseries in life and can never be fullfilled

धूमेनाव्रियते वह्निर्यथादर्शो मलेन च।
यथोल्बेनावृतो गर्भस्तथा तेनेदमावृतम् ॥38॥

dhūmenāvriyate vahnir yathādarśo malena ca
yatholbenāvṛto garbhas tathā tenedam āvṛtam

The Supreme Lord said: It is desire (lust and *kama*) which is born out of passion (*rajas*) that becomes anger due to unfulfilled desire. Desire is insatiable, very harmful and consider this as the enemy. (3.37)

Just as fire is covered by smoke, as a mirror by dust, and as an embryo by the womb, similarly the Self-Knowledge (*Brahma-Jnana*) of the living entity is covered by desire. (3.38)

Q Who is the eternal enemy of the wise?

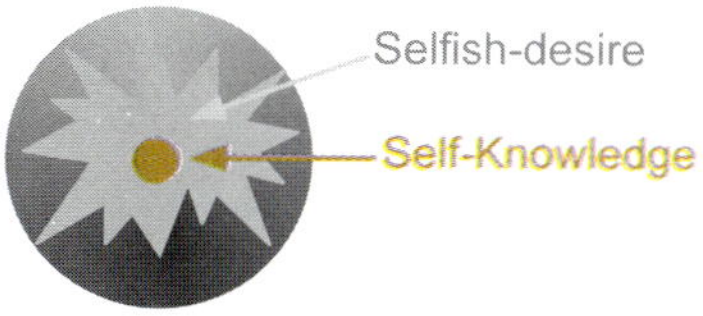

आवृतं ज्ञानमेतेन ज्ञानिनो नित्यवैरिणा।
कामरूपेण कौन्तेय दुष्पूरेणानलेन च ॥ 39 ॥

āvṛtaṁ jñānam etena jñānino nitya-vairiṇā
kāma-rūpeṇa kaunteya duṣpūreṇānalena ca

O Arjuna, Insatiable desire is the eternal enemy of the wise, for Self Knowledge (Pure Consciousness, Wisdom) gets coverd by it (3.39)

Q Where do desires live and how harmful are they?

इन्द्रियाणि मनो बुद्धिरस्याधिष्ठानमुच्यते।
एतैर्विमोहयत्येष ज्ञानमावृत्य देहिनम् ॥ 40 ॥

indriyāṇi mano buddhir asyādhiṣṭhānam ucyate
etair vimohayaty eṣa jñānam āvṛtya dehinam

The senses, the mind, and the intellect are said to be the seat of lust and desire. These desire delude the embodied soul by enveloping his wisdom. (3.40)

Q How to control selfish desires?

तस्मात्त्वमिन्द्रियाण्यादौ नियम्य भरतर्षभ।
पाप्मानं प्रजहि ह्येनं ज्ञानविज्ञाननाशनम् ॥ 41 ॥

tasmāt tvam indriyāṇy ādau niyamya bharatarṣabha
pāpmānaṁ prajahi hy enaṁ jñāna-vijñāna-nāśanam

O Arjuna, therefore kill this sinful destroyer by controlling your senses from the very beginning which obstructs Knowledge, Wisdom and Discrimination. (3.41)

Q What is the relationship of body, mind and spirit?

इन्द्रियाणि पराण्याहुरिन्द्रियेभ्यः परं मनः।
मनसस्तु परा बुद्धिर्यो बुद्धेः परतस्तु सः ॥ 42 ॥

indriyāṇi parāṇy āhur indriyebhyaḥ paraṁ manaḥ
manasas tu parā buddhir yo buddheḥ paratas tu saḥ

The senses are said to be higher than the body, the mind is higher than the senses, the intellect is still higher than the mind, but *Atma*/Spirit, Self is even higher than the intellect. (3.42)

Body < Senses < Mind < Intellect < Spirit

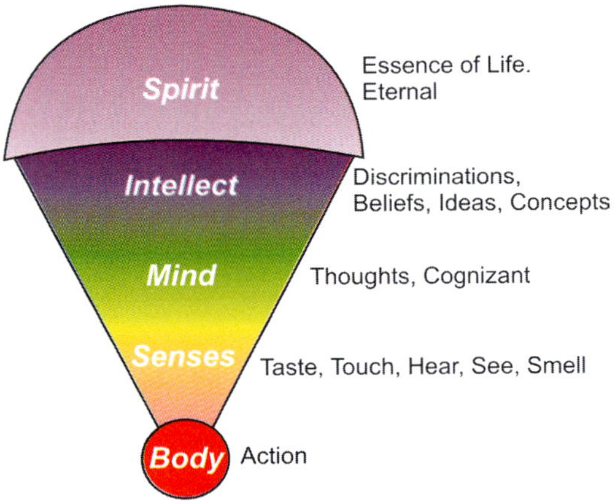

Fig. 3.2 *Relationship of body, mind and Spirit*

Q How to put Transcendental Knowledge into practice?

एवं बुद्धेः परं बुद्ध्वा संस्तभ्यात्मानमात्मना ।
जहि शत्रुं महाबाहो कामरूपं दुरासदम् ।। 43 ।।

evaṁ buddheḥ paraṁ buddhvā
saṁstabhyātmānam ātmanā
jahi śatruṁ mahā-bāho
kāma-rūpaṁ durāsadam

Spiritual practices lead to calmness of mind

Knowing the Self to be superior to intellect, mind and senses, one should purify and steady the mind through regular spiritual practices. Thus with this spiritual strength one must kill this insatiable enemy of lust that is very difficult to conquer, O Arjuna. (3.43)

Lessons to learn and practice in daily life

Do your duty selflessly and renounce the fruit of action

1. Focus on yourself and your responsiblities and not blame others for your problems as Lord Krishna never mentioned Duryodhana's faults to Arjuna but guided Arjuna to focus on his duty.
2. Do every activity in life that brings everlasting Peace, Happiness and leads to the Supreme goal of life, *Sat Chit Ananda*
3. Lead a spiritual lifestyle like a *Karma Yogi* (*Sadhaka*) and perform your duty as *Sadhana* (Offering to God, *Yajna*)
4. Take full responsibility for your action, fulfill your commitment, and perform your prescribed duty cheerfully.
5. Since having too many worldly desires is the biggest obstacle to *Karma Yoga* and attaining Self-Realization, one must control selfish desires by substituting all worldly desires with the desire to serve God's creation and attain Him.
6. Help and respect others, and practice Goodness.
7. Become a noble person and a mentor to others.
8. Only when Self-Knowledge is practiced with action, then it can be experienced and realized. Therefore, we must use all of our resources (body and mind) to perform *Karma Yoga* and attain Self-Knowledge.

Attaining Anandam is the purpose of our life, Spreading Love, Peace and Anandam to others is our Karma Yoga and being in Peace and Anandam is our Sadhana

Fig. 3.3 *Kamadhenu/milch cow (3.10)*

ॐ तत्सदिति श्रीमद्भगवद्गीतासूपनिषत्सु ब्रह्मविद्यायां योगशास्त्रे
श्रीकृष्णार्जुनसंवादे कर्मयोगो नाम तृतीयोऽध्यायः ॥

AUM TAT SAT

Thus ends the third chapter named "*Karma Yoga*"
The Path of Right Action
in the *Upanishad* of the glorious Bhagavad Gita, the scripture of Yoga,
the science of the Absolute (*Brahman*), in the form of the dialogue
between Lord Krishna and Arjuna

Aum Shanti, Shanti, Shantihi

What is My Duty (Svadharma)?

Being happy and spreading the happiness to others is my duty.
Developing good qualities is my duty.
Developing WISDOM is my duty.
Thinking good is my duty.
Seeing good is my duty.
Hearing good is my duty.
Speaking the truth is my duty.
Eating good is my duty.
Doing good is my duty.
Controlling my senses is my duty.
Helping others is my duty.
Respecting others is my duty.
Sharing with others is my duty.
Loving others is my duty.
Doing selfless service is my duty.
Taking care of myself is my duty.
Taking care of my responsibilities is my duty.
God/Self-Realization is my duty.

"Being in peace and making this world a peaceful place to live is my duty"

JNANA-KARMA-SANYASA YOGA

The Path of Knowledge, Action and Renunciation

Union with God (Self-Realization) through the path of action with knowledge of renunciation

The Gita is Timeless Wisdom that awakens our own guru within

In this chapter Lord Krishna explains the remote history of the Gita and the importance of passing this knowledge from generation to generation (father to son). However, when this tradition of passing down of the wisdom is interrupted then the decline of *Dharma*/righteousness takes place. Codes of Righteous Living are not followed (*adharma*), and people become more selfish and start operating based on their negative emotions, resulting from their desires and perform evil acts.

Lord Krishna declares the purpose and reason of His periodic reincarnation (descending) into the materialistic world and the importance of having a guru (Self-realized teacher). He further explains that the Self-Knowledge purifies and leads to Liberation. Such knowledge is the fruit of selfless action (*Karma Yoga*).

Q What is Dharma?

Codes of righteous living are followed (Righteousness) and one's own prescribed duty (*svadharma*) is fullfiled, and ethical behavior is practiced.

Dharma leads to Light and Liberation
(Anandam, Eternal Happiness and Peace)

Dharma is love in action.

—Sathya Sai Baba

Q What is adharma?

Codes of righteous living are not followed (unrighteousness), not fulfilling own obligatory duty (responsibility) and unethical behavior is practiced.

Adharma leads to darkness, miseries, sorrow and bondage (rebirth)

- Hurting others is adharma
- Self-rejection and self-destruction is adharma
- Not working toward Self-Realization is adharma
- Greed is adharma
- Excessive use of natural resources without concern for others is adharma.
- Laziness and idleness is adharma
- Anything working against the law of existence (nature) is adharma.

Respecting others is Dharma but insulting others is adharma
Loving others is Dharma but hating others is adharma
Sharing with others is Dharma but snatching from others is adharma

Q What are the causes of *adharma*?

Adharma is caused by any of the following:

- Ignorance
- Confusion
- Dejection
- Stress
- Desires
- Greed
- Ego
- Anger
- Envy
- Hatred
- Lack of faith
- Disconnection with one's inner voice (Voice of God, Higher Self).

Decline in moral values and increase of vices prevail during *adharma*.

Q What are the causes of one's disconnection with Higher Self?

- When one becomes more selfish and starts operating based on negative emotions, resulting from impurities, i.e. 5+2 Enemies (desires, ego, attachment, greed, anger, envy and hatred).
- When person is unfocused on the Supreme purpose of his life, for more material gains and name and fame, his ego and possessiveness increase (I-ness and my-ness), he thinks only of his body and not the spirit. He becomes more selfish and thinks of himself first. Lying, cheating, hurting others and showing off become his lifestyle and thus results to disconnection with Higher Self.

- When one is disconnected from the Supreme Consciousness (Higher Self) one is also disconnected from the needs of others and cannot recognize one's duty/*svadharma*.
- This also leads to corruption in society and in nations and results in the downfall of morality in the world.

All starts from within

Therefore, it is very important to live in God/Self-Consciousness, develop awareness and do one's own duty (follow/*svadharma*).

Guidance and knowledge from the Higher Self come only when one is connected with the Higher Self/Supreme Consciousness

Connection comes only when one is pure. Therefore, one must have pure thoughts and expressions. Purity comes when one performs action with knowledge and love.

Process of Self-Realization:

Karma Yoga → Self-Purification and Self-Transformation → Connection with Higher Self → Self-Knowledge (Wisdom) → Self-Realization

Main Message

Attain Oneness with God through knowledge, action and renunciation

- The reason for God to manifest is to establish the righteousness and protect virtues.
- *Karma Yoga* is the precursor for Self-Knowledge.
- Self-Knowledge (Transcendental) purifies and liberates one from worldly miseries.
- Do your action with knowledge and contribute towards establishing righteousness in the world.
- Sacrifices (*Yajnas*, spiritual practices) can be performed in many different ways, e.g. worship, offerings, listening and self-control.
- In order to attain Self-Knowledge, one must have faith, not doubt.

Self-Knowledge is a Perennial Knowledge and must be practiced to fight the battle of life

Chapter Overview

01–04	History of the Gita
05–15	Purpose of God's incarnation, His glories and attributes
16–17	Selfish, selfless and forbidden action
18–23	Attributes and glories of yogis and sages
24–32	Different types of sacrifices (spiritual practices) and their benefits
33–42	The power of Self-Knowledge

History of the Gita

Q To whom did God teach Self-Knowledge first, second and third?

श्रीभगवानुवाच
इमं विवस्वते योगं प्रोक्तवानहमव्ययम्।
विवस्वान्मनवे प्राह मनुरिक्ष्वाकवेऽब्रवीत्॥1॥

śrī-bhagavān uvāca
imaṁ vivasvate yogaṁ proktavān aham avyayam
vivasvān manave prāha manur ikṣvākave 'bravīt

Ancient tradition of passing down the torch of knowledge to next generation

The Supreme Lord said: I taught this imperishable science of Yoga to King Vivasan (Sun god). Vivasan taught it to his son Manu (the Father of Mankind) and Manu taught it to his son Ikshvaku. (4.01)

Q How was the Supreme Knowledge lost from the world?

एवं परम्पराप्राप्तमिमं राजर्षयो विदुः।
स कालेनेह महता योगो नष्टः परंतप॥2॥

evaṁ paramparā-prāptam imaṁ rājarṣayo viduḥ
sa kāleneha mahatā yogo naṣṭaḥ parantapa

Thus the Supreme science was preserved and understood by saintly kings by passing it down from father to son. However, in the course of time the succession was broken and it was lost from this earth, O Arjuna. (4.02)

Q Why did Lord Krishna choose Arjuna to be the fourth one to receive the Self-Knowledge?

स एवायं मया तेऽद्य योगः प्रोक्तः पुरातनः।
भक्तोऽसि मे सखा चेति रहस्यं ह्येतदुत्तमम् ॥3॥

sa evāyaṁ mayā te 'dya yogaḥ proktaḥ purātanaḥ
bhakto 'si me sakhā ceti rahasyaṁ hy etad uttamam

Today, I have imparted to you the very same ancient Yoga because you are my sincere and dear friend. This is a Supreme secret. (4.03)

Q Why did Arjuna not believe that Lord Krishna taught Self-Knowledge to the Sun god first?

अर्जुन उवाच
अपरं भवतो जन्म परं जन्म विवस्वतः।
कथमेतद्विजानीयां त्वमादौ प्रोक्तवानिति ॥4॥

arjuna uvāca
aparaṁ bhavato janma paraṁ janma vivasvataḥ
katham etad vijānīyāṁ tvam ādau proktavān iti

Arjuna said: You are recent born but King Vivasan was born in ancient times. How, then, am I to understand that You taught this Yoga in the beginning of the creation? (4.04)

Purpose of God's incarnation, His glories and attributes

Q How did Lord Krishna convince Arjuna that they had known each other for many previous lifetimes?

श्रीभगवानुवाच
बहूनि मे व्यतीतानि जन्मानि तव चार्जुन।
तान्यहं वेद सर्वाणि न त्वं वेत्थ परंतप ॥5॥

śrī-bhagavān uvāca
bahūni me vyatītāni janmāni tava cārjuna
tāny ahaṁ veda sarvāṇi na tvaṁ vettha parantapa

The Supreme Lord said: Both you and I have taken many births. I do remember them all but you do not, O Arjuna. (4.05)

Q How and when does God manifest Himself?

अजोऽपि सन्नव्ययात्मा भूतानामीश्वरोऽपि सन्।
प्रकृतिं स्वामधिष्ठाय संभवाम्यात्ममायया ॥6॥

ajo 'pi sann avyayātmā
bhūtānām īśvaro 'pi san
prakṛtiṁ svām adhiṣṭhāya
sambhavāmy ātma-māyayā

God takes Avatara/ forms because of our sins

यदा यदा हि धर्मस्य ग्लानिर्भवति भारत।
अभ्युत्थानमधर्मस्य तदात्मानं सृजाम्यहम् ॥7॥

yadā yadā hi dharmasya glānir bhavati bhārata
abhyutthānam adharmasya tadātmānaṁ sṛjāmy aham

Though I am birthless and deathless, and the Lord of all beings, yet, to govern My Own Nature (*Prakriti*), I incarnate myself though My divine potential energy (*Yoga-Maya*). (4.06)

Whenever and wherever there is a decline of Righteousness (*Dharma*) and a rise of unrighteousness (*adharma*), O Arjuna, then I manifest Myself (Incarnate). (4.07)

Q Why does God manifest Himself in the form of human body (*Avatara*)?

परित्राणाय साधूनां विनाशाय च दुष्कृताम्।
धर्मसंस्थापनार्थाय संभवामि युगे युगे ॥8॥

paritrāṇāya sādhūnāṁ vināśāya ca duṣkṛtām
dharma-saṁsthāpanārthāya sambhavāmi yuge yuge

For the protection of the virtuous (devotees), for destruction of the wicked, and for re-establishment of Righteousness (*Dharma*), I appear from time to time. (4.08)

Q What are the benefits of attaining Self-Knowledge?

जन्म कर्म च मे दिव्यमेवं यो वेत्ति तत्त्वतः।
त्यक्त्वा देहं पुनर्जन्म नैति मामेति सोऽर्जुन ॥9॥

janma karma ca me divyam
evaṁ yo vetti tattvataḥ
tyaktvā dehaṁ punar janma
naiti mām eti so 'rjuna

Wow! What a power of Self-Knowledge

One who truly understands My divine birth and work (Creation, maintenance, and dissolution) is not reborn in this materialistic world after casting off the body but attains My Supreme Abode, O Arjuna. (4.09)

Q How does one attain God's bliss and has anyone attained it yet?

वीतरागभयक्रोधा मन्मया मामुपाश्रिताः।
बहवो ज्ञानतपसा पूता मद्भावमागताः॥ 10॥

vīta-rāga-bhaya-krodhā man-mayā mām upāśritāḥ
bahavo jñāna-tapasā pūtā mad-bhāvam āgatāḥ

Freed from attachment, fear and anger, fully absorbed in My Consciousness, taking refuge in Me and purified by the fire of Self-Knowledge, many have attained My being (Nirvana, Self/God-Realization). (4.10)

Q Why do people approach God?

ये यथा मां प्रपद्यन्ते तांस्तथैव भजाम्यहम्।
मम वर्त्मानुवर्तन्ते मनुष्याः पार्थ सर्वशः॥ 11॥

ye yathā māṁ prapadyante
tāṁs tathaiva bhajāmy aham
mama vartmānuvartante
manuṣyāḥ pārtha sarvaśaḥ

Everyone has his own purpose to worship God

O Arjuna for whatever reason people worship Me, I honor their wishes accor...
Everyone worships Me for different reasons. (4.11)

Q Why do people worship demi-gods?

काङ्क्षन्तः कर्मणां सिद्धिं यजन्त इह देवताः।
क्षिप्रं हि मानुषे लोके सिद्धिर्भवति कर्मजा॥ 12॥

kāṅkṣantaḥ karmaṇāṁ siddhiṁ yajanta iha devatāḥ
kṣipraṁ hi mānuṣe loke siddhir bhavati karma-jā

Those who desire success in their work worship the demi-gods (*devas*) and succeed in their work quickly in this materialistic world. (4.12)

Q Why did God create divisions of human society and what role does He play?

चातुर्वर्ण्यं मया सृष्टं गुणकर्मविभागशः।
तस्य कर्तारमपि मां विद्ध्यकर्तारमव्ययम्॥ 13॥

cātur-varṇyaṁ mayā sṛṣṭaṁ
guṇa-karma-vibhāgaśaḥ
tasya kartāram api māṁ
viddhy akartāram avyayam

God is a non-doer

The four divisions of human society (*Varnas*: *Brahmins*-guiding, *Kshatriyas*—ruling goodness, *Vaisyas*—trading-passion, and *Sudras*—labor-service) were created by Me based upon aptitude and vocation (*Gunas* and work). Though I am the creator of this system of this division, one should know that I am a non-doer and changeless. (4.13)

Q Why is God not bound by *karma*?

न मां कर्माणि लिम्पन्ति न मे कर्मफले स्पृहा।
इति मां योऽभिजानाति कर्मभिर्न स बध्यते ।। 14 ।।

na māṁ karmāṇi limpanti na me karma-phale spṛhā
iti māṁ yo 'bhijānāti karmabhir na sa badhyate

Actions or *karmas* do not bind Me, because I have no desire for the fruit of actions. One who fully understands and practices this reality is also not bound by actions-*karmas*. (4.14)

Q How does one follow the foot prints of ancient, Self-realized souls to fulfill responsibilities in modern times?

एवं ज्ञात्वा कृतं कर्म पूर्वैरपि मुमुक्षुभिः।
कुरु कर्मैव तस्मात्त्वं पूर्वैः पूर्वतरं कृतम् ।। 15 ।।

evaṁ jñātvā kṛtaṁ karma
pūrvair api mumukṣubhiḥ
kuru karmaiva tasmāt tvaṁ
pūrvaiḥ pūrvataraṁ kṛtam

Be a liberated soul from this very moment

With similar understanding, the ancient seekers of Liberation performed their duties as well. Therefore, you should also perform your duty as the ancient seekers of the Liberation did in their times. (4.15)

Selfish, selfless and forbidden action

Q Why is it important to know different type of actions?

किं कर्म किमकर्मेति कवयोऽप्यत्र मोहिताः।
तत्ते कर्म प्रवक्ष्यामि यज्ज्ञात्वा मोक्ष्यसेऽशुभात् ।। 16 ।।

kiṁ karma kim akarmeti kavayo 'py atra mohitāḥ
tat te karma pravakṣyāmi yaj jñātvā mokṣyase 'śubhāt

What is action and what is inaction? Even the wise are confused about it. Therefore, I must clearly explain to you about action, by knowing that one will be liberated from its evil effect (birth and death). (4.16)

Q How many different types of actions are there? What is Action that binds (*karma*), Action that does not bind (*Akarma*) and Forbidden action (*vikarma*)?

कर्मणो ह्यपि बोद्धव्यं बोद्धव्यं च विकर्मण: ।
अकर्मणश्च बोद्धव्यं गहना कर्मणो गति: ।। 17 ।।

karmaṇo hy api boddhavyaṁ
boddhavyaṁ ca vikarmaṇaḥ
akarmaṇaś ca boddhavyaṁ
gahanā karmaṇo gatiḥ

Law of karma, "cause and effect"

The true nature of action is very difficult to understand. Therefore, one must be able to fully discriminate and understand what is attached action (*karma* that binds), what is detached action (*Akarma* that does not bind), and also what is forbidden action (*vikarma*). (4.17)

Attributes and glories of yogis and sages

Q How does a yogi (wise person) see action and inaction?

कर्मण्यकर्म य: पश्येदकर्मणि च कर्म य: ।
स बुद्धिमान्मनुष्येषु स युक्त: कृत्स्नकर्मकृत् ।। 18 ।।

karmaṇy akarma yaḥ paśyed
akarmaṇi ca karma yaḥ
sa buddhimān manuṣyeṣu
sa yuktaḥ kṛtsna-karma-kṛt

One who sees inaction in action and also action in inaction is a wise person. Such a person is a yogi, although engaged in all sorts of activities. (4.18)

Q Who is called a sage by the Wise (*Pandit*)?

यस्य सर्वे समारम्भा: कामसंकल्पवर्जिता: ।
ज्ञानाग्निदग्धकर्माणं तमाहु: पण्डितं बुधा: ।। 19 ।।

yasya sarve samārambhāḥ
kāma-saṅkalpa-varjitāḥ
jñānāgni-dagdha-karmāṇaṁ
tam āhuḥ paṇḍitaṁ budhāḥ

Pure soul is called Wise

One whose every undertaking is free from selfish desires and whose actions have been purified by the fire of Self-Knowledge is called a sage by the wise. (4.19)

Q Who does not incur any sins and is free from consequences of his action/*karma*?

त्यक्त्वा कर्मफलासङ्गं नित्यतृप्तो निराश्रयः।
कर्मण्यभिप्रवृत्तोऽपि नैव किंचित्करोति सः ॥20॥

tyaktvā karma-phalāsaṅgaṁ nitya-tṛpto nirāśrayaḥ
karmaṇy abhipravṛtto 'pi naiva kiñcit karoti saḥ

One who has renounced selfish attachment to the fruits of action and remains ever content and dependent on no one but God, such a person does not do anything (*Akarta*) though fully engaged in all kind of actions. (4.20)

Q Who is free from the consequences of his actions and what is his mental makeup?

निराशीर्यतचित्तात्मा त्यक्तसर्वपरिग्रहः।
शारीरं केवलं कर्म कुर्वन्नाप्नोति किल्बिषम् ॥21॥

nirāśīr yata-cittātmā tyakta-sarva-parigrahaḥ
śārīraṁ kevalaṁ karma kurvan nāpnoti kilbiṣam

The basic needs of the body must be met

यदृच्छालाभसंतुष्टो द्वन्द्वातीतो विमत्सरः।
समः सिद्धावसिद्धौ च कृत्वापि न निबध्यते ॥22॥

yadṛcchā-lābha-santuṣṭo dvandvātīto vimatsaraḥ
samaḥ siddhāv asiddhau ca kṛtvāpi na nibadhyate

One who is free from desires, whose mind and senses are fully under control and who has renounced the desires for all proprietorship and performs only the necessary actions for the body, incurs no sins and any *karmic* reaction. (4.21)

Content with whatever gains come naturally by His will, free from duality (pairs of opposites), free from envy, undisturbed by success and failure, although engaged in work, such a *Karma Yogi* is not bound by *karma*. (4.22)

Q Whose *karmas* are completely dissolved?

गतसङ्गस्य मुक्तस्य ज्ञानावस्थितचेतसः।
यज्ञायाचरतः कर्म समग्रं प्रविलीयते ॥23॥

gata-saṅgasya muktasya jñānāvasthita-cetasaḥ
yajñāyācarataḥ karma samagraṁ pravilīyate

A philanthropic person (*Karma Yogi*), who is free from attachment, whose mind is established in Self-Knowledge and who does work as a selfless service (sacrifice) to God, his entire *karma* dissolves away. (4.23)

Different types of sacrifices (spiritual practices) and their benefits

Q Who is *Brahman* and what are the four essentials of *Yajna*?

ब्रह्मार्पणं ब्रह्म हविर्ब्रह्माग्नौ ब्रह्मणा हुतम् ।
ब्रह्मैव तेन गन्तव्यं ब्रह्मकर्मसमाधिना ।। 24 ।।

brahmārpaṇaṁ brahma havir
brahmāgnau brahmaṇā hutam
brahmaiva tena gantavyaṁ
brahma-karma-samādhinā

Everything is a part of Brahman-God

The act of offering (sacrifice) is *Brahman* (God, Ultimate Truth) and the offering itself (clarified butter) is *Brahman*. The one who offers is *Brahman* and the sacred fire into which the offering is made is also *Brahman*. Thus, one who always lives in the Consciousness of *Brahman* and considers everything as His manifestation and His act will realize *Brahman*. (4.24)

Q How do yogis/the wise offer their sacrifices?

दैवमेवापरे यज्ञं योगिनः पर्युपासते ।
ब्रह्माग्नावपरे यज्ञं यज्ञेनैवोपजुह्वति ।। 25 ।।

daivam evāpare yajñaṁ yoginaḥ paryupāsate
brahmāgnāv apare yajñaṁ yajñenaivopajuhvati

Some yogis perform sacrifice-*Yajna* as worship to demi-gods (minor deities, *devas*), while others perform sacrifices (selfless service) into the fire of the Supreme (*Brahman*). (4.25)

Q How are offerings (Spiritual practices) made by hearing?

श्रोत्रादीनीन्द्रियाण्यन्ये संयमाग्निषु जुह्वति ।
शब्दादीन्विषयानन्य इन्द्रियाग्निषु जुह्वति ।। 26 ।।

śrotrādīnīndriyāṇy anye saṁyamāgniṣu juhvati
śabdādīn viṣayān anya indriyāgniṣu juhvati

Some offer hearing and other senses as sacrifice into the fires of restraint by contemplating sound vibrations (like *mantras*) while others offer sound and other objects of the senses (as sacrifice) in the fires of the senses. (4.26)

Q How are the offerings made by controlling the mind and senses?

सर्वाणीन्द्रियकर्माणि प्राणकर्माणि चापरे ।
आत्मसंयमयोगाग्नौ जुह्वति ज्ञानदीपिते ।। 27 ।।

sarvāṇīndriya-karmāṇi prāṇa-karmāṇi cāpare
ātma-saṁyama-yogāgnau juhvati jñāna-dīpite

Others who are interested in achieving Self-Realization through control of mind and senses, offer all functions of the senses, and do *Pranayama* (breathing exercises) as sacrifice into the fire of self-restraint. (4.27)

Q What are the other types of offerings?

द्रव्ययज्ञास्तपोयज्ञा योगयज्ञास्तथापरे ।
स्वाध्यायज्ञानयज्ञाश्च यतयः संशितव्रताः ।। 28 ।।

dravya-yajñās tapo-yajñā yoga-yajñās tathāpare
svādhyāya-jñāna-yajñāś ca yatayaḥ saṁśita-vratāḥ

Others give charity and offer their wealth as a sacrifice and in practice of Yoga as sacrifice while the ascetics with strict vows offer their study of Vedas and scriptures and Transcendental Knowledge as sacrifice. (4.28)

Q How are the offerings made by *Pranayama* (the science of breath control)?

अपाने जुह्वति प्राणं प्राणेऽपानं तथापरे ।
प्राणापानगती रुद्ध्वा प्राणायामपरायणाः ।। 29 ।।

apāne juhvati prāṇaṁ prāṇe 'pānaṁ tathāpare
prāṇāpāna-gatī ruddhvā prāṇāyāma-parāyaṇāḥ

Still others, who are engaged in Yogic practices, reach the breathless state of trance (*Samadhi*) by offering inhalation into exhalation (*Prana* into *Apana*) and exhalation into inhalation as a sacrifice (*Pranayama*, the science of breath control). (4.29)

Q Why should one do offerings and how do they help to attain Self-Realization?

अपरे नियताहाराः प्राणान्प्राणेषु जुह्वति ।
सर्वेऽप्येते यज्ञविदो यज्ञक्षपितकल्मषाः ।। 30 ।।

apare niyatāhārāḥ prāṇān prāṇeṣu juhvati
sarve 'py ete yajña-vido yajña-kṣapita-kalmaṣāḥ

Yet others regulate their diet and offer their life breaths into the life breaths as sacrifice (*Pranayama*). All these people who know the meaning of sacrifice destroy their sins by their sacrifice and become purified. (4.30)

Q How to attain worldly happiness, Self-Knowledge and Self-Realization?

यज्ञशिष्टामृतभुजो यान्ति ब्रह्म सनातनम्।
नायं लोकोऽस्त्ययज्ञस्य कुतोऽन्यः कुरुसत्तम ॥ 31 ॥

yajña-śiṣṭāmṛta-bhujo
yānti brahma sanātanam
nāyaṁ loko 'sty ayajñasya
kuto 'nyaḥ kuru-sattama

Selfless service leads to happiness in this world and beyond

O Arjuna, those who perform selfless service (*Seva, Yajna*) obtain the nectar of Self-Knowledge as a result of their sacrifice and attain the eternal state of Self-Realization. Even this world is not a happy place for the one who does not perform sacrifice, how then can he have happiness in the other world. (4.31)

Selfless service (Karma Yoga) → Self-Knowledge → Self-Realization

Q What roles do body, mind and senses play in the spiritual practices to attain Liberation?

एवं बहुविधा यज्ञा वितता ब्रह्मणो मुखे।
कर्मजान्विद्धि तान्सर्वानेवं ज्ञात्वा विमोक्ष्यसे ॥ 32 ॥

evaṁ bahu-vidhā yajñā
vitatā brahmaṇo mukhe
karma-jān viddhi tān sarvān
evaṁ jñātvā vimokṣyase

Spiritual discipline of body, mind and senses lead to Liberation

All these different types of spiritual disciplines (*Yajna*, sacrifice) are approved by the Vedas and all of them are born of different types of *karma* or the action of body, mind, and senses. Knowing thus, you will be free from the bondage of *karma* and attain Salvation (Liberation, *Nirvana*). (4.32)

The Power of Self-Knowledge

Q Why is the sacrifice and sharing of knowledge superior?

श्रेयान् द्रव्यमयाद्यज्ञाज्ज्ञानयज्ञः परंतप।
सर्वं कर्माखिलं पार्थ ज्ञाने परिसमाप्यते ॥ 33 ॥

śreyān dravya-mayād yajñāj
jñāna-yajñaḥ parantapa
sarvaṁ karmākhilaṁ pārtha
jñāne parisamāpyate

Sharing of knowledge is superior to any other sacrifice

O Arjuna, the sacrifice and sharing of knowledge is superior to any sacrifice of material objects because all spiritual activities purify mind and lead to Self-Knowledge/Transcendental-Knowledge and Self-Realization (Supreme goal of life). (4.33)

Karma Yoga → Purity of Mind → Self-Knowledge → Self-Realization

Q From whom and how should I acquire Self-Knowledge (Transcendental Knowledge)?

तद्विद्धि प्रणिपातेन परिप्रश्नेन सेवया।
उपदेक्ष्यन्ति ते ज्ञानं ज्ञानिनस्तत्त्वदर्शिनः ॥ 34 ॥

tad viddhi praṇipātena
paripraśnena sevayā
upadekṣyanti te jñānaṁ
jñāninas tattva-darśinaḥ

One must have a spiritual master/ mentor

Attain this Transcendental Knowledge from a Self-realized person, a spiritual master, by humble reverence, by sincere inquiry and by service. The Self-realized soul will teach you that knowledge. (4.34)

Q Why should I gain Transcendental Knowledge and how will I benefit from it?

यज्ज्ञात्वा न पुनर्मोहमेवं यास्यसि पाण्डव।
येन भूतान्यशेषेण द्रक्ष्यस्यात्मन्यथो मयि ॥ 35 ॥

yaj jñātvā na punar moham evaṁ yāsyasi pāṇḍava
yena bhūtāny aśeṣāṇi drakṣyasy ātmany atho mayi

After obtaining the real knowledge from a Self-realized soul, O Arjuna, you will not again be deluded like this. Through this knowledge, you will see the entire universe within yourself and also within Me. (4.35)

Q Can a sinner benefit from Self-Knowledge?

अपि चेदसि पापेभ्यः सर्वेभ्यः पापकृत्तमः।
सर्वं ज्ञानप्लवेनैव वृजिनं संतरिष्यसि ॥ 36 ॥

api ced asi pāpebhyaḥ
sarvebhyaḥ pāpa-kṛt-tamaḥ
sarvaṁ jñāna-plavenaiva
vṛjinaṁ santariṣyasi

Self- Knowledge is for all

Even if you are the most sinful of all sinners you will certainly cross over the ocean of miseries and sins by the boat of Self-Knowledge alone. (4.36)

Q What does Self-Knowledge do?

यथैधांसि समिद्धोऽग्निर्भस्मसात्कुरुतेऽर्जुन ।
ज्ञानाग्निः सर्वकर्माणि भस्मसात्कुरुते तथा ।। 37 ।।

yathaidhāṁsi samiddho 'gnir bhasma-sāt kurute 'rjuna
jñānāgniḥ sarva-karmāṇi bhasma-sāt kurute tatha

Just as the blazing fire turns wood to ashes, similarly the fire of Self-Knowledge reduces all bonds of *karma*/action to ashes, O Arjuna. (4.37)

Q What is the greatest purifier?

न हि ज्ञानेन सदृशं पवित्रमिह विद्यते ।
तत्स्वयं योगसंसिद्धः कालेनात्मनि विन्दति ।। 38 ।।

na hi jñānena sadṛśaṁ
pavitram iha vidyate
tat svayaṁ yoga-saṁsiddhaḥ
kālenātmani vindati

Self-Knowledge can be discovered within

Certainly, there is no purifier in this world like the Self-Knowledge (Transcendental Knowledge, *Jnana*). One who becomes purified by Yoga discovers this knowledge within naturally, in due course of time. (4.38)

Q Who attains Supreme Peace and how?

श्रद्धावाँल्लभते ज्ञानं तत्परः संयतेन्द्रियः ।
ज्ञानं लब्ध्वा परां शान्तिमचिरेणाधिगच्छति ।। 39 ।।

śraddhāvāl labhate jñānaṁ tat-paraḥ saṁyatendriyaḥ
jñānaṁ labdhvā parāṁ śāntim acireṇādhigacchati

One who has faith, does yogic practices sincerely and has control over one's senses attains this Transcendental Knowledge. Having attained this knowledge, he immediately attains Supreme Peace. (4.39)

Self-Knowledge → Supreme Peace

Q What happens to one who has no faith and is full of doubts?

अज्ञश्चाश्रद्दधानश्च संशयात्मा विनश्यति ।
नायं लोकोऽस्ति न परो न सुखं संशयात्मनः ।। 40 ।।

ajñaś cāśraddadhānaś ca
saṁśayātmā vinaśyati
nāyaṁ loko 'sti na paro
na sukhaṁ saṁśayātmanaḥ

Doubts lead to confusion and confusion leads no where

The man who is ignorant and irrational, has no faith and is possessed by doubts, goes to destruction. For the doubting soul there is neither this world nor the world beyond nor any happiness. (4.40)

Q Who is ultimately not bound by *karma*?

योगसंन्यस्तकर्माणं ज्ञानसंछिन्नसंशयम्।
आत्मवन्तं न कर्माणि निबध्नन्ति धनंजय॥41॥

yoga-sannyasta-karmāṇaṁ
jñāna-sañchinna-saṁśayam
ātmavantaṁ na karmāṇi
nibadhnanti dhanañjaya

O Arjuna, *karma* (work) does not bind one who has dedicated all of one's actions to God and has renounced the fruits of actions in the spirit of *Karma Yoga*, whose doubts have been completely destroyed by Self-Knowledge and who is poised in the Self. (4.41)

Q What did Lord Krishna finally advise Arjuna?

तस्मादज्ञानसंभूतं हृत्स्थं ज्ञानासिनात्मनः।
छित्त्वैनं संशयं योगमातिष्ठोत्तिष्ठ भारत॥42॥

tasmād ajñāna-sambhūtaṁ
hṛt-sthaṁ jñānāsinātmanaḥ
chittvainaṁ saṁśayaṁ yogam
ātiṣṭhottiṣṭha bhārata

Fight the battle of life with desireless action

Therefore, cut these self doubts in your heart which are born of ignorance by the sword of Transcendental Knowledge, resort to *Karma Yoga* with Equanimity and get up for the war, O Arjuna. (4.42)

Lessons to learn and practice in daily life

Every action of ours must lead us to Self-Knowledge and Self-Realization

1. We should make the best use of our time, body and all resources only to attain the Supreme goal of our life, Self-Realization.
2. We must not waste our time and efforts on changing others but focus only on transforming ourselves.
3. We should follow *Dharma* (Righteousness) and avoid *adharma* (unrighteousness).

4. We should always perform our obligatory duty and help establish righteousness.
5. We should always fulfill our commitments in life toward ourselves, family, society, nation and the world as parents, as children, as employees, etc.
6. Parents should pass on knowledge, family values and culture to their children and this tradition must carry on preserving righteousness in the universe.
7. We should raise our children with a good value system.
8. We should always keep in mind the best interest of the entire mankind and not just ourselves and our near and dear ones.
9. We should be loyal to our nation but always protect the interest of the entire universe.
10. We should get spiritual knowledge only from a qualified individual.

The Gita is the path to connect with Supreme Consciousness

ॐ तत्सदिति श्रीमद्भगवद्गीतासूपनिषत्सु ब्रह्मविद्यायां योगशास्त्रे
श्रीकृष्णार्जुनसंवादे ज्ञानकर्मसंन्यासयोगो नाम चतुर्थोऽध्यायः ।।

AUM TAT SAT

Thus ends the fourth chapter named "*Jnana-Karma-Sanyasa Yoga*",
The Path of Knowledge, Action and Renunciation
in the *Upanishad* of the glorious Bhagavad Gita, the scripture of Yoga,
the science of the Absolute (*Brahman*), in the form of the dialogue
between Lord Krishna and Arjuna.

Aum Shanti, Shanti, Shantihi

Union with God—Self-Realization

One who performs all of his actions as an offering to God and gives up all attachment to the results. He is not touched by Karmic reaction, just as a lotus leaf is never wet by water. (5.10)

Self-Purification and Transformation through
True Renunciation

KARMA-SANYASA YOGA

The Path of Action and Renunciation

Union with God (Self-Realization) through the path of true renunciation

The Gita is a guide to the righteous path

Previously, Lord Krishna had praised both correct action (*Karma Yoga*) and renunciation of action (*Sanyasa Yoga*). So, Arjuna got confused and wanted to know which one was better for him, to follow the path of *karma* or renouncing his *karma* as a warrior and follow the path of *Sanyasa*?

Therefore, in this chapter, Lord Krishna imparts the knowledge to eliminate Arjuna's confusion about the two different yogas. Lord Krishna leads Arjuna on the path of *karma*/action Yoga to fulfill his duty which leads to control over one's mind and to abandonment all desires and anger (self-transformation, self-purification), thus attaining Liberation and *Anandam* (Supreme Bliss).

Sanyasa Yoga is the renunciation of action while *Karma Yoga* is engaging in action without concern or desire for the fruits of action.

Lord Krishna assures Arjuna that both the paths lead to the Supreme goal of life, Self-Realization; however, *Karma Yoga* is superior to renunciation of action, *Sanyasa Yoga*.

Main Message

Attain Union with God through action and renunciation of the fruit of action

- Do action with renunciation of the fruits of action. It will become Action Yoga, *Karma Yoga* that will benefit others and bring everlasting peace and happiness.
- Externally perform all the actions but internally renounce the fruit of those actions (no desires/expectation of any personal gain, name, fame, money or favors, etc.).

Desires/Expectations → Unhappiness/Darkness → Disasters/Miseries

- *Karma Yoga* is a better and easier path for active people than renunciation of action (*Karma Sanyasa*) to attain Self-Realization.
- In *Sanyasa Yoga*, one purifies himself through meditation, acquires Self-Knowledge; and attains detachment (non-attachment, *vairagya*), self-control, patience, Higher vision, Supreme Peace and Bliss/*Anandam*.
- *Karma Yoga* is the precursor for Self-Knowledge; therefore, both yogas lead to Liberation.
- *Karma Yogi*: Frees himself from 5 + 2 Enemies by performing *Karma Yoga*
- *Sankhya Yogi*: Frees himself from 5 + 2 Enemies by acquiring Self-Knowledge (Transcendental Knowledge) through meditation.
- Peace is within and one who realizes it attains Supreme Peace.

Karma Yoga → Self-Knowledge → Ultimate Peace/Liberation

Chapter Overview

01–06 Should one follow the Yoga of Renunciation or the Yoga of Action
07–12 Marks of Renunciant Yogi (*Sanyasi*) and *Karma Yogi*
13–19 The Path of Self-Knowledge
20–26 Attaining the Supreme Bliss
27–29 The Path of Meditation and Devotion

Should one follow the Yoga of Renunciation or the Yoga of Action

Q What is the difference between the two spiritual paths and which one is better to follow?

अर्जुन उवाच
संन्यासं कर्मणां कृष्ण पुनर्योगं च शंससि ।
यच्छ्रेय एतयोरेकं तन्मे ब्रूहि सुनिश्चितम् ।। 1 ।।

arjuna uvāca
sannyāsaṁ karmaṇāṁ kṛṣṇa punar yogaṁ ca śaṁsasi
yac chreya etayor ekaṁ tan me brūhi su-niścitam

Arjuna said: O Krishna, first You praise renunciation of action, *Sanyasa Yoga* (Self-Knowledge) and then you recommend the path of action (Selfless service, *Karma Yoga*). Please, tell me clearly, which one of the two is more beneficial for Self-Realization? (5.01)

Q Why is *Karma Yoga* superior to renunciation of action (*Karma Sanyasa*)?

श्रीभगवानुवाच
संन्यासः कर्मयोगश्च निःश्रेयसकरावुभौ ।
तयोस्तु कर्मसंन्यासात्कर्मयोगो विशिष्यते ।। 2 ।।

śrī-bhagavān uvāca
sannyāsaḥ karma-yogaś ca
niḥśreyasa-karāv ubhau
tayos tu karma-sannyāsāt
karma-yogo viśiṣyate

Selfless action is better than renunciation of action

The Supreme Lord said: The path of renunciation and the path of action both lead to the Supreme Bliss, *Sat Chit Ananda*. But of the two, *Karma Yoga* is superior to the path of renunciation (*Karma Sanyasa*). (5.02)

Q Who is a true Sanyasi?

ज्ञेयः स नित्यसंन्यासी यो न द्वेष्टि न काङ्क्षति।
निर्द्वन्द्वो हि महाबाहो सुखं बन्धात्प्रमुच्यते ॥3॥

jñeyaḥ sa nitya-sannyāsī yo na dveṣṭi na kāṅkṣati
nirdvandvo hi mahā-bāho sukhaṁ bandhāt pramucyate

One should be considered a true renunciant (*Sanyasi*), who neither likes nor dislikes, and who has transcended the pairs of opposites. O Arjuna, he is easily liberated from *karmic* consequences and its bondage. (5.03)

Q Are these two paths of spirituality different from each other?

सांख्ययोगौ पृथग्बालाः प्रवदन्ति न पण्डिताः।
एकमप्यास्थितः सम्यगुभयोर्विन्दते फलम् ॥4॥

sāṅkhya-yogau pṛthag bālāḥ pravadanti na paṇḍitāḥ
ekam apy āsthitaḥ samyag ubhayor vindate phalam

Only the ignorant and not the learned consider the path of renunciation, *Karma Sanyasa* and the path of selfless service, *Karma Yoga* as different from each other. The person who has truly learned will achieve the benefits of both. (5.04)

Q Do both paths lead to Supreme Bliss and the Supreme goal of life?

यत्सांख्यैः प्राप्यते स्थानं तद्योगैरपि गम्यते।
एकं सांख्यं च योगं च यः पश्यति स पश्यति ॥5॥

yat sāṅkhyaiḥ prāpyate sthānaṁ
tad yogair api gamyate
ekaṁ sāṅkhyaṁ ca yogaṁ ca
yaḥ paśyati sa paśyati

Both paths lead to union with Self/God

Both the renunciant, *Sanyasi* and the *Karma Yogi* attain the same goal of Liberation. Therefore, the one who considers both the path of Self-Knowledge and the path of action the same reaches his Supreme goal of life and unites with the Supreme Being. (5.05)

Q What is the easiest and quickest way to attain the Supreme?

संन्यासस्तु महाबाहो दुःखमाप्तुमयोगतः।
योगयुक्तो मुनिर्ब्रह्म न चिरेणाधिगच्छति ॥6॥

sannyāsas tu mahā-bāho duḥkham āptum ayogataḥ
yoga-yukto munir brahma na cireṇādhigacchati

O Arjuna, true renunciation is difficult to achieve without first engaging in selfless action (*Karma Yoga*). A sage whose mind is always focused on God while doing selfless service with devotion (*Karma Yoga*), he easily and quickly attains *Nirvana* (*Brahman*, Supreme). (5.06)

Marks of Renunciant Yogi (*Sanyasi*) and *Karma Yogi*

Q Who attains Liberation from action/*karma* and how?

योगयुक्तो विशुद्धात्मा विजितात्मा जितेन्द्रियः।
सर्वभूतात्मभूतात्मा कुर्वन्नपि न लिप्यते ॥7॥

yoga-yukto viśuddhātmā vijitātmā jitendriyaḥ
sarva-bhūtātma-bhūtātmā kurvann api na lipyate

A *Karma Yogi* who is pure at heart, whose body, mind and senses are under control and who sees own Self as the Self (God) in all beings is not bound by his *karma* though engaged in work. (5.07)

Q How does an enlightened soul perceive his daily actions and remain detached?

नैव किंचित्करोमीति युक्तो मन्येत तत्त्ववित्।
पश्यञ्शृण्वन्स्पृशञ्जिघ्रन्नश्नन्गच्छन्स्वपञ्श्वसन् ॥8॥

naiva kiñcit karomīti
yukto manyeta tattva-vit
paśyañ śṛṇvan spṛśañ jighrann
aśnan gacchan svapan śvasan

प्रलपन् विसृजन्गृह्णन्नुन्मिषन्निमिषन्नपि।
इन्द्रियाणीन्द्रियार्थेषु वर्तन्त इति धारयन् ॥9॥

pralapan visṛjan gṛhṇann unmiṣan nimiṣann api
indriyāṇīndriyārtheṣu vartanta iti dhārayan

One who is united with the Supreme and who knows the truth thinks 'I do nothing at all'. Such an enlightened soul perceives that only the senses are engaged while doing their function in seeing, hearing, touching, smelling, eating, walking, sleeping, breathing, speaking, excreting, and opening and closing the eyes. He believes that only the senses are occupied with the objects of the senses, therefore, he is detached from them. (5.08–09)

Q What is the right kind of attitude towards work and what is the symbolism of the lotus flower in Hindu scriptures?

ब्रह्मण्याधाय कर्माणि सङ्गं त्यक्त्वा करोति यः।
लिप्यते न स पापेन पद्मपत्रमिवाम्भसा ॥10॥

brahmaṇy ādhāya karmāṇi saṅgaṁ tyaktvā karoti yaḥ
lipyate na sa pāpena padma-patram ivāmbhasā

One who performs all of his actions as an offering to God and gives up all attachment to the fruit of action. He is not touched by sin or *karmic* reaction, just as a lotus leaf is never wet by water. (5.10)

Q Why does a *Karma Yogi* perform actions?

कायेन मनसा बुद्ध्या केवलैरिन्द्रियैरपि।
योगिनः कर्म कुर्वन्ति सङ्गं त्यक्त्वात्मशुद्धये ॥11॥

kāyena manasā buddhyā
kevalair indriyair api
yoginaḥ karma kurvanti
saṅgaṁ tyaktvātma-śuddhaye

Karma Yogi works only for self-purification

The *Karma Yogis* perform all of their actions with their body, mind, intellect, and senses, without any selfish attachment, only for the purification of their mind and intellect (Self-purification). (5.11)

Q Who attains Supreme Peace and who becomes bound?

युक्तः कर्मफलं त्यक्त्वा शान्तिमाप्नोति नैष्ठिकीम्।
अयुक्तः कामकारेण फले सक्तो निबध्यते ॥12॥

yuktaḥ karma-phalaṁ tyaktvā śāntim āpnoti naiṣṭhikīm
ayuktaḥ kāma-kāreṇa phale sakto nibadhyate

A *Karma Yogi* attains Supreme Peace in the form of God-Realization by offering the fruits of action to God, while others who work for selfish motives and attached to the fruits of work under the impulsion of desires become bound. (5.12)

The Path of Self-Knowledge

Q How does a self-controlled person lead his life?

सर्वकर्माणि मनसा संन्यस्यास्ते सुखं वशी।
नवद्वारे पुरे देही नैव कुर्वन्न कारयन्॥13॥

sarva-karmāṇi manasā sannyasyāste sukhaṁ vaśī
nava-dvāre pure dehī naiva kurvan na kārayan

When the self-controlled embodied soul (*jivatma*) mentally renounces the doership of all actions completely, he resides *happily and peacefully* in the city of nine gates (physical body), neither working nor causing others to work. (5.13)

Q What drives one to work?

न कर्तृत्वं न कर्माणि लोकस्य सृजति प्रभुः।
न कर्मफलसंयोगं स्वभावस्तु प्रवर्तते॥14॥

na kartṛtvaṁ na karmāṇi
lokasya sṛjati prabhuḥ
na karma-phala-saṁyogaṁ
svabhāvas tu pravartate

Our innate nature is responsible for our actions

God does not create activities nor does He persuade people to act, nor does He create the attachment to the fruits of action. All these are done by the power of Material Nature. (5.14)

Q Is God responsible for our actions?

नादत्ते कस्यचित्पापं न चैव सुकृतं विभुः।
अज्ञानेनावृतं ज्ञानं तेन मुह्यन्ति जन्तवः॥15॥

nādatte kasyacit pāpaṁ na caiva sukṛtaṁ vibhuḥ
ajñānenāvṛtaṁ jñānaṁ tena muhyanti jantavaḥ

The Omnipresent Lord is not responsible for the good or bad (sinful) deeds of anybody. When the Self-Knowledge of people is covered by ignorance, they get confused and do evil deeds. (5.15)

Q What uncovers the Supreme Consciousness within?

ज्ञानेन तु तदज्ञानं येषां नाशितमात्मनः।
तेषामादित्यवज्ज्ञानं प्रकाशयति तत्परम्॥16॥

jñānena tu tad ajñānaṁ yeṣāṁ nāśitam ātmanaḥ
teṣām āditya-vaj jñānaṁ prakāśayati tat param

Transcendental Knowledge destroys the ignorance of the individual and unveils the Supreme Consciousness as the rising sun lights up everything in the morning. (5.16)

Q Who else attains the Supreme goal of his life and how does purity help?

तद्‌बुद्धयस्तदात्मानस्तन्निष्ठास्तत्परायणाः ।
गच्छन्त्यपुनरावृत्तिं ज्ञाननिर्धूतकल्मषाः ॥ 17 ॥

tad-buddhayas tad-ātmānas tan-niṣṭhās tat-parāyaṇāḥ
gacchanty apunar-āvṛttiṁ jñāna-nirdhūta-kalmaṣāḥ

A person whose mind and intellect are completely merged with God, who is fully devoted to Him, who has full faith in Him, and has God-Realization and Self-Realization as the Supreme goal of his life. Then, his impurities and sins are totally destroyed by Self-Knowledge and thus he becomes very pure and reaches the Supreme Consciousness State from which there is no return. (5.17)

Q How does a Self-realized person (Enlightened person) treat all the other living beings?

विद्याविनयसंपन्ने ब्राह्मणे गवि हस्तिनि ।
शुनि चैव श्वपाके च पण्डिताः समदर्शिनः ॥ 18 ॥

vidyā-vinaya-sampanne
brāhmaṇe gavi hastini
śuni caiva śva-pāke ca
paṇḍitāḥ sama-darśinaḥ

Impartiality toward everyone is enlightenment

An enlightened person (*Jnana Yogi*) looks impartially with an equal eye (love) at a learned and humble *Brahmana*, an outcast, even a cow, an elephant, or a dog and perceives God in all. (5.18)

Enlightened person = no partiality, respects and loves all

Q How does one attain *Brahman* in this life?

इहैव तैर्जितः सर्गो येषां साम्ये स्थितं मनः ।
निर्दोषं हि समं ब्रह्म तस्माद्‌ब्रह्मणि ते स्थिताः ॥ 19 ॥

ihaiva tair jitaḥ sargo yeṣāṁ sāmye sthitaṁ manaḥ
nirdoṣaṁ hi samaṁ brahma tasmād brahmaṇi te sthitāḥ

Those whose minds are steady, established in Equanimity have already accomplished everything in this very life and have realized the Supreme Being (*Brahman*, God). *Brahman* is flawless and equal in all, therefore, they are established in *Brahman*. (5.19)

Attaining the Supreme Bliss

Q Who is established in Supreme Consciousness *Brahman*?

न प्रहृष्येत्प्रियं प्राप्य नोद्विजेत्प्राप्य चाप्रियम्।
स्थिरबुद्धिरसंमूढो ब्रह्मविद् ब्रह्मणि स्थितः ।।20।।

na prahṛṣyet priyaṁ prāpya
nodvijet prāpya cāpriyam
sthira-buddhir asammūḍho
brahma-vid brahmaṇi sthitaḥ

One who neither rejoices on getting something desirable nor grieves on getting something undesirable, who is free from doubt and is undeluded, such a knower of Supreme is established in Supreme Consciousness and lives eternally in Supreme Bliss, *Sat Chit Ananda*. (5.20)

Q Who is always happy and blissful?

बाह्यस्पर्शेष्वसक्तात्मा विन्दत्यात्मनि यत्सुखम्।
स ब्रह्मयोगयुक्तात्मा सुखमक्षयमश्नुते ।।21।।

bāhya-sparśeṣv asaktātmā
vindaty ātmani yat sukham
sa brahma-yoga-yuktātmā
sukham akṣayam aśnute

One who is not attracted to external senses of pleasure but finds pleasure and happiness within. Such a liberated soul is united with Supreme Consciousness and enjoys Transcendental Bliss and Ultimate Happiness by the contemplation of the Supreme. (5.21)

Q What is the source of misery and how to avoid it?

ये हि संस्पर्शजा भोगा दुःखयोनय एव ते।
आद्यन्तवन्तः कौन्तेय न तेषु रमते बुधः ।।22।।

ye hi saṁsparśa-jā bhogā
duḥkha-yonaya eva te
ādy-antavantaḥ kaunteya
na teṣu ramate budhaḥ

O Arjuna, the sensual pleasures are, certainly a source of misery and have a beginning and an end. Therefore, the wise do not rejoice in them. (5.22)

Q Who is a happy man?

शक्नोतीहैव यः सोढुं प्राक्शरीरविमोक्षणात्।
कामक्रोधोद्भवं वेगं स युक्तः स सुखी नरः ॥23॥

śaknotīhaiva yaḥ soḍhuṁ
prāk śarīra-vimokṣaṇāt
kāma-krodhodbhavaṁ vegaṁ
sa yuktaḥ sa sukhī naraḥ

Number of desires are directly proportionate to the no. of miseries in life

One who is able to resist the impulses of desires and anger even in this world before giving up his physical body is a and a happy man. (5.23)

Q Who else attains Supreme Peace and *Brahma-Nirvana*, the Purpose of life?

योऽन्तःसुखोऽन्तरारामस्तथान्तर्ज्योतिरेव यः।
स योगी ब्रह्मनिर्वाणं ब्रह्मभूतोऽधिगच्छति ॥24॥

yo 'ntaḥ-sukho 'ntar-ārāmas tathāntar-jyotir eva yaḥ
sa yogī brahma-nirvāṇaṁ brahma-bhūto 'dhigacchati

लभन्ते ब्रह्मनिर्वाणमृषयः क्षीणकल्मषाः।
छिन्नद्वैधा यतात्मानः सर्वभूतहिते रताः ॥25॥

labhante brahma-nirvāṇam ṛṣayaḥ kṣīṇa-kalmaṣāḥ
chinna-dvaidhā yatātmānaḥ sarva-bhūta-hite ratāḥ

One who finds his happiness within, who rejoices within himself and who is illuminated by the inner light of Self-Knowledge, such a yogi becomes one with God and ultimately attains *Brahma-Nirvana*. (5.24)

The sages whose sins (imperfections) are destroyed, whose doubts (dualities have been dispelled by Self-Knowledge, whose minds are disciplined and who are engaged in the welfare of all beings attain *Brahma-Nirvana* (Supreme Peace). (5.25)

Q Who experiences the presence and bliss of God?

कामक्रोधवियुक्तानां यतीनां यतचेतसाम्।
अभितो ब्रह्मनिर्वाणं वर्तते विदितात्मनाम् ॥26॥

kāma-krodha-vimuktānāṁ yatīnāṁ yata-cetasām
abhito brahma-nirvāṇaṁ vartate viditātmanām

The people who are totally above selfish desires and anger and who have subdued their mind and senses experience *Brahma-Nirvana* and Eternal Bliss everywhere. (5.26)

The Path of Meditation and Devotion

Q How does a sage attain, Liberation (*Sat Chit Ananda*)?

स्पर्शान्कृत्वा बहिर्बाह्यांश्चक्षुश्चैवान्तरे भ्रुवोः।
प्राणापानौ समौ कृत्वा नासाभ्यन्तरचारिणौ ।। 27 ।।

sparśān kṛtvā bahir bāhyāṁś cakṣuś caivāntare bhruvoḥ
prāṇāpānau samau kṛtvā nāsābhyantara-cāriṇau

यतेन्द्रियमनोबुद्धिर्मुनिर्मोक्षपरायणः।
विगतेच्छाभयक्रोधो यः सदा मुक्त एव सः ।। 28 ।।

yatendriya-mano-buddhir munir mokṣa-parāyaṇaḥ
vigatecchā-bhaya-krodho yaḥ sadā mukta eva saḥ

A sage certainly liberates himself and attains Liberation (Supreme Bliss, *Sat Chit Ananda*) by:

1. Renouncing all sense enjoyment
2. Fixing the eye and vision between the two eyebrows (third eye, eye to enlightenment)
3. Regulating inward and outward breath (*Prana* and *Apana*) by *Pranayama*
4. Maintaining senses, mind, and intellect under control
5. Having Self-Realization (Liberation, *Moksha*) as the Supreme goal of his life and becoming totally free from desire, fear and anger. (5.27–28)

Q Who attains Peace?

भोक्तारं यज्ञतपसां सर्वलोकमहेश्वरम्।
सुहृदं सर्वभूतानां ज्ञात्वा मां शान्तिमृच्छति ।। 29 ।।

bhoktāraṁ yajña-tapasāṁ sarva-loka-maheśvaram
suhṛdaṁ sarva-bhūtānāṁ jñātvā māṁ śāntim ṛcchati

One attains peace by knowing Me (Supreme Being) as the great Lord of the entire universe, the friend and well wisher of all beings the enjoyer of all the offerings, sacrifices and austerities. (5.29)

Lessons to learn and practice in daily life

Do your action but renounce the fruit of action (no expectations)

1. We must focus on achieving the Supreme goal of our life (attaining everlasting Peace and Happiness within).
2. We should not renounce (*Tyaga*) our work but renounce our expectation from the fruit of our work.
3. We should substitute our worldly desires with desires for divinity.
4. We should focus on self-purifying and self-transforming (reprogramming our preconditioned mind) with spiritual practices.
5. We should live according to the code of ethics.
6. We must read the Gita or any other scriptures daily and practice its teachings every moment in all our actions.

ॐ तत्सदिति श्रीमद्भगवद्गीतासूपनिषत्सु ब्रह्मविद्यायां योगशास्त्रे
श्रीकृष्णार्जुनसंवादे कर्मसंन्यासयोगो नाम पञ्चमोऽध्यायः ॥

AUM TAT SAT

Thus ends the fifth chapter named "*Karma-Sanyasa Yoga*"
The Path of Action and Renunciation
in the *Upanishad* of the glorious Bhagavad Gita, the scripture of Yoga,
the science of the Absolute (*Brahman*), in the form of the dialogue
between Lord Krishna and Arjuna.

Aum Shanti, Shanti, Shantihi

Union with God—Self-Realization

The Person of discipline and settled Mind attains eternal happiness, Supreme Peace and Merges with Me (Nirvana). (6.15)

Self-Purification and Transformation through Self-Discipline and Meditation

Meditation

Meditation is the way to discipline the Mind
Meditation is the pathway for self-purification
Meditation is the way to reprogram the mind
Meditation is the way to calm the mind
Meditation is the pathway to get rid off the old habits
Meditation is the pathway to eliminate anger
Meditation is the pathway to lower blood pressure
Meditation is the pathway to go within
Meditation is the pathway to attain Equanimity
Meditation is the pathway to merge with God
Meditation is the way to communicate with God
Meditation is the pathway to God/Self-Realization
Meditation is the pathway to Nirvana
Meditation is the pathway to Oneness
Meditation is the way to experience love, peace—Anandam
Meditation is the surest way to liberation

"Meditation is the best medication for all the agitations"
—H.H. Pujya Swami Chidanand Saraswatiji

DHYANA YOGA

The Path of Self-discipline and Meditation

Union with God (Self-Realization) through the path of Self-discipline and meditation

The Gita is a spiritual guide to Self-discipline; and Meditation is the way to discipline the Mind

In the previous chapters, Lord Krishna imparted the knowledge of *Karma Yoga*, one performs one's actions but renounces the fruit of action thus purifying the mind. He also briefly introduced the concept of meditation.

In this chapter Lord Krishna gives more detailed knowledge of the path of Self-discipline and meditation, to attain Union with God and Self-Realization. He explains the difficulties of the mind and details methods of meditation by which one can master one's mind.

Meditation is the best way to discipline and purify the mind. During meditation, transformation takes place at the conscious level, one goes within, connects and communicates with the Supreme (God), attains Equanimity (*Sthitha-Prajna*) and Self-Realization. The Supreme can only be experienced and realized when the mind is serene and totally calm (just as the bottom of a lake can only be seen if the water is calm and has no waves) and that can be achieved only by meditation.

The self-transformation must take place at the conscious level first before it can be expressed at the action or behavior level

When the change takes place at the conscious level then transformation occurs within. Once that happens our transformed behavior starts reflecting in the external world.

Transformation at the Conscious level → Transformation within → Transformed behavior → Expressed in the External World

This Yoga provides additional method to answer one of the basic questions, '*How to realize God and fulfill the Supreme goal of life.*'

Main Message

Meditation is the best yoga for self-purification and self-transformation

- The mind is a very powerful tool
- The mind is nothing but a bundle of thoughts and a memory bank of past experiences and impressions (*Sanskaras*). It is the master of a human being. Mind can be the best friend or worst enemy that can lead one to Higher Self or lower self (6.07–08)

Thought is a pen for writing your Destiny. —Dada Vaswani

Mind → Thoughts → Speech → Action → Habits → Destiny

Higher Self ↓ ↑ Lower Self

Mind as an enemy:

Bad thoughts lead to turmoil within, in the society and in the world.

Bad thoughts → Bad Speech → Bad Action → Bad Habits → Bad society → Turmoil in the World

Mind as a friend:

Good thoughts lead to Higher Self and Peace within, in the society and world

Good Thoughts → Pleasant Speech → Good Action → Inner peace and good health → Peace in the society and in the world

Flow chart 6.1 *Relationship of thoughts, action and destiny*

It all starts with one's mind

- Simple yet very effective techniques of meditation are described: Control of the mind and senses; and contemplation on the Supreme Consciousness, practice finally culminates in *Samadhi*, full Consciousness of the Supreme.
- One can uplift oneself by controlling the mind and focusing on the Supreme Consciousness, then one's mind is gradually transformed, tranquilized and finally reaches *Samadhi*.
- Controlling the restless mind requires non-attachment, constant spiritual practice, leading a balanced life and meditation.
- It is a very slow but steady process and requires self-discipline, continuous practice and a lot of patience.

Hell and Heaven are here and tranquility of mind is heaven and misery is hell

Chapter Overview

01–04	Yoga of Action (*Karma Yoga*) and hallmarks of a *Karma Yogi*
05–06	Power of self (mind)
07–10	Lifestyle of a yogi and Lord Krishna's encouragement to Arjuna to become a yogi
11–26	Meditation, its pre-requisities, method and benefits
27–32	Description of a Yogi
33–36	Method to control the monkey mind
37–45	Destination of an unsuccessful spiritual practitioner
46–47	The Best Yogi

Yoga of Action (*Karma Yoga*) and Hallmarks of a *Karma Yogi*

Q Who is a renunciant, *Sanyasi*, and who is a *Karma Yogi*?

श्रीभगवानुवाच
अनाश्रितः कर्मफलं कार्यं कर्म करोति यः।
स संन्यासी च योगी च न निरग्निर्न चाक्रियः॥1॥

śrī-bhagavān uvāca
anāśritaḥ karma-phalaṁ kāryaṁ karma karoti yaḥ
sa sannyāsī ca yogī ca na niragnir na cākriyaḥ

The Supreme Lord said: "One who performs the obligatory duty without depending on and seeking its fruit (for personal enjoyment) is a true renunciant (*Sanyasi*) and a *Karma Yogi*; and not the one who has merely given up the sacred fire and has refrained from action. (6.01)

Q Is renunciation same as Yoga?

यं संन्यासमिति प्राहुर्योगं तं विद्धि पाण्डव।
न ह्यसंन्यस्तसंकल्पो योगी भवति कश्चन॥2॥

yaṁ sannyāsam iti prāhur yogaṁ taṁ viddhi pāṇḍava
na hy asannyasta-saṅkalpo yogī bhavati kaścana

O Arjuna, what is called renunciation is also known as Yoga. No one can become a yogi without renouncing selfish desires and selfish motives. (6.02)

Q What is the role of action and Equanimity in attaining Self-Realization?

आरुरुक्षोर्मुनेर्योगं कर्म कारणमुच्यते ।
योगारूढस्य तस्यैव शमः कारणमुच्यते ॥ 3 ॥

āruruksor muner yogaṁ karma kāraṇam ucyate
yogārūḍhasya tasyaiva śamaḥ kāraṇam ucyate

For the beginner sage, the Muni, who wishes to attain Yoga, action is considered to be the means; after he has attained Yoga, Equanimity (serenity of the mind) is considered to be the means (for Self-Realization). (6.03)

Karma Yoga (Selfless action) → Equanimity → Self-Realization

Q What are the characteristics of a yogi?

यदा हि नेन्द्रियार्थेषु न कर्मस्वनुषज्जते ।
सर्वसंकल्पसंन्यासी योगारूढस्तदोच्यते ॥ 4 ॥

yadā hi nendriyārtheṣu na karmasv anuṣajjate
sarva-saṅkalpa-sannyāsī yogārūḍhas tadocyate

A person is said to be established in Yoga when he has given up:

1. All material desire
2. All sensual pleasures
3. All attachment to the fruits of work
4. Renounced all thoughts of personal selfish motives. (6.04)

Power of self (mind)

Q How can the self /mind be our friend or enemy?

उद्धरेदात्मनात्मानं नात्मानमवसादयेत् ।
आत्मैव ह्यात्मनो बन्धुरात्मैव रिपुरात्मनः ॥ 5 ॥

uddhared ātmanātmānaṁ nātmānam avasādayet
ātmaiva hy ātmano bandhur ātmaiva ripur ātmanaḥ

बन्धुरात्मात्मनस्तस्य येनात्मैवात्मना जितः ।
अनात्मनस्तु शत्रुत्वे वर्तेतात्मैव शत्रुवत् ॥ 6 ॥

bandhur ātmātmanas tasya yenātmaivātmanā jitaḥ
anātmanas tu śatrutve vartetātmaiva śatru-vat

Our mind-self could be our dearest friend or our worst enemy

One must uplift himself by himself and not degrade himself. The self alone is his friend and self alone is his enemy. For him, who has conquered his lower self (5+2 Enemies) by the Higher Self, his self is a friend. But for one who has not conquered his self, his self is an enemy. (6.05–06)

Lifestyle of a yogi and Lord Krishna's encouragement to Arjuna to become a yogi

Q Who is a balanced person?

जितात्मनः प्रशान्तस्य परमात्मा समाहितः।
शीतोष्णसुखदुःखेषु तथा मानापमानयोः ॥7॥

jitātmanaḥ praśāntasya paramātmā samāhitaḥ
śītoṣṇa-sukha-duḥkheṣu tathā mānāpamānayoḥ

The self-disciplined person, who has control over the lower self (mind, senses and body) and remains firmly established in the Supreme-Self, has attained tranquility and everlasting peace. Such a person is always balanced in heat and cold, in pleasure and pain, and also in honor and dishonor. (6.07)

Q Who is a yogi and what are his characteristics?

ज्ञानविज्ञानतृप्तात्मा कूटस्थो विजितेन्द्रियः।
युक्त इत्युच्यते योगी समलोष्टाश्मकाञ्चनः ॥8॥

jñāna-vijñāna-tṛptātmā kūṭa-stho vijitendriyaḥ
yukta ity ucyate yogī sama-loṣṭrāśma-kāñcanaḥ

A person is called a yogi and Self-realized soul:

1. who is fully satisfied with knowledge and experiential wisdom of the Self
2. who is steadfast
3. who is a master of his own mind and senses and
4. who has the same value for a lump of clay, a stone and gold. (6.08)

Q What are the marks of an enlightened person, a Self-realized soul?

सुहृन्मित्रार्युदासीनमध्यस्थद्वेष्यबन्धुषु।
साधुष्वपि च पापेषु समबुद्धिर्विशिष्यते ॥9॥

suhṛn-mitrāry-udāsīna-madhyastha-dveṣya-bandhuṣu
sādhuṣv api ca pāpeṣu sama-buddhir viśiṣyate

Calmness of mind is a sign of spirituality

A person is regarded more advanced in spirituality who is equal-minded toward well-wishers, friends, enemies, haters, relatives, saints and sinners. (6.09)

Q How should a yogi lead his life?

योगी युञ्जीत सततमात्मानं रहसि स्थितः।
एकाकी यतचित्तात्मा निराशीरपरिग्रहः ॥ 10 ॥

yogī yuñjīta satatam ātmānaṁ rahasi sthitaḥ
ekākī yata-cittātmā nirāśīr aparigrahaḥ

A yogi should always meditate on God while living alone in a secluded place, controlling his mind and body and giving up desires and feelings of possessiveness (proprietorship). (6.10)

Meditation, its pre-requisities, method and benefits

Q How should one practice meditation and why?

शुचौ देशे प्रतिष्ठाप्य स्थिरमासनमात्मनः।
नात्युच्छ्रितं नातिनीचं चैलाजिनकुशोत्तरम् ॥ 11 ॥

śucau deśe pratiṣṭhāpya sthiram āsanam ātmanaḥ
nāty-ucchritaṁ nāti-nīcaṁ cailājina-kuśottaram

A pure thought leads to self-purification

तत्रैकाग्रं मनः कृत्वा यतचित्तेन्द्रियक्रियः।
उपविश्यासने युञ्ज्याद्योगमात्मविशुद्धये ॥ 12 ॥

tatraikāgraṁ manaḥ kṛtvā yata-cittendriya-kriyaḥ
upaviśyāsane yuñjyād yogam ātma-viśuddhaye

To practice meditation, one should choose a clean spot and sit on a firm seat that is neither too high nor too low, covered with grass, a deerskin and a cloth. Sitting in a comfortable position on his prepared seat and concentrating the mind on one point, controlling the thoughts and the activities of the senses, he should practice meditation (Yoga) for self-purification. (6.11–12)

Q How should one sit, focus and do meditation?

समं कायशिरोग्रीवं धारयन्नचलं स्थिरः।
संप्रेक्ष्य नासिकाग्रं स्वं दिशश्चानवलोकयन् ॥ 13 ॥

samaṁ kāya-śiro-grīvaṁ dhārayann acalaṁ sthiraḥ
samprekṣya nāsikāgraṁ svaṁ diśaś cānavalokayan

प्रशान्तात्मा विगतीभीर्ब्रह्मचारिव्रते स्थित: ।
मन: संयम्य मच्चितो युक्त आसीत मत्पर: ।। 14 ।।

praśāntātmā vigata-bhīr brahmacāri-vrate sthitaḥ
manaḥ saṁyamya mac-citto yukta āsīta mat-paraḥ

One should sit still, steady and straight by holding his body, spine, chest, neck, and head erect, fix his eyes and mind steadily on the tip or front of his nose without looking in any other direction. (6.13)

Thus, serene and peaceful, fearless, firm in the practice of celibacy and mind under full control; one should meditate on Me, and make Me the Supreme goal of his life. (6.14)

Q What is the benefit of meditation?

Meditation is the surest way to Liberation

युञ्जन्नेवं सदात्मानं योगी नियतमानस: ।
शान्तिं निर्वाणपरमां मत्संस्थामधिगच्छति ।। 15 ।।

yuñjann evaṁ sadātmānaṁ yogī niyata-mānasaḥ
śāntiṁ nirvāṇa-paramāṁ mat-saṁsthām adhigacchati

Thus, by always concentrating on Me, the yogi of disciplined and settled mind attains Eternal Supreme Peace and merges with Me (*Nirvana*). (6.15)

Q Who will not be able to do meditation?

नात्यश्नतस्तु योगोऽस्ति न चैकान्तमनश्नत: ।
न चाति स्वप्नशीलस्य जाग्रतो नैव चार्जुन ।। 16 ।।

nāty-aśnatas 'tu yogo 'sti na caikāntam anaśnataḥ
na cāti-svapna-śīlasya jāgrato naiva cārjuna

This Yoga is not possible for one who eats too much or eats too little, who sleeps too much or sleeps too little, O Arjuna. (6.16)

Q How can one lead a balanced life and what are the benefits?

A balanced lifestyle is mandatory for Yoga

युक्ताहारविहारस्य युक्तचेष्टस्य कर्मसु ।
युक्तस्वप्नावबोधस्य योगो भवति दु:खहा ।। 17 ।।

yuktāhāra-vihārasya yukta-ceṣṭasya karmasu
yukta-svapnāvabodhasya yogo bhavati duḥkha-hā

Yoga, the destroyer of pains and miseries is achieved only by a person who is disciplined, moderates and balances his:

1. Eating
2. Recreation
3. Working
4. Sleeping
5. Walking (6.17)

Fig. 6.1 *Balanced lifestyle is the prerequisite for meditation*

Q Who is established in Yoga (Union with God)?

यदा विनियतं चित्तमात्मन्येवावतिष्ठते।
नि:स्पृह: सर्वकामेभ्यो युक्त इत्युच्यते तदा ।। 18 ।।

yadā viniyataṁ cittam ātmany evāvatiṣṭhate
nispṛhaḥ sarva-kāmebhyo yukta ity ucyate tadā

A person is said to be established in Yoga, union with God, when his mind is completely controlled, becomes free from all worldly desires and becomes situated in transcendence/*Samadhi*. (6.18)

Q What are the additional benefits of a disciplined mind and meditation?

यथा दीपो निवातस्थो नेङ्गते सोपमा स्मृता।
योगिनो यतचित्तस्य युञ्जतो योगमात्मन: ।। 19 ।।

yathā dīpo nivāta-stho neṅgate sopamā smṛtā
yogino yata-cittasya yuñjato yogam ātmanaḥ

Meditation is the best yoga for self-purification and self-transformation

यत्रोपरमते चित्तं निरुद्धं योगसेवया।
यत्र चैवात्मनात्मानं पश्यन्नात्मनि तुष्यति ।। 20 ।।

yatroparamate cittaṁ niruddhaṁ yoga-sevayā
yatra caivātmanātmānaṁ paśyann ātmani tuṣyati

As a lamp in a windless place does not flicker so the yogi with a conquered mind does not tremble with worldly desires, who focuses and meditates on the Self. (6.19)

When the mind is completely restrained from worldly thoughts, becomes steady and peaceful by practicing meditation, one certainly develops the ability to see the Self by the pure mind and rejoices in the Self and becomes satisfied in the Self alone. (6.20)

Self-Discipline → Meditation → Self-Realization

Q What happens after experiencing the Supreme Bliss?

सुखमात्यन्तिकं यत्तद्बुद्धिग्राह्यमतीन्द्रियम्।
वेत्ति यत्र न चैवायं स्थितश्चलति तत्त्वतः ॥ 21 ॥

sukham ātyantikaṁ yat tad buddhi-grāhyam atīndriyam
vetti yatra na caivāyaṁ sthitaś calati tattvataḥ

यं लब्ध्वा चापरं लाभं मन्यते नाधिकं ततः।
यस्मिन्स्थितो न दुःखेन गुरुणापि विचाल्यते ॥ 22 ॥

yaṁ labdhvā cāparaṁ lābhaṁ manyate nādhikaṁ tataḥ
yasmin sthito na duḥkhena guruṇāpi vicālyate

Supreme Bliss is the highest achievement in life

When one experiences the Transcendental Happiness, *Anandam* (State of Bliss), that is derived from deep meditation through the subtle intellect, and that is beyond the reach of the senses, one is never separated from the Absolute Truth. (6.21)

After attaining such a Supreme State of Bliss, *Sat Chit Ananda*—one does not consider any other gain superior to the blissful state and once established in that state, the individual is not shaken even by the greatest calamity. (6.22)

Q What is the state of freedom?

तं विद्याद्दुःखसंयोगवियोगं योगसंज्ञितम्।
स निश्चयेन योक्तव्यो योगोऽनिर्विण्णचेतसा ॥ 23 ॥

taṁ vidyād duḥkha-saṁyoga-viyogaṁ yoga-saṁjñitam
sa niścayena yoktavyo yogo 'nirviṇṇa-cetasā

The state of freedom from all sorrow, miseries arising from material contact, is called Yoga. This Yoga should be practiced with firm determination and an undistracted mind. (6.23)

Q What is the process of developing tranquility and serenity of the mind?

संकल्पप्रभवान् कामांस्त्यक्त्वा सर्वानशेषतः।
मनसैवेन्द्रियग्रामं विनियम्य समन्ततः ॥ 24 ॥

saṅkalpa-prabhavān kāmāṁs tyaktvā sarvān aśeṣataḥ
manasaivendriya-grāmaṁ viniyamya samantataḥ

शनैः शनैरुपरमेद् बुद्ध्या धृतिगृहीतया।
आत्मसंस्थं मनः कृत्वा न किंचिदपि चिन्तयेत् ॥ 25 ॥

śanaiḥ śanair uparamed buddhyā dhṛti-gṛhītayā
ātma-saṁsthaṁ manaḥ kṛtvā na kiñcid api cintayet

Self -Realization is not an instant gain but a gradual process

1. By totally abandoning all selfish desires arising from worldly thoughts
2. By fully controlling all the senses and mind from all sides by intellect
3. By keeping the mind fully engaged in God's Consciousness
4. By thinking of nothing else at all

Little by little through practice, one gradually attains peace and tranquility of the mind. (6.24–25)

Q What should I do when my mind wanders during meditation?

यतो यतो निश्चरति मनश्चञ्चलमस्थिरम्।
ततस्ततो नियम्यैतदात्मन्येव वशं नयेत् ॥ 26 ॥

yato yato niścalati manaś cañcalam asthiram
tatas tato niyamyaitad ātmany eva vaśaṁ nayet

Focusing on Self is the beginning of the process

Due to its flickering and unsteady nature, wherever this restless and unsteady mind wanders during meditation, one must certainly bring it back by repeatedly concentrating on the Self. (6.26)

Description of a Yogi

Q How to achieve Supreme happiness?

प्रशान्तमनसं ह्येनं योगिनं सुखमुत्तमम्।
उपैति शान्तरजसं ब्रह्मभूतमकल्मषम् ॥ 27 ॥

praśānta-manasaṁ hy enaṁ yoginaṁ sukham uttamam
upaiti śānta-rajasaṁ brahma-bhūtam akalmaṣam

The Supreme Happiness (Ultimate Bliss, *Anandam*) comes to the Self-realized Yogi whose mind is perfectly calm, tranquil and fixed on Me, whose mode of passion is subdued, and who is free from all the sin. (6.27)

Q Who attains Union (Oneness) with God?

युञ्जन्नेवं सदात्मानं योगी विगतकल्मषः।
सुखेन ब्रह्मसंस्पर्शमत्यन्तं सुखमश्नुते ॥28॥

yuñjann evaṁ sadātmānaṁ yogī vigata-kalmaṣaḥ
sukhena brahma-saṁsparśam atyantaṁ sukham aśnute

Thus, a self-disciplined yogi, who is constantly living in Supreme Consciousness through meditation and other spiritual practices, becomes free from sins and easily attains the Infinite Bliss of Oneness with *Brahman* (Union with Self, God). (6.28)

Q How does a yogi perceive others?

सर्वभूतस्थमात्मानं सर्वभूतानि चात्मनि।
ईक्षते योगयुक्तात्मा सर्वत्र समदर्शनः ॥29॥

sarva-bhūta-stham ātmānaṁ sarva-bhūtāni cātmani
īkṣate yoga-yuktātmā sarvatra sama-darśanaḥ

One who is established in Yoga and united with the Supreme Consciousness (Self-realized Soul), sees every being with an equal eye, and sees himself in all beings, and all beings in him. (6.29)

Q How to stay closer to God?

यो मां पश्यति सर्वत्र सर्वं च मयि पश्यति।
तस्याहं न प्रणश्यामि स च मे न प्रणश्यति ॥30॥

yo māṁ paśyati sarvatra sarvaṁ ca mayi paśyati
tasyāhaṁ na praṇaśyāmi sa ca me na praṇaśyati

Those who see Me everywhere, and see everyone in Me are not out of my sight, and I am not out of their sight. (6.30)

Q Who resides in God?

सर्वभूतस्थितं यो मां भजत्येकत्वमास्थितः।
सर्वथा वर्तमानोऽपि स योगी मयि वर्तते ॥31॥

sarva-bhūta-sthitaṁ yo māṁ bhajaty ekatvam āsthitaḥ
sarvathā vartamāno 'pi sa yogī mayi vartate

One who is established in Oneness, worships Me as residing in all beings, that yogi though engaged in all forms of activities, will always reside in Me in all circumstances. (6.31)

Q Who is a perfect yogi?

आत्मौपम्येन सर्वत्र समं पश्यति योऽर्जुन।
सुखं वा यदि वा दुःखं स योगी परमो मतः ।। 32 ।।

ātmaupamyena sarvatra samaṁ paśyati yo 'rjuna
sukhaṁ vā yadi vā duḥkhaṁ sa yogī paramo mataḥ

A perfect yogi is the one who considers every being like himself, applies the same standards for others as he applies to himself and who can feel the pain and pleasures of others as his own, O Arjuna. (6.32)

Method to control the monkey mind

Q How does Arjuna describe the mind?

अर्जुन उवाच
योऽयं योगस्त्वया प्रोक्तः साम्येन मधुसूदन।
एतस्याहं न पश्यामि चञ्चलत्वात्स्थितिं स्थिराम् ।। 33 ।।

arjuna uvāca
yo 'yaṁ yogas tvayā proktaḥ sāmyena madhusūdana
etasyāhaṁ na paśyāmi cañcalatvāt sthitiṁ sthirām

चञ्चलं हि मनः कृष्ण प्रमाथि बलवद्दृढम्।
तस्याहं निग्रहं मन्ये वायोरिव सुदुष्करम् ।। 34 ।।

cañcalaṁ hi manaḥ kṛṣṇa pramāthi balavad dṛḍham
tasyāhaṁ nigrahaṁ manye vāyor iva su-duṣkaram

Arjuna said: O Krishna, this Yoga of Equanimity of mind described by you, I do not perceive it as steady and lasting due to the restless nature of the mind. (6.33)

O Krishna, the mind indeed is very restless, turbulent, powerful, and stubborn. I think controlling the mind is as difficult as controlling the wind. (6.34)

Q How can one control the restless mind?

श्रीभगवानुवाच
असंशयं महाबाहो मनो दुर्निग्रहं चलम्।
अभ्यासेन तु कौन्तेय वैराग्येण च गृह्यते ।। 35 ।।

Right practice makes one perfect

śrī-bhagavān uvāca
asaṁśayaṁ mahā-bāho mano durnigrahaṁ calam
abhyāsena tu kaunteya vairāgyeṇa ca gṛhyate

Lord Krishna said: Certainly, O Arjuna, the mind is restless and extremely difficult to control, but it can be controlled by constant spiritual practice (Meditation) and by non-attachment, O Arjuna. (6.35)

Q Who can achieve Yoga (Oneness with God) and how?

असंयतात्मना योगो दुष्प्राप इति मे मतिः।
वश्यात्मना तु यतता शक्योऽवाप्तुमुपायतः ॥ 36 ॥

asaṁyatātmanā yogo duṣprāpa iti me matiḥ
vaśyātmanā tu yatatā śakyo 'vāptum upāyataḥ

Yoga (Equanimity) is difficult to achieve for the one whose mind is uncontrolled and unsettled, but it is attainable by the person of controlled mind who strives ceaselessly through proper practice. That is My opinion. (6.36)

Destination of an unsuccessful spiritual practitioner

Q What was Arjuna's question about the destiny of an unsuccessful spiritual practitioner?

अर्जुन उवाच
अयतिः श्रद्धयोपेतो योगाच्चलितमानसः।
अप्राप्य योगसंसिद्धिं कां गतिं कृष्ण गच्छति ॥ 37 ॥

arjuna uvāca
ayatiḥ śraddhayopeto yogāc calita-mānasaḥ
aprāpya yoga-saṁsiddhiṁ kāṁ gatiṁ kṛṣṇa gacchati

कच्चिन्नोभयविभ्रष्टश्छिन्नाभ्रमिव नश्यति।
अप्रतिष्ठो महाबाहो विमूढो ब्रह्मणः पथि ॥ 38 ॥

kaccin nobhaya-vibhraṣṭaś chinnābhram iva naśyati
apratiṣṭho mahā-bāho vimūḍho brahmaṇaḥ pathi

एतन्मे संशयं कृष्ण छेत्तुमर्हस्यशेषतः।
त्वदन्यः संशयस्यास्य छेत्ता न ह्युपपद्यते ॥ 39 ॥

etan me saṁśayaṁ kṛṣṇa chettum arhasy aśeṣataḥ
tvad-anyaḥ saṁśayasyāsya chettā na hy upapadyate

Arjuna said: O Krishna, what is the destiny of the one, who in the beginning, starts on the path of Self-Realization with full faith but later, at the time of death, discontinues due to his uncontrolled mind and thus fails to attain the highest perfection (Self-Realization)? (6.37)

O Krishna, one who is lost from the path of Yoga, does he not loses both spiritual and material success (God-Realization and worldly enjoyment) and without support disappears like a dispersing cloud? (6.38)

This is my doubt, O Krishna, I ask you to dispel it completely, because there is none other than You who can eradicate such a doubt. (6.39)

Q How does one carry the credit of good deeds from one life to the next?

श्रीभगवानुवाच
पार्थ नैवेह नामुत्र विनाशस्तस्य विद्यते।
न हि कल्याणकृत्कश्चिद् दुर्गतिं तात गच्छति ॥ 40 ॥

śrī-bhagavān uvāca
pārtha naiveha nāmutra vināśas tasya vidyate
na hi kalyāṇa-kṛt kaścid durgatiṁ tāta gacchati

The Supreme Lord said: O Arjuna, there is no destruction for one who is engaged in virtuous deeds (yogi), neither in this material world nor in the next life. He is never put to grief, My dear friend. (6.40)

Q What will happen to a yogi if he falls short on his spiritual practices (unsuccessful seeker)?

प्राप्य पुण्यकृतां लोकानुषित्वा शाश्वतीः समाः।
शुचीनां श्रीमतां गेहे योगभ्रष्टोऽभिजायते ॥ 41 ॥

prāpya puṇya-kṛtāṁ lokān uṣitvā śāśvatīḥ samāḥ
śucīnāṁ śrīmatāṁ gehe yoga-bhraṣṭo 'bhijāyate

अथवा योगिनामेव कुले भवति धीमताम्।
एतद्धि दुर्लभतरं लोके जन्म यदीदृशम् ॥ 42 ॥

atha vā yogināṁ eva kule bhavati dhīmatām
etad dhi durlabhataraṁ loke janma yad īdṛśam

The unsuccessful yogi (who has fallen from Yoga) attains a Higher World (Heaven) to which the men of meritorious deeds alone are entitled and lives there for countless years. Then he will be born in a family of enlightened, spiritually-advanced yogi. However, such a birth is very difficult, actually, to obtain in this world. (6.41–42)

Q What kind of destiny will an unsuccessful seeker have?

तत्र तं बुद्धिसंयोगं लभते पौर्वदेहिकम्।
यतते च ततो भूयः संसिद्धौ कुरुनन्दन ॥ 43 ॥

tatra taṁ buddhi-saṁyogaṁ labhate paurva-dehikam
yatate ca tato bhūyaḥ saṁsiddhau kuru-nandana

पूर्वाभ्यासेन तेनैव ह्रियते ह्यवशोऽपि सः।
जिज्ञासुरपि योगस्य शब्दब्रह्मातिवर्तते ।। 44 ।।

pūrvābhyāsena tenaiva hriyate hy avaśo 'pi saḥ
jijñāsur api yogasya śabda-brahmātivartate

There he automatically regains spiritual insight (latent Knowledge) that was acquired in the previous life, and strives much more than before to achieve perfection (Self-Realization), O Arjuna. (6.43)

The unsuccessful yogi feels compulsively, automatically and instinctively drawn toward the spiritual path by invisible forces of former impressions, *Samsakara*, acquired in previous lives by Yogic practices. Such a seeker always rises above those who duly perform all Vedic rituals. (6.44)

Q What does a yogi finally accomplish?

प्रयत्नाद्यतमानस्तु योगी संशुद्धकिल्बिषः।
अनेकजन्मसंसिद्धस्ततो याति परां गतिम् ।। 45 ।।

prayatnād yatamānas tu yogī saṁśuddha-kilbiṣaḥ
aneka-janma-saṁsiddhas tato yāti parāṁ gatim

But the yogi who sincerely strives for further progress becomes completely free from all sins, (purified), gradually achieves perfection through many births and reaches the Supreme Abode. (6.45)

The Best Yogi

Q Why should you strive to be a yogi?

तपस्विभ्योऽधिको योगी ज्ञानिभ्योऽपि मतोऽधिकः।
कर्मिभ्यश्चाधिका योगी तस्माद्योगी भवार्जुन ।। 46 ।।

tapasvibhyo 'dhiko yogī jñānibhyo 'pi mato 'dhikaḥ
karmibhyaś cādhiko yogī tasmād yogī bhavārjuna

A yogi is superior to the ascetics. The yogi is considered greater than the Vedic scholars, those with only with bookish knowledge, and the yogi is certainly far above the ritualists (those who perform their actions with expectations of reward). Therefore, O Arjuna, you be a yogi. (6.46)

Q Who is the greatest yogi?

योगिनामपि सर्वेषां मद्गतेनान्तरात्मना ।
श्रद्धावान् भजतेयो मां स मे युक्ततमो मत: ॥ 47 ॥

yoginām api sarveṣāṁ mad-gatenāntar-ātmanā
śraddhāvān bhajate yo māṁ sa me yuktatamo mataḥ

One who always lives in God Conciousness is the greatest Yogi

Among all the Yogis the one who worship me with full faith and devotion, whose mind is totally absorbed in Me, single-pointed concentration (lives in God Consciousness), I consider him to be the greatest yogi. (6.47)

Lessons to learn and practice in daily life

Spirituality is not just an activity but a lifestyle; therefore it must be practiced every day

1. We must discipline ourselves and lead a balanced life in all respects (eating, working, entertaining and sleeping.)
2. We must have a healthy body and a calm mind to lead our day-to-day life.
3. We must feed good thoughts to our mind by reading good books (scriptures), surrounding ourselves with good company and watching only good programs on TV.
4. We should only perform action that uplifts ourselves, others and the whole society (His creation).
5. We must perform daily spiritual practices—selfless service (*Karma Yoga*), *Asanas*, *Pranayam*, *meditation*, etc.

When we perform daily spiritual practices, gradually we will attain peace and Anandam within and also experience in our external life

ॐ तत्सदिति श्रीमद्भगवद्गीतासूपनिषत्सु ब्रह्मविद्यायां योगशास्त्रे
श्रीकृष्णार्जुनसंवादे ध्यानयोगो नाम षष्ठोऽध्यायः ।।

AUM TAT SAT

Thus ends the sixth chapter named "*Dhyana Yoga*"
The Path of Self-discipline and Meditation
in the *Upanishad* of the glorious Bhagavad Gita, the scripture of Yoga,
the science of the Absolute (*Brahman*), in the form of the dialogue
between Lord Krishna and Arjuna.

Aum Shanti, Shanti, Shantihi

Union with God—Self-Realization

"God is the Essence for All"

Self-Purification and Transformation through
Metaphysical Knowledge

JNANA-VIJNANA YOGA

The Path of Knowing and Experiencing God

Union with God (Self-Realization) through the path of knowing God, and experiencing His presence (Realized Knowledge/Science)

The Gita is a bridge between science and spirituality

In the previous chapter, Lord Krishna declares that the greatest yogi is the one who worships Him with full faith and single-pointed concentration. However, this can be done only by knowing Him as Omnipresent, Omniscient and Omnipotent.

In this chapter, Lord Krishna enlightens Arjuna by revealing that,"God (Divinity) is the essential core and sustaining force of the entire creation, both material and spiritual" (Metaphysical Knowledge). Therefore, He is everywhere (Omnipresent) and He can be found and seen everywhere (*kan kan me*). Pious souls surrender unto Him, however, impious souls divert their mind to other objects of worship.

Jnana Vijnana Yoga: *Jnana* is the theoretical knowledge and *Vijnana* is the realized knowledge. Therefore, it is also called, "*Yoga of Realization*," or experiential knowledge.

Theoretical spiritual knowledge can be received by many means—studying scriptures, listening to learned people. However, realized Knowledge (Wisdom) can be obtain only through one's own experiences, feelings and intuitions, just as swimming cannot be learned by studying books but only by practicing. By knowing and experiencing one gets to know his real and eternal affinity with God. He realizes that he is God and he is not seperate from God.

The Truth has to be known and experienced.

—Sathya Sai Baba

Main Message

Union with God through Wisdom and Self-Realized Knowledge

- First, we must gain theoretical knowledge of the Yogas, and then practice it by the selfless service (*Seva*). Finally, we must realize it through meditation and *Samadhi*.

Theoretical Knowledge → Selfless Service (Seva) →
Meditation → Realization

- God can be realized in any form as worshipped by His devotee.
- This creation of God (Matter, Divine illusion, *Maya*) that consists of three states of mind (*Gunas*, qualities), is extremely difficult to transcend. But it can be achieved only by surrendering to Him.

Chapter Overview

01–07 Ultimate knowledge is Knowing God-Divinity in Essence

08–12 Supreme Power-God is the basis of everything

13–15 Divine illusion (*Maya*) and *Gunas*

16–19 Four types of devotees but who is the best devotee

20–23 Worship of demi-gods

24–30 Criticism of those who do not know the glory of God and praise for those who do

Ultimate Knowledge is Knowing God-Divinity in Essence

Q How to know God?

श्रीभगवानुवाच
मय्यासक्तमनाः पार्थ योगं युञ्जन्मदाश्रयः।
असंशयं समग्रं मां यथा ज्ञास्यसि तच्छृणु ॥1॥

śrī-bhagavān uvāca
mayy āsakta-manāḥ pārtha
yogaṁ yuñjan mad-āśrayaḥ
asaṁśayaṁ samagraṁ māṁ
yathā jñāsyasi tac chṛṇu

The Supreme Lord said: O Arjuna, now listen, how you will know Me entirely without any doubt is by practicing Yoga with your mind completely focused on Me and taking total refuge in me. (7.01)

Q What is Ultimate Knowledge?

ज्ञानं तेऽहं सविज्ञानमिदं वक्ष्याम्यशेषतः।
यज्ज्ञात्वा नेह भूयोऽन्यज्ज्ञातव्यमवशिष्यते ॥2॥

jñānaṁ te 'haṁ sa-vijñānam
idaṁ vakṣyāmy aśeṣataḥ
yaj jñātvā neha bhūyo 'nyaj
jñātavyam avaśiṣyate

God is the only purpose of Life

I will now reveal to you in detail wisdom along with experiential knowledge (*Vijnana*, Science). After knowing that, nothing else remains to be known in this world. (7.02)

Q Do many people know God?

मनुष्याणां सहस्रेषु कश्चिद्यतति सिद्धये।
यततामपि सिद्धानां कश्चिन्मां वेत्ति तत्त्वतः ॥3॥

manuṣyāṇāṁ sahasreṣu
kaścid yatati siddhaye
yatatām api siddhānāṁ
kaścin māṁ vetti tattvataḥ

Only one in thousand want to realize God

Among thousands of men, very rarely one strives for perfection and from those who strive and succeed; again a rare one truly knows Me in Essence. (7.03)

Q What constitutes the eight-fold division of God's Nature (*Prakriti*, Material energy)?

भूमिरापोऽनलो वायुः खं मनो बुद्धिरेव च।
अहंकार इतीयं मे भिन्ना प्रकृतिरष्टधा ॥4॥

bhūmir āpo 'nalo vāyuḥ khaṁ mano buddhir eva ca
ahaṅkāra itīyaṁ me bhinnā prakṛtir aṣṭadhā

Earth, water, fire, air, ether, mind, intelligence and ego constitute the eight-fold division of My Nature (*Prakriti*, Material energy). (7.04)

Q How is the entire universe sustained?

अपरेयमितस्त्वन्यां प्रकृतिं विद्धि मे पराम्।
जीवभूतां महाबाहो ययेदं धार्यते जगत् ॥5॥

apareyam itas tv anyāṁ prakṛtiṁ viddhi me parām
jīva-bhūtāṁ mahā-bāho yayedaṁ dhāryate jagat

This *Prakriti* (Material energy) is My lower nature (*Apara-Shakti*), but you should also know My Higher Nature, the essence of life principle (*Para-Shakti*, Spirit) by which the entire universe is sustained, O Arjuna. (7.05)

Q Who is the originator of the universe?

एतद्योनीनि भूतानि सर्वाणीत्युपधारय।
अहं कृत्स्नस्य जगतः प्रभवः प्रलयस्तथा ॥6॥

etad-yonīni bhūtāni
sarvāṇīty upadhāraya
ahaṁ kṛtsnasya jagataḥ
prabhavaḥ pralayas tatha

The universe is made with matter and Spirit

Know that all beings have evolved from this two-fold energy (material and spirit, matter and energy, temporary and permanent) and I am the source of both the origin and the dissolution of the entire universe. (7.06)

Matter + Spirit (Energy) = Universe (Cosmos)

Q Who is the Supreme binding power in the universe?

मत्तः परतरं नान्यत्किञ्चिदस्ति धनंजय।
मयि सर्वमिदं प्रोतं सूत्रे मणिगणा इव ।। 7 ।।

mattaḥ parataraṁ nānyat
  kiñcid asti dhanañjaya
mayi sarvam idaṁ protaṁ
  sūtre maṇi-gaṇā iva

God is the essence of all

O Arjuna, there is nothing else besides Me. Everything in the universe is strung on Me like pearls on the string of a necklace. (7.07)

Supreme Power-God is the basis of everything

Q Where can one find God?

रसोऽहमप्सु कौन्तेय प्रभास्मि शशिसूर्ययोः।
प्रणवः सर्ववेदेषु शब्दः खे पौरुषं नृषु ।। 8 ।।

raso 'ham apsu kaunteya
  prabhāsmi śaśi-sūryayoḥ
praṇavaḥ sarva-vedeṣu
  śabdaḥ khe pauruṣaṁ nṛṣu

God is everything and everything is God

पुण्यो गन्धः पृथिव्यां च तेजश्चास्मि विभावसौ।
जीवनं सर्वभूतेषु तपश्चास्मि तपस्विषु ।। 9 ।।

puṇyo gandhaḥ pṛthivyāṁ ca tejaś cāsmi vibhāvasau
jīvanaṁ sarva-bhūteṣu tapaś cāsmi tapasviṣu

O Arjuna:

1. I am the taste in water
2. I am the radiance in the sun and the moon.
3. I am the sacred syllable 'ॐ *AUM*' in the Vedic *mantras*
4. I am the sound in the ether
5. I am potency in men

6. I am the pure fragrance in earth
7. I am the heat in the fire
8. I am the life in all living beings
9. I am the austerity in the ascetics. (7.08–09)

Q Who is God?

बीजं मां सर्वभूतानां विद्धि पार्थ सनातनम् ।
बुद्धिर्बुद्धिमतामस्मि तेजस्तेजस्विनामहम् ॥ 10 ॥

bījaṁ māṁ sarva-bhūtānāṁ
viddhi pārtha sanātanam
buddhir buddhimatām asmi
tejas tejasvinām aham

बलं बलवतां चाहं कामरागविवर्जितम् ।
धर्माविरुद्धो भूतेषु कामोऽस्मि भरतर्षभ ॥ 11 ॥

balaṁ balavatāṁ cāhaṁ
kāma-rāga-vivarjitam
dharmāviruddho bhūteṣu
kāmo 'smi bharatarṣabha

The Gita is the Universal Mother

O Arjuna:

1. I am the eternal seed of all beings
2. I am the intelligence of the intelligent
3. I am the brilliance of the brilliant
4. I am the strength of the strong that is devoid of passion and selfish attachment
5. I am the sexual desire in human beings that is not contrary to righteousness (*Dharma*), O Arjuna. (7.10–11)

Q From where do the three modes of *Gunas*, the qualities of nature arise?

ये चैव सात्त्विका भावा राजसास्तामसाश्च ये ।
मत्त एवेति तान्विद्धि न त्वहं तेषु ते मयि ॥ 12 ॥

ye caiva sāttvikā bhāvā rājasās tāmasāś ca ye
matta eveti tān viddhi na tv ahaṁ teṣu te mayi

Know that all three modes of Material Nature (*Gunas*, attributes)—*Sattva* (Goodness), *Rajas* (passion) and *Tamas* (ignorance) originate from Me alone. I am not affected by them or depend on them but they depend on Me. (7.12)

Divine illusion (*Maya*) and *Gunas*

Q Why is it difficult to recognize God?

त्रिभिर्गुणमयैर्भावैरेभिः सर्वमिदं जगत्।
मोहितं नाभिजानाति मामेभ्यः परमव्ययम् ।। 13 ।।

tribhir guṇa-mayair bhāvair ebhiḥ sarvam idaṁ jagat
mohitaṁ nābhijānāti mām ebhyaḥ param avyayam

The whole world is deluded by these three qualities (*Gunas-Sattva*, *Rajas*, and *Tamas*) originating from the *Prakriti*. Therefore, people do not recognize Me; who is above these qualities, Imperishable and the Supreme. (7.13)

Q How can one transcend His divine illusion, *Maya* (Three modes of *Gunas*)?

दैवी ह्येषा गुणमयी मम माया दुरत्यया।
मामेव ये प्रपद्यन्ते मायामेतां तरन्ति ते ।। 14 ।।

daivī hy eṣā guṇa-mayī
mama māyā duratyayā
mām eva ye prapadyante
māyām etāṁ taranti te

Everyone is a puppet of mother nature except the one who surrenders to Me

This divine illusion (*Maya*) of Mine, consists of three states of mind (*Gunas*) and is extremely difficult to transcend. However, those who surrender only to Me easily cross beyond this divine illusion. (7.14)

Q Why do some people not worship God?

न मां दुष्कृतिनो मूढाः प्रपद्यन्ते नराधमाः।
माययापहृतज्ञाना आसुरं भावमाश्रिताः ।। 15 ।।

na māṁ duṣkṛtino mūḍhāḥ prapadyante narādhamāḥ
māyayāpahṛta-jñānā āsuraṁ bhāvam āśritāḥ

The evil doers, the ignorant, the lowest among mankind, whose discriminating power (Wisdom) has been taken away by divine illusive power (*Maya*) and who have adopted the demonic nature. They do not worship me or take refuge in Me. (7.15)

Four types of devotees but who is the best devotee

Q Who takes refuge in God, worships Him and why?

चतुर्विधा भजन्ते मां जनाः सुकृतिनोऽर्जुन ।
आर्तो जिज्ञासुरर्थार्थी ज्ञानी च भरतर्षभ ।। 16 ।।

catur-vidhā bhajante māṁ
janāḥ sukṛtino 'rjuna
ārto jijñāsur arthārthī
jñānī ca bharatarṣabha

The four types of devotees

O Arjuna, there are four kinds of virtuous men who worship Me:

1. The distressed
2. The seeker of Self-Knowledge
3. The seeker of wealth
4. The enlightened man of wisdom (7.16)

Q Who is the best devotee among these virtuous four?

तेषां ज्ञानी नित्ययुक्त एकभक्तिर्विशिष्यते ।
प्रियो हि ज्ञानिनोऽत्यर्थमहं स च मम प्रियः ।। 17 ।।

teṣāṁ jñānī nitya-yukta
eka-bhaktir viśiṣyate
priyo hi jñānino 'tyartham
ahaṁ sa ca mama priyaḥ

The wise one is the best and most dear to God

Of these, the best is the man of wisdom, the enlightened devotee, who is ever united with Me and whose devotion is single-minded. I am extremely dear to the man of wisdom and he is very dear to Me. (7.17)

Q Who does God consider the best?

उदाराः सर्व एवैते ज्ञानी त्वात्मैव मे मतम् ।
आस्थितः स हि युक्तात्मा मामेवानुत्तमां गतिम् ।। 18 ।।

udārāḥ sarva evaite
jñānī tv ātmaiva me matam
āsthitaḥ sa hi yuktātmā
mām evānuttamāṁ gatim

One who sets God as "the goal of his life" is the wisest

All these are indeed very noble but I consider the man of wisdom to be My very own Self because he is firmly established in Me and for him, I am the Supreme goal. (7.18)

Q Who is a great soul and why is it rare?

बहूनां जन्मनामन्ते ज्ञानवान्मां प्रपद्यते ।
वासुदेवः सर्वमिति स महात्मा सुदुर्लभः ।। 19 ।।

bahūnāṁ janmanām ante
jñānavān māṁ prapadyate
vāsudevaḥ sarvam iti
sa mahātmā su-durlabhaḥ

Very rare to find pure souls

At the end of many births, the wise one comes to Me by realizing that "*Vasudeva* (Supreme Being) is all there is." However, such a great soul (Mahatma) is very rare. (7.19)

Worship of demi-gods

Q Who worships demi-gods (*devas*)?

कामैस्तैस्तैर्हृतज्ञानाः प्रपद्यन्तेऽन्यदेवताः ।
तं तं नियममास्थाय प्रकृत्या नियताः स्वया ।। 20 ।।

kāmais tais tair hṛta-jñānāḥ prapadyante 'nya-devatāḥ
taṁ taṁ niyamam āsthāya prakṛtyā niyatāḥ svayā

Those, whose discrimination has been distorted by worldly desires driven by their own inherent nature (*karmic* impression), worship demi-gods (*devas*) by various rituals. (7.20)

Q Whom should I worship?

यो यो यां यां तनुं भक्तः श्रद्धयार्चितुमिच्छति ।
तस्य तस्याचलां श्रद्धां तामेव विदधाम्यहम् ।। 21 ।।

yo yo yāṁ yāṁ tanuṁ bhaktaḥ
śraddhayārcitum icchati
tasya tasyācalāṁ śraddhāṁ
tām eva vidadhāmy aham

God can be visualized in any form

स तया श्रद्धया युक्तस्तस्या राधनमीहते ।
लभते च ततः कामान्मयैव विहितान्हि तान् ।। 22 ।।

sa tayā śraddhayā yuktas tasyārādhanam īhate
labhate ca tataḥ kāmān mayaiva vihitān hi tān

Whatever form, name and method a devotee chooses to worship with faith, I make his faith steady in that very form. Endowed with such steadfast faith, he worships that deity and gains his wishes which are, in reality, granted by Me only. (7.21–22)

Q What is the fate of demi-god (*devas*) worshippers?

अन्तवत्तु फलं तेषां तद्भवत्यल्पमेधसाम्।
देवान्देवयजो यान्ति मद्भक्ता यान्ति मामपि ॥ 23 ॥

antavat tu phalaṁ teṣāṁ tad bhavaty alpa-medhasām
devān deva-yajo yānti mad-bhaktā yānti mām api

The material gains of these men of poor intellect are temporary. The worshippers of demi-gods go to *devas*, but My devotees surely come to Me. (7.23)

Criticism of those who do not know the glory of God and praise for those who do

Q What does an ignorant person think of God?

अव्यक्तं व्यक्तिमापन्नं मन्यन्ते मामबुद्धयः।
परं भावमजानन्तो ममाव्ययमनुत्तमम् ॥ 24 ॥

avyaktaṁ vyaktim āpannaṁ manyante mām abuddhayaḥ
paraṁ bhāvam ajānanto mamāvyayam anuttamam

The ignorant one unaware of My Infinite, Transcendental, Supreme and Imperishable nature thinks of Me only in terms of my perishable and finite form. (7.24)

Q Why don't people recognize the true Nature of God?

नाहं प्रकाशः सर्वस्य योगमायासमावृतः।
मूढोऽयं नाभिजानाति लोको मामजमव्ययम् ॥ 25 ॥

Ignorant cannot recognize God

nāhaṁ prakāśaḥ sarvasya
  yoga-māyā-samāvṛtaḥ
mūḍho 'yaṁ nābhijānāti
  loko mām ajam avyayam

Veiled by My *Yoga-Maya* (Divine Power), I do not reveal Myself to such ignorant ones. Therefore, they do not recognize me as the Unborn, Eternal, Imperishable, Transcendental and Supreme Spirit. (7.25)

Q Does any one know God?

वेदाहं समतीतानि वर्तमानानि चार्जुन।
भविष्याणि च भूतानि मां तु वेद न कश्चन ॥ 26 ॥

God knows all

vedāhaṁ samatītāni vartamānāni cārjuna
bhaviṣyāṇi ca bhūtāni māṁ tu veda na kaścana

O Arjuna, I know all the beings of the past, the present, and even those to come in the future but no one knows Me completely. (7.26)

Q Who worships God with full faith and determination?

इच्छाद्वेषसमुत्थेन द्वन्द्वमोहेन भारत ।
सर्वभूतानि संमोहं सर्गे यान्ति परंतप ।। 27 ।।

icchā-dveṣa-samutthena dvandva-mohena bhārata
sarva-bhūtāni sammohaṁ sarge yānti parantapa

येषां त्वन्तगतं पापं जनानां पुण्यकर्मणाम् ।
ते द्वन्द्वमोहनिर्मुक्ता भजन्ते मां दृढव्रताः ।। 28 ।।

yeṣāṁ tv anta-gataṁ pāpaṁ janānāṁ puṇya-karmaṇām
te dvandva-moha-nirmuktā bhajante māṁ dṛḍha-vratāḥ

O Arjuna, in this world, all beings are born in utter ignorance due to the delusion of dualities, (pairs of opposites, likes and dislikes) arising from likes and dislikes (desire and hate). But persons of selfless, pious and virtuous deeds, whose sins are completely eradicated, become free from the delusion of pairs of opposites and worship Me with full determination. (7.27–28)

Q Who can realize one's true nature?

जरामरणमोक्षाय मामाश्रित्य यतन्ति ये ।
ते ब्रह्म तद्विदुः कृत्स्नमध्यात्मं कर्म चाखिलम् ।। 29 ।।

jarā-maraṇa-mokṣāya
māṁ āśritya yatanti ye
te brahma tad viduḥ kṛtsnam
adhyātmaṁ karma cākhilam

Yoga of surrender is the best path to attain Liberation

साधिभूताधिदैवं मां साधियज्ञं च ये विदुः ।
प्रयाणकालेऽपि च मां ते विदुर्युक्तचेतसः ।। 30 ।।

sādhibhūtādhidaivaṁ māṁ sādhiyajñaṁ ca ye viduḥ
prayāṇa-kāle 'pi ca māṁ te vidur yukta-cetasaḥ

Those who strive for Liberation from the cycles of birth, old age, and death by taking refuge in Me, fully realize the Supreme Spirit (*Brahman*, Eternal Being), the nature of Self, and the entire field of actions (*karma*) and His creative power. (7.29)

Those who live in full Consciousness of Me and know Me as the God of material manifestations (*Adhibhuta*), the God of demi-gods, (*Adhidaiva*) and also the God of Sacrifice (*Adhiyajna*) can attain Me even at the time of death. (7.30)

Lessons to learn and practice in daily life

God is the essence of everything in the universe

1. We should see Divinity, God's presence in everything and in every situation.
2. Surrender is the basic requirement and the best Yoga to attain God. Therefore, we should learn to surrender to Him and always live in His Consciousness (Awareness).

ॐ तत्सदिति श्रीमद्भगवद्गीतासूपनिषत्सु ब्रह्मविद्यायां योगशास्त्रे
श्रीकृष्णार्जुनसंवादे ज्ञानविज्ञानयोगो नाम सप्तमोऽध्यायः ।।

AUM TAT SAT

Thus ends the seventh chapter named "*Jnana-Vijnana Yoga*"
The Path of Knowing and Experiencing God
in the *Upanishad* of the glorious Bhagavad Gita, the scripture of Yoga,
the science of the Absolute (*Brahman*), in the form of the dialogue
between Lord Krishna and Arjuna.

Aum Shanti, Shanti, Shantihi

Self-Purification and Transformation through ॐ Mantra

AUM

ॐ

AUM is Cosmic Sound
AUM is the music of soul
AUM is sound of universe
AUM is divinity, infinite
AUM is past, present and future
AUM is Brahma, Vishnu, and Mahesh
AUM is creation, preservation and destruction
AUM is conscious, sub-conscious and Super-Conscious
AUM is Durga, Laxmi and Saraswati
AUM is awareness, awakening
AUM is your inner voice
AUM is your real name
AUM is you
AUM is me
AUM is every thing
AUM is all in one and one in all!
ॐ AUM is Love, Peace and Anandam

AKSARA-BRAHMA YOGA

The Path of the Eternal Brahman

Union with God (Self-Realization) through the path of constantly remembering God and reciting ॐ AUM mantra

ॐ *AUM is an Eternal Mantra*

In this chapter, Arjuna requested Lord Krishna to enlighten him with clarification of eight questions (based upon Lord Krishna's statements in previous chapter). He also wanted to know the one specific path that is simple and easy to practice in daily life, even at the time of death. Lord Krishna guided Arjuna to build direct communication and connection with God, experience His presence (feel *Anandam*) in every moment of life and even at the time of death by constantly remembering Him and reciting, 'ॐ *AUM*.' It is the simplest method to attain God-Realization and Self-Realization. However, the recitation must be done from the heart and with feelings not just by lips.

ॐ *AUM is the Ocean of Anandam*

One does not have to wait until the last moment of life (death), to remember and realize God. One can start experiencing, feeling, seeing Him and feeling happy and peaceful immediately, even in this busy and hectic lifestyle, only by constantly remembering Him and reciting 'ॐ *AUM*.' When *AUM* is recited with feelings (*Bhava*), its vibration generates everlasting Peace and *Anandam* within.

Main Message

Remembering God every moment of our life by reciting 'ॐ AUM,' is the simplest Yoga

- According to Lord Krishna, there are two eternal paths in the world, one leads to salvation and the other to bondage.
- Lord Krishna again emphasized the techniques of focusing, contemplating, and meditating on Him, because these techniques not only help to lead a happy and peaceful life in the materialistic world, but also lead to Union with God even at the very last moment of life as well.

Chapter Overview

01–04 Arjuna's eight questions of Self-Realization and Lord Krishna's answers

05–06 How to experience God's presence at the time of death

08–22 Self-Realization by meditating on God and constant uttering of ॐ *AUM*

23–28 Two Eternal paths: Light and Dark

Arjuna's eight questions of Self-Realization and Lord Krishna's answers

Q What are Arjuna's eight questions related to God-Realization and Self-Realization?

अर्जुन उवाच
किं तद् ब्रह्म किमध्यात्मं किं कर्म पुरुषोत्तम।
अधिभूतं च किं प्रोक्तमधिदैवं किमुच्यते ॥1॥

arjuna uvāca
kiṁ tad brahma kim adhyātmaṁ kiṁ karma puruṣottama
adhibhūtaṁ ca kiṁ proktam adhidaivaṁ kim ucyate

अधियज्ञः कथं कोऽत्र देहेऽस्मिन्मधुसूदन।
प्रयाणकाले च कथं ज्ञेयोऽसि नियतात्मभिः ॥2॥

adhiyajñaḥ kathaṁ ko 'tra dehe 'smin madhusūdana
prayāṇa-kāle ca kathaṁ jñeyo 'si niyatātmabhiḥ

Arjuna asked: O Krishna

1. What is *Brahman*?
2. What is *Adhyatma*?
3. What is *Karma*?
4. What is called *Adhibhuta*?
5. What is termed *Adhidaiva*?
6. Who is the *Adhiyajna*?
7. How does He dwell in the body?
8. How can You, the Supreme be realized at the time of death by the self-controlled, O Krishna? (8.01–02)

Q What are the Lord Krishna's answers?

श्रीभगवानुवाच
अक्षरं ब्रह्म परमं स्वभावोऽध्यात्ममुच्यते।
भूतभावोद्भवकरो विसर्गः कर्मसंज्ञितः ॥3॥

śrī-bhagavān uvāca
akṣaraṁ brahma paramaṁ svabhāvo 'dhyātmam ucyate
bhūta-bhāvodbhava-karo visargaḥ karma-saṁjñitaḥ

अधिभूतं क्षरो भावः पुरुषश्चाधिदैवतम्।
अधियज्ञोऽहमेवात्र देहे देहभृतां वर ॥4॥

adhibhūtaṁ kṣaro bhāvaḥ puruṣaś cādhidaivatam
adhiyajño 'ham evātra dehe deha-bhṛtāṁ vara

The Supreme Lord said, O Arjuna:

1. *Brahman* is Godhead, Supreme, Super Spirit, Eternal Being, Imperishable, Infinite and Absolute, *Purushottama*.
2. *Adhyatm* is God's Essential Nature: Godhead existing in all individual beings (embodied soul, self). It can be known by spiritual practices.
3. *Karma* (action with consequences) is the creative force of the Supreme-Spirit that causes living beings into manifestation. (8.03)
4. *Adhibhuta* is the God of the elements-material manifestation. All perishable objects are called *Adhibhuta*.
5. *Adhiyajna* is the Lord of Sacrifice, spirit of selfless service.
6. *Adhidaiva-Purusha*, is the God of demi-gods (*devas*, divine beings) He resides as the Supreme Consciousness and inner witness in the body (heart) of every being – He is all in all. (8.04)

How to experience God's presence at the time of death

Q What should one contemplate at the time of death and why?

अन्तकाले च मामेव स्मरन्मुक्त्वा कलेवरम्।
यः प्रयाति स मद्भावं याति नास्त्यत्र संशयः ॥5॥

anta-kāle ca mām eva smaran muktvā kalevaram
yaḥ prayāti sa mad-bhāvaṁ yāti nāsty atra saṁśayaḥ

The art of dying is just as important as the art of living

यं यं वापि स्मरन्भावं त्यजत्यन्ते कलेवरम्।
तं तमेवैति कौन्तेय सदा तद्भावभावितः ॥6॥

yaṁ yaṁ vāpi smaran bhāvaṁ tyajaty ante kalevaram
taṁ tam evaiti kaunteya sadā tad-bhāva-bhāvitaḥ

One who remembers Me even while leaving the body at the time of death certainly merges with Me and attains My Being, there is no doubt about this. (8.05)

O Arjuna, whatever object and whoever contemplates at the time of death, while leaving his body, attains that very object and goes into that very form in the next birth, as he has been constantly absorbed in that thought throughout his life. (8.06)

Q What is the simplest method of God and Self-Realization?

तस्मात्सर्वेषु कालेषु मामनुस्मर युध्य च।
मय्यर्पितमनोबुद्धिर्मामेवैष्यस्यसंशयः ॥7॥

tasmāt sarveṣu kāleṣu
māṁ anusmara yudhya ca
mayy arpita-mano-buddhir
māṁ evaiṣyasy asaṁśayaḥ

Therefore, always remember Me, do your prescribed duty and fight the battle with your mind and intellect fixed on me. You shall without doubt come to Me. (8.07)

Self-Realization by meditating on God and constant uttering of ॐ *AUM*

Q What is the role of the mind and meditation in realizing God?

अभ्यासयोगयुक्तेन चेतसा नान्यगामिना।
परमं पुरुषं दिव्यं याति पार्थानुचिन्तयन् ॥8॥

abhyāsa-yoga-yuktena
cetasā nānya-gāminā
paramaṁ puruṣaṁ divyaṁ
yāti pārthānucintayan

One can attain God by practicing meditation

One certainly attains the Supreme Divine by constant practice of meditation on the Supreme Being, and not thinking of anything else, O Arjuna. (8.08)

Q Who can realize God and how?

कविं पुराणमनुशासितार मणोरणीयांसमनुस्मरेद्यः।
सर्वस्य धातारमचिन्त्यरूप मादित्यवर्णं तमसः परस्तात् ॥9॥

kaviṁ purāṇam anuśāsitāram
aṇor aṇīyāṁsam anusmared yaḥ
sarvasya dhātāram acintya-rūpam
āditya-varṇaṁ tamasaḥ parastāt

प्रयाणकाले मनसाचलेन भक्तया युक्तो योगबलेन चैव।
भ्रुवोर्मध्ये प्राणमावेश्य सम्यक् स तं परं पुरुषमुपैति दिव्यम् ॥ 10 ॥

prayāṇa-kāle manasācalena
bhaktyā yukto yoga-balena caiva
bhruvor madhye prāṇam āveśya samyak
sa taṁ paraṁ puruṣam upaiti divyam

One who contemplates and meditates on the Omniscient, Supreme Being, (*Para-Brahman*) as the oldest, the ruler of the entire universe, smaller than the smallest atom (bigger than the biggest), the sustainer of all, the inconceivable, that shines like the sun and beyond the darkness of ignorance. One, who at the time of death, with single-minded devotion and by the power of Yoga, draws the flow of life breath, (*Prana*) between the two eyebrows and holding there, will surely attain Me, the Supreme Divine. (8.09–10)

Q What role does celibacy play in attaining Self-Realization?

यदक्षरं वेदविदो वदन्ति विशन्ति यद्यतयो वीतरागाः।
यदिच्छन्तो ब्रह्मचर्यं चरन्ति तत्ते पदं संग्रहेण प्रवक्ष्ये ॥ 11 ॥

yad akṣaraṁ veda-vido vadanti
viśanti yad yatayo vīta-rāgāḥ
yad icchanto brahmacaryaṁ caranti
tat te padaṁ saṅgraheṇa pravakṣye

Now I shall briefly describe to you that state which the knowers of the Vedas call the Eternal Goal (God-Realization, Self-Realization), in which the seeker practices detachment (non-attachment) and self-control, celibacy in order to attain the Supreme Goal. (8.11)

Meditation is the surest way to Liberation

Q How does one merge with God at the time of death?

सर्वद्वाराणि संयम्य मनो हृदि निरुध्य च।
मूर्ध्न्याधायात्मनः प्राणमास्थितो योगधारणाम् ॥ 12 ॥

sarva-dvārāṇi saṁyamya
mano hṛdi nirudhya ca
mūrdhny ādhāyātmanaḥ prāṇam
āsthito yoga-dhāraṇām

ओमित्येकाक्षरं ब्रह्म व्याहरन्मामनुस्मरन्।
यः प्रयाति त्यजन्देहं स याति परमां गतिम् ॥ 13 ॥

oṁ ity ekākṣaraṁ brahma
vyāharan mām anusmaran
yaḥ prayāti tyajan dehaṁ
sa yāti paramāṁ gatim

'ॐ AUM' the simplest and easiest mantra to attain God

Whoever leaves the body by remebring Me, having closed all the gates of the body (controlling all the senses), focusing the mind on Me in the heart (God) and fixing the *Prana* (life energy) at the top of the head (crown, cerebellum), meditating on Me and vibrating the sacred monosyllable 'ॐ *AUM*'—with this Supreme combination of letters (Sound power of Supreme Being, Brahman), one certainly attains the Supreme Goal (Self-Realization). (8.12–13)

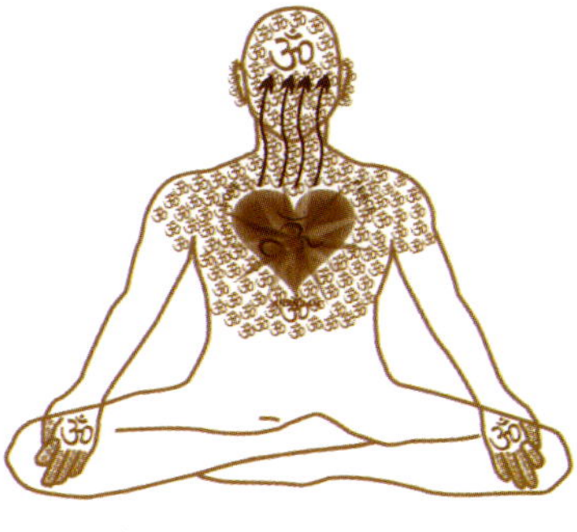

Fig. 8.1 *How to die*

Q Is it easy to realize God and if so by whom?

अनन्यचेताः सततं यो मां स्मरति नित्यशः।
तस्याहं सुलभः पार्थ नित्ययुक्तस्य योगिनः॥14॥

ananya-cetāḥ satataṁ yo māṁ smarati nityaśaḥ
tasyāhaṁ sulabhaḥ pārtha nitya-yuktasya yoginaḥ

Gita not only teaches how to live but also how to die

"O Arjuna, I am easily attainable by one who always thinks of Me alone with undivided attention because he is always united with me" (Yoga). (8.14)

Q Does one come back to the universe after attaining God?

मामुपेत्य पुनर्जन्म दुःखालयमशाश्वतम्।
नाप्नुवन्ति महात्मानः संसिद्धिं परमां गताः॥15॥

mām upetya punar janma duḥkhālayam aśāśvatam
nāpnuvanti mahātmānaḥ saṁsiddhiṁ paramāṁ gatāḥ

After attaining Me, these great souls are not reborn again in this miserable, transitory world because they have attained the highest perfection. (8.15)

Q Is there any rebirth after attaining God?

आब्रह्मभुवनाल्लोकाः पुनरावर्तिनोऽर्जुन।
मामुपेत्य तु कौन्तेय पुनर्जन्म न विद्यते॥16॥

ā-brahma-bhuvanāl lokāḥ
punar āvartino 'rjuna
mām upetya tu kaunteya
punar janma na vidyate

Every one in the universe will be reborn

O Arjuna, everyone from all the worlds, including the world of Brahma, the Creator, to the lowest are subject to rebirth. But, after attaining Me, O son of Kunti, there is no rebirth. (8.16)

Q What are the Cosmic day and night (day and night of Brahma, the Creator)?

सहस्रयुगपर्यन्तमहयद्ब्रह्मणो विदु: ।
रात्रिं युगसहस्रान्तां तेऽहोरात्रविदो जना: ।। 17 ।।

sahasra-yuga-paryantam ahar yad brahmaṇo viduḥ
rātriṁ yuga-sahasrāntāṁ te 'ho-rātra-vido janāḥ

Those who know that the Cosmic day and the Cosmic night (day and night of Brahma, the Creator) last one thousand Yugas each knows the reality of time (One Yuga = 4.32 billion years). (8.17)

Q How does the Cosmic evolution take place?

अव्यक्ताद्व्यक्तय: सर्वा: प्रभवन्त्यहरागमे ।
रात्र्यागमे प्रलीयन्ते तत्रैवाव्यक्तसंज्ञके ।। 18 ।।

avyaktād vyaktayaḥ sarvāḥ prabhavanty ahar-āgame
rātry-āgame pralīyante tatraivāvyakta-saṁjñake

At the coming of the Cosmic manifestation day (Brahma's day), all living beings emerge from the unmanifested state and at the coming of the unmanifestation day (Brahma's night), all of them merge back into the same, unmanifested state, subtle body of Brahma. (8.18)

भूतग्राम: स एवायं भूत्वा भूत्वा प्रलीयते ।
रात्र्यागमेऽवश: पार्थ प्रभवत्यहरागमे ।। 19 ।।

bhūta-grāmaḥ sa evāyaṁ bhūtvā bhūtvā pralīyate
rātry-āgame 'vaśaḥ pārtha prabhavaty ahar-āgame

O Arjuna, that very multitude of beings comes into existence again and again under compulsion from *Prakriti* at the beginning of the Cosmic manifestation day (Brahma's day, Creator) and are dissolved helplessly at the coming of Brahma's night. (8.19)

Q Is there any other existence besides creation and dissolution (cycle of birth and death)?

परस्तस्मात्तु भावोऽन्योऽव्यक्तोऽव्यक्तात्सनातन: ।
य: स सर्वेषु भूतेषु नश्यत्सु न विनश्यति ।। 20 ।।

Heaven is not the final destination, Supreme Abode is

paras tasmāt tu bhāvo 'nyo
'vyakto 'vyaktāt sanātanaḥ
yaḥ sa sarveṣu bhūteṣu
naśyatsu na vinaśyati

अव्यक्तोऽक्षर इत्युक्तस्तमाहुः परमां गतिम् ।
यं प्राप्य न निवर्तन्ते तद्धाम परमं मम ।। 21 ।।

avyakto 'kṣara ity uktas tam āhuḥ paramāṁ gatim
yaṁ prāpya na nivartante tad dhāma paramaṁ mama

Beyond this unmanifest state (into which all beings dissolve) there is yet another Eternal Unmanifest, Supreme Divine in nature that does not perish even when all others perish. This Unmanifest is called Imperishable, the Supreme Abode (*Parama-dhama*, Eternal Being). Upon attaining it, one does not return to the manifested universe. (8.20–21)

Q How does one reach the Supreme Abode?

पुरुषः स परः पार्थ भक्त्या लभ्यस्त्वनन्यया ।
यस्यान्तः स्थानि भूतानि येन सर्वमिदं ततम् ।। 22 ।।

puruṣaḥ sa paraḥ pārtha bhaktyā labhyas tv ananyayā
yasyāntaḥ-sthāni bhūtāni yena sarvam idaṁ tatam

O Arjuna, that Supreme Abode is attainable by undivided devotion to only Me alone, within whom all beings reside and by whom all this universe is pervaded. (8.22)

Two Eternal paths: Light and Dark

Q When does one attain freedom from the cycle of life and death (auspicious time to die)?

यत्र काले त्वनावृत्तिमावृत्तिं चैव योगिनः ।
प्रयाता यान्ति तं कालं वक्ष्यामि भरतर्षभ ।। 23 ।।

yatra kāle tv anāvṛttim
 āvṛttiṁ caiva yoginaḥ
prayātā yānti taṁ kālaṁ
 vakṣyāmi bharatarṣabha

Choose your path carefully

अग्निर्ज्योतिरहः शुक्लः षण्मासा उत्तरायणम् ।
तत्र प्रयाता गच्छन्ति ब्रह्म ब्रह्मविदो जनाः ।। 24 ।।

agnir jyotir ahaḥ śuklaḥ ṣaṇ-māsā uttarāyaṇam
tatra prayātā gacchanti brahma brahma-vido janāḥ

O Arjuna, now I will describe to you the different times when Yogis do not return after their death and also the time when they do return. (8.23)

Those, who depart from this world during the day time, the lunar fortnight, the influence of the *devas* and the six months of the northern path of the sun, *Uttarayana*, and know the Supreme *Brahman*, go to *Brahman*—Unite with God. (8.24)

Q When does one not attain freedom from the cycle of life and death (inauspicious time to die)?

धूमो रात्रिस्तथा कृष्णः षण्मासा दक्षिणायनम् ।
तत्र चान्द्रमसं ज्योतिर्योगी प्राप्य निवर्तते ।। 25 ।।

dhūmo rātris tathā kṛṣṇaḥ ṣaṇ-māsā dakṣiṇāyanam
tatra cāndramasaṁ jyotir yogī prāpya nivartate

Departing from this world during the time of smoke, night, the dark lunar fortnight, the six months of the southern path of the sun, the yogis attain the moon planet (lunar abode) or heaven, and reincarnate in the mortal world. (8.25)

Q How many Eternal paths are there?

शुक्लकृष्णे गती ह्येते जगतः शाश्वते मते ।
एकया यात्यनावृत्तिमन्ययावर्तते पुनः ।। 26 ।।

śukla-kṛṣṇe gatī hy ete jagataḥ śāśvate mate
ekayā yāty anāvṛttim anyayāvartate punaḥ

In the world, there are considered to be two Eternal paths; the path of light (Spiritual practice, Self-Knowledge) and path of darkness (Materialism, Ignorance). The one leads to salvation (Liberation, Nirvana), but the other leads to bondage and rebirth. (8.26)

Light → Liberation

Light → Darkness → Bondage

Q Which path should I choose?

नैते सृती पार्थ जानन्योगी मुह्यति कश्चन ।
तस्मात्सर्वेषु कालेषु योगयुक्तो भवार्जुन ।। 27 ।।

naite sṛtī pārtha jānan yogī muhyati kaścana
tasmāt sarveṣu kāleṣu yoga-yukto bhavārjuna

Knowing the reality of these two paths, the yogi is not deluded. Therefore, O Arjuna, be established in Yoga at all times, live in God's Consciousness and strive to attain Self-Realization. (8.27)

Q What is the importance of realizing the Absolute Truth?

वेदेषु यज्ञेषु तपःसु चैव दानेषु यत्पुण्यफलं प्रदिष्टम् ।
अत्येति तत्सर्वमिदं विदित्वा योगी परं स्थानमुपैति चाद्यम् ।। 28 ।।

vedeṣu yajñeṣu tapaḥsu caiva
dāneṣu yat puṇya-phalaṁ pradiṣṭam
atyeti tat sarvam idaṁ viditvā
yogī paraṁ sthānam upaiti cādyam

Self-Knowledge leads to salvation (Moksha)

The yogi who realizes this Absolute Truth certainly transcends all the rewards that arise from the study of Vedas, performance of sacrifices, austerities and giving charities and attains *Parama-dhama*, the Supreme Eternal Abode (Supreme goal of life, Self-Realization). (8.28)

Lessons to learn and practice in daily life

The Gita is Ananadmayi, the Source of Anandam (Ultimate Bliss)

1. Always live in God's Consciousness (Awareness of His presence)
2. Constantly recite 'ॐ *AUM*' (Not just verbally but with feeling)
3. Meditate daily, thus build communication and relationship with God (Inner Self)
4. Lead a self-disciplined life (practice celibacy and non-attachment)
5. Strive to attain the Supreme goal of life—Self-Realization

ॐ तत्सदिति श्रीमद्भगवद्गीतासूपनिषत्सु ब्रह्मविद्यायां योगशास्त्रे
श्रीकृष्णार्जुनसंवादे तारकब्रह्मयोगो नामाष्टमोऽध्यायः ।।

AUM TAT SAT

Thus ends the eighth chapter named "*Aksara-Brahma Yoga*"
The Path of the Eternal Brahman
in the *Upanishad* of the glorious Bhagavad Gita, the scripture of Yoga,
the science of the Absolute (*Brahman*), in the form of the dialogue
between Lord Krishna and Arjuna.

Aum Shanti, Shanti, Shantihi

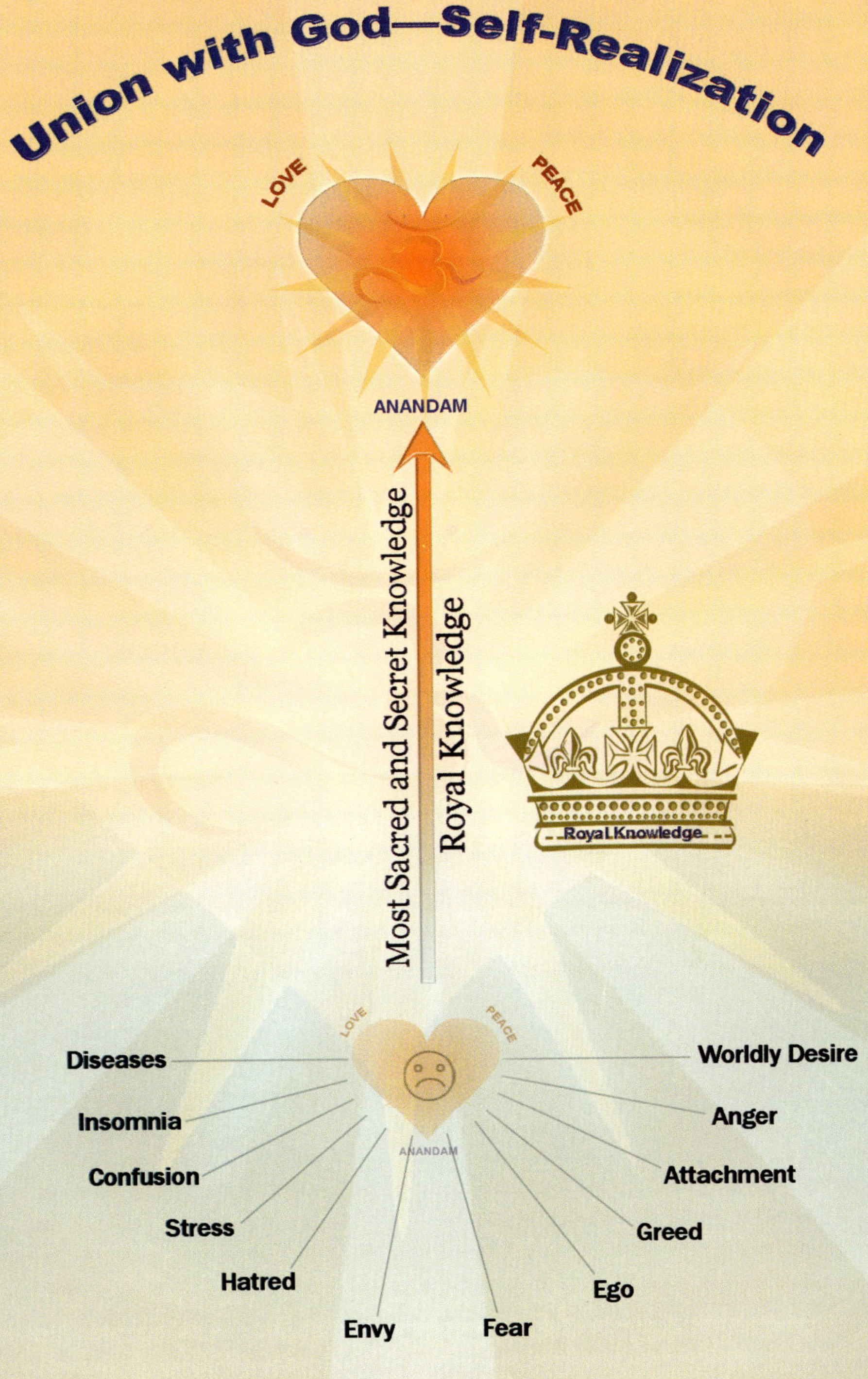

Self-Purification and Transformation through Royal Knowledge

RAJAVIDYA-RAJAGUHYA YOGA

The Path of the Most Secret and Sacred Knowledge

Union with God (Self-Realization) through the path of most secret and most sacred knowledge

The Gita is the Ocean of Eternal Knowledge

In this chapter, Lord Krishna imparts the knowledge of the sacred truth of His Divine mystery and is called the King of Knowledge (Supreme Knowledge) and most Secret Knowledge. He declares to Arjuna that:

Supreme Knowledge is the Highest Knowledge of all

He explains that the entire material existence is created, pervaded, maintained and annihilated by His external energy and all beings ascend and descend under His supervision.

Lord Krishna guided and motivated Arjuna to fulfill his duty. "You should fight the righteous war to establish Righteousness in My creation with the sense of offering to Me and not for your own sake. By doing so, you will also attain the Supreme goal of life, *Sat Chit Ananda* (Self-Realization, Supreme Bliss).

Main Message

Supreme Knowledge is the Royal Path to Liberation

- Supreme Knowledge is the king of all kinds of knowledge and also the most confidential Knowledge.
- God originates the world due to cause and effect.
- Everything is God's manifestation.
- One can also attain Self-Realization by *Bhakti/Devotion Yoga.*
- God Himself fulfills both worldly and spiritual needs of His devotees and also provides them with security of their possessions.
- God does not require any fancy things except our pure love and devotion. Therefore, our offering to Him must be pure and with Love and Devotion.
- Everyone including a sinner, who lives in God's Consciousness, worships Him with full devotion, and does all actions for Him and will be united with Him.

Chapter Overview

01–06	Wisdom (Self-Knowledge) and its glories
07–10	Creation and annihilation of the universe
11–15	Criticism of ignorant people and praise of the wise
16–19	Everything is God's manifestation
20–25	Worship of God and gods
26–28	God accepts things only from a pure heart with love
29–31	A sinner can also become a saint
32–34	Glories of selfless devotion

Wisdom (Self-Knowledge) and its glories

Q What is the highest knowledge of all?

श्रीभगवानुवाच

इदं तु ते गुह्यतमं प्रवक्ष्याम्यनसूयवे।
ज्ञानं विज्ञानसहितं यज्ज्ञात्वा मोक्ष्यसेऽशुभात्॥1॥

śrī-bhagavān uvāca
idaṁ tu te guhyatamaṁ
pravakṣyāmy anasūyave
jñānaṁ vijñāna-sahitaṁ
yaj jñātvā mokṣyase 'śubhāt

The divine mystery is unveiled

The Supreme Lord said: Since you do not envy Me, I shall disclose to you the most profound and most Secret Knowledge together with Transcendental experience, Self-realized Knowledge. By knowing this you will be free from the sorrows of life, birth and death. (9.01)

Q What is the nature of Transcendental Knowledge and can this be easily practiced?

राजविद्या राजगुह्यं पवित्रमिदमुत्तमम्।
प्रत्यक्षावगमं धर्म्यं सुसुखं कर्तुमव्ययम्॥2॥

rāja-vidyā rāja-guhyaṁ
pavitram idam uttamam
pratyakṣāvagamaṁ dharmyaṁ
su-sukhaṁ kartum avyayam

Transcendental Knowledge is the king of all knowledge

This Self-Knowledge is the sovereign of all knowledge. It is the most secret, Supreme Purifier and is easy to understand by direct experience (Sovereign Science) and fully in accordance with Righteousness (*Dharma*). It is Imperishable, Everlasting, and Enjoyable, and is also very easy to practice. (9.02)

Q Who does not attain God?

अश्रद्दधानाः पुरुषा धर्मस्यास्य परंतप ।
अप्राप्य मां निवर्तन्ते मृत्युसंसारवर्त्मनि ।। 3 ।।

aśraddadhānāḥ puruṣā dharmasyāsya parantapa
aprāpya māṁ nivartante mṛtyu-saṁsāra-vartmani

O Arjuna, people with no faith and reverence in this Sacred Knowledge do not attain Me but return to the path of life and death in this material world. (9.03)

Q Does God depend on His creation and dwell in it?

मया ततमिद् सर्वं धजगदव्यक्तमूर्तिना ।
मत्स्थानि सर्वभूतानि न चाहं तेष्ववस्थितः ।। 4 ।।

mayā tatam idaṁ sarvaṁ jagad avyakta-mūrtinā
mat-sthāni sarva-bhūtāni na cāhaṁ teṣv avasthitaḥ

न च मत्स्थानि भूतानि पश्य मे योगमैश्वरम् ।
भूतभृन्न च भूतस्थो ममात्मा भूतभावनः ।। 5 ।।

na ca mat-sthāni bhūtāni paśya me yogam aiśvaram
bhūta-bhṛn na ca bhūta-stho mamātmā bhūta-bhāvanaḥ

This entire cosmos is an expansion of My Non-Manifested form. All beings abide in Me but I am not abiding in them. (9.04)

Look at the wonderful power of My Divine Yoga. Though I am the sustainer and creator of all beings yet, I do not dwell in them, nor do they dwell in Me. (9.05)

Q How do all living beings abide in God?

यथाकाशस्थितो नित्यं वायुः सर्वत्रगो महान् ।
तथा सर्वाणि भूतानि मत्स्थानीत्युपधारय ।। 6 ।।

yathākāśa-sthito nityaṁ vāyuḥ sarvatra-go mahān
tathā sarvāṇi bhūtāni mat-sthānīty upadhāraya

Just as the mighty wind blows everywhere while always resting in the sky, know that all beings rest in Me. (9.06)

Creation and annihilation of the universe

Q How did creation come into existence?

सर्वभूतानि कौन्तेय प्रकृतिं यान्ति मामिकाम्।
कल्पक्षये पुनस्तानि कल्पादौ विसृजाम्यहम्॥7॥

sarva-bhūtāni kaunteya
prakṛtiṁ yānti māmikām
kalpa-kṣaye punas tāni
kalpādau visṛjāmy aham

God is the best designer. He customizes and creates us based upon our karms/deeds

प्रकृतिं स्वामवष्टभ्य विसृजामि पुनः पुनः।
भूतग्राममिमं कृत्सनमवशं प्रकृतेर्वशात्॥8॥

prakṛtiṁ svām avaṣṭabhya visṛjāmi punaḥ punaḥ
bhūta-grāmam imaṁ kṛtsnam avaśaṁ prakṛter vaśāt

O Arjuna, at the end of a *Kalpa* (Time cycle, *Brahma's* day) all beings merge into My *Prakriti* (Nature that is part of me) and at the beginning of the next Time cycle I create them again. (9.07)

Due to My Material Nature (*Prakriti* or *Maya*), I automatically create again and again this whole multitude of beings, reincarnating them (according to their respective *karma*) and subject to the influence of their own nature. (9.08)

Q Why does God, as Creator not bound by His act of creation (His *karma*)?

न च मां तानि कर्माणि निबध्नन्ति धनंजय।
उदासीनवदासीनमसक्तं तेषु कर्मसु॥9॥

na ca māṁ tāni karmāṇi nibadhnanti dhanañjaya
udāsīna-vad āsīnam asaktaṁ teṣu karmasu

O Arjuna, these acts of creation do not bind Me, because I remain neutral and unattached to these actions. (9.09)

Q How does God and *Prakriti* work together to create the universe?

मयाध्यक्षेण प्रकृतिः सूयते सचराचरम्।
हेतुनानेन कौन्तेय जगद्विपरिवर्तते॥10॥

mayādhyakṣeṇa prakṛtiḥ sūyate sa-carācaram
hetunānena kaunteya jagad viparivartate

Under My direction and supervision, the Material Nature (*Prakriti*), My divine energy produces the whole of creation both moving and non-moving beings (animate and inanimate), O Arjuna. Thus by this means, the whole universe is created and annihilated again and again. (9.10)

Criticism of ignorant people and praise of the wise

Q Why can't an ignorant person recognize God?

अवजानन्ति मां मूढा मानुषीं तनुमाश्रितम्।
परं भावमजानन्तो मम भूतमहेश्वरम्॥11॥

avajānanti māṁ mūḍhā mānuṣīṁ tanum āśritam
paraṁ bhāvam ajānanto mama bhūta-maheśvaram

मोघाशा मोघकर्माणो मोघज्ञाना विचेतसः।
राक्षसीमासुरीं चैव प्रकृतिं मोहिनीं श्रिताः॥12॥

moghāśā mogha-karmāṇo mogha-jñānā vicetasaḥ
rākṣasīm āsurīṁ caiva prakṛtiṁ mohinīṁ śritāḥ

Fools disregard Me when I descend in the human form because they do not know My Supreme nature as the great Lord of all beings (taking Me for an ordinary human being). (9.11)

They have vain hopes, futile actions and vain knowledge, therefore they have adopted delusions and demonic (evil) qualities. Due to the lack of discriminating power they are unable to recognize Me. (9.12)

Q Who can recognize God?

महात्मानस्तु मां पार्थ दैवीं प्रकृतिमाश्रिताः।
भजन्त्यनन्यमनसो ज्ञात्वा भूतादिमव्ययम्॥13॥

mahātmānas tu māṁ pārtha daivīṁ prakṛtim āśritāḥ
bhajanty ananya-manaso jñātvā bhūtādim avyayam

O Arjuna, great souls who possess divine qualities know Me as the prime source of creation and worship Me constantly with undivided mind, love and devotion. (9.13)

Q How do people worship Manifested/*Suguna* (with Form) God?

सततं कीर्तयन्तो मां यतन्तश्च दृढव्रताः।
नमस्यन्तश्च मां भक्त्या नित्युयुक्ता उपासते॥14॥

satataṁ kīrtayanto māṁ yatantaś ca dṛḍha-vratāḥ
namasyantaś ca māṁ bhaktyā nitya-yuktā upāsate

These great souls of divine nature make firm vows to worship Me with devotion and great determination. They constantly chant My names and glories, bowing down before Me with devotion and perpetually striving to realize Me. (9.14)

Q How do people worship Unmanifest (Formless) God ?

ज्ञानयज्ञेन चाप्यन्ये यजन्तो मामुपासते ।
एकत्वेन पृथक्त्वेन बहुधा विश्वतोमुखम् ।। 15 ।।

jñāna-yajñena cāpy anye yajanto mām upāsate
ekatvena pṛthaktvena bahudhā viśvato-mukham

Others worship Me as the Oneness of Self (non-duality, unmanifested God) by offering integral, Transcendental Knowledge, yet others worship Me in My Universal Form (manifested) thinking of Me as distinct from them (duality) and the manifold facing in all directions. (9.15)

Everything is God's manifestation

Q Who is God and what does He do?

अहं क्रतुरहं यज्ञः स्वधाहमहमौषधम् ।
मन्त्रोऽहमहमेवाज्यमहमग्निरहं हुतम् ।। 16 ।।

ahaṁ kratur ahaṁ yajñaḥ
svadhāham aham auṣadham
mantro 'ham aham evājyam
aham agnir ahaṁ hutam

पिताहमस्य जगतो माता धाता पितामहः ।
वेद्यं पवित्रमोंकार ऋक्सामयजुरेव च ।। 17 ।।

pitāham asya jagato
mātā dhātā pitāmahaḥ
vedyaṁ pavitram oṁkāra
ṛk sāma yajur eva ca

God is everything and every thing is His manifestation

गतिर्भर्ता प्रभुः साक्षी निवासः शरणं सुहृत् ।
प्रभवः प्रलयः स्थानं निधानं बीजमव्ययम् ।। 18 ।।

gatir bhartā prabhuḥ sākṣī
nivāsaḥ śaraṇaṁ suhṛt
prabhavaḥ pralayaḥ sthānaṁ
nidhānaṁ bījam avyayam

1. I am the Vedic ritual
2. I am the offering (Sacrifice, *Yajna*)
3. I am the medicinal herb
4. I am the *mantra*
5. I am the clarified butter
6. I am the fire
7. I am the oblation (*Ahuti*- the offering to the fire) (9.16)
8. I am the Father, the Mother, the Sustainer, and the Grandfather of the universe
9. I am the object of sacred knowledge
10. I am the sacred syllable ॐ '*AUM*'
11. I am also the *Rig*, the *Sama*, and the *Yajur Vedas** (9.17)
12. I am the Supreme Goal
13. I am the Supporter
14. I am the Great Lord
15. I am the Witness
16. I am the Abode
17. I am the Refuge
18. I am the Friend
19. I am the Origin
20. I am the End
21. I am the Foundation
22. I am the Treasure house
23. I am the Imperishable Seed (9.18)

* *Rig, Sama, Yajur Vedas are principal Vedas. Rig* is devoted to verses of praise, *Sama* to mantras, and *Yajur* to ritual formulae.

तपाम्यहमहं वर्षं निगृह्णाम्युत्सृजामि च ।
अमृतं चैव मृत्युश्च सदसच्चाहमर्जुन ।। 19 ।।

tapāmy aham ahaṁ varṣaṁ nigṛhṇāmy utsṛjāmi ca
amṛtaṁ caiva mṛtyuś ca sad asac cāham arjuna

O Arjuna, I give heat. I withhold as well as send forth the rain. I am Immortality as well as Death. I am also both the Absolute (*Sat* or *Aksara*, Spirit, Being) and the temporal (*Asat*, matter, non-being). (9.19)

Worship of God and gods

Q How does one attain heaven?

त्रैविद्या मां सोमपाः पूतपापा
यज्ञैरिष्ट्वा स्वर्गतिं प्रार्थयन्ते।
ते पुण्यमासाद्य सुरेन्द्रलोक
मश्नन्ति दिव्यान्दिवि देवभोगान् ।। 20 ।।

trai-vidyā māṁ soma-pāḥ pūta-pāpā
yajñair iṣṭvā svar-gatiṁ prārthayante
te puṇyam āsādya surendra-lokam
aśnanti divyān divi deva-bhogān

Those who perform some rituals as described in the three Vedas (*Rig, Sama, Yajur*), and drink *Soma* juice, are purified of all sins and worship Me by performing sacrifice (*Yajna*) for the attainment of heaven. As a result of their good deeds, they certainly obtain heaven (where gods reside) and enjoy godly pleasures. (9.20)

Q Can one stay in heaven forever?

ते तं भुक्त्वा स्वर्गलोकं विशालं
क्षीणे पुण्ये मर्त्यलोकं विशन्ति।
एवं त्रैधर्म्यमनुप्रपन्ना
गतागतं कामकामा लभन्ते ।। 21 ।।

Heaven is not the final destination

te taṁ bhuktvā svarga-lokaṁ viśālaṁ
kṣīṇe puṇye martya-lokaṁ viśanti
evaṁ trayī-dharmam anuprapannā
gatāgataṁ kāma-kāmā labhante

After enjoying the wide world of heavenly pleasures thus exhausting their good *karma* (*Punya*), they return to the mortal world. Thus, conforming to the injunctions of the three Vedas and desirous of enjoyment, they repeatedly come and go from the mortal world to heaven and back. (9.21)

Q Can a devotee rely 100 percent on God?

अनन्याश्चिन्तयन्तो मां ये जनाः पर्युपासते।
तेषां नित्याभियुक्तानां योगक्षेमं वहाम्यहम् ।। 22 ।।

ananyāś cintayanto māṁ ye janāḥ paryupāsate
teṣāṁ nityābhiyuktānāṁ yoga-kṣemaṁ vahāmy aham

Devotees who always worships me with undivided devotion and are ever united in thoughts with me (meditating on me, living in my Consciousness i.e. lives conscious of my presence), I personally take care of their spiritual and material needs and bring prosperity and security to them. (9.22)

Q Should one worship other gods/*devas*?

येऽप्यन्यदेवता भक्ता यजन्ते श्रद्धयान्विताः।
तेऽपि मामेव कौन्तेय यजन्त्यविधिपूर्वकम् ॥ 23 ॥

ye 'py anya-devatā-bhaktā yajante śraddhayānvitāḥ
te 'pi mām eva kaunteya yajanty avidhi-pūrvakam

O Arjuna, even those devotees who worship other gods with faith, they too worship only Me but in an improper method (due to ignorance). (9.23)

Q What happens to Atheists, who do not know or recognize God?

अहं हि सर्वयज्ञानां भोक्ता च प्रभुरेव च।
न तु मामभिजानन्ति तत्त्वेनातश्च्यवन्ति ते ॥ 24 ॥

ahaṁ hi sarva-yajñānāṁ bhoktā ca prabhur eva ca
na tu mām abhijānanti tattvenātaś cyavanti te

I, the Lord of universe, am alone the Receiver and the Enjoyer of all sacrificial services made (*Yajna*). But these people do not recognize Me in reality and so they fall (to the mortal world of birth and death). (9.24)

Q What is the result of worshipping demi-gods (*devas*) and not Him (Supreme Being)?

यान्ति देवव्रता देवान्पितॄन्यान्ति पितृव्रताः।
भूतानि यान्ति भूतेज्या यान्ति मद्याजिनोऽपि माम् ॥ 25 ॥

yānti deva-vratā devān
pitṝn yānti pitṛ-vratāḥ
bhūtāni yānti bhūtejyā
yānti mad-yājino 'pi mām

You get what you pray for—God or ghost

Energy follows thoughts

The worshippers of demi-gods (*devas*) go to the demi-gods, the worshippers of ancestors go to the ancestors and the worshippers of ghosts (evil spirits) go to the ghosts (take birth among them) Those who worship Me attain Me (freedom from the cycle of birth and death). (9.25)

God accepts things only from a pure heart with love

Q What should I offer God and how?

पंत्र पुष्पं फलं तोयं यो मे भक्त्या प्रयच्छति ।
तदहं भक्त्युपहृतमश्नामि प्रयतात्मन: ।। 26 ।।

patraṁ puṣpaṁ phalaṁ toyaṁ
yo me bhaktyā prayacchati
tad ahaṁ bhakty-upahṛtam
aśnāmi prayatātmanaḥ

God wants only our PURE HEART, not fancy things

Whosoever offers Me a leaf, a flower, a fruit, or water, with love and devotion from a pure heart, I accept that pious offering of the pure minded with great pleasure and love. (9.26)

Q How do I offer my services to God?

यत्करोषि यदश्नासि यज्जुहोषि ददासि यत् ।
यत्तपस्यसि कौन्तेय तत्कुरुष्व मदर्पणम् ।। 27 ।।

yat karoṣi yad aśnāsi yaj juhoṣi dadāsi yat
yat tapasyasi kaunteya tat kuruṣva mad-arpaṇam

O Arjuna, whatever you do, whatever you eat, whatever you offer as an oblation to the sacred fire (*Yajna*), whatever you give as charity, whatever you practice as austerity, perform all these as an offering to Me. (9.27)

Q How to be free from the consequences of action?

शुभाशुभफलैरेवं मोक्ष्यसे कर्मबन्धनै: ।
संन्यासयोगयुक्तात्मा विमुक्तो मामुपैष्यसि ।। 28 ।।

śubhāśubha-phalair evaṁ
mokṣyase karma-bandhanaiḥ
sannyāsa-yoga-yuktātmā
vimukto mām upaiṣyasi

In this way you will be totally released from the bondage of action and its auspicious and inauspicious results (good and bad consequences). Thus, with your mind firmly established in the Yoga of renunciation, you will be liberated and come to Me. (9.28)

A sinner can also become a saint

Q Who is close to God and who is He close to?

समोऽहं सर्वभूतेषु न मे द्वेष्योऽस्ति न प्रियः।
ये भजन्ति तु मां भक्त्या मयि ते तेषु चाप्यहम् ॥29॥

samo 'haṁ sarva-bhūteṣu
na me dveṣyo 'sti na priyaḥ
ye bhajanti tu māṁ bhaktyā
mayi te teṣu cāpy aham

God is as close to us as we want Him to be

I am equal to all beings. There is none hateful nor dear to Me (favorite and non-favorite). However, those who worship Me (follow and practice my teachings) with love and devotion are very near and dear to Me. I am also very near and dear to them. (9.29)

Q Can a sinner worship God and become His devotee and a saint?

अपि चेत्सुदुराचारो भजते मामनन्यभाक्।
साधुरेव स मन्तव्यः सम्यग्व्यवसितो हि सः॥30॥

api cet su-durācāro
bhajate mām ananya-bhāk
sādhur eva sa mantavyaḥ
samyag vyavasito hi saḥ

No one is exluded from God's Grace

क्षिप्रं भवति धर्मात्मा शश्वच्छान्तिं निगच्छति।
कौन्तेय प्रतिजानीहि न मे भक्तः प्रणश्यति॥31॥

kṣipraṁ bhavati dharmātmā
śaśvac-chāntiṁ nigacchati
kaunteya pratijānīhi
na me bhaktaḥ praṇaśyati

Even if the most sinful person worships Me with undivided devotion, he should certainly be regarded as righteous for making the right resolution. (9.30)

Soon he becomes virtuous (righteous) and attains Eternal Peace. O Arjuna, know for certain that My devotee is never ruined. (9.31)

Glories of selfless devotion

Q Is anyone excluded from approaching and attaining God?

मां हि पार्थ व्यपाश्रित्य येऽपि स्युः पापयोनयः।
स्त्रियोवैश्यास्तथा शूद्रास्तेऽपि यान्ति परां गतिम् ॥ 32 ॥

māṁ hi pārtha vyapāśritya ye 'pi syuḥ pāpa-yonayaḥ
striyo vaiśyās tathā śūdrās te 'pi yānti parāṁ gatim

O Arjuna, anybody, including even those born of sinful parents, women*, traders (*Vaisyas*) and laborers (*Sudras*) can attain the Supreme Goal of their life just by surrendering unto My will with love and devotion. (9.32)

Q What are the two easiest and simplest ways to attain God?

किं पुनर्ब्राह्मणाः पुण्या भक्ता राजर्षयस्तथा।
अनित्यमसुखं लोकमिमं प्राप्त भजस्व माम् ॥ 33 ॥

kiṁ punar brāhmaṇāḥ puṇyā
bhaktā rājarṣayas tathā
anityam asukhaṁ lokam
imaṁ prāpya bhajasva mām

Surrender and selfless service will lead to Liberation

How much easier it is then for the righteous *Brahmanas* and the royal sages, who are entirely devoted to Me, to attain the Supreme State. Therefore, now that you are in this temporary, miserable world, seek refuge in Me and devote yourself to worshiping Me alone. (9.33)

***Note:** Since Draupadi, the queen of the family was treated disrespectfully, Lord Krishna reemphasized to make sure that women are also part of Him and must be treated fairly and with respect.

One of the most disgraceful incidents in the Mahabharata was the public humiliation and disrobing of Draupadi (wife of Pandavas) by the Kauravas. After Yudhishtara, the eldest brother of Pandavas loses everything including his kingdom, brothers and wife in the game of dice, the Kauravas wanted to avenge themselves by dishonoring Draupadi. One of the Kaurava brothers drags her by the hair into the court. Nobody responds to Draupadi's cries for help—the elders in the family, the sages, the learned; none at all. Draupadi then prays to Lord Krishna. The Lord saves her dignity and honor by giving her an endless sari. The Lord wanted everyone to know that a woman is also a part of His creation and Him. She should be treated with respect and not exploited and objectified.

Q How to worship God and why should one set the Supreme Goal of his Life to merge with Him?

मन्मना भव मद्भक्तो मद्याजी मां नमस्कुरु।
मामेवैष्यसि युक्त्वैवमात्मानं मत्परायण: ।। 34 ।।

man-manā bhava mad-bhakto mad-yājī māṁ namaskuru
mām evaiṣyasi yuktvaivam ātmānaṁ mat-parāyaṇaḥ

Fix your mind on Me, be devoted to Me, worship Me and bow down to Me (surrender) thus, uniting yourself with Me and setting Me as your Supreme Goal, you will certainly come to Me. (9.34)

Lessons to learn and practice in daily life

Everything is God's manifestation and He can be seen in everything and everywhere (kan kan me)

1. We must set the Supreme goal of life, Self-Realization and perform every activity in life to attain God.
2. Since everything is God manifestation, try to see him in everything.
3. We must serve His creation with love and devotion and with the attitude that we are performing every action for Him.
4. Consider "work as worship," as if we are doing it for Him (Higher cause) and our every action must be an offering to Him (*Puja*).
5. All of our offerings (thoughts and actions to God must be totally pure, free from the 5 + 2 Enemies) as a Prasad to Him.
6. We should pray to and worship God to attain Self-Realization and not just for worldly things.
7. We must have faith in God and fully trust Him that He knows the best and He will do the best for us.

The Lord is more than His creation.

—Dr. Radhakrishna

ॐ तत्सदिति श्रीमद्भगवद्गीतासूपनिषत्सु ब्रह्मविद्यायां योगशास्त्रे
श्रीकृष्णार्जुनसंवादे राजविद्याराजगुह्ययोगो नाम नवमोऽध्यायः ।।

AUM TAT SAT

Thus ends the ninth chapter named "*Rajavidya-Rajaguhya Yoga*"
The Path of the Most Secret and Sacred Knowledge
in the *Upanishad* of the glorious Bhagavad Gita, the scripture of Yoga,
the science of the Absolute (*Brahman*), in the form of the dialogue
between Lord Krishna and Arjuna.

Aum Shanti, Shanti, Shantihi

The Ultimate Purpose of Life

What is the Purpose of Life/Supreme goal of life (one of the basic question): Answers could be many but ultimate is only one, "Be Happy, peaceful and live in Anandam"

Attain freedom from miseries and stress

Attain freedom from, anger, fear and stress

Lead Balanced Life

Do Self-Purification and Self-Realization

Remove vices and develop virtues

Attain Supreme Satisfaction and Contentment

Unite with Supreme-Conscious (Super-Conscious)

See God equally in all beings

Attain that Supreme state, where one does not return again

Attain Liberation (Moksha)

Live in Love

Live in Peace and Anandam

Attain God/Self-Realization

Realize my true nature, 'SAT CHIT ANANDAM'

The Ultimate Goal of Life is
"Be happy, live in Peace, and Anandam and spread the same to others"

GOD is the

Best of the Best
Best of the Best
Best of the Best
Best of the Best
Best of the Best
Best of the Best
Best of the Best
Best of the Best

Lord
KRISHNA

VIBHUTI YOGA

The Path of Divine Glories and Manifestations

Union with God (Self-Realization) through the path of knowing His Divine Manifestations (Glories)

God is everything and everything is God

In the previous chapter, Lord Krishna guided Arjuna regarding how to serve Him in a manner that would lead to a Union with Him. He emphasized that what we offer Him is not important, but how we make offerings to Him is the most important. He only wants our love, not fancy things from us, therefore, whatever we can afford to offer Him, we must do it with love and devotion.

In this chapter, Lord Krishna enlightened Arjuna by further revealing who HE (God) is, where He lives and how to see Him. Lord Krishna declared that everything in the universe is His Manifestation and His Power (*Yoga-Maya, Shakti*), and made it easier for us to see God everywhere and relate to Him.

God is Omnipotent, Omniscient and Omnipresent

Therefore, we do not have to look hard or go far to find Him. He is present wherever we are, in every shape and form, from space to earth, mountain to river, water to food and animal to people, etc. We just have to be aware of Him and His presence. We should feel Him, see Him, hear Him and then we will find Him everywhere in the universe. Therefore, one could easily serve Him only by serving His creation.

Everything in the universe is because of God. No matter where you look, you will see nothing but God

Main Message

God is the source of All. To know Him is to know All

—Dr. Radhakrishna

1. God is the cause of everything in the universe.
2. The entire universe (both the material world and the spiritual world) is His expression which is only a partial manifestation of His energy (Yogic Power/ *Shakti*) and His majesty. (10.42)
3. All the qualities in human beings arise from God.

Chapter Overview

01–07	God's glories and His Yogic Power (Supreme Energy)
08–11	Devotion Yoga – its fruit and glories
12–18	Arjuna's praises of God's glories and His Yogic Power
19–42	Lord Krishna describes His glories and power of Yoga

God's glories and His Yogic Power (Supreme Energy)

Q What else did Lord Krishna tell Arjuna and why?

श्रीभगवानुवाच
भूय एव महाबाहो श‍ृणु मे परमं वचः।
यत्तेऽहं प्रीयमाणाय वक्ष्यामि हितकाम्यया॥1॥

śrī-bhagavān uvāca
bhūya eva mahā-bāho
śṛṇu me paramaṁ vacaḥ
yat te 'haṁ prīyamāṇāya
vakṣyāmi hita-kāmyayā

God is the origin and the reason of everything

The Supreme Lord said: O Arjuna, once again listen to My Supreme word. As you are very dear to Me, I will speak to you for your benefit. (10.01)

Q Does anyone know the origin of God?

न मे विदुः सुरगणाः प्रभवं न महर्षयः।
अहमादिर्हि देवानां महर्षीणां च सर्वशः॥2॥

na me viduḥ sura-gaṇāḥ prabhavaṁ na maharṣayaḥ
aham ādir hi devānāṁ maharṣīṇāṁ ca sarvaśaḥ

Neither demi-gods (*devas*) nor the great sages know the secret of My origin because I am the origin of all the gods and also of great sages in all respects. (10.02)

Q Who is a wise person and what are the benefits of being wise?

यो मामजमनादिं च वेत्ति लोकमहेश्वरम्।
असंमूढः स मर्त्येषु सर्वपापैः प्रमुच्यते॥3॥

yo mām ajam anādiṁ ca vetti loka-maheśvaram
asammūḍhaḥ sa martyeṣu sarva-pāpaiḥ pramucyate

One who knows Me as Unborn, without beginning and as the Supreme Lord of the universe is regarded learned among the mortals and is liberated from all sins (the bondage of *karma*). (10.03)

Q What are the various qualities and where do they come from?

बुद्धिर्ज्ञानमसंमोहः क्षमा सत्यं दमः शमः।
सुखं दुःखं भवोऽभावो भयं चाभयमेव च ॥4॥

buddhir jñānam asammohaḥ
kṣamā satyaṁ damaḥ śamaḥ
sukhaṁ duḥkhaṁ bhavo 'bhāvo
bhayaṁ cābhayam eva ca

All the attributes originate from God

अहिंसा समता तुष्टिस्तो दानं यशोऽयशः।
भवन्ति भावा भूतानां मत्त एव पृथग्विधाः ॥5॥

ahiṁsā samatā tuṣṭis tapo dānaṁ yaśo 'yaśaḥ
bhavanti bhāvā bhūtānāṁ matta eva pṛthag-vidhāḥ

1. Discrimination
2. Wisdom
3. Non-delusion
4. Forgiveness
5. Truthfulness
6. Control over the mind and senses
7. Tranquility
8. Joy
9. Sorrow
10. Evolution and dissolution (birth and death)
11. Fear, fearlessness
12. Nonviolence
13. Equanimity
14. Contentment
15. Austerity
16. Charity
17. Fame and ill fame

All of these diverse qualities in human beings originate from Me alone. (10.04–05)

Q How did all the creatures of the world come into existence?

महर्षयः सप्त पूर्वे चत्वारो मनवस्तथा।
मद्भावा मानसा जाता येषां लोक इमाः प्रजाः ॥6॥

maharṣayaḥ sapta pūrve catvāro manavas tathā
mad-bhāvā mānasā jātā yeṣāṁ loka imāḥ prajāḥ

The seven great sages (*Maharishis*), and before them, four *Sanakas* and the *Manus* (progenitors of mankind), possessed power like Me, were born from my mind (potential energy) and from them all the creatures of the world were born. (10.06)

Q What is the benefit of knowing the glory of His manifestation and His Yogic Power?

एतां विभूतिं योगं च मम यो वेत्ति तत्त्वतः।
सोऽविकम्पेन योगेन युज्यते नात्र संशयः॥7॥

etāṁ vibhūtiṁ yogaṁ ca mama yo vetti tattvataḥ
so 'vikalpena yogena yujyate nātra saṁśayaḥ

One who truly understands the Supreme glory of My manifestation (Macrocosm) and Yogic Power (Microcosm) is united with Me by unshakeable Yoga, there is no doubt about it. (10.07)

Devotion Yoga – its fruit and glories

Q Why do the wise worship God?

अहं सर्वस्व प्रभवो मत्तः सर्वं प्रवर्तते।
इति मत्वा भजन्ते मां बुधा भावसमन्विताः॥8॥

ahaṁ sarvasya prabhavo mattaḥ sarvaṁ pravartate
iti matvā bhajante māṁ budhā bhāva-samanvitāḥ

I am the source of all creation (spiritual and material worlds). Everything evolves from Me. Understanding this, the wise worship Me with hearts full of love and devotion. (10.08)

Q How can one worship God and develop the feeling of His existence?

मच्चित्ता मद्गतप्राणा बोधयन्तः परस्परम्।
कथयन्तश्च मां नित्यं तुष्यन्ति च रमन्ति च॥9॥

mac-cittā mad-gata-prāṇā
bodhayantaḥ parasparam
kathayantaś ca māṁ nityaṁ
tuṣyanti ca ramanti ca

Divine souls enjoy talking about God to others

Those pure devotees remain ever content and delighted whose minds remain absorbed in Me and who have surrendered their lives to Me. They always enlighten each other by talking about Me. (10.09)

Q What does God grant His devotees?

तेषां सततयुक्तानां भजतां प्रीतिपूर्वकम्।
ददामि बुद्धियोगं तं येन मामुपयान्ति ते ।। 10 ।।

teṣāṁ satata-yuktānāṁ
bhajatāṁ prīti-pūrvakam
dadāmi buddhi-yogaṁ taṁ
yena māṁ upayānti te

God gives wisdom to His devotees

तेषामेवानुकम्पार्थमहमज्ञानजं तमः।
नाशयाम्यात्मभावस्थो ज्ञानदीपेन भास्वता ।। 11 ।।

teṣām evānukampārtham aham ajñāna-jaṁ tamaḥ
nāśayāmy ātma-bhāva-stho jñāna-dīpena bhāsvatā

To those who are ever united with Me with devotion and worship me with love, I grant the Yoga of understanding-integral wisdom (Transcendental Knowledge) by which they attain Me. (10.10)

Out of mere compassion for them, I dwell within their inner psyche (heart) as Consciousness and destroy the darkness born of ignorance by the luminous lamp of wisdom (Self-Knowledge). (10.11)

Arjuna's praises of God's glories and His Yogic Power

Q Why is God known as the Eternal Divine?

अर्जुन उवाच
परं ब्रह्म परं धाम पवित्रं परमं भवान्।
पुरुषं शाश्वतं दिव्यमादिदेवमजं विभुम् ।। 12 ।।

arjuna uvāca
paraṁ brahma paraṁ dhāma pavitraṁ paramaṁ bhavān
puruṣaṁ śāśvataṁ divyam ādi-devam ajaṁ vibhum

आहुस्त्वामृषयः सर्वे देवर्षिर्नारदस्तथा।
असितो देवलो व्यासः स्वयं चैव ब्रवीषि मे ।। 13 ।।

āhus tvām ṛṣayaḥ sarve devarṣir nāradas tathā
asito devalo vyāsaḥ svayaṁ caiva bravīṣi me

Arjuna said: You are:

1. The Supreme Brahman
2. The Supreme Abode
3. The Supreme Purifier

4. The Absolute Truth
5. The Eternal Divine Being
6. The Primal God
7. The Unborn
8. The Omnipresent

All the great sages including the celestial sages such as *Narada*, *Asita*, *Devala* and *Vyasa* have thus declared You as the Eternal Divine, and now You Yourself are telling the same to me. (10.12–13)

Q Does anyone understand the real nature of God?

सर्वमेतदृतं मन्ये यन्मां वदसि केशव।
न हि ते भगवन्व्यक्तिं विदुर्देवा न दानवाः ।। 14 ।।

sarvam etad ṛtaṁ manye yan māṁ vadasi keśava
na hi te bhagavan vyaktiṁ vidur devā na dānavāḥ

I believe all this to be true, O Supreme Lord neither the demi-gods (*devas*) nor the demons fully understand Your manifestation (Real nature). (10.14)

Q Who knows God's manifestation?

स्वयमेवात्मनात्मानं वेत्थ त्वं पुरुषोत्तम।
भूतभावन भूतेश देवदेव जगत्पते ।। 15 ।।

svayam evātmanātmānaṁ
vettha tvaṁ puruṣottama
bhūta-bhāvana bhūteśa
deva-deva jagat-pate

No one knows the real nature of God except God Himself

O greatest of all beings (*Purushottama*), O Supreme person, O origin of all, O Lord of everything, God of all gods (demi-gods, *devas*) and Lord of the entire universe, only You know Yourself by Your own internal potency (Divine Power/*Shakti*). (10.15)

Q Can anyone describe God?

वक्तुमर्हस्यशेषेण दिव्या ह्यात्मविभूतयः।
याभिर्विभूतिभिर्लोकानिमांस्त्वं व्याप्य तिष्ठसि ।। 16 ।।

vaktum arhasy aśeṣeṇa divyā hy ātma-vibhūtayaḥ
yābhir vibhūtibhir lokān imāṁs tvaṁ vyāpya tiṣṭhasi

Therefore, only You alone can tell me about Your divine glories or the manifestations by which You pervade all the universe. (10.16)

Q Why did Arjuna want to know more about Lord Krishna's glories?

कथं विद्यामहं योगिंस्त्वां सदा परिचिन्तयन्।
केषु केषु च भावेषु चिन्त्योऽसि भगवन्मया ।। 17 ।।

kathaṁ vidyām ahaṁ yogiṁs tvāṁ sadā paricintayan
keṣu keṣu ca bhāveṣu cintyo 'si bhagavan mayā

विस्तरेणात्मनो योगं विभूतिं च जनार्दन।
भूयः कथय तृप्तिर्हि शृण्वतो नास्ति मेऽमृतम् ।। 18 ।।

vistareṇātmano yogaṁ vibhūtiṁ ca janārdana
bhūyaḥ kathaya tṛptir hi śṛṇvato nāsti me 'mṛtam

O Master of Yoga, how may I know You through constant contemplation and meditation? In what particular form of yours shall I contemplate on You, O Lord? (10.17)

O Lord Krishna, please tell me again in full detail of Your power of Yoga and Your divine manifestations (Glories, *Vibhuties*) because I am not yet satiated by hearing Your nectar-like speech. (10.18)

Lord Krishna describes His glories and power of Yoga

Q Is there any limit to the Lord's manifestations?

श्रीभगवानुवाच
हन्त ते कथयिष्यामि दिव्या ह्यात्मविभूतयः।
प्राधान्यतः कुरुश्रेष्ठ नास्त्यन्तो विस्तरस्य मे ।। 19 ।।

śrī-bhagavān uvāca
hanta te kathayiṣyāmi
divyā hy ātma-vibhūtayaḥ
prādhānyataḥ kuru-śreṣṭha
nāsty anto vistarasya me

Everything in the univese is God's manifestation

The Supreme Lord said: O Arjuna, now I will tell you My Divine Manifestations but only main ones, because there is no end to My Manifestations. (10.19)

Q What is God's true nature?

अहमात्मा गुडाकेश सर्वभूताशयस्थितः।
अहमादिश्च मध्यं च भूतानामन्त एव च ।। 20 ।।

aham ātmā guḍākeśa
sarva-bhūtāśaya-sthitaḥ
aham ādiś ca madhyaṁ ca
bhūtānām anta eva ca

God lives in the heart of all

O Arjuna, I am the Supreme-Soul (Supreme Spirit, God) seated in the hearts (inner psyche) of all living beings. I am also the beginning, the middle, and indeed the end of all beings. (10.20)

Q What are God's manifestations (Attributes, Divine Glories)?

आदित्यानामहं विष्णुर्ज्योतिषां रविरंशुमान्।
मरीचिर्मरुतामस्मि नक्षत्राणामहं शशी ।। 21 ।।

ādityānām ahaṁ viṣṇur jyotiṣāṁ ravir aṁśumān
marīcir marutām asmi nakṣatrāṇām ahaṁ śaśī

वेदानां सामवेदोऽस्मि देवानामस्मि वासवः।
इन्द्रियाणां मनश्चास्मि भूतानामस्मि चेतना ।। 22 ।।

vedānāṁ sāma-vedo 'smi devānām asmi vāsavaḥ
indriyāṇāṁ manaś cāsmi bhūtānām asmi cetanā

रुद्राणां शङ्करश्चास्मि वित्तेशो यक्षरक्षसाम्।
वसूनां पावकश्चास्मि मेरुः शिखरिणामहम् ।। 23 ।।

rudrāṇāṁ śaṅkaraś cāsmi vitteśo yakṣa-rakṣasām
vasūnāṁ pāvakaś cāsmi meruḥ śikhariṇām aham

पुरोधसां च मुख्यं मां विद्धि पार्थ बृहस्पतिम्।
सेनानीनामहं स्कन्दः सरसामस्मि सागरः ।। 24 ।।

purodhasāṁ ca mukhyaṁ māṁ
viddhi pārtha bṛhaspatim
senānīnām ahaṁ skandaḥ
sarasām asmi sāgaraḥ

God's glories are unlimited

महर्षीणां भृगुरहं गिरामस्म्येकमक्षरम्।
यज्ञानां जपयज्ञोऽस्मि स्थावराणां हिमालयः ।। 25 ।।

maharṣīṇāṁ bhṛgur ahaṁ girām asmy ekam akṣaram
yajñānāṁ japa-yajño 'smi sthāvarāṇāṁ himālayaḥ

अश्वत्थः सर्ववृक्षाणां देवर्षीणां च नारदः।
गन्धर्वाणां चित्ररथः सिद्धानां कपिलो मुनिः ।। 26 ।।

aśvatthaḥ sarva-vṛkṣāṇāṁ devarṣīṇāṁ ca nāradaḥ
gandharvāṇāṁ citrarathaḥ siddhānāṁ kapilo muniḥ

उच्चैःश्रवसमश्वानां विद्धि माममृतोद्भवम्।
ऐरावतं गजेन्द्राणां नराणां च नराधिपम् ।। 27 ।।

uccaiḥśravasam aśvānāṁ viddhi mām amṛtodbhavam
airāvataṁ gajendrāṇāṁ narāṇāṁ ca narādhipam

God is the best of the best

आयुधानामहं वज्रं धेनूनामस्मि कामधुक् ।
प्रजनश्चास्मि कन्दर्पः सर्पाणामस्मि वासुकिः ।। 28 ।।

āyudhānām ahaṁ vajraṁ dhenūnām asmi kāmadhuk
prajanaś cāsmi kandarpaḥ sarpāṇām asmi vāsukiḥ

अनन्तश्चास्मि नागानां वरुणो यादसामहम् ।
पितृणामर्यमा चास्मि यमः संयमतामहम् ।। 29 ।।

anantaś cāsmi nāgānāṁ varuṇo yādasām aham
pitṝṇām aryamā cāsmi yamaḥ saṁyamatām aham

प्रह्लादाश्चास्मि दैत्यानां कालः कलयतामहम् ।
मृगाणां च मृगेन्द्रोऽहं वैनतेयश्च पक्षिणाम् ।। 30 ।।

prahlādaś cāsmi daityānāṁ kālaḥ kalayatām aham
mṛgāṇāṁ ca mṛgendro 'haṁ vainateyaś ca pakṣiṇām

पवनः पवतामस्मि रामः शस्त्रभृतामहम् ।
झषाणां मकरश्चास्मि स्रोतसामस्मि जाह्नवी ।। 31 ।।

God is Omnipotent, Omniscient and Omnipresent

pavanaḥ pavatām asmi
rāmaḥ śastra-bhṛtām aham
jhaṣāṇāṁ makaraś cāsmi
srotasām asmi jāhnavī

सर्गाणामादिरन्तश्च मध्यं चैवाहमर्जुन ।
अध्यात्मविद्या विद्यानां वादः प्रवदतामहम् ।। 32 ।।

sargāṇām ādir antaś ca madhyaṁ caivāham arjuna
adhyātma-vidyā vidyānāṁ vādaḥ pravadatām aham

अक्षराणामकारोऽस्मि द्वन्द्वः सामासिकस्य च ।
अहमेवाक्षयः कालो धाताहं विश्वतोमुखः ।। 33 ।।

akṣarāṇām a-kāro 'smi dvandvaḥ sāmāsikasya ca
aham evākṣayaḥ kālo dhātāhaṁ viśvato-mukhaḥ

मृत्युः सर्वहरश्चाहमुद्भवश्च भविष्यताम् ।
कीर्तिः श्रीर्वाक्च नारीणां स्मृतिर्मेधा धृतिः क्षमा ।। 34 ।।

mṛtyuḥ sarva-haraś cāham
udbhavaś ca bhaviṣyatām
kīrtiḥ śrīr vāk ca nārīṇāṁ
smṛtir medhā dhṛtiḥ kṣamā

बृहत्साम तथा साम्नां गायत्री छन्दसामहम् ।
मासानां मार्गशीर्षोऽहमृतूनां कुसुमाकरः ।। 35 ।।

bṛhat-sāma tathā sāmnāṁ gāyatrī chandasām aham
māsānāṁ mārga-śīrṣo 'ham ṛtūnāṁ kusumākaraḥ

द्यूतं छलयतामस्मि तेजस्तेजस्विनामहम् ।
जयोऽस्मि व्यवसायोऽस्मि सत्त्वं सत्त्ववतामहम् ।। 36 ।।

dyūtaṁ chalayatām asmi tejas tejasvinām aham
jayo 'smi vyavasāyo 'smi sattvaṁ sattvavatām aham

वृष्णीनां वासुदेवोऽस्मि पाण्डवानां धनंजयः ।
मुनीनामप्यहं व्यासः कवीनामुशना कविः ।। 37 ।।

vṛṣṇīnāṁ vāsudevo 'smi pāṇḍavānāṁ dhanañjayaḥ
munīnām apy ahaṁ vyāsaḥ kavīnām uśanā kaviḥ

दण्डो दमयतामस्मि नीतिरस्मि जिगीषताम् ।
मौनं चैवास्मि गुह्यानां ज्ञानं ज्ञानवतामहम् ।। 38 ।।

daṇḍo damayatām asmi nītir asmi jigīṣatām
maunaṁ caivāsmi guhyānāṁ jñānaṁ jñānavatām aham

O Arjuna,

1. I am Vishnu (Sustainer) among the (twelve) sons of Aditi (*Adityas*).
2. I am the Radiant Sun among the luminaries.
3. I am Marici among the supernatural controllers of wind (*Maruts – Gods of wind and storm*).
4. I am the moon among the stars. (10.21)
5. I am *Sama Veda* among the Vedas
6. I am Indra (the celestial ruler, the king of Heaven—god of rain), among the gods (*devas*).
7. I am the mind among the senses
8. I am the Consciousness (living force) in living beings. (10.22)
9. I am Lord Shiva among the Rudras (gods of destruction)
10. I am Kubera (Lord of wealth) among the Yakshas (celestial beings) and demons
11. I am Pavaka (god of fire-purifier) among the Vasus (gods of elements)
12. I am Meru among the mountains. (10.23)
13. I am the chief Brhaspati among the priests
14. I am Skanda (Kartikeya) among the army generals of the celestial controllers
15. I am the ocean, O Arjuna among the bodies of water. (10.24)
16. I am Bhrgu among the great sages
17. I am the monosyllable Cosmic sound (most sacred), ॐ '*AUM*' among the words.
18. I am *Japa-Yajna* (constant repetition of God's name-mantra) among the *Yajna* (sacrifices).
19. I am the Himalaya among the immovables. (10.25)
20. I am the holy banyan tree (Ashwattha) among all the trees.
21. I am Narada among the celestial sages.

22. I am Citraratha among the *Gandharvas* (Celestial musicians).
23. I am Kapila among the *Siddhas*/perfected sage. (10.26)
24. I am the celestial horse Uccaihsravas, born during the churning of the ocean along with nectar among the horses.
25. I am Airavata among the celestial elephants.
26. I am the King among men.
27. I am the thunderbolt among the weapons.
28. I am celestial wish–granting cow Kamadhenu among cows.
29. I am Cupid (Kandarpah, god of love) among progenitors.
30. I am Vasuki among the serpents. (10.27–28)
31. I am Ananta among *Nagas* (serpents, snakes).
32. I am god Varun among the water-gods.
33. I am Aryam among the manes (ancestors).
34. I am Yama (God of death) among the governors.
35. I am devoted Prahlad (*Daitya*-demon (enemy of gods), who defected from demons, became pious and worshipped Lord Vishnu), among the *Daitya*.
36. I am Time among calculators.
37. I am the Lion among beasts.
38. I am Garuda (the vehicle of Lord Vishnu) among the birds. (10.29–30)
39. I am the wind among the purifiers.
40. I am Lord Rama among the warriors.
41. I am the crocodile among the fishes.
42. I am the holy Ganga among the rivers. (10.31)
43. I am the beginning, the middle, and the end of all creation, O Arjuna.
44. I am the Science of Self (Supreme knowledge, Spiritual knowledge) among sciences (all knowledge).
45. I am the logic among debtors. (10.32)
46. I am the letter "A" (first letter of alphabets) among the alphabet.
47. I am the dual compound among compound words.
48. I am endless time (*Aksaya Kala*). I am the all-pervading sustainer/preserver, with My face in all directions (I am omniscient). (10.33)
49. I am the all-devouring death and the origin of future beings.
50. In the feminine virtues (seven Goddess qualities), I am-
    a. Fame (*Kirtih*)
    b. Prosperity (*Sri*)
    c. Speech (*Vak*)
    d. Memory (*Smritih*)
    e. Intelligence/wisdom (*Medha*)
    f. Firmness (*Dhritih*)
    g. Forgiveness (*Ksama*) (10.34)

51. I am Brihat Sama among the *Sama* hymns
52. I am Gayatri among the Vedic mantras
53. I am Marghsirsh (Name of the month sacred for worship-mid November to mid December) among the months
54. I am flower-bearing spring among the seasons. (10.35)
55. I am the gambling amongst deceitful practices.
56. I am the glory of the glorious
57. I am the victory of the victorious
58. I am the determination of the determined
59. I am the Goodness of the good (Truth of the truth-tellers). (10.36)
60. I am Vasudeva (another name of Lord Krishna) among the *Vrishnis* family
61. I am Arjuna among the Pandavas
62. I am Vyasa among the sages (One who compiled the Vedas and is also the author of Puranas and Mahabharata – Hindu scriptures from India).
63. I am Usana among the poets. (10.37)
64. I am the ruling power in rulers
65. I am the righteousness of those who seek victory
66. I am silence, the protector of worthwhile secrets
67. I am the wisdom of the wise (10.38)

Q Where do all beings originate from?

यच्चापि सर्वभूतानां बीजं तदहमर्जुन।
न तदस्ति विना यत्स्यान्मया भूतं चराचरम् ।। 39 ।।

yac cāpi sarva-bhūtānāṁ
bījaṁ tad aham arjuna
na tad asti vinā yat syān
mayā bhūtaṁ carācaram

God is the source of everything

O Arjuna, I am also the origin or seed of all beings. There is nothing, moving or non-moving (living beings and non-living beings) that can exist without Me. (10.39)

Q Is there any limit to His attributes?

नान्तोऽस्ति मम दिव्यानां विभूतीनां परंतप।
एष तूद्देशत: प्रोक्तो विभूतेर्विस्तरो मया ।। 40 ।।

nānto 'sti mama divyānāṁ vibhūtīnāṁ parantapa
eṣa tūddeśataḥ prokto vibhūter vistaro maya

O mighty conqueror of enemies (Arjuna), there is no limit to My Divine Attributes (*Vibhuties*). This is only a brief description by Me of the extent (just a sample) of My Divine Manifestations. (10.40)

Q Where does all the glory and beauty of the universe come from?

यद्यद्विभूतिमत्सत्त्वं श्रीमदूर्जितमेव वा।
तत्तदेवावगच्छ त्वं मम तेजोंऽशसंभवम् ॥41॥

yad yad vibhūtimat sattvaṁ
śrīmad ūrjitam eva vā
tat tad evāvagaccha tvaṁ
mama tejo-'ṁśa-sambhavam

This universe is only a small fraction of God's manifestation

Whatever is glorious, beautiful and powerful, know that all have manifested from a minuscule part of My limitless splendor. (10.41)

Q How much do we really need to know about God?

अथवा बहुनैतेन किं ज्ञातेन तवार्जुन।
विष्टभ्याहमिदं कृत्स्नमेकांशेन स्थितो जगत् ॥42॥

atha vā bahunaitena kiṁ jñātena tavārjuna
viṣṭabhyāham idaṁ kṛtsnam ekāṁśena sthito jagat

What is the need for you to know all this in detail, O Arjuna? It is enough for you to know that I continually support this entire universe with a small fraction of My Divine Power (*Yoga-Maya*). (10.42)

Lessons to learn and practice in daily life

1. See God everywhere
2. Feel God everywhere
3. Listen to Him through your own inner voice (Supreme Consciousness)
4. See Him through His creation (Material Nature) in every situation, feel Him (through own intuitions), and worship Him every moment by serving His creation with love and devotion, and without any expectation of the fruit of action
5. Always live in His Consciousness/Awareness

God is in everything and in every moment
(Bhagvan Kan kan me hai, chan chan me hai)

ॐ तत्सदिति श्रीमद्भगवद्गीतासूपनिषत्सु ब्रह्मविद्यायां योगशास्त्रे
श्रीकृष्णार्जुनसंवादे विभूतियोगो नाम दशमोऽध्यायः ॥

AUM TAT SAT

Thus ends the tenth chapter named "*Vibhuti Yoga*"
The Path of Divine Glories and Manifestations
in the *Upanishad* of the glorious Bhagavad Gita, the scripture of Yoga,
the science of the Absolute (*Brahman*), in the form of the dialogue
between Lord Krishna and Arjuna.

Aum Shanti, Shanti, Shantihi

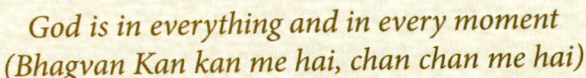

Cosmic Form

Self-Purification and Transformation through Divine Vision

VISVARUPA-DARSANA YOGA

The Path of the Divine Vision of the Cosmic Form

Union with God (Self-Realization) through the path of divine vision of His Cosmic Form

The Gita is the Vehicle to attain Self-Realization

Arjuna was so impressed with Lord Krishna's description of His manifestation and His Powers (*Shakti*) in the previous chapter that he wanted to actually see Him in that very form. Therefore, he requested Lord Krishna to show Himself in His Cosmic Form (Universal Form).

Lord Krishna granted his wish and gave Arjuna divine vision (Divya Jyoti) to see His Unlimited Universal Form because he could not be seen with regular vision.

God-Realization and Self-Realization is the Purpose and Supreme goal of our life

Main Message

Purity leads to divinity and divinity leads to unity (Union with God)

- One can get the divine vision of God (*Divya Jyoti*) only by God's grace if one has a pure conscience and devotion (no negativity, no I-ness/arrogance or my-ness/ possessiveness, none of the 5+2 enemies). No amount of spiritual studies, giving gifts or doing austerities and scarifies will entitle one to find such grace.

God's grace requires nothing but only purity of heart, love and devotion

- The last verse of this chapter (11.55) summarizes the teachings of the entire Gita, the purpose of human existence and the way to attain it. One can realize God and Self, if one sets Self-Realization and God-Realization as the Supreme goal of his life, does selfless service with love and devotion, eliminates the 5+2 enemies (impurities), is friendly to all and always lives in God's Consciousness.

The last shloka of this chapter is the essence of the whole Gita.

—Sri Shankarachaya

Selfless service with love (Karma Yoga) + Spiritual Practices (Sadhana) → Purity → Divinity → Unity (Union with God, Self-Realization)

Chapter Overview

01–04	Arjuna's request to see Lord Krishna's Cosmic Form
05–08	God's Cosmic Form and Arjuna's divine vision
09–14	Description of Lord Krishna's Cosmic Form
15–31	Arjuna's confusion, fear and praise of Lord's Cosmic Form
32–34	Lord Krishna describes His majestic power to Arjuna and encourages him to fulfill his duty
35–50	Arjuna's request to see Lord Krishna's four armed form
51–55	The vision of God can be obtained only through undivided devotion

Arjuna's request to see Lord Krishna's Cosmic Form

Q How did Arjuna's delusion vanish?

अर्जुन उवाच
मदनुग्रहाय परमं गुह्यमध्यात्मसंज्ञितम् ।
यत्त्वयोक्तं वचस्तेन मोहोऽयं विगतो मम ॥1॥

arjuna uvāca
mad-anugrahāya paramaṁ guhyam adhyātma-saṁjñitam
yat tvayoktaṁ vacas tena moho 'yaṁ vigato mama

भवाप्ययौ हि भूतानां श्रुतौ विस्तरशो मया ।
त्वत्तः कमलपत्राक्ष माहात्म्यमपि चाव्ययम् ॥2॥

bhavāpyayau hi bhūtānāṁ śrutau vistaraśo mayā
tvattaḥ kamala-patrākṣa māhātmyam api cāvyayam

Arjuna said to Lord Krishna: My delusion is gone by Your most profound and secret words of spiritual wisdom that You have spoken to me as an act of compassion. (11.01)

O Krishna, I have heard from You the origin and dissolution of beings in detail and Your immortal glory. (11.02)

Q How and why did Arjuna request to see Lord Krishna's Cosmic Form?

एवमेतद्यथात्थ त्वमात्मानं परमेश्वर।
द्रष्टुमिच्छामि ते रूपमैश्वरं पुरुषोत्तम ॥3॥

evam etad yathāttha tvam
  ātmānaṁ parameśvara
draṣṭum icchāmi te rūpam
  aiśvaraṁ puruṣottama

Prayer to see God in physical form

मन्यसे यदि तच्छक्यं मया द्रष्टुमिति प्रभो।
योगेश्वर ततो मे त्वं दर्शयात्मानमव्ययम् ॥4॥

manyase yadi tac chakyaṁ mayā draṣṭum iti prabho
yogeśvara tato me tvaṁ darśayātmānam avyayam

O Supreme Lord, You are precisely what you declared Yourself to be, yet I wish to see Your divine and mighty Cosmic Form, O *Purusottama* (Supreme Being). (11.03)

O Lord, if You think it is possible for me to see Your imperishable form then, O Lord of the Yoga (All Mystic Power), please reveal to me your Cosmic Form (Transcendental). (11.04)

God's Cosmic Form and Arjuna's divine vision

Q What did Lord Krishna's Cosmic Form look like?

श्रीभगवानुवाच
पश्य मे पार्थ रूपाणि शतशोऽथ सहस्रशः।
नानाविधानि दिव्यानि नानावर्णाकृतीनि च ॥5॥

śrī-bhagavān uvāca
paśya me pārtha rūpāṇi śataśo 'tha sahasraśaḥ
nānā-vidhāni divyāni nānā-varṇākṛtīni ca

पश्यादित्यान्वसून्रुद्रानश्विनौ मरुतस्तथा।
बहून्यदृष्टपूर्वाणि पश्याश्चर्याणि भारत ॥6॥

paśyādityān vasūn rudrān aśvinau marutas tathā
bahūny adṛṣṭa-pūrvāṇi paśyāścaryāṇi bhārata

इहैकस्थं जगत्कृत्स्नं पश्याद्य सचराचरम्।
मम देहे गुडाकेश यच्चान्यद्द्रष्टुमिच्छसि ॥7॥

ihaika-sthaṁ jagat kṛtsnaṁ paśyādya sa-carācaram
mama dehe guḍākeśa yac cānyad draṣṭum icchasi

The Supreme Lord said: O Arjuna, see now hundreds and thousands of My multifarious divine forms of different colors and different shapes. (11.05)

O Arjuna, see here the different manifestations of all the other gods (Adityas, Vasus, Rudras, two Asvin Kumaras and Maruts) and many wonders which have never been seen or heard before. (11.06)

O Arjuna, behold at once here within this body of Mine, the entire universe, animate, inanimate (living and non living beings) and whatever else you like to see now and also whatever you may want to see in the future. (11.07)

Q Could Arjuna see Lord Krishna's Cosmic Form (His Supreme divinity) with his physical eyes?

न तु मां शक्यसे द्रष्टुमनेनैव स्वचक्षुषा।
दिव्यं ददामि ते चक्षुः पश्य मे योगमैश्वरम्॥8॥

na tu māṁ śakyase draṣṭum anenaiva sva-cakṣuṣā
divyaṁ dadāmi te cakṣuḥ paśya me yogam aiśvaram

God can be seen only with divine vision

But certainly you can not see Me with your normal eyes (physical). Therefore, I bless you with Divine vision to see the power of Yoga. (11.08)

Description of Lord Krishna's Cosmic Form

Q Did Sanjaya share the information of Lord Krishna's Cosmic Form with King Dhritarastra?

संजय उवाच
एवमुक्त्वा ततो राजन्महायोगेश्वरो हरिः।
दर्शयामास पार्थाय परमं रूपमैश्वरम्॥9॥

sañjaya uvāca
evam uktvā tato rājan mahā-yogeśvaro hariḥ
darśayām āsa pārthāya paramaṁ rūpam aiśvaram

Sanjaya said: Having thus said, O King, Lord Krishna, the great Lord of Yoga, then revealed His Supreme Divine Form to Arjuna. (11.09)

Q What did Arjuna see in Lord Krishna's Cosmic Form?

अनेकवक्त्रनयनमनेकाद्भुतदर्शनम्।
अनेकदिव्याभरणं दिव्यानेकोद्यतायुधम्॥10॥

aneka-vaktra-nayanam anekādbhuta-darśanam
aneka-divyābharaṇaṁ divyānekodyatāyudham

दिव्यमाल्याम्बरधरं दिव्यगन्धानुलेपनम् ।
सर्वाश्चर्यमयं देवमनन्तं विश्वतोमुखम् ।। 11 ।।

divya-mālyāmbara-dharaṁ divya-gandhānulepanam
sarvāścarya-mayaṁ devam anantaṁ viśvato-mukham

दिवि सूर्यसहस्रस्य भवेद्युगपदुत्थिता ।
यदि भाः सदृशी सा स्याद्भासस्तस्य महात्मनः ।। 12 ।।

divi sūrya-sahasrasya bhaved yugapad utthitā
yadi bhāḥ sadṛśī sā syād bhāsas tasya mahātmanaḥ

तत्रैकस्थं जगत्कृत्स्नं प्रविभक्तमनेकधा ।
अपश्यद्देवदेवस्य शरीरे पाण्डवस्तदा ।। 13 ।।

tatraika-sthaṁ jagat kṛtsnaṁ pravibhaktam anekadhā
apaśyad deva-devasya śarīre pāṇḍavas tadā

Arjuna saw the Cosmic Form of the Lord possessing many mouths and eyes, presenting many wonderful sights, with numerous divine ornaments, holding many divine weapons, wearing divine garlands and garments, anointed with divine sandal-pastes, full of all wonders, boundless and facing in all directions. (11.10–11)

If hundreds of thousands of suns were to blaze forth all at once in the sky, even their radiance would not resemble the splendor of that Mighty Lord (Supreme Being) in that Cosmic Form. (11.12)

There, Arjuna saw the entire universe, though divided in many folds, resting in one place in the transcendental body of Lord Krishna, the God of gods. (11.13)

Q How did Arjuna feel upon seeing His Cosmic Form?

ततः स विस्मयाविष्टो हृष्टरोमा धनंजयः ।
प्रणम्य शिरसा देवं कृताञ्जलिरभाषत ।। 14 ।।

tataḥ sa vismayāviṣṭo hṛṣṭa-romā dhanañjayaḥ
praṇamya śirasā devaṁ kṛtāñjalir abhāṣata

Upon seeing the Cosmic Form of the Lord Krishna, Arjuna was amazed and his hair was standing on end. Bowing his head, he began to pray with folded hands to the Lord. (11.14)

Arjuna's confusion, fear and praise of Lord's Cosmic Form

Q Which gods and additional features did Arjuna see in His Cosmic body?

अर्जुन उवाच
पश्यामि देवांस्तव देव देहे सर्वांस्तथा भूतविशेषसङ्घान्।
ब्रह्माणमीशं कमलासनस्थ मृषींश्च सर्वानुरगांश्च दिव्यान्॥ 15॥

arjuna uvāca
paśyāmi devāṁs tava deva dehe
sarvāṁs tathā bhūta-viśeṣa-saṅghān
brahmāṇam īśaṁ kamalāsana-stham
ṛṣīṁś ca sarvān uragāṁś ca divyān

अनेकबाहूदरवक्त्रनेत्रं पश्यामि त्वां सर्वतोऽनन्तरूपम्।
नान्तं न मध्यं न पुनस्तवादिं पश्यामि विश्वेश्वर विश्वरूप॥ 16॥

aneka-bāhūdara-vaktra-netraṁ
paśyāmi tvāṁ sarvato 'nanta-rūpam
nāntaṁ na madhyaṁ na punas tavādiṁ
paśyāmi viśveśvara viśva-rūpa

God has no beginning and no end

किरीटिनं गदिनं चक्रिणं च तेजोराशिं सर्वतोदीप्तिमन्तम्।
पश्यामि त्वां दुर्निरीक्ष्यं समन्ताद्दीप्तानलार्कद्युतिमप्रमेयम्॥ 17॥

kirīṭinaṁ gadinaṁ cakriṇaṁ ca
tejo-rāśiṁ sarvato dīptimantam
paśyāmi tvāṁ durnirīkṣyaṁ samantād
dīptānalārka-dyutim aprameyam

Arjuna said: O Lord, I see all the gods in Your body and also various living beings, Lord Brahma, the Lord of creation (One of the god of Hindu trinity) seated on the lotus flower, Lord Shiva, all the great sages and divine serpents. (11.15)

O Lord of the Universe, I see Your Infinite Form everywhere with numerous arms, stomachs, faces and eyes. O Cosmic Form, I see neither Your beginning nor the middle nor the end. (11.16)

I see You with crown, club, discus, and massive radiance, shining everywhere, hard to look at, all around blazing like fire and sun, dazzling and immeasurable on all sides. (11.17)

Q What did Arjuna think about Lord Krishna while watching His Cosmic Form?

त्वमक्षरं परमं वेदितव्यं
त्वमस्य विश्वस्य परं निधानम्।
त्वमव्ययः शाश्वतधर्मगोप्ता
सनातनस्त्वं पुरुषो मतो मे ।। 18 ।।

tvam akṣaraṁ paramaṁ veditavyaṁ
tvam asya viśvasya paraṁ nidhānam
tvam avyayaḥ śāśvata-dharma-goptā
sanātanas tvaṁ puruṣo mato me

God is the protector of Righteousness

I believe that you are the Eternal Being to be realized. You are the Imperishable, Supreme Being (*Para-Brahma*). You are the Ultimate resort of the universe and you are the protector of the eternal order (*Dharma* and Righteousness). You are the Everlasting Being (*Atma*, Spirit). (11.18)

Q What amazed Arjuna about His Cosmic Form and what did he tell Lord Krishna?

अनादिमध्यान्तमनन्तवीर्यमनन्तबाहुं शशिसूर्यनेत्रम्।
पश्यामि त्वां दीप्तहुताशवक्त्रं स्वतेजसा विश्वमिदं तपन्तम् ।। 19 ।।

anādi-madhyāntam ananta-vīryam
ananta-bāhuṁ śaśi-sūrya-netram
paśyāmi tvāṁ dīpta-hutāśa-vaktraṁ
sva-tejasā viśvam idaṁ tapantam

God is the Supreme Power

द्यावापृथिव्योरिदमन्तरं हि व्याप्तं त्वयैकेन दिशश्च सर्वाः।
दृष्ट्वाद्भुतं रूपमुग्रं तवेदं लोकत्रयं प्रव्यथितं महात्मन् ।। 20 ।।

dyāv ā-pṛthivyor idam antaraṁ hi
vyāptaṁ tvayaikena diśaś ca sarvāḥ
dṛṣṭvādbhutaṁ rūpam ugraṁ tavedaṁ
loka-trayaṁ pravyathitaṁ mahātman

अमी हि त्वां सुरसङ्घा विशन्ति केचिद्भीताः प्राञ्जलयो गृणन्ति।
स्वस्तीत्युक्त्वा महर्षिसिद्धसङ्घाः स्तुवन्ति त्वां स्तुतिभिः पुष्कलाभिः ।। 21 ।।

amī hi tvāṁ sura-saṅghā viśanti
kecid bhītāḥ prāñjalayo gṛṇanti
svastīty uktvā maharṣi-siddha-saṅghāḥ
stuvanti tvāṁ stutibhiḥ puṣkalābhiḥ

रुद्रादित्या वसवो ये च साध्या विश्वेऽश्विनौ मरुतश्चोष्मपाश्च।
गन्धर्वयक्षासुरसिद्धसङ्घा वीक्षन्ते त्वां विस्मिताश्चैव सर्वे ॥ 22 ॥

rudrādityā vasavo ye ca sādhyā
viśve 'śvinau marutaś coṣmapāś ca
gandharva-yakṣāsura-siddha-saṅghā
vīkṣante tvāṁ vismitāś caiva sarve

I see You, without beginning, middle, or end with infinite power, with infinite arms with the sun and the moon as Your eyes. I see you with blazing fire coming forth from your mouth, heating the entire universe with Your radiance. (11.19)

O Krishna, although You are one, the entire space between heaven and earth and in all quarters is indeed filled by You. Seeing Your most marvelous form and also fearsome form, all the three worlds* are trembling with fear. (11.20)

*(Planet, heaven and earth in between; and the three state of Consciousness—walking, dream and deep sleep state)

All the hosts of gods are surrendering before you and entering into You, some with folded hands in fear are chanting Your Thy names and glories. The multitudes of sages and perfected ones are saying "All peace!" and praying to You by singing the Vedic hymns and devotional praises. (11.21)

All the various manifestations of the Lord – *Shiva, the Rudras, Adityas, Vasus, Sadhyas, Visava devas, Asvins, Maruts, Usmapas, Gandharvas, Yaksas, Asuras,* and *Siddhas* (the perfected gods) are gazing at You in great amazement. (For detail of names see 10.38) (11.22)

Q Why did Arjuna become so fearful by looking at His Cosmic Form?

रूपं महत्ते बहुवक्त्रनेत्रं महाबाहो बहुबाहूरुपादम्।
बहूदरं बहुदंष्ट्राकरालं दृष्ट्वा लोकाः प्रव्यथितास्तथाहम् ॥ 23 ॥

rūpaṁ mahat te bahu-vaktra-netraṁ
mahā-bāho bahu-bāhūru-pādam
bahūdaraṁ bahu-daṁṣṭrā-karālaṁ
dṛṣṭvā lokāḥ pravyathitās tathāham

One may not be prepared to see God

नभःस्पृशं दीप्तमनेकवर्णं व्यात्ताननं दीप्तविशालनेत्रम्।
दृष्ट्वा हि त्वां प्रव्यथितान्तरात्मा धृतिं न विन्दामि शमं च विष्णो ॥ 24 ॥

nabhaḥ-spṛśaṁ dīptam aneka-varṇaṁ
vyāttānanaṁ dīpta-viśāla-netram
dṛṣṭvā hi tvāṁ pravyathitāntar-ātmā
dhṛtiṁ na vindāmi śamaṁ ca viṣṇo

O Mighty Lord, seeing your Infinite Form with numerous mouths, eyes, many arms and thighs, feet, stomachs, and many terrifying teeth, the whole world is shaking with fear and so am I. (11.23)

Seeing Your very bright and colorful form touching the sky, Your mouth wide open and large shining eyes, I am very disturbed and frightened and find neither steadiness nor peace, O Krishna. (11.24)

Q What else did Arjuna tell Lord Krishna upon seeing His Cosmic Form?

दंष्ट्राकरालानि च ते मुखानि दृष्ट्वा कालानलसन्निभानि।
दिशो न जाने न लभे च शर्म प्रसीद देवेश जगन्निवास ।। 25 ।।

damṣṭrā-karālāni ca te mukhāni
dṛṣṭvaiva kālānala-sannibhāni
diśo na jāne na labhe ca śarma
prasīda deveśa jagan-nivāsa

Seeing Your faces with fearful teeth, resembling the raging fire at the time of Cosmic dissolution, I have totally lost my sense of direction and peace of mind. O Lord of demi-gods (*devas*), O Abode of the universe, please have mercy on me. (11.25)

Q What were the great warriors doing in His Cosmic body and what happened to them?

अमी च त्वां धृतराष्ट्रस्य पुत्राः सर्वे सहैवावनिपालसङ्घैः।
भीष्मो द्रोणः सूतपुत्रस्तथासौ सहास्मदीयैरपि योधमुख्यैः ।। 26 ।।

amī ca tvāṁ dhṛtarāṣṭrasya putrāḥ
sarve sahaivāvani-pāla-saṅghaiḥ
bhīṣmo droṇaḥ sūta-putras tathāsau
sahāsmadīyair api yodha-mukhyaiḥ

वक्त्राणि ते त्वरमाणा विशन्ति दंष्ट्राकरालानि भयानकानि।
केचिद्विलग्ना दशनान्तरेषु संदृश्यन्ते चूर्णितैरुत्तमाङ्गैः ।। 27 ।।

vaktrāṇi te tvaramāṇā viśanti
damṣṭrā-karālāni bhayānakāni
kecid vilagnā daśanāntareṣu
sandṛśyante cūrṇitair uttamāṅgaiḥ

यथा नदीनां बहवोऽम्बुवेगाः समुद्रमेवाभिमुखा द्रवन्ति।
तथा तवामी नरलोकवीरा विशन्ति वक्त्राण्यभिविज्वलन्ति ।। 28 ।।

yathā nadīnāṁ bahavo 'mbu-vegāḥ
samudram evābhimukhā dravanti
tathā tavāmī nara-loka-vīrā
viśanti vaktrāṇy abhivijvalanti

यथा प्रदीप्तं ज्वलनं पतङ्गा विशन्ति नाशाय समृद्धवेगाः।
तथैव नाशाय विशन्ति लोका स्तवापि वक्त्राणि समृद्धवेगाः ।। 29 ।।

yathā pradīptaṁ jvalanaṁ pataṅgā
viśanti nāśāya samṛddha-vegāḥ
tathaiva nāśāya viśanti lokās
tavāpi vaktrāṇi samṛddha-vegāḥ

All the sons of Dhritarastra, along with many other kings, Bhisma, Drona, and Karna together with chief warriors on our side also, are quickly entering into Your terrifying mouths with fearsome teeth. Some are trapped with their heads crushed between the teeth. (11.26–27)

These great warriors of the mortal world are entering into Your blazing mouths as the many torrents of rivers flow toward the ocean. (11.28)

As the moths rush with great speed into the blazing flame for their own destruction, all these people are also rapidly rushing into Your mouths for destruction. (11.29)

Q What was being seen in Lord Krishna's Cosmic Form?

लेलिह्यसे ग्रसमानः समन्ताल्लोकान्समग्रान्वदनैर्ज्वलद्भिः।
तेजोभिरापूर्य जगत्समग्रं भासस्तवोग्राः प्रतपन्ति विष्णो ।। 30 ।।

lelihyase grasamānaḥ samantāl
lokān samagrān vadanair jvaladbhiḥ
tejobhir āpūrya jagat samagraṁ
bhāsas tavograḥ pratapanti viṣṇo

O Krishna, You are swallowing all the worlds and licking them up with Your flaming mouths from all directions. Your powerful brilliance is filling it with radiance and burning the entire universe. (11.30)

Q What did Arjuna ask Lord Krishna while seeing His Cosmic Form?

आख्याहि मे को भवानुग्ररूपो नमोऽस्तु ते देववर प्रसीद।
विज्ञातुमिच्छामि भवन्तमाद्यं न हि प्रजानामि तव प्रवृत्तिम् ।। 31 ।।

ākhyāhi me ko bhavān ugra-rūpo
namo 'stu te deva-vara prasīda
vijñātum icchāmi bhavantam ādyaṁ
na hi prajānāmi tava pravṛttim

O Supreme God, please tell me who are You in such a fierce form? My salutations to You, be merciful! I wish to know You, O Primal being, I do not comprehend Your intention and Your mission. (11.31)

Lord Krishna describes His majestic power to Arjuna and encourages him to fulfill his duty

Q Why did Lord Krishna incarnate into human form?

श्रीभगवानुवाच
कालोऽस्मि लोकक्षयकृत्प्रवृद्धो लोकान्समाहर्तुमिह प्रवृत्तः।
ऋतेऽपि त्वां न भविष्यन्ति सर्वे येऽवस्थिताः प्रत्यनीकेषु योधाः॥32॥

śrī-bhagavān uvāca
kālo 'smi loka-kṣaya-kṛt pravṛddho
lokān samāhartum iha pravṛttaḥ
ṛte 'pi tvāṁ na bhaviṣyanti sarve
ye 'vasthitāḥ pratyanīkeṣu yodhāḥ

God has His own system to clean up the world

The Supreme Lord said: I am *Kala* (Time death), the mighty destroyer of the world. I have come here to destroy all these people. All these warriors standing arrayed in the opposing armies are going to die, even without your participation in the war. (11.32)

Q Why did He advice Arjuna to fight the righteous war and how did He motivate him?

तस्मात्त्वमुत्तिष्ठ यशो लभस्व जित्वा शत्रून्भुङ्क्ष्व राज्यं समृद्धम्।
मयैवैते निहताः पूर्वमेव निमित्तमात्रं भव सव्यसाचिन्॥33॥

tasmāt tvam uttiṣṭha yaśo labhasva
jitvā śatrūn bhuṅkṣva rājyaṁ samṛddham
mayaivaite nihatāḥ pūrvam eva
nimitta-mātraṁ bhava savya-sācin

We are only His instruments

द्रोणं च भीष्मं च जयद्रथं च कर्णं तथान्यानपि योधवीरान्।
मया हतांस्त्वं जहि मा व्यथिष्ठा युध्यस्व जेतासि रणे सपत्नान्॥34॥

droṇaṁ ca bhīṣmaṁ ca jayadrathaṁ ca
karṇaṁ tathānyān api yodha-vīrān
mayā hatāṁs tvaṁ jahi mā vyathiṣṭhā
yudhyasva jetāsi raṇe sapatnān

We should focus on our duty and leave the rest to God

Therefore, you must get up and gain the glory, conquer your enemies and enjoy a prosperous kingdom. I have already destroyed all these warriors but You are merely an instrument, O Arjuna. (11.33)

Slay Drona, Bhisma, Jayadratha, Karna, and other great warriors who have already been killed by Me. Do not fear. Just fight. You will surely conquer the enemies in the battle. (11.34)

Arjuna's request to see Lord Krishna's four armed form

Q What did Arjuna do after listening to Lord Krishna's advice?

संजय उवाच
एतच्छ्रुत्वा वचनं केशवस्य कृताञ्जलिर्वेपमानः किरीटी।
नमस्कृत्वा भूय एवाह कृष्णं सगद्गदं भीतभीतः प्रणम्य ॥35॥

sañjaya uvāca
etac chrutvā vacanaṁ keśavasya
kṛtāñjalir vepamānaḥ kirītī
namaskṛtvā bhūya evāha kṛṣṇaṁ
sa-gadgadaṁ bhīta-bhītaḥ praṇamya

Sanjaya said: After hearing these words from Krishna, the crowned Arjuna, trembling and with folded hands once again fearfully spoke to Krishna in a choked voice. (11.35)

Q What was happening in His Cosmic body?

अर्जुन उवाच
स्थाने हृषीकेश तव प्रकीर्त्या जगत्प्रहृष्यत्यनुरज्यते च।
रक्षांसि भीतानि दिशो द्रवन्ति सर्वे नमस्यन्ति च सिद्धसङ्घाः ॥36॥

arjuna uvāca
sthāne hṛṣīkeśa tava prakīrtyā
jagat prahṛṣyaty anurajyate ca
rakṣāṁsi bhītāni diśo dravanti
sarve namasyanti ca siddha-saṅghāḥ

Arjuna said: O Krishna, the world rightly delights and rejoices in glorifying You. The terrified demons flee in all directions, while all perfected ones bow to You in adoration. (11.36)

Q Why were the *Siddhas* (perfected ones) bowing to Him in adoration?

कस्माच्च ते न नमेरन्महात्मन् गरीयसे ब्रह्मणोऽप्यादिकर्त्रे ।
अनन्त देवेश जगन्निवास त्वमक्षरं सदसत्तत्परं यत् ।। 37 ।।

kasmāc ca te na nameran mahātman
garīyase brahmaṇo 'py ādi-kartre
ananta deveśa jagan-nivāsa
tvam akṣaraṁ sad-asat tat paraṁ yat

God is beyond existence and non-existence

O great Supreme-Soul, why should they not bow to You, the original creator who is even greater than Brahma, the creator of material worlds? O infinite Lord, O God of gods, O Abode of the universe, You are Imperishable, both Sat (Eternal) and Asat (Temporal) and the Supreme Being (Para-Brahman) that is beyond both Sat and Asat. (11.37)

Q How exulted did Arjuna become and how did he describe Lord Krishna?

त्वमादिदेवः पुरुषः पुराणस्त्वमस्य विश्वस्य परं निधानम् ।
वेत्तासि वेद्यं च परं च धाम त्वया ततं विश्वमनन्तरूप ।। 38 ।।

tvam ādi-devaḥ puruṣaḥ purāṇas
tvam asya viśvasya paraṁ nidhānam
vettāsi vedyaṁ ca paraṁ ca dhāma
tvayā tataṁ viśvam ananta-rūpa

वायुर्यमोऽग्निर्वरुणः शशाङ्कः प्रजापतिस्त्वं प्रपितामहश्च ।
नमो नमस्तेऽस्तु सहस्रकृत्वः पुनश्च भूयोऽपि नमो नमस्ते ।। 39 ।।

vāyur yamo 'gnir varuṇaḥ śaśāṅkaḥ
prajāpatis tvaṁ prapitāmahaś ca
namo namas te 'stu sahasra-kṛtvaḥ
punaś ca bhūyo 'pi namo namas te

नमः पुरस्तादथ पृष्ठतस्ते नमोऽस्तु ते सर्वत एव सर्व ।
अनन्तवीर्यामितविक्रमस्त्वं सर्वं समाप्नोषि ततोऽसि सर्वः ।। 40 ।।

namaḥ purastād atha pṛṣṭhatas te
namo 'stu te sarvata eva sarva
ananta-vīryāmita-vikramas tvaṁ
sarvaṁ samāpnoṣi tato 'si sarvaḥ

You are the primal God, the most ancient Person (*Purusha*), the ultimate resort of the entire universe. You are the Knower, the Knowable and the Supreme Abode. It is You by who the entire universe (Cosmic Manifestation) is pervaded, O Lord of the Infinite Form. (11.38)

You are Vayu (wind god), Yama (god of death), Agni (god of fire), Varuna (sea god), Sasanka (the moon), and creator (Brahma) as well as the father of Brahma. Salutations to You, a thousand times and again and again salutations to You. (11.39)

O Lord of infinite prowess, my salutations to You from front and from behind. O soul of all, my salutes to You from all sides. You, who possess limitless might that pervades all, therefore You are all. (11.40)

Q Why did Arjuna feel so foolish and how did he ask Lord Krishna for His forgiveness?

सखेति मत्वा प्रसभं यदुक्तं हे कृष्ण हे यादव हे सखेति।
अजानता महिमानं तवेदं मया प्रमादात्प्रणयेन वापि ॥ 41 ॥

sakheti matvā prasabhaṁ yad uktaṁ
he kṛṣṇa he yādava he sakheti
ajānatā mahimānaṁ tavedaṁ
mayā pramādāt praṇayena vāpi

यच्चावहासार्थमसत्कृतोऽसि विहारशय्यासनभोजनेषु।
एकोऽथवाप्यच्युत तत्समक्षं तत्क्षामये त्वामहमप्रमेयम् ॥ 42 ॥

yac cāvahāsārtham asat-kṛto 'si
vihāra-śayyāsana-bhojaneṣu
eko 'tha vāpy acyuta tat-samakṣaṁ
tat kṣāmaye tvām aham aprameyam

पितासि लोकस्य चराचरस्य त्वमस्य पूज्यश्च गुरुर्गरीयान्।
न त्वत्समोऽस्त्यभ्यधिकः कुतोऽन्यो लोकत्रयेऽप्यप्रतिमप्रभाव ॥ 43 ॥

pitāsi lokasya carācarasya
tvam asya pūjyaś ca gurur garīyān
na tvat-samo 'sty abhyadhikaḥ kuto 'nyo
loka-traye 'py apratima-prabhāva

तस्मात्प्रणम्य प्रणिधाय कायं प्रसादये त्वामहमीशमीड्यम्।
पितेव पुत्रस्य सखेव सख्युः प्रियः प्रियायार्हसि देव सोढुम् ॥ 44 ॥

tasmāt praṇamya praṇidhāya kāyaṁ
prasādaye tvām aham īśam īḍyam
piteva putrasya sakheva sakhyuḥ
priyaḥ priyāyārhasi deva soḍhum

Asking for His forgiveness is the path to His Grace

Regarding You as my friend, without knowing Your greatness, merely out of affection or ignorance, I have foolishly addressed You as O Krishna, O Yadava, O Friend, etc. (11.41)

In whatever way I may have disrespected You, teased you while playing, relaxing, sitting, or eating in privacy or in public, O Krishna, the Unshaken and Infinite One, please forgive me for all those offenses. (11.42)

You are the Father and the greatest *Guru* (Supreme Spiritual Master) of this complete Cosmic creation (Universe), of the animate and inanimate and highly adorable. O Lord of incomparable and unmatched power, there is no one equal to You in all the three worlds. How then could there be anyone greater than You? (11.43)

Therefore, my dear Lord, I seek Your grace by bowing down and prostrating my body before You so please forgive me as a father to his son, as a friend to a friend and as a lover to his beloved, O Lord. (11.44)

Q Why did Arjuna want to see His original Divine Form?

अदृष्टपूर्वं हृषितोऽस्मि दृष्ट्वा भयेन च प्रव्यथितं मनो मे।
तदेव मे दर्शय देव रूपं प्रसीद देवेश जगन्निवास ॥ 45 ॥

adṛṣṭa-pūrvaṁ hṛṣito 'smi dṛṣṭvā
bhayena ca pravyathitaṁ mano me
tad eva me darśaya deva rūpaṁ
prasīda deveśa jagan-nivāsa

किरीटिनं गदिनं चक्रहस्तमिच्छामि त्वां द्रष्टुमहं तथैव।
तेनैव रूपेण चतुर्भुजेन सहस्रबाहो भव विश्वमूर्ते ॥ 46 ॥

kirīṭinaṁ gadinaṁ cakra-hastam
icchāmi tvāṁ draṣṭum ahaṁ tathaiva
tenaiva rūpeṇa catur-bhujena
sahasra-bāho bhava viśva-mūrte

Having seen what has never been seen before, I am delighted and yet my mind is tormented with fear. Therefore, O God of gods, O Abode of the universe, please have mercy on me and show me again Your previous Divine Form. (11.45)

I wish to see You as before with Your crown, holding mace and a discus in Your hands. Therefore, O Krishna, thousand-armed and Cosmic Being, please appear again in the same four-armed form. (11.46)

Q Did Lord Krishna show His Cosmic Form to any one else before?

श्रीभगवानुवाच
मया प्रसन्नेन तवार्जुनेदं रूपं परं दर्शितमात्मयोगात्।
तेजोमयं विश्वमनन्तमाद्यं यन्मे त्वदन्येन न दृष्टपूर्वम् ॥ 47 ॥

śrī-bhagavān uvāca
maya prasannena tavārjunedaṁ
rūpaṁ paraṁ darśitam ātma-yogāt
tejo-mayaṁ viśvam anantam ādyaṁ
yan me tvad anyena na dṛṣṭa-pūrvam

न वेदयज्ञाध्ययनैर्न दानैर्न च क्रियाभिर्न तपोभिरुग्रैः।
एवंरूपः शक्य अहं नृलोके द्रष्टुं त्वदन्येन कुरुप्रवीर ।। 48 ।।

na veda-yajñādhyayanair na dānair
na ca kriyābhir na tapobhir ugraiḥ
evaṁ-rūpaḥ śakya ahaṁ nṛ-loke
draṣṭuṁ tvad anyena kuru-pravīra

The Supreme Lord said: by My grace, O Arjuna, I have shown you, through My own Yogic Power, this supreme, radiant, infinite, primeval Cosmic Form of Mine that has never been seen before by anyone else except you. (11.47)

Neither by studying the Vedas nor by *Yajnas* (sacrifice) nor by charity nor by rituals and neither by severe austerities can I be seen in this Cosmic Form in this materialistic world by anyone else except you, O Arjuna. (11.48)

Q How did Lord Krishna console Arjuna and regain His original form?

मा ते व्यथा मा च विमूढभावो दृष्ट्वा रूपं घोरमीदृङ्ममेदम्।
व्यपेतभीः प्रीतमनाः पुनस्त्वं तदेव मे रूपमिदं प्रपश्य: ।। 49 ।।

mā te vyathā mā ca vimūḍha-bhāvo
dṛṣṭvā rūpaṁ ghoram īdṛṅ mamedam
vyapeta-bhīḥ prīta-manāḥ punas tvaṁ
tad eva me rūpam idaṁ prapaśya

संजय उवाच
इत्यर्जुनं वासुदेवस्तथोक्त्वा स्वकं रूपं दर्शयामास भूयः।
आश्वासयामास च भीतमेनं भूत्वा पुनः सौम्यवपुर्महात्मा ।। 50 ।।

sañjaya uvāca
ity arjunaṁ vāsudevas tathoktvā
svakaṁ rūpaṁ darśayām āsa bhūyaḥ
āśvāsayām āsa ca bhītam enaṁ
bhūtvā punaḥ saumya-vapur mahātmā

Do not be afraid and perplexed by seeing this terrifying form of Mine. Without fear and with a loving heart, now see once again the former four-armed form of Mine (with conch, crown, mace and discus/*Chakra* in My hands). (11.49)

Sanjaya said: Having spoken like this to Arjuna, Lord Krishna once again revealed His four-armed form to him. Then, assuming His pleasant and gentle human form (two-armed), Lord Krishna, Supreme-Soul, consoled and comforted terrified Arjuna. (11.50)

The vision of God can be obtained only through undivided devotion

Q Did Arjuna regain his composure after seeing His original form?

अर्जुन उवाच
दृष्ट्वेदं मानुषं रूपं तव सौम्यं जनार्दन।
इदानीमस्मि संवृत्तः सचेताः प्रकृतिं गतः ।।51।।

arjuna uvāca
dṛṣṭvedaṁ mānuṣaṁ rūpaṁ
tava saumyaṁ janārdana
idānīm asmi saṁvṛttaḥ
sa-cetāḥ prakṛtiṁ gataḥ

Arjuna said: O Krishna, after seeing this serene human form of Yours, I have now become composed and my normal self again. (11.51)

Q How difficult is it to see His Cosmic Form?

श्रीभगवानुवाच
सुदुर्दर्शमिदं रूपं दृष्ट्वानसि यन्मम।
देवा अप्यस्य रूपस्य नित्यं दर्शनकाङ्क्षिणः ।।52।।

śrī-bhagavān uvāca
su-durdarśam idaṁ rūpaṁ
dṛṣṭavān asi yan mama
devā apy asya rūpasya
nityaṁ darśana-kāṅkṣiṇaḥ

नाहं वेदैर्न तपसा न दानेन न चेज्यया।
शक्य एवंविधो द्रष्टुं दृष्टवानसि मां यथा ।।53।।

nāhaṁ vedair na tapasā
na dānena na cejyayā
śakya evaṁ-vidho draṣṭuṁ
dṛṣṭavān asi māṁ yathā

The Supreme Lord said: It is very difficult indeed to see this form of Mine (Cosmic and Four Armed) that you have just seen. Even the gods (*devas*) are always eager to see this form. (11.52)

Neither by the study of Vedas, nor by austerity, nor by acts of charity, nor by the performance of rituals, can I be seen in this form as you have just seen me with your transcendental eyes. (11.53)

Q How can one see His Cosmic Form?

भक्त्या त्वनन्यया शक्य अहमेवंविधोऽर्जुन।
ज्ञातुं द्रष्टुं च तत्त्वेन प्रवेष्टुं च परंतप ॥54॥

bhaktyā tv ananyayā śakya
aham evaṁ-vidho 'rjuna
jñātuṁ draṣṭuṁ ca tattvena
praveṣṭuṁ ca parantapa

God can only be realized by undivided devotion

Yet, through undivided devotion (focus) alone, I can be seen in this form, can be known in essence and can also be experienced and realized (Union with God), O Arjuna. (11.54)

Q Who can experience, realize and attain God?

मत्कर्मकृन्मत्परमो मद्भक्तः सङ्गवर्जितः।
निर्वैरः सर्वभूतेषु यः स मामेति पाण्डव ॥55॥

mat-karma-kṛn mat-paramo
mad-bhaktaḥ saṅga-varjitaḥ
nirvairaḥ sarva-bhūteṣu
yaḥ sa mām eti pāṇḍava

The Essence of Gita

1. One who performs all his actions for Me
2. One who makes Me the Supreme goal of his life
3. One who is fully devoted to Me and always lives in My Consciousness
4. One who has no attachments
5. One who is free from enmity (malice) towards all beings
6. One who is friendly to all,
   Certainly attains Me, O Arjuna. (11.55)

Lessons to learn and practice in daily life

1. The only purpose of human birth is to realize God (Self-Realization)
2. We must set the Supreme goal of our life to attain unity with God and then work toward achieving it by self-discipline, selfless service with love (*Karma Yoga*) and spiritual practices (*Sadhana*)

ॐ तत्सदिति श्रीमद्भगवद्गीतासूपनिषत्सु ब्रह्मविद्यायां योगशास्त्रे
श्रीकृष्णार्जुनसंवादे विश्वरूपदर्शनं नामैकादशोऽध्यायः ।।

AUM TAT SAT

Thus ends the chapter named "*Visvarupa-Darsana Yoga*"
The Path of the Divine Vision of the Cosmic Form
in the *Upanishad* of the glorious Bhagavad Gita, the scripture of Yoga,
the science of the Absolute (*Brahman*) in the form of the dialogue
between Lord Krishna and Arjuna.

Aum Shanti, Shanti, Shantihi

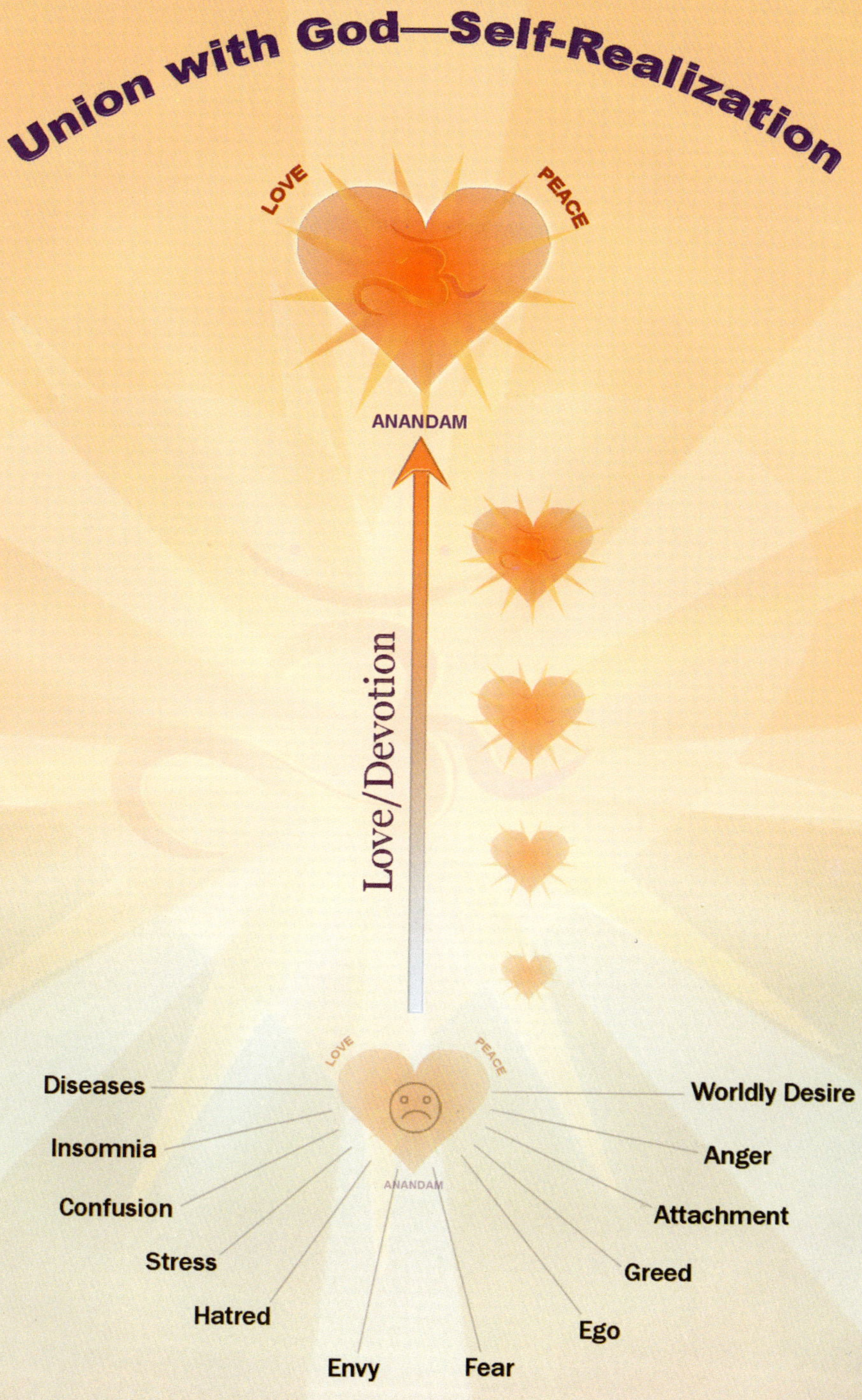

Self-Purification and Transformation through Love and Devotion

BHAKTI YOGA

The Path of Love and Devotion

Union with God (Self-Realization) through the path of Love and Devotion

The Gita is a journey from sorrow to Supreme Bliss through love and devotion

In this chapter, Lord Krishna imparts to Arjuna the knowledge to eliminate his confusion about worshiping manifested or unmanifested God to attain God-Realization and the different forms of spiritual disciplines. He explains to Arjuna that the path of devotion is the highest and most expeditious path to attain His Supreme Bliss. He further explains that those who follow this path develop divine qualities and virtues, (hallmarks of divinity) and become his true devotees and extremely dear to God.

Bhakti yoga is The Heart of Gita.

—Swami H. H. Hari Harji Maharaj

Bhakti Yoga is a very enjoyable path. In this path one **builds an emotional bond, straight from heart to heart with God.** It is a path of duality, where one easily establishes communication and builds a relationship with the manifested God (*Saguna*) through worshipping idols, praying, singing devotional songs expressing one's emotions, and performing selfless services.

Therefore, worshipping manifested God is better than meditating on the unmanifested and formless God, whereby one has no association with any object and it requires only contemplation by mind. However, the mind is very difficult to control.

Formula for Devotion Yoga

Work + compassion/love/devotion = Bhakti Yoga

Benefits of *Bhakti Yoga*: *Bhakti Yoga* is one of the easiest path for self-purification and self-transformation, where one develops divine qualities and becomes very dear to God

Bhakti/Devotion Yoga → Divine Qualities → God-Realization (Sat Chit Ananda)

The Yoga of building a relationship with God and His people through love and selfless service

Main Message

The Path of Love and Devotion (extreme love for God)

Bhakti Yoga is the easiest, the highest and the most expedient method to attain God

- On this path, faith and feelings of love (emotions-Heart) are the driving force for building the relationship, communication and union with God.
- One who lives every moment in God's Consciousness merges with Him, e.g. *Meera* always lived in His Consciousness and became *Krishna-mayi.*
- Four methods of worshipping God to attain Ultimate Peace (Self-Realization) and their order of merit.

The order of merit from lowest to highest: 1. Ritual practices 2. Knowledge 3. Meditation 4. Renunciation (*Tyaga*)

Ritual practices < Knowledge < Meditation < Renunciation (Tyaga) → Ultimate Peace (Self-Realization)

- There are thirty nine hallmarks of a true devotee
- By following the path of devotion, the devotee sincerely works to develop the divine qualities/virtues by eliminating his bad qualities and vices. Thus, the devotee putting his best efforts forward becomes extremely dear to God and finally attains God-Realization.

Love and devotion → Self-Purification → Divine Qualities (Purity of Heart) → Dear to God → God and Self-Realization

Chapter Overview

01–05	Should one worship, the manifested or the unmanifested form of God
06–12	Respective merits of worshippers and four paths to Ultimate Peace (God-Realization)
13–19	Hallmarks of the most loved and true devotee
20	Benefit: Become God's beloved

Should one worship, the manifested or the unmanifested form of God

Q What did Arjuna want to know about worshiping God with Form (*Saguna*) and without form (*Nirguna*)?

अर्जुन उवाच
एवं सततयुक्ता ये भक्तास्त्वां पर्युपासते।
ये चाप्यक्षरमव्यक्तं तेषां के योगवित्तमाः ॥1॥

arjuna uvāca
evaṁ satata-yuktā ye bhaktās tvāṁ paryupāsate
ye cāpy akṣaram avyaktaṁ teṣāṁ ke yoga-vittamāḥ

Arjuna asked: Which of the devotees are better versed in Yoga, those who worship you Manifested (Your personal form-*Saguna*) with ever steadfast devotion or those who worship the Imperishable and the Unmanifested (Formless God-*Nirguna*)? (12.01)

Q Who is the best yogi (Devotee)?

श्रीभगवानुवाच
मय्यावेश्य मनो ये मां नित्ययुक्ता उपासते।
श्रद्धया परयोपेतास्ते मे युक्ततमा मताः ॥2॥

śrī-bhagavān uvāca
mayy āveśya mano ye māṁ nitya-yuktā upāsate
śraddhayā parayopetās te me yuktatamā matāḥ

One who always lives in God's Consciousness is the best Yogi

The Supreme Lord said: I consider those to be the best Yogis (Devotees, Most divine) who contemplate on Me every moment (ever steadfast) and worship me with Supreme faith. (12.02)

Q Can God be attained by worshipping formless, Unmanifested God?

ये त्वक्षरमनिर्देश्यमव्यक्तं पर्युपासते ।
सर्वत्रगमचिन्त्यं च कूटस्थमचलं ध्रुवम् ।।3।।

ye tv akṣaram anirdeśyam avyaktaṁ paryupāsate
sarvatra-gam acintyaṁ ca kūṭa-stham acalaṁ dhruvam

संनियम्येन्द्रियग्रामं सर्वत्र समबुद्धयः ।
ते प्राप्नुवन्ति मामेव सर्वभूतहिते रताः ।।4।।

sanniyamyendriya-grāmaṁ sarvatra sama-buddhayaḥ
te prāpnuvanti mām eva sarva-bhūta-hite ratāḥ

But those who worship:

1. The Imperishable
2. The Indefinable
3. The Unmanifested
4. The Omnipresent
5. The Unthinkable
6. The Unchanging
7. The Immovable
8. The Eternal

Fully restraining all the senses, with (even-tempered under all circumstances) and engaged in the welfare of all, they also attain Me. (12.03–04)

Q How difficult is it to attain the Supreme goal of life "Self-Realization" by worshipping unmanifested God (*Nirguna*)?

Attaining God through His manifested form is easier

क्लेशोऽधिकतरस्तेषामव्यक्तासक्तचेतसाम् ।
अव्यक्ता हि गतिर्दुःखं देहवद्भिरवाप्यते ।।5।।

kleśo 'dhikataras teṣām avyaktāsakta-cetasām
avyaktā hi gatir duḥkhaṁ dehavadbhir avāpyate

The path of focusing the mind on the Formless (Non-manifested) is full of obstacles, slow and very difficult to comprehend. Therefore, it is an extremely difficult path for attaining the Goal of Self-Realization by embodied beings (*jivatma*). (12.05)

Respective merits of worshippers and four paths to Ultimate Peace (God-Realization)

Q How does God help His devotee to attain the Supreme goal of life (Liberation)?

ये तु सर्वाणि कर्माणि मयि संन्यस्य मत्पराः।
अनन्येनैव योगेन मां ध्यायन्त उपासते ॥6॥

ye tu sarvāṇi karmāṇi mayi sannyasya mat-parāḥ
ananyenaiva yogena māṁ dhyāyanta upāsate

तेषामहं समुद्धर्ता मृत्युसंसारसागरात्।
भवामि न चिरात्पार्थ मय्यावेशितचेतसाम् ॥7॥

teṣām ahaṁ samuddhartā mṛtyu-saṁsāra-sāgarāt
bhavāmi na cirāt pārtha mayy āveśita-cetasām

God always takes care of His devotees

Arjuna, but those who worship Me (as their personal God, *Saguna*):

1. With undivided devotion
2. Surrender all their action to Me
3. Regard me as their Supreme Goal
4. Constantly meditate on Me with single minded devotion (always live in My Consciousness)

I become their savior and I quickly rescue them (liberate) from the materialistic world that is the ocean of birth and death. (12.06–07)

Q Why should I always live in God Consciousness (focus on God)?

मय्येव मन आधत्स्व मयि बुद्धिं निवेशय।
निवसिष्यसि मय्येव अत ऊर्ध्वं न संशयः ॥8॥

mayy eva mana ādhatsva mayi buddhiṁ niveśaya
nivasiṣyasi mayy eva ata ūrdhvaṁ na saṁśayaḥ

Therefore, fix your mind on Me alone and let your intellect dwell in Me. Then, you will surely live in Me alone, there is no doubt about this. (12.08)

Q If I cannot focus on You then what else would you recommend to attain You ?

अथ चित्तं समाधातुं न शक्नोषि मयि स्थिरम्।
अभ्यासयोगेन ततो मामिच्छाप्तुं धनंजय ॥9॥

atha cittaṁ samādhātuṁ na śaknoṣi mayi sthiram
abhyāsa-yogena tato mām icchāptuṁ dhanañjaya

If you are unable to focus your mind steadily on Me, then seek to attain Me, O Arjuna, by Yoga of practice of your own choice that suits you (any spiritual discipline/*sadhana*). (12.09)

Q If I cannot do any spiritual practices then what else would You recommend?

अभ्यासेऽप्यसमर्थोऽसि मत्कर्मपरमो भव ।
मदर्थमपि कर्माणि कुर्वन्सिद्धिमवाप्स्यसि ।। 10 ।।

abhyāse 'py asamartho 'si mat-karma-paramo bhava
mad-artham api karmāṇi kurvan siddhim avāpsyasi

अथैतदप्यशक्तोऽसि कर्तुं मद्योगमाश्रितः ।
सर्वकर्मफलत्यागं ततः कुरु यतात्मवान् ।। 11 ।।

athaitad apy aśakto 'si kartuṁ mad-yogam āśritaḥ
sarva-karma-phala-tyāgaṁ tataḥ kuru yatātmavān

One has full freedom to chose his spiritual path

If you are unable even to do any type of spiritual practice (*sadhana*), then do all of your work as if you are doing it for Me only. Even just by working for Me, you will attain perfection (work only as an instrument, just to serve and please Me, without selfish motives). (12.10)

However, if you are unable to even work for Me, then just take refuge in Me with Equanimity (complete surrender to My will) and renounce the fruits of all action (accept all results as My Grace/Prasad). (12.11)

Q What is the best way to attain Supreme Peace?

श्रेयो हि ज्ञानमभ्यासाज्ज्ञानाद्ध्यानं विशिष्यते ।
ध्यानात्कर्मफलत्यागस्त्यागाच्छान्तिरनन्तरम् ।। 12 ।।

śreyo hi jñānam abhyāsāj jñānād dhyānaṁ viśiṣyate
dhyānāt karma-phala-tyāgas tyāgāc chāntir anantaram

Renunciation is the ultimate path to Supreme Peace

Knowledge of scriptures is better than only ritualistic practice (without proper insight); meditation is superior to knowledge; *Tyaga* or renunciation of the fruits of work is even superior to meditation; and Peace follows immediately after renunciation . (12.12)

Ritual practices < Knowledge < Meditation < Tyaga (Renunciation)

Tyaga (Renunciation) → Ultimate Peace (Self-Realization)

Hallmarks of the most loved and true devotee

Q Who is God's true devotee and very dear to Him (His favorite) and what are his hallmarks?*

अद्वेष्टा सर्वभूतानां मैत्रः करुण एव च।
निर्ममो निरहंकारः समदुःखसुखः क्षमी ।। 13 ।।

advesṭā sarva-bhūtānāṁ maitraḥ karuṇa eva ca
nirmamo nirahaṅkāraḥ sama-duḥkha-sukhaḥ kṣamī

Any one of the attributes is enough to become a devotee of God

संतुष्टः सततं योगी यतात्मा दृढनिश्चयः।
मय्यर्पितमनोबुद्धिर्यो मद्भक्तः स मे प्रियः ।। 14 ।।

santuṣṭaḥ satataṁ yogī yatātmā dṛḍha-niścayaḥ
mayy arpita-mano-buddhir yo mad-bhaktaḥ sa me priyaḥ

यस्मान्नोद्विजते लोको लोकान्नोद्विजते च यः।
हर्षामर्षभयोद्वेगैर्मुक्तो यः स च मे प्रियः ।। 15 ।।

yasmān nodvijate loko lokān nodvijate ca yaḥ
harṣāmarṣa-bhayodvegair mukto yaḥ sa ca me priyaḥ

अनपेक्षः शुचिर्दक्ष उदासीनो गतव्यथः।
सर्वारम्भपरित्यागी यो मद्भक्तः स मे प्रियः ।। 16 ।।

anapekṣaḥ śucir dakṣa udāsīno gata-vyathaḥ
sarvārambha-parityāgī yo mad-bhaktaḥ sa me priyaḥ

यो न हृष्यति न द्वेष्टि न शोचति न काङ्क्षति।
शुभाशुभपरित्यागी भक्तिमान्यः स म प्रियः ।। 17 ।।

yo na hṛṣyati na dveṣṭi na śocati na kāṅkṣati
śubhāśubha-parityāgī bhaktimān yaḥ sa me priyaḥ

समः शत्रौ च मित्रे च तथा मानापमानयोः।
शीतोष्णसुखदुःखेषु समः सङ्गविवर्जितः ।। 18 ।।

samaḥ śatrau ca mitre ca tathā mānāpamānayoḥ
śītoṣṇa-sukha-duḥkheṣu samaḥ saṅga-vivarjitaḥ

तुल्यनिन्दास्तुतिर्मौनी संतुष्टो येन केनचित्।
अनिकेतः स्थिरमतिर्भक्तिमान्मे प्रियो नरः ।। 19 ।।

tulya-nindā-stutir maunī santuṣṭo yena kenacit
aniketaḥ sthira-matir bhaktimān me priyo naraḥ

The devotee who has following attributes is dear to God.

1. Free from envy (ill will) to all living beings
2. Friendly
3. Compassionate
4. Free from egoism
5. Attachments (I-ness/arrogance and my-ness/possessiveness)
6. Even-minded in pain and pleasure
7. Forgiving (12.13)
8. Always content in all circumstances
9. Steady in meditation (mentally united with me)
10. Self-controlled (body, mind and spirit)
11. Very firm and determined
12. Surrender his mind and intellect to me, such a devotee of mine is dear to me. (12.13–14)
13. Does not agitate others
14. And is not agitated by others
15. Free from joy
16. Free from envy
17. Free from fear
18. Free from disappointments (12.15)
19. Has no expectations (free from desires)
20. Pure
21. Wise
22. Impartial
23. Free from anxiety
24. Has renounced the feeling of doer ship in all undertakings, such a devotee is dear to me. (12.16)
25. Does not rejoice
26. Does not hate
27. Does not grieve
28. Has no desires
29. Has renounced both the good and the evil, full of devotion, is dear to me (12.17)
30. Alike to an enemy or a friend
31. Alike in honor or disgrace
32. Same in heat and cold
33. Same in pleasure or pain
34. Indifferent to criticism or praise
35. Quiet (practice silence)

36. Content with whatever he has
37. Unattached to a place (a country, or a house)
38. Equanimous (even tempered)
39. Full of devotion (12.18–19)

Benefit: Become God's beloved

Q Who is extremely dear to God (His most favorite)?

ये तु धर्म्यामृतमिदं यथोक्तं पर्युपासते।
श्रद्दधाना मत्परमा भक्तास्तेऽतीव मे प्रियाः ॥20॥

ye tu dharmāmṛtam idaṁ yathoktaṁ paryupāsate
śraddadhānā mat-paramā bhaktās te 'tīva me priyāḥ

But those who set Me as their Supreme goal and follow faithfully the above mentioned nectar of moral values (or at least put their best effort to develop these), those devotees are extremely dear to Me. (12.20)

One who sets God as his Supreme goal and puts his best efforts to realize Him, is extremely dear to Him

Lessons to learn and practice in daily life

Start your day with love, fill your day with love and end your day with love
—Sathya Sai Baba

1. Build Relationships: The Yoga of Devotion not only teaches us how to build relations with God but also with others in the world by applying the same teachings, knowing their likes and dislikes and following them accordingly. Thus, becoming dear to Him and to others, one can enjoy life in the material world and also attain God/Self-Realization. Most of the miseries in the world are due to bad relationships. If we follow these teachings, they will help us make our surroundings and the world a happier and more peaceful place.
2. Divine qualities: We must develop divine qualities and apply them in our daily life thus we become extremely dear to God.
3. We should always live in God's Consciousness.

Work with compassion is the only way to God

4. Develop pure love for others: *Bhakti Yoga* teaches how to love others without any expectation in return.
5. We should always practice Devotion Yoga and put love into every action we do. Therefore, just add love to whatever you do, e.g. when cooking food, add love with the thought that you are preparing food for God. As icing on a cake it will taste better too.

The whole universe is His creation, so we should "Love All, Serve All."

—Sathya Sai Baba

Love is the only bond that keeps people, family, society, nations and the world together

ॐ तत्सदिति श्रीमद्भगवद्गीतासूपनिषत्सु ब्रह्मविद्यायां योगशास्त्रे
श्रीकृष्णार्जुनसंवादे भक्तियोगो नाम द्वादशोऽध्यायः ।।

AUM TAT SAT

Thus ends the twelfth chapter named "*Bhakti Yoga*"
The Path of Love and Devotion
in the *Upanishad* of the glorious Bhagavad Gita, the scripture of Yoga, the science of the Absolute (*Brahman*) in the form of the dialogue between Lord Krishna and Arjuna.

Aum Shanti, Shanti, Shantihi

The Creator and His Creation

Self-Transformation and Purification through Knowing the Body, Spirit and the Supreme Spirit

KSETRA-KSETRAJNA VIBHAGA YOGA

The Path of knowing the Field and the Knower of the Field

Union with God (Self-Realization) through the path of knowing body, spirit and Supreme Spirit

The Lord is more than His creation.
—Dr. Radhakrishna

In the previous dialogues, *Karma Yoga* and *Bhakti Yoga* (Chapters 1–12), Lord Krishna explained how one can attain God through selfless service with love and devotion without expecting any fruit of action. One worships manifested God (*Saguna*), develops noble qualities and becomes His beloved.

In Knowledge Yoga (*Jnana Yoga*, Chapters 13–18), He explains how one can realize Self and become One with *Brahman*, Supreme Reality (Unmanifested/Formless God). Oneness/Union with God/Self-Realization can be attained by transcending oneself (lower self) to Self (Higher Self) through self-awareness, self-analysis, self-purification and self-transformation.

In this first chapter of Knowledge Yoga, Lord Krishna enlightens Arjuna by imparting the knowledge of the physical body (field, Cosmos, *Prakriti*, creation, Nature, matter, miniature universe) and the Creator of the body (Knower of the field, Consciousness, Supreme Spirit, God, *Purusha*), and to know the difference between them.

Lord Krishna explains to Arjuna that the physical body is transitory and spirit is Eternal. The body is like a field that yields the ambrosial fruit. When a seeker knows the importance of the field and the difference between the field (body, creation, matter) and the knower of the field (Consciousness, Spirit, Energy, Unmanifested Form), he finally attains True Knowledge and realizes God.

The Lord also gives the precise knowledge about the individual soul and the Ultimate Soul. Whatever we see around us is the combination of matter and Spirit, *Prakriti* and *Purusha*, body and Spirit. God is the knower of the field who dwells in all the bodies. The fields, individuals (embodied soul, *jivatma*), are many but the dweller of the field, God (*Parmatma*) is only one.

In human nature, there are two opposing forces that are always working together; one leads toward God, the other toward ignorance. The individual who is ignorant of soul lives in body consciousness due to his three *Gunas* (Goodness, passion and ignorance). However, the one who is aware of Supreme Spirit, lives in God's Consciousness and dedicates his life to attains Union with God.

This knowledge also answers some of the basic questions of "Where did I come from and where will I go from here and how?"

Main Message

The path of knowing the Creator and His Creation

Everyone is made up of matter and energy, body and soul

- Knowledge of both the Creator and Creation is called Transcendental Knowledge (Integral Knowledge, True Knowledge or Metaphysical Knowledge).
- The human body (field, microcosm) is only a fragment of the macrocosm (universe), therefore whatever is present in the microcosm is also present in the body, e.g. a drop of water in the ocean.
- The whole universe is operated by *Purushottama* (Higher Self, Supreme Consciousness).
- The human body and the Spirit are different from each other.
- The body (field) is constituted of 24 principles.
- The body is the field (vehicle) for all the activities of the soul. The soul resides inside the body, enjoys the material world (*Maya*) and gets entangled due to its *Gunas* (Goodness, passion and ignorance).
- The Soul/Spirit knows and witnesses all the actions of its body therefore it is called the knower of the body (field). The spirit knows only its own body but the Supreme-Soul knows all the bodies in Creation.
- One who knows the difference between the body, individual soul and the Supreme-Soul is the knower of the Self-Knowledge (Wisdom). Developing divine qualities (virtues) is the prerequisite to attaining Self-Knowledge.

Body (jiva, field) + Soul (Knower of the field) = Jivatma-Individual being → Divine Qualities → Self/True-Knowledge (Wisdom)

Chapter Overview

01–06 Creation and the Creator (Field and the Knower of the field)

07–11 The True Knowledge

12–34 Knowledge of the Field and the Knower of the Field (*Prakriti* and *Purusha*)

Creation and the Creator (Field and the Knower of the field)

Q What is creation (Kshetra) and who is the Creator (Kshetrajna)?

श्रीभगवानुवाच
इदं शरीरं कौन्तेय क्षेत्रमित्यभिधीयते।
एतद्यो वेत्ति तं प्राहुः क्षेत्रज्ञ इति तद्विदः ॥1॥

śrī-bhagavān uvāca
idaṁ śarīraṁ kaunteya kṣetram ity abhidhīyate
etad yo vetti taṁ prāhuḥ kṣetra-jña iti tad-vidaḥ

Be the Knower of the field

The Supreme Lord said: O Arjuna, this body is called the field of action (*Kshetra*, creation, miniature universe). One who knows this field is called the knower of the field (***Kshetrajna***, Creator, Spirit). (13.01)

Q Who is the knower of the field?

क्षेत्रज्ञं चापि मां विद्धि सर्वक्षेत्रेषु भारत।
क्षेत्रक्षेत्रज्ञयोर्ज्ञानं यत्तज्ज्ञानं मतं मम ॥2॥

kṣetra-jñaṁ cāpi māṁ viddhi sarva-kṣetreṣu bhārata
kṣetra-kṣetrajñayor jñānaṁ yat taj jñānaṁ mataṁ mama

Transcedental Knowledge is knowing both oneself and God

O Arjuna, know Me as the Creator of the field of all the fields (creation). The knowledge of the field and the knower of the field (Creator and creation, Spirit and matter) are considered to be the True Knowledge (Transcendental, Metaphysical Knowledge) by me. (13.02)

Q How did Lord Krishna describe to Arjuna the creation and the Creator?

तत्क्षेत्रं यच्च यादृक्च यद्विकारि यतश्च यत्।
स च यो यत्प्रभावश्च तत्समासेन मेश्रृणु ॥3॥

tat kṣetraṁ yac ca yādṛk ca yad-vikāri yataś ca yat
sa ca yo yat-prabhāvaś ca tat samāsena me śṛṇu

Please listen to my brief description of both creation and the Creator. What is that creation (*Kshetra*), what it is like, what are its changes (transformations, modifications) and where is it produced? Who is that Creator (*Kshetrajna*) and what are His powers? (13.03)

Q Where can these details be found?

ऋषिभिर्बहुधा गीतं छन्दोभिर्विविधैः पृथक् ।
ब्रह्मसूत्रपदैश्चैव हेतुमद्भिर्विनिश्चितैः ।।4।।

ṛṣibhir bahudhā gītaṁ chandobhir vividhaiḥ pṛthak
brahma-sūtra-padaiś caiva hetumadbhir viniścitaiḥ

The great sages have sung and described the truth about the creation and the Creator very distinctively with many different ways in different Vedic hymns and also in the conclusive and convincing verses of the *Vedanta-Sutra*. (13.04)

Q What are the 24 elements and their modifications (Cosmos, body, field, *Kshetra, Prakriti*)?

महाभूतान्यहंकारो बुद्धिरव्यक्तमेव च ।
इन्द्रियाणि दशैकं च पञ्च चेन्द्रियगोचराः ।।5।।

mahā-bhūtāny ahaṅkāro buddhir avyaktam eva ca
indriyāṇi daśaikaṁ ca pañca cendriya-gocarāḥ

इच्छा द्वेषः सुखं दुःखं संघातश्चेतना धृतिः ।
एतत्क्षेत्रं समासेन सविकारमुदाहृतम् ।।6।।

icchā dveṣaḥ sukhaṁ duḥkhaṁ saṅghātaś cetanā dhṛtiḥ
etat kṣetraṁ samāsena sa-vikāram udāhṛtam

The primary material Nature, the entire Cosmic creation (Cosmic, body, *Prakriti*) consists of total of 24 elements and their modifications:

1. Ego
2. Intellect (*buddhi*)
3. Non-manifest (primordial matter, nature).
4. Mind

5–9. Five basic elements such as air, fire, earth, water and ether
10–19. Ten organs of sensation (*indriyas*) and their actions
20–24. Five objects of the senses (sound, touch, sight, taste and smell) (13.05)

Their modifications (*vikaras*) are:

1. Desire
2. Hatred
3. Pleasure

4. Pain
5. Physical body
6. Consciousness
7. Steadfastness

This is the brief description of the entire creation (body) along with its transformations. (13.06)

The True Knowledge

Q What is the True Knowledge and how can I acquire it?

अमानित्वमदम्भित्वमहिंसा क्षान्तिरार्जवम् ।
आचार्योपासनं शौचं स्थैर्यमात्मविनिग्रहः ।। 7 ।।

amānitvam adambhitvam ahiṁsā kṣāntir ārjavam
ācāryopāsanaṁ śaucaṁ sthairyam ātma-vinigrahaḥ

इन्द्रियार्थेषु वैराग्यमनहंकार एव च ।
जन्ममृत्युजराव्याधिदुःखदोषानुदर्शनम् ।। 8 ।।

indriyārtheṣu vairāgyam anahaṅkāra eva ca
janma-mṛtyu-jarā-vyādhi-duḥkha-doṣānudarśanam

असक्तिरनभिष्वङ्गः पुत्रदारगृहादिषुः ।
नित्यं च समचित्तत्वमिष्टानिष्टोपपत्तिषु ।। 9 ।।

asaktir anabhiṣvaṅgaḥ putra-dāra-gṛhādiṣu
nityaṁ ca sama-cittatvam iṣṭāniṣṭopapattiṣu

मयि चानन्ययोगेन भक्तिरव्यभिचारिणी ।
विविक्तदेशसेवित्वमरतिर्जनसंसदि ।। 10 ।।

mayi cānanya-yogena bhaktir avyabhicāriṇī
vivikta-deśa-sevitvam aratir jana-saṁsadi

True knowledge leads to God

अध्यात्मज्ञाननित्यत्वं तत्त्वज्ञानार्थदर्शनम् ।
एतज्ज्ञानमिति प्रोक्तमज्ञानं यदतोऽन्यथा ।। 11 ।।

adhyātma-jñāna-nityatvaṁ tattva-jñānārtha-darśanam
etaj jñānam iti proktam ajñānaṁ yad ato 'nyathā

The Ultimate Knowledge is:

1. Humility, Absence of arrogance
2. Non violence with body, mind and speech
3. Forgiveness
4. Honesty

5. Service to a spiritual-guru
6. Purity (of thought, word and deed)
7. Firmness in spiritual discipline
8. Self-control
9. Dispassion towards sense objects
10. Absence of ego (modesty)
11. Constant reflection in mind of the pain and suffering inherent in birth, old age, disease and death
12. Detachment or non-attachment (*vairagya*)
13. Non-possessiveness for son, wife, home, etc.
14. Constant evenness of mind (Equanimity) both in favorable and unfavorable circumstances (attainment of the desirable and the undesirable)
15. Constant devotion to Me through single-minded contemplation
16. Taste for solitude
17. Distaste for social gatherings and gossips
18. Steadfastness in acquiring knowledge of Self (Eternal Being)
19. Seeing the omnipresent Supreme Being everywhere

All this is said to be Knowledge (Wisdom, *Jnana*) and whatever is contrary to this is called ignorance. (13.07–11)

Knowledge of the Field and the Knower of the Field (*Prakriti* and *Purusha*)

Q What one must one know in order to gain Supreme Bliss and Immortality?

ज्ञेयं यत्तत्प्रवक्ष्यामि यज्ज्ञात्वामृतमश्नुते ।
अनादिमत्परं ब्रह्म न सत्तन्नासदुच्यते ॥ 12 ॥

jñeyaṁ yat tat pravakṣyāmi yaj jñātvāmṛtam aśnute
anādi mat-paraṁ brahma na sat tan nāsad ucyate

God is beyond imagination

Now, I will explain to you that which is to be known and by knowing that one attains Supreme Bliss and Immortality. It is Supreme Brahman (God, Spirit, Supreme Being) who is without beginning and is called neither Eternal (*Sat*) nor non-being/temporal (*asat*). (13.12)

Q How can God be Omnipresent?

सर्वत:पाणिपादं तत्सर्वतोऽक्षिशिरोमुखम् ।
सर्वत:श्रुतिमल्लोके सर्वमावृत्य तिष्ठति ॥ 13 ॥

sarvataḥ pāṇi-pādaṁ tat sarvato 'kṣi-śiro-mukham
sarvataḥ śrutimal loke sarvam āvṛtya tiṣṭhati

सर्वेन्द्रियगुणाभासं सर्वेन्द्रियविवर्जितम् ।
असक्तं सर्वभृच्चैव निर्गुणं गुणभोक्तृ च ।। 14 ।।

sarvendriya-guṇābhāsaṁ sarvendriya-vivarjitam
asaktaṁ sarva-bhṛc caiva nirguṇaṁ guṇa-bhoktṛ ca

बहिरन्तश्च भूतानामचरं चरमेव च ।
सूक्ष्मत्वात्तदविज्ञेयं दूरस्थं चान्तिके च तत् ।। 15 ।।

bahir antaś ca bhūtānām acaraṁ caram eva ca
sūkṣmatvāt tad avijñeyaṁ dūra-sthaṁ cāntike ca tat

अविभक्तं च भूतेषु विभक्तमिव च स्थितम् ।
भूतभर्तृ च तज्ज्ञेयं ग्रसिष्णु प्रभविष्णु च ।। 16 ।।

avibhaktaṁ ca bhūteṣu vibhaktam iva ca sthitam
bhūta-bhartṛ ca taj jñeyaṁ grasiṣṇu prabhaviṣṇu ca

The Supreme-Soul has His hands, feet, eyes, head, mouth, and ears everywhere. He is pervading all and Omnipresent. (13.13)

He possesses the function of all the senses yet He is without all physical senses. He is unattached, yet the sustainer of all; free from *Gunas* of material nature (free of attribute) and yet the Enjoyer of the attributes by becoming a living entity. (*jivatma*) (13.14)

He exists inside as well as outside all beings and constitutes both animate and inanimate creation (living and non-living). Since He is subtle, He is Incomprehensible (beyond the power of the senses to see or to know). Because He is Omnipresent, He is far away (in the Supreme Abode, *Parama-dhama*) and yet so near (residing in one's inner psyche). (13.15)

He is Undivided like space, yet appears to be divided among all living and non-living beings. He is to be understood as He is the Creator (Generator–*Brahma*) of all beings; Sustainer (*Operator*) Vishnu, and He is also the *Demolisher* (Shiva) of all; the Trinity. (13.16)

Generator + Operator + Destroyer = GOD

Q What is the source of light (Wisdom, Knowledge, *Jnana*)?

Consciousness within is God

ज्योतिषामपि तज्जयोतिस्तमसः परमुच्यते ।
ज्ञानं ज्ञेयं ज्ञानगम्यं हृदि सर्वस्य विष्ठितम् ।। 17 ।।

jyotiṣām api taj jyotis tamasaḥ param ucyate
jñānaṁ jñeyaṁ jñāna-gamyaṁ hṛdi sarvasya viṣṭhitam

The Supreme is also the source of all light (luminous objects). He is said to be beyond darkness of ignorance. He is the Self-Knowledge, object of knowledge and the goal of knowledge (Realized Knowledge), He is seated in the inner psyche of all beings (the causal heart as Consciousness of all beings). (13.17)

Q Why is it important to know the creation and the Creator?

इति क्षेत्रं तथा ज्ञानं ज्ञेयं चोक्तं समासतः।
मद्भक्त एतद्विज्ञाय मद्भावायोपपद्यते ।। 18 ।।

iti kṣetraṁ tathā jñānaṁ jñeyaṁ coktaṁ samāsataḥ
mad-bhakta etad vijñāya mad-bhāvāyopapadyate

God can be attained by knowing both creation and His creator

Thus, I have briefly described creation as well as knowledge and the object of knowledge. By knowing and understanding this, My devotee attains My Supreme Abode (Self-Realization, God-Realization, Lord Krishna). (13.18)

Q From where do the *Gunas* originate?

प्रकृतिं पुरुषं चैव विद्ध्यनादी उभावपि।
विकारांश्च गुणांश्चैव विद्धि प्रकृतिसंभवान् ।। 19 ।।

prakṛtiṁ puruṣaṁ caiva viddhy anādī ubhāv api
vikārāṁś ca guṇāṁś caiva viddhi prakṛti-sambhavān

Understand that both matter (Nature, *Prakriti*) and Soul are beginning-less; also understand that all modifications and three modes of *Gunas* (attributes, qualities) are born of Material Nature alone. (13.19)

Q What is the cause of creation and the cause of experiences (pleasure and pain)?

कार्यकरणकर्तृत्वे हेतुः प्रकृतिरुच्यते।
पुरुषः सुखदुःखानां भोक्तृत्व हेतुरुच्यते ।। 20 ।।

kārya-kāraṇa-kartṛtve hetuḥ prakṛtir ucyate
puruṣaḥ sukha-duḥkhānāṁ bhoktṛtve hetur ucyate

Material nature is the cause of existence of the human body

Material Nature is said to be the cause of production of the physical body and the senses (all material causes and effects) while Supreme Consciousness (Supreme-Soul) is said to be the cause of experience of pleasure and pain. (13.20)

Q What determines the type of parents one will have in the next life?

पुरुषः प्रकृतिस्थो हि भुङ्क्ते प्रकृतिजान्गुणान् ।
कारणं गुणसङ्गोऽस्य सदसद्योनिजन्मसु ॥ 21 ॥

puruṣaḥ prakṛti-stho hi bhuṅkte prakṛti-jān guṇān
kāraṇaṁ guṇa-saṅgo 'sya sad-asad-yoni-janmasu

While seated in the body, the Soul/Spirit enjoys the association, experiences and attachment to the *Gunas* (Goodness, passion, ignorance) and this becomes the cause of his birth in good and evil wombs. (13.21)

Q What are some other names of the Supreme-Soul (God)?

उपद्रष्टानुमन्ता च भर्ता भोक्ता महेश्वरः ।
परमात्मेति चाप्युक्तो देहेऽस्मिन्पुरुषः परः ॥ 22 ॥

upadraṣṭānumantā ca bhartā bhoktā maheśvaraḥ
paramātmeti cāpy ukto dehe 'smin puruṣaḥ paraḥ

The Supreme-Soul, while dwelling in the body, is also called the Witness, the Guide, the Counselor, the Supporter, the Experience of pleasure and pain, the Great Lord and also the Supreme-Self. (13.22)

Q What will I gain by knowing both Purusha (Spirit-Soul) and the Prakriti (Material Nature)?

य एवं वेत्ति पुरुषं प्रकृतिं च गुणैः सह ।
सर्वथा वर्तमानोऽपि न स भूयोऽभिजायते ॥ 23 ॥

ya evaṁ vetti puruṣaṁ prakṛtiṁ ca guṇaiḥ saha
sarvathā vartamāno 'pi na sa bhūyo 'bhijāyate

One who thoroughly understands the inter-relationship of the Spiritual Spirit (*Purusha*) and the Material Nature (*Prakriti*) with its three modes (*Gunas*, qualities) is sure to attain Liberation (never born again) regardless of their work and lifestyle. (13.23)

Q In how many ways can God be realized?

ध्यानेनात्मनि पश्यन्ति केचिदात्मानमात्मना ।
अन्ये सांख्येन योगेन कर्मयोगेन चापरे ॥ 24 ॥

dhyānenātmani paśyanti kecid ātmānam ātmanā
anye sāṅkhyena yogena karma-yogena cāpare

God is only One but the methods to realizing Him are many

अन्ये त्वेवमजानन्तः श्रुत्वान्येभ्य उपासते।
तेऽपि चातितरन्त्येव मृत्युं श्रुतिपरायणाः ॥25॥

anye tv evam ajānantaḥ śrutvānyebhya upāsate
te 'pi cātitaranty eva mṛtyuṁ śruti-parāyaṇāḥ

Some perceive the Self (Supreme-Soul) within self through meditation, others by Yoga of knowledge and still others by Yoga of action (Selfless service). (13.24)

Yet others, not knowing these paths of Yogas (meditation, Yoga of knowledge and Yoga of action), worship Him as they have heard from others (as mentioned in the scriptures by the saints and sages). They also cross beyond death by their devotion to what they have heard. (13.25)

Q How are living beings and non-living beings born?

यावत्संजायते किंचित्सत्त्वं स्थावरजङ्गमम्।
क्षेत्रक्षेत्रज्ञसंयोगात्तद्विद्धि भरतर्षभ ॥26॥

yāvat sañjāyate kiñcit sattvaṁ sthāvara-jaṅgamam
kṣetra-kṣetrajña-saṁyogāt tad viddhi bharatarṣabha

Everything in the universe is the combination of matter and Spirit/Energy

O Arjuna, whatever is born animate or is inanimate; you must understand that they are born from the Union of Spirit (*Purusha*) and matter (*Prakriti*, Material Nature). (13.26)

Q Who is the real seer and what is his real gain?

समं सर्वेषु भूतेषु तिष्ठन्तं परमेश्वरम्।
विनश्यत्स्वविनश्यन्तं यः पश्यति स पश्यति ॥27॥

samaṁ sarveṣu bhūteṣu tiṣṭhantaṁ parameśvaram
vinaśyatsv avinaśyantaṁ yaḥ paśyati sa paśyati

Almighty is present in everyone

समं पश्यन्हि सर्वत्र समवस्थितमीश्वरम्।
न हिनस्त्यात्मनात्मानं ततो याति परां गतिम् ॥28॥

samaṁ paśyan hi sarvatra samavasthitam īśvaram
na hinasty ātmanātmānaṁ tato yāti parāṁ gatim

One who sees the same Imperishable Supreme-Soul dwelling and abiding equally in all perishable beings is a true seer. (13.27)

By seeing the same Lord existing equally in all beings, he does not degrade, harm, hurt and kill himself or anybody else and therefore, he attains the Supreme Abode, Supreme goal of his life, God-Realization and Self-Realization. (13.28)

Q Who is a doer and who is a non-doer?

प्रकृत्यैव च कर्माणि क्रियमाणानि सर्वशः ।
यः पश्यति तथात्मानमकर्तारं स पश्यति ॥ 29 ॥

prakṛtyaiva ca karmāṇi kriyamāṇāni sarvaśaḥ
yaḥ paśyati tathātmānam akartāraṁ sa paśyati

One is the puppet of his innate qualities

One who clearly sees that all actions are done by the power of *Gunas* (*Prakriti*, Material Nature) alone and the Soul/Self is not the doer, he truly sees. (13.29)

Q When and how can a person become one with God?

यदा भूतपृथग्भावमेकस्थमनुपश्यति ।
तत एव च विस्तारं ब्रह्म संपद्यते तदा ॥ 30 ॥

yadā bhūta-pṛthag-bhāvam eka-stham anupaśyati
tata eva ca vistāraṁ brahma sampadyate tadā

God and I are One

When a person discovers that the entire diversity of beings is actually rooted in *One* and further has emerged from that *One* alone, he becomes that very *One* (*Brahman*) himself. (13.30)

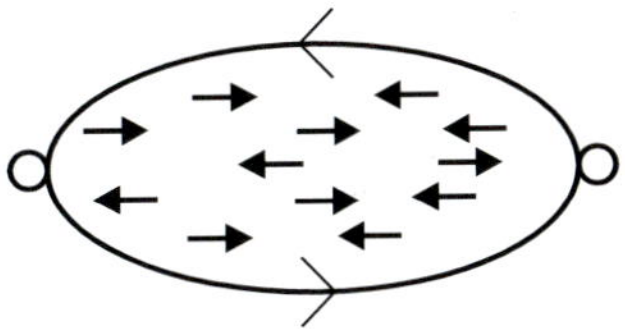

Q Can Soul (*Atma*) be contaminated when seated in the human body?

अनादित्वान्निर्गुणत्वात्परमात्मायमव्ययः ।
शरीरस्थोऽपि कौन्तेय न करोति न लिप्यते ॥ 31 ॥

anāditvān nirguṇatvāt paramātmāyam avyayaḥ
śarīra-stho 'pi kaunteya na karoti na lipyate

यथा सर्वगतं सौक्ष्म्यादाकाशं नोपलिप्यते ।
सर्वत्रावस्थितो देहे तथात्मा नोपलिप्यते ॥ 32 ॥

yathā sarva-gataṁ saukṣmyād ākāśaṁ nopalipyate
sarvatrāvasthito dehe tathātmā nopalipyate

O Arjuna, the Imperishable Supreme-Soul (*Parmatma*), is without beginning and without the *Gunas* (qualities), though dwelling in the body (*jivatma*), neither does anything nor gets contaminated. (13.31)

Although ether (sky) is all-pervading, due to its subtle nature it is not contaminated by anything. Similarly, the soul (*Atma*) pervading everywhere in the body, does not mix with the body and is not contaminated. (13.32)

Q What does the Soul (*Atma*, Spirit) do?

यथा प्रकाशयत्येकः कृत्स्नं लोकमिमं रविः ।
क्षेत्रं क्षेत्री तथा कृत्स्नं प्रकाशयति भारत ॥ 33 ॥

yathā prakāśayaty ekaḥ kṛtsnaṁ lokam imaṁ raviḥ
kṣetraṁ kṣetrī tathā kṛtsnaṁ prakāśayati bhārata

O Arjuna, as one sun illuminates this entire universe (field, creation), so does the Spirit (*Atma*) illuminate the entire field (body). (13.33)

Q What is the benefit of knowing both *Kshetra* (field, creation, body) and the *Kshetrajna* (Knower of the field, Creator, Spirit)?

क्षेत्रक्षेत्रज्ञयोरेवमन्तरं ज्ञानचक्षुषा ।
भूतप्रकृतिमोक्षं च ये विदुर्यान्ति ते परम् ॥ 34 ॥

kṣetra-kṣetrajñayor evam antaraṁ jñāna-cakṣuṣā
bhūta-prakṛti-mokṣaṁ ca ye vidur yānti te param

Those who attain the Supreme (Self-Realization), who perceive with the eye of wisdom the distinction between creation (Body) and the Creator (Knower of the body, Spirit) also know the paths of Liberation from the bondage of Material Nature (any one of the five paths—Selfless service, Knowledge, Devotion, Meditation, and Surrender). (13.34)

Lessons to learn and practice in daily life

Divine Qualities lead to True knowledge and Self-Realization

1. Since the human body is the carrier for the soul, we must take good care of the body and other worldly matters. However, must not get too attached to them and spend all of our time just taking care of them.
2. We should always make the best use of our body; i.e., we should use our body only for knowing the Creator of our body (Supreme Being, Supreme Spirit, Super-Soul).
3. Since human birth is the cause and effect of one's own actions, we should perform only those actions that will take us toward God-Realization and Self-Realization.

4. We should put a conscious effort into developing the divine qualities (precursor for God-Realization) as they lead to God/Self-Realization.

ॐ तत्सदिति श्रीमद्भगवद्गीतासूपनिषत्सु ब्रह्मविद्यायां योगशास्त्रे
श्रीकृष्णार्जुनसंवादे क्षेत्रक्षेत्रज्ञयोगो नाम त्रयोदशोऽध्यायः ।।

AUM TAT SAT

Thus ends the thirteenth chapter named "*Ksetra-Ksetrajna Vibhaga Yoga*"
The Path of knowing the Field and the Knower of the Field
in the *Upanishad* of the glorious Bhagavad Gita, the scripture of Yoga,
the science of the Absolute (*Brahman*), in the form of the dialogue
between Lord Krishna and Arjuna.

Aum Shanti, Shanti, Shantihi

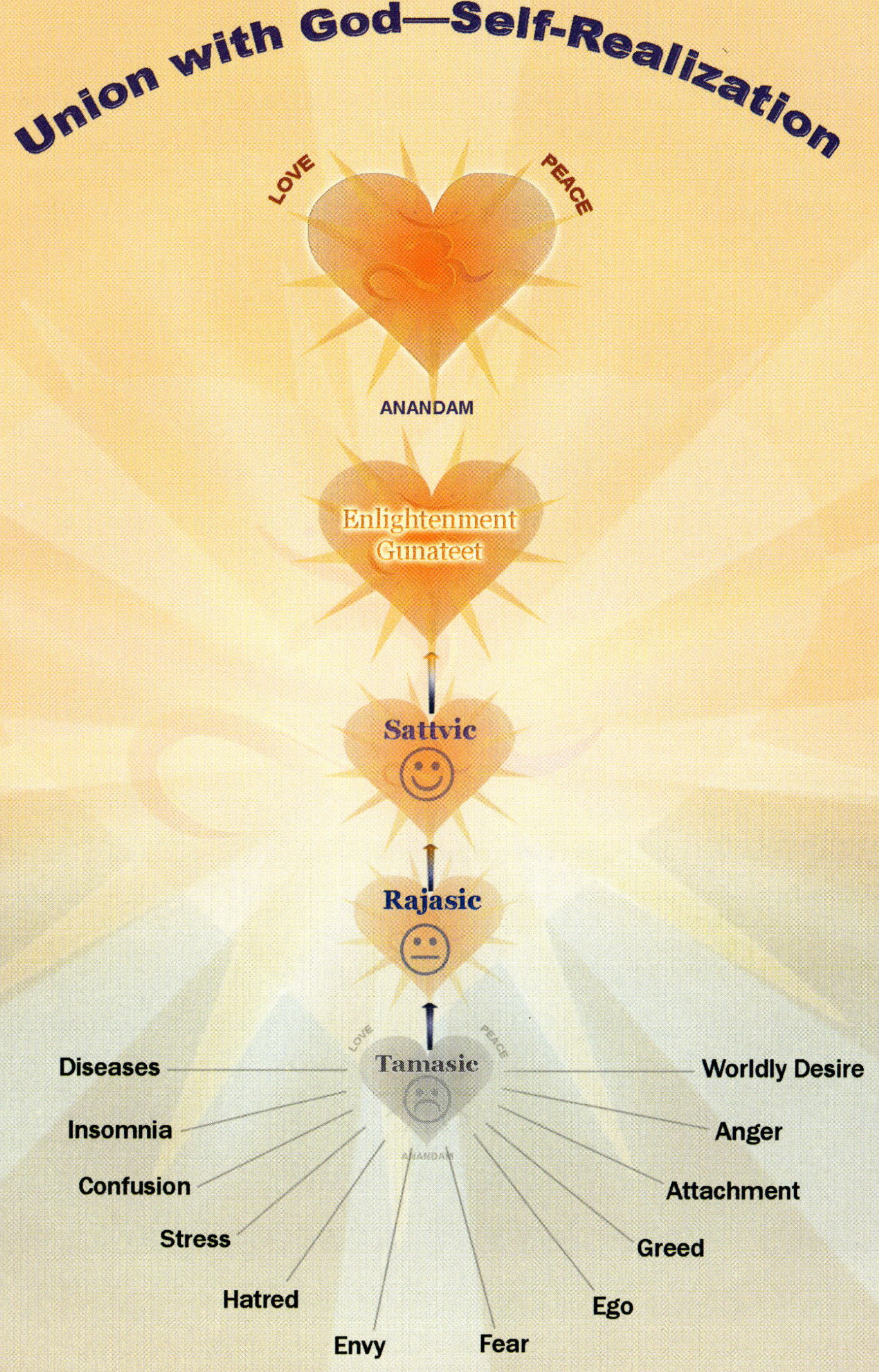

Self-Purification and Transformation through Transcending Gunas

GUNA-TRAYA VIBHAGA YOGA

The Path of the Division of the Three Gunas

Union with God (Self-Realization) through the path of transcending three Gunas

The Gita is a guide to take you beyond your limitations

In this chapter, Lord Krishna enlightens Arjuna with the knowledge of the three modes of nature, *Gunas* (*Sattva*-Goodness, *Rajas*-Passion, *Tamas*-Ignorance), their qualities and how to differentiate between them. How the evolution of the world takes place from *Prakriti* (Material Nature) and *Purush* (Spirit, God). How to realize God by transcending *Gunas* (Self-Transformation) and what are the hallmarks of the one who has reached the State of Transcendence (Supreme Bliss).

Reprogram the software of mind and attain Liberation

Main Message

Jivatma → Mahatma → Paramatma

Everything in this universe is bound by the law of Material Nature (Gunas)

- Every human being (embodied soul) is made of body and soul (*jiva* + *Atma* = *jivatma*). Everyone, in this world, is under the influence of following three modes of Material Nature (Attributes/qualities/*Gunas*):

    1. Goodness, Purity (*Sattvic*) (binds to happiness and goodness, it can be harnessed by selfless action)

    2. Passion (*Rajasic*) (can be harnessed by dedication to one's own duty/ *svadharma*)

    3. Ignorance, darkness (*Tamasic*) (can be conquered by *Karma Yoga*)

- These *Gunas*/modes bind to soul and are responsible for the downfall or upliftment of the individuals (embodied soul, *jivatma*).
- Here Lord Krishna advises to free oneself from ignorance and passion and adopt the path of goodness, purity until one acquires the ability to transcend them completely.
- One can attain Liberation by transcending these modes of Material Nature (attributes)
- One can transcend the *Gunas* by performing selfless service with unwavering devotion.

Union with God through Self-Purification and Self-Transformation

Chapter Overview

01–04	Origin of Universe by union of *Prakriti* (Material Nature) and *Purusha* (Soul)
05–09	Three *Gunas* (Material Nature) bind the Spirit-Soul to the body
10–13	*Gunas*, the qualities of *three modes of nature* (*Sattva*, *Rajas* and *Tamas*)
14–20	Transcending the *Gunas* is the way to *Nirvana*, Self-Realization
21–25	The hallmarks of one who has transcended the *Gunas*
26–27	Transcending from the *Gunas* can be achieved through *Love* and *Devotion*

Origin of Universe by union of *Prakriti* (Material Nature) and *Purusha* (Soul)

Q Why did Lord Krishna talk about Supreme Knowledge again?

श्रीभगवानुवाच
परं भूयः प्रवक्ष्यामि ज्ञानानां ज्ञानमुत्तमम् ।
यज्ज्ञात्वा मुनयः सर्वे परां सिद्धिमितो गताः ॥1॥

śrī-bhagavān uvāca
paraṁ bhūyaḥ pravakṣyāmi jñānānāṁ jñānam uttamam
yaj jñātvā munayaḥ sarve parāṁ siddhim ito gatāḥ

The Supreme Lord said: I will proclaim once again that Supreme Knowledge is the greatest of all wisdoms. By acquiring which all the sages have achieved Liberation from the mundane world and have attained the highest perfection. (14.01)

Q What are the benefits of acquiring Transcendental Knowledge?

इदं ज्ञानमुपाश्रित्य मम साधर्म्यमागताः ।
सर्गेऽपि नोपजायन्ते प्रलये न व्यथन्ति च ॥2॥

idaṁ jñānam upāśritya mama sādharmyam āgatāḥ
sarge 'pi nopajāyante pralaye na vyathanti ca

Attaining Supreme knowledge is equivalent to attaining God

Those who have acquired this Transcendental Knowledge have attained transcendental nature like My own and have become one with Me. They are neither born at the beginning of every Cosmic cycle nor disturbed at the time of final dissolution. (14.02)

Q How does *jivatma* come into existence?

मम योनिर्महद् ब्रह्म तस्मिन्गर्भं दधाम्यहम् ।
संभवः सर्वभूतानां ततो भवति भारत ।। 3 ।।

mama yonir mahad brahma
tasmin garbhaṁ dadhāmy aham
sambhavaḥ sarva-bhūtānāṁ
tato bhavati bhārata

All living beings are born by the union of Spirit/Energy and matter

O Arjuna, My material Nature is My womb wherein I place the seed (of Consciousness, Spirit). The birth of all beings follows from this Union of Matter and Spirit. (*jiva* + *Atma* = *jivatma*) (14.03)

Q Who is the universal mother and the father?

सर्वयोनिषु कौन्तेय मूर्तयः संभवन्ति याः ।
तासां ब्रह्म महद्योनिरहं बीजप्रदः पिता ।। 4 ।।

sarva-yoniṣu kaunteya mūrtayaḥ sambhavanti yāḥ
tāsāṁ brahma mahad yonir ahaṁ bīja-pradaḥ pitā

Nature is our mother and God is our father

O Arjuna, all the beings that are born from different wombs, Nature (*Prakriti*) is their body-giving mother and I (Supreme Consciousness) am the seed and life-giving father. (14.04)

Three *Gunas* (Material Nature) bind the Spirit-Soul to the body

Q What do the three modes of nature (*Gunas*) do?

सत्त्वं रजस्तम इति गुणाः प्रकृतिसंभवाः ।
निबध्नन्ति महाबाहो देहे देहिनमव्ययम् ।। 5 ।।

sattvaṁ rajas tama iti guṇāḥ prakṛti-sambhavāḥ
nibadhnanti mahā-bāho dehe dehinam avyayam

Sattva (Goodness, purity), *Rajas* (Passion, activity), and *Tamas* (darkness, ignorance, inertia), these qualities born of material nature bind the Eternal Soul to the body, O Arjuna. (14.05)

Q How does the *Sattvic* mode of nature bind the soul to the body?

तत्र सत्त्वं निर्मलत्वात्प्रकाशकमनामयम्।
सुखसङ्गेन बध्नाति ज्ञानसङ्गेन चानघ ॥6॥

tatra sattvaṁ nirmalatvāt prakāśakam anāmayam
sukha-saṅgena badhnāti jñāna-saṅgena cānagha

O Arjuna, *Sattva* (mode of goodness) being pure, is luminous and free from sickness and yet in its own way binds the soul to the body (*jiva*, embodied beings, individuals) by creating attachment to happiness and wisdom. (14.06)

Q How does the *Rajasic* mode of nature bind the soul to the body?

रजो रागात्मकं विद्धि तृष्णासङ्गसमुद्भवम्।
तन्निबध्नाति कौन्तेय कर्मसङ्गेन देहिनम् ॥7॥

rajo rāgātmakaṁ viddhi tṛṣṇā-saṅga-samudbhavam
tan nibadhnāti kaunteya karma-saṅgena dehinam

O Arjuna, *Rajas* (mode of passion) on the other hand, is born by intense craving and therefore is the source of desire and attachment. It binds the embodied beings (*jiva*) by attachment to the fruit of action. (14.07)

Q How does the *Tamasic* mode of nature bind the soul to the body?

तमस्त्वज्ञानजं विद्धि मोहनं सर्वदेहिनाम्।
प्रमादालस्यनिद्राभिस्तन्निबध्नाति भारत ॥8॥

tamas tv ajñāna-jaṁ viddhi mohanaṁ sarva-dehinām
pramādālasya-nidrābhis tan nibadhnāti bhārata

O Arjuna, but know that *Tamas* (the mode of darkness) is born of ignorance and the delusion of all embodied beings (*jiva*). It binds the *jiva* by negligence, laziness, and excessive sleep. (14.08)

Q What do the Gunas (*Sattvic, Rajasic* and *Tamasic*) do to individuals?

सत्त्वं सुखे संजयति रजः कर्मणि भारत।
ज्ञानमावृत्य तु तमः प्रमादे संजयत्युत ॥9॥

sattvaṁ sukhe sañjayati rajaḥ karmaṇi bhārata
jñānam āvṛtya tu tamaḥ pramāde sañjayaty uta

O Arjuna, *Sattva* (mode of goodness) attaches one to happiness of learning and knowing the Spirit. *Rajas* (mode of passion) stimulates vigorous action while *Tamas* (the mode of ignorance) obscures Self-Knowledge, clouds discrimination, creates negligence and triggers wrong action. (14.09)

Gunas, the qualities of _three modes of nature_ (_Sattva_, _Rajas_ and _Tamas_)

Q How do these *Gunas* prevail?

रजस्तमश्चाभिभूय सत्त्वं भवति भारत।
रजः सत्त्वं तमश्चैव तमः सत्त्वं रजस्तथा ॥ 10 ॥

rajas tamaś cābhibhūya sattvaṁ bhavati bhārata
rajaḥ sattvaṁ tamaś caiva tamaḥ sattvaṁ rajas tathā

Sattva (Goodness) dominates by suppressing *Rajas* (passion) and (*Tamas*) ignorance. Passion (*Rajas*) dominates by suppressing goodness and ignorance and ignorance dominates by suppressing goodness and passion, O Arjuna. (14.10)

Ignorance (Tamas) < Passion (Rajas) < Goodness (Sattva)

Q What are the signs when goodness (*Sattva*) prevails?

सर्वद्वारेषु देहेऽस्मिन्प्रकाश उपजायते।
ज्ञानं यदा तदा विद्याद्विवृद्धं सत्त्वमित्युत ॥ 11 ॥

sarva-dvāreṣu dehe 'smin prakāśa upajāyate
jñānaṁ yadā tadā vidyād vivṛddhaṁ sattvam ity uta

When the light of Self-Knowledge (Wisdom) radiates through every gate of the body (all the senses) then it should be known that *Sattva* (Goodness, purity) has increased. (14.11)

Q What are the signs when passion (*Rajas*) prevails?

लोभः प्रवृत्तिरारम्भः कर्मणामशमः स्पृहा।
रजस्येतानि जायन्ते विवृद्धे भरतर्षभ ॥ 12 ॥

lobhaḥ pravṛttir ārambhaḥ karmaṇām aśamaḥ spṛhā
rajasy etāni jāyante vivṛddhe bharatarṣabha

O Arjuna, when *Rajas* (passion) predominates:

1. Greed
2. Overexertion
3. Undertaking of action with selfish motives
4. Restlessness and uncontrollable desire arise. (14.12)

Q What are the signs when inertia (*Tamas*) prevails?

अप्रकाशोऽप्रवृत्तिश्च प्रमादो मोह एव च।
तमस्येतानि जायन्ते विवृद्धे कुरुनन्दन ।। 13 ।।

aprakāśo 'pravṛttiś ca pramādo moha eva ca
tamasy etāni jāyante vivṛddhe kuru-nandana

O Arjuna, when inertia (*Tamas*) predominates, ignorance, darkness, lack of effort, carelessness and delusion arise. (14.13)

Transcending the *Gunas* is the way to *Nirvana*, Self-Realization

Q What is the future of the *Sattvic* individual?

यदा सत्त्वे प्रवृद्धे तु प्रलयं याति देहभृत।
तदोत्तमविदां लोकानमलान्प्रतिपद्यते ।। 14 ।।

yadā sattve pravṛddhe tu pralayaṁ yāti deha-bhṛt
tadottama-vidāṁ lokān amalān pratipadyate

Goodness leads to heaven

One who dies when goodness dominates in him, goes to heaven, the world of those who are pure and of great wisdom (Noble ones). (14.14)

Q What is the future of *Rajasic* and *Tamasic* individuals?

रजसि प्रलयं गत्वा कर्मसङ्गिषु जायते।
तथा प्रलीनस्तमसि मूढयोनिषु जायते ।। 15 ।।

rajasi pralayaṁ gatvā karma-saṅgiṣu jāyate
tathā pralīnas tamasi mūḍha-yoniṣu jāyate

One who dies when passion (*Rajas*) dominates in him, is born among those engaged in fruit-oriented activities. One who dies when ignorance (*Tamas*) dominates is born in the animal kingdom as a lower creature. (14.15)

Q What are the results of different actions of the different *Gunas* (qualities)?

कर्मणः सुकृतस्याहुः सात्त्विकं निर्मलं फलम्।
रजसस्तु फलं दुःखमज्ञानं तमसः फलम् ।। 16 ।।

karmaṇaḥ sukṛtasyāhuḥ sāttvikaṁ nirmalaṁ phalam
rajasas tu phalaṁ duḥkham ajñānaṁ tamasaḥ phalam

The fruit of good/virtuous action (*Sattva*) is purity, the fruit of passionate action (*Rajas*) is misery, pain and sorrow and the fruit of ignorant action (*Tamas*) is ignorance. (14.16)

Q What kind of attributes does one develop from the different modes of *Gunas*?

सत्त्वात्संजायते ज्ञानं रजसो लोभ एव च।
प्रमादमोहौ तमसो भवतोऽज्ञानमेव च ॥ 17 ॥

sattvāt sañjāyate jñānaṁ rajaso lobha eva ca
pramāda-mohau tamaso bhavato 'jñānam eva ca

Greed leads to disaster

From the mode of goodness (*Sattva*) develops Self-Knowledge (Wisdom); from the mode of passion (*Rajas*) develops greed, and from the mode of ignorance (*Tamas*) develops negligence, delusion and madness. (14.17)

Q What determines the destiny of the individual?

ऊर्ध्वं गच्छन्ति सत्त्वस्था मध्ये तिष्ठन्ति राजसाः।
जघन्यगुणवृत्तिस्था अधो गच्छन्ति तामसाः ॥ 18 ॥

ūrdhvaṁ gacchanti sattva-sthā
madhye tiṣṭhanti rājasāḥ
jaghanya-guṇa-vṛtti-sthā
adho gacchanti tāmasāḥ

One's future is in one's own hand

Sattvic, those who are established in goodness go to heaven or higher world; *Rajasic* or passionate persons are reborn in the mortal world and dwell in the middle; and *Tamasic* or those abiding in ignorance, go to lower planets or hell. (14.18)

Q Who attains His Divine Nature (Self-Realization)?

नान्यं गुणेभ्यः कर्तारं यदा द्रष्टानुपश्यति।
गुणेभ्यश्च परं वेत्ति मद्भावं सोऽधिगच्छति ॥ 19 ॥

nānyaṁ guṇebhyaḥ kartāraṁ
yadā draṣṭānupaśyati
guṇebhyaś ca paraṁ vetti
mad-bhāvaṁ so 'dhigacchati

Everything in this universe is bound by law of nature, "Cause and effect"

When a person perceives that everything in the Material Nature is but a play of the *Gunas* and clearly perceives the beyond the *Gunas* (qualities, attributes), he attains my Divine Nature (Self-Realization, *Nirvana*). (14.19)

Q How can one be free from miseries of the world and attain immortality (salvation, *Mukti*)?

Transcending the gunas is the path to Nirvana

गुणानेतानतीत्य त्रीन्देही देहसमुद्भवान् ।
जन्ममृत्युजरादु:खैर्विमुक्तोऽमृतमश्नुते ।। 20 ।।

guṇān etān atītya trīn dehī deha-samudbhavān
janma-mṛtyu-jarā-duḥkhair vimukto 'mṛtam aśnute

When one transcends the three *Gunas* that created the body, one is free from the pains of birth, old age, death, pains and miseries and can enjoy the Supreme Bliss (Nectar) even in this life and also attain immortality (Salvation). (14.20)

Ignorance (Tamas) → Passion (Rajas) → Goodness (Sattva) → Supreme Peace/Nirvana

The hallmarks of one who has transcended the *Gunas*

Q What are the three most important questions Arjuna asked about *Gunas*?

अर्जुन उवाच
कैर्लिङ्गैस्त्रीन्गुणानेतानतीतो भवति प्रभो ।
किमाचारः कथं चैतांस्त्रीन्गुणानतिवर्तते ।। 21 ।।

arjuna uvāca
kair liṅgais trīn guṇān etān atīto bhavati prabho
kim ācāraḥ kathaṁ caitāṁs trīn guṇān ativartate

Arjuna said: O Lord Krishna, what are the hallmarks of one who has transcended the three modes of Material Nature (*Gunas*) and how does he behave? How does one transcend above these three *Gunas* (qualities)? (14.21)

Q What are the hallmarks of one who has transcended above the *Gunas* and how does he achieve it?

श्रीभगवानुवाच
प्रकाशं च प्रवृत्तिं च मोहमेव च पाण्डव ।
न द्वेष्टि संप्रवृत्तानि न निवृत्तानि काङ्क्षति ।। 22 ।।

śrī-bhagavān uvāca
prakāśaṁ ca pravṛttiṁ ca moham eva ca pāṇḍava
na dveṣṭi sampravṛttāni na nivṛttāni kāṅkṣati

उदासीनवदासीनो गुणैर्यो न विचाल्यते।
गुणा वर्तन्त इत्येव योऽवतिष्ठति नेङ्गते ॥ 23 ॥

udāsīna-vad āsīno guṇair yo na vicālyate
guṇā vartanta ity evaṁ yo 'vatiṣṭhati neṅgate

समदुःखसुखः स्वस्थः समलोष्टाश्मकाञ्चनः।
तुल्यप्रियाप्रियो धीरस्तुल्यनिन्दात्मसंस्तुतिः ॥ 24 ॥

sama-duḥkha-sukhaḥ sva-sthaḥ sama-loṣṭāśma-kāñcanaḥ
tulya-priyāpriyo dhīras tulya-nindātma-saṁstutiḥ

मानापमानयोस्तुल्यस्तुल्यो मित्रारिपक्षयोः।
सर्वारम्भपरित्यागी गुणातीतः स उच्यते ॥ 25 ॥

mānāpamānayos tulyas tulyo mitrāri-pakṣayoḥ
sarvārambha-parityāgī guṇātītaḥ sa ucyate

The Supreme Lord said: O Arjuna, a person is said to have transcended the *Gunas* (modes of Material Nature), when one does not hate the presence of enlightening activity, nor does he desire for them when they are absent. He, who remains like a witness without being affected by *Gunas* and stays firmly attached to the Lord. He understands that only the *Gunas* are that act, so he remains firmly established in God (Self) without wavering. (14.22–23)

And who is alike in pain and pleasure, Self-dwelling; who sees clay, a stone, and gold as of equal value; to whom the dear and the unfriendly are equal; who is steadfast; who is calm and maintains his balance in honor (praise) and disgrace (blame, criticism); who is impartial to friends and foes and treats them alike and who has renounced the sense of doer-ship in all undertakings, such a person is said to have transcended the *Gunas* (modes of Material Nature). (14.24–25)

Transcending from the *Gunas* can be done through *Love* and *Devotion*

Q Who qualifies for *Brahma-Nirvana* (Liberation/*Moksha*)?

मां च योऽव्यभिचारेण भक्तियोगेन सेवते।
स गुणान्समीत्यैतान्ब्रह्मभूयाय कल्पते ॥ 26 ॥

māṁ ca yo 'vyabhicāreṇa bhakti-yogena sevate
sa guṇān samatītyaitān brahma-bhūyāya kalpate

One who constantly serves Me with love and devotion (unfailing in all circumstances) transcends the three modes of Material Nature (attributes) and thus becomes eligible for *Nirvana* (Liberation/*Moksha*, Oneness with God. (14.26)

Jivatma → *Parmatma*

Q Who is Eternal Being (*Brahman*), Righteousness (*Dharma*) and Supreme Bliss (*Anandam*)?

ब्रह्मणो हि प्रतिष्ठाहममृतस्याव्ययस्य च ।
शाश्वतस्य च धर्मस्य सुखस्यैकान्तिकस्य च ।। 27 ।।

brahmaṇo hi pratiṣṭhāham amṛtasyāvyayasya ca
śāśvatasya ca dharmasya sukhasyaikāntikasya ca

For certain, I am the Abode of Imperishable *Brahman*; Immortal and Everlasting Righteousness (*Dharma*) and of Supreme Bliss. (14.27)

Lessons to learn and practice in daily life

O Arjuna, transcend the three Gunas

Since the purpose of our life is to rise to the highest perfection (Higher Self), therefore, we must transcend the three *Gunas* (*Sattva*-Goodness, *Rajas*-Passion, *Tamas*-Ignorance) by performing selfless service with unwavering devotion and practicing goodness to attain the Transcendental State (*Brahmic State*, Oneness with God). (2.45, 2.72)

Attaining Unity with God (Liberation) is a long but enjoyable journey

ॐ तत्सदिति श्रीमद्भगवद्गीतासूपनिषत्सु ब्रह्मविद्यायां योगशास्त्रे
श्रीकृष्णार्जुनसंवादे गुणत्रयविभागयोगो नाम चतुर्दशोऽध्यायः ।।

AUM TAT SAT

Thus ends the fourteenth chapter named "*Guna-Traya Vibhaga Yoga*"
The Path of the Division of the Three Gunas
in the *Upanishad* of the glorious Bhagavad Gita, the scripture of Yoga,
the science of the Absolute (*Brahman*), in the form of the dialogue
between Lord Krishna and Arjuna.

Aum Shanti, Shanti, Shantihi

My True Nature is Sat Chit Ananda

Anger is not my true nature; my true nature is Sat Chit Ananda
Hatred is not my true nature; my true nature is Sat Chit Ananda
Resentment is not my true nature; my true nature is Sat Chit Ananda
Jealousy is not my true nature; my true nature is Sat Chit Ananda
Dejection is not my true nature; my true nature is Sat Chit Ananda
Restless is not my true nature; my true nature is Sat Chit Ananda
Laziness is not my true nature; my true nature is Sat Chit Ananda
Sickness is not my true nature; my true nature is Sat Chit Ananda
I am not sick, I am not lazy, I am not stupid; I am Sat Chit Ananda
I am love, I am peace, I am Anandam

From now on, do not call yourself, I am lazy, sick, boring, lifeless,
stupid, etc. because you are none of these
you are Sat Chit Ananda

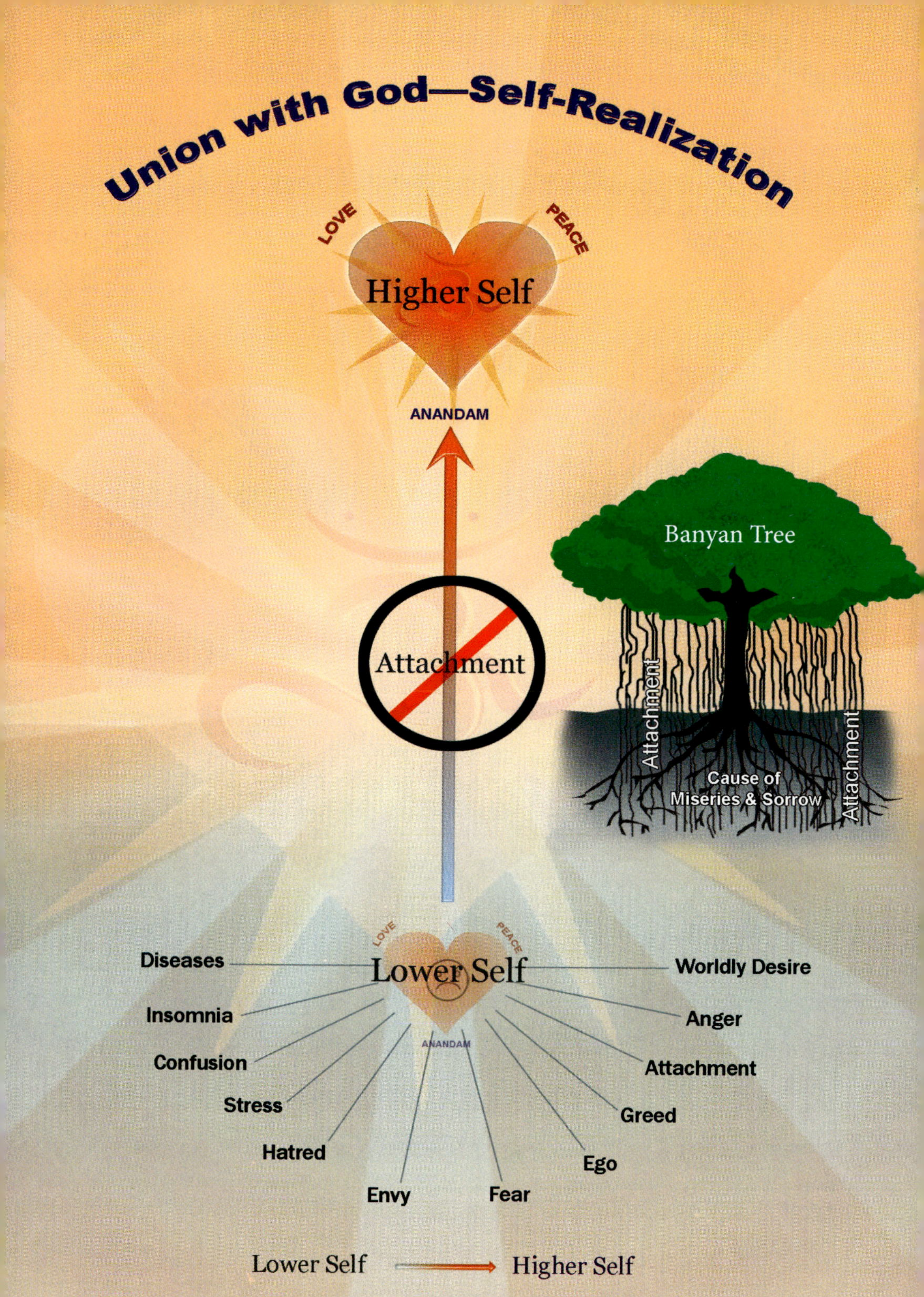

Self-Purification and Transformation through Detachment

PURUSHOTTAMA YOGA

The Path of the Supreme Person

Union with God (Self-Realization) through the path of realizing God as the Supreme-Self

The Gita is the Guide to Higher Self

In this chapter, Lord Krishna enlightened Arjuna by imparting the knowledge about His true nature as a Higher Self (*Purushottama*, Supreme-Self) and the means to attain, Union with Him. He also declared that the ultimate purpose of human life is to detach oneself from the materialistic world and to understand that God is the Supreme personality of Godhead. One who understands His Divine Nature, His Divine Power, and surrenders to Him, lives happily and peacefully in the materialistic world, without being obsessed with it and also attains Oneness with God, Self-Realization (Supreme Bliss).

Thus, this chapter answers very concisely one of the basic question: What is the purpose of life and how to achieve it.

Main Message

Path to transcend from lower self to Higher Self

Lower self → Higher Self

- The human body, the entire Cosmos/universe is a tree of *sanskaras* (past deeds) that is changing every moment. However, it can be cut down with the weapons of non-attachment.
- A *jivatma* (embodied soul, individual soul, lower self) is a fragment, a small part of the Supreme-Soul, Higher Self (His Divine Power).
- One must understand that the purpose of one's existence is to realize the true nature of God, who is the (Higher Self, *Purushottama*, *Para-Brahman*,

Parmatma, Supreme Being, Supreme Consciousness, the Absolute, Truth, *Sat*, Supreme-Soul, *Supreme Purusha*, etc.)

- The main stumbling block to realizing God is our own arrogance (false pride, ego, I-ness) and undue attachment to the materialistic world (My-ness, possessiveness). Whoever can cross these stumbling blocks by constantly dwelling on Him, achieves the Supreme Abode, Higher Self (Self-Realization, the Imperishable Supreme state, *Nirvana*).
- God is present in the heart of all beings and He is the source of all Wisdom.
- God needs to be known and constantly worshipped (by selfless service, Self-Knowledge, Love and Devotion).
- One who understands this most profound and secret science of Self-Knowledge (Experiential Knowledge, *Brahma-vidya*) becomes enlightened (Wise) and attains self-satisfaction, complete contentment, Ultimate Peace and Eternal Happiness; *Sat Chit Ananda*—Oneness with Higher Self and attatins the Supreme goal of life.

Chapter Overview

01–02	Universe as a banyan tree (tree of *Sanskaras-Karmas*-past deeds)
03–06	Attain Self-salvation by detachment and Self-Knowledge
07–11	Journey of the *jivatma*-individual soul
12–15	God-Spirit is the essence of all
16–20	Who is *jivatma*-individual soul, *Atma*-Spirit and the *Paramatma*-Supreme-Soul

Universe as a banyan tree (tree of *Sanskaras-Karmas*-past deeds)

Q What is the relationship of *Asvattha* (banyan tree) and universe and who comprehends the nature of this tree?

श्रीभगवानुवाच
ऊर्ध्वमूलमधःशाखमश्वत्थं प्राहुरव्ययम्।
छन्दांसि यस्य पर्णानि यस्तं वेद स वेदवित्॥1॥

śrī-bhagavān uvāca
ūrdhva-mūlam adhaḥ-śākham aśvatthaṁ prāhur avyayam
chandāṁsi yasya parṇāni yas taṁ veda sa veda-vit

The Supreme Lord said: This creation (universe and body) resembles an eternal tree (Banyan tree-*Asvattha*), that has its roots above in the Supreme Being (God) and its branches below in the cosmos. Its leaves are the Vedic hymns (*mantras*). One who fully understands the nature of this tree is the knower of the Vedas. (15.01)

Q How is this tree being nourished?

अधश्चोर्ध्वं प्रसृतास्तस्य शाखा गुणप्रवृद्धा विषयप्रवालाः।
अधश्च मूलान्यनुसंततानि कर्मानुबन्धीनि मनुष्यलोके॥2॥

adhaś cordhvaṁ prasṛtās tasya śākhā
guṇa-pravṛddhā viṣaya-pravālāḥ
adhaś ca mūlāny anusantatāni
karmānubandhīni manuṣya-loke

The branches of this Cosmic tree (*Maya*, Illusion) are spread all over the cosmos (downward and upward). The tree is being nourished by the energy of *Gunas* (Goodness, Passion, Ignorance, Material Nature). The sense objects (pleasures) are its buds and its roots of ego and desires stretch downwards into the world of men, binding the soul to their *karma* (action) and causing *karmic* bondage. (15.02)

Attain Self-salvation by detachment and Self-Knowledge

Q Can anyone understand this tree and how can one cut it down?

न रूपमस्येह तथोपलभ्यते नान्तो च चादिर्न च संप्रतिष्ठा।
अश्वत्थमेनं सुविरुढमूलमसङ्गशस्त्रेण दृढेन छित्त्वा ॥3॥

na rūpam asyeha tathopalabhyate
nānto na cādir na ca sampratiṣṭhā
aśvattham enaṁ su-virūḍha-mūlam
asaṅga-śastreṇa dṛḍhena chittvā

Non-attachment is the key to Liberation

The real form of this tree cannot be perceived in this world. No one can understand where it ends, where it begins or where its foundation is. However, this firmly rooted tree can be cut down with the strong axe of non-attachment. (15.03)

Q What kind of goal should one have in life?

ततः पदं तत्परिमार्गितव्यं यस्मिन्गता न निवर्तन्ति भूयः।
तमेव चाद्यं पुरुषं प्रपद्ये यतः प्रवृत्तिः प्रसृता पुराणी ॥4॥

tataḥ padaṁ tat parimārgitavyaṁ
yasmin gatā na nivartanti bhūyaḥ
tam eva cādyaṁ puruṣaṁ prapadye
yataḥ pravṛttiḥ prasṛtā purāṇī

Self-Realization must be the Supreme Goal of Life

Then, one must have the Supreme goal and seek to attain that Supreme state (Higher Self), where one does not return. The prayers must be: I surrender to that Supreme Being (Primal *Purusha*) from whom this creation has emanated since ancient times. (15.04)

Q Who attains the Imperishable Supreme State (Supreme goal of life)?

निर्मानमोहा जितसङ्गदोषा
अध्यात्मनित्या विनिवृत्तकामाः।
द्वन्द्वैर्विमुक्ताः सुखदुःखसंज्ञै-
र्गच्छन्त्यमूढाः पदमव्ययं तत् ॥5॥

nirmāna-mohā jita-saṅga-doṣā
adhyātma-nityā vinivṛtta-kāmāḥ
dvandvair vimuktāḥ sukha-duḥkha-saṁjñair
gacchanty amūḍhāḥ padam avyayam tat

Freedom from I-ness and My-ness leads to Ultimate Liberation

Those who are free from egoism (arrogance, I-ness) and delusion, who have conquered the evil of attachment, who are totally free from selfish desires and dualities like pleasure and pain and dwelling constantly in the Supreme-Self, such delusion–free ones attain the Supreme State, Oneness with God, *Sat Chit Ananda* (Eternal Goal). (15.05)

Q What is God's Supreme Abode?

न तद्भासयते सूर्यो न शशाङ्को न पावकः।
यद्गत्वा न निवर्तन्ते तद्धाम परमं मम्॥6॥

na tad bhāsayate sūryo na śaśāṅko na pāvakaḥ
yad gatvā na nivartante tad dhāma paramaṁ mama

Attaining God is the ultimate destination

My Supreme Abode is the place from where one does not return to the material world after reaching (He merges with me and attains Oneness with Me). It cannot be illuminated by the sun, the moon or the fire.(15.06)

Journey of the *jivatma*-individual soul

Q Does the eternal soul in the human body represent the entire Supreme-Soul?

ममैवांशो जीवलोके जीवभूतः सनातनः।
मनःषष्ठानीन्द्रियाणि प्रकृतिस्थानि कर्षति॥7॥

mamaivāṁśo jīva-loke jīva-bhūtaḥ sanātanaḥ
manaḥ-ṣaṣṭhānīndriyāṇi prakṛti-sthāni karṣati

The Spirit (*Atma*) in the body is an essential part of Myself. Once it enters the body, it becomes *jivatma*, (embodied soul) and draws around itself the five senses with mind as the sixth, which resides in Nature (*Prakriti*). (15.07)

Q What does soul take from one body to next body?

शरीरं यदवाप्नोति यच्चाप्युत्क्रामतीश्वरः।
गृहीत्वैतानि संयाति वायुर्गन्धानिवाशयात्॥8॥

śarīraṁ yad avāpnoti yac cāpy utkrāmatīśvaraḥ
gṛhītvaitāni saṁyāti vāyur gandhān ivāśayāt

When the individual soul leaves the body (*jivatma*), it takes his different conceptions and experiences of life (by mind and senses from the world) from one body to another just as the air carries aroma away from the flower. (15.08)

Q How does *jivatma* experience worldly pleasure?

श्रोत्रं चक्षुः स्पर्शनं च रसनं घ्राणमेव च।
अधिष्ठाय मनश्चायं विषयानुपसेवते ॥9॥

śrotraṁ cakṣuḥ sparśanaṁ ca rasanaṁ ghrāṇam eva ca
adhiṣṭhāya manaś cāyaṁ viṣayān upasevate

While dwelling in the body, *jivatma* (living being, individual being) experiences and enjoys sense objects, using six sensory faculties: hearing (ears), sight (eyes), touch, taste, smell and mind. (15.09)

Q Who can experience/perceive and observe the Soul (Spirit)?

उत्क्रामन्तं स्थितं वापि भुञ्जानं वा गुणान्वितम्।
विमूढा नानुपश्यन्ति पश्यन्ति ज्ञानचक्षुषः ॥10॥

utkrāmantaṁ sthitaṁ vāpi bhuñjānaṁ vā guṇānvitam
vimūḍhā nānupaśyanti paśyanti jñāna-cakṣuṣaḥ

Purity leads to Liberation

यतन्तो योगिनश्चैनं पश्यन्त्यात्मन्यवस्थितम्।
यतन्तोऽप्यकृतात्मानो नैनं पश्यन्त्यचेतसः ॥11॥

yatanto yoginaś cainaṁ paśyanty ātmany avasthitam
yatanto 'py akṛtātmāno nainaṁ paśyanty acetasaḥ

The deluded do not perceive the Soul while departing from or dwelling in the body and experiencing the objects of senses in association with the *Gunas*. But only those who possess the eye of Wisdom can truly see Him. (15.10)

The Yogis who are striving for perfection, can perceive the Soul (Self) that is seated in their inner psyche (Consciousness) but the ignorant, whose hearts are not pure, even though they may try very hard, do not perceive Him. (15.11)

Purity → Oneness with God, Sat Chit Ananda

God-Spirit is the essence of all

Q Where does the brilliance in the sun and moon come from?

यदादित्यगतं तेजो जगद्भासयतेऽखिलम्।
यच्चन्द्रमसि यच्चाग्नौ तत्तेजो विद्धि मामकम् ॥12॥

yad āditya-gataṁ tejo jagad bhāsayate 'khilam
yac candramasi yac cāgnau tat tejo viddhi māmakam

Everything originates from God

The brilliance in the sun which brightens the whole universe, the brilliance in the moon and also is in the fire, know that brilliance comes only from Me. (15.12)

Q What does the vital energy that comes from God do?

गामाविश्य च भूतानि धारयाम्यहमोजसा।
पुष्णामि चौषधीः सर्वाः सोमो भूत्वा रसात्मकः ॥ 13 ॥

gām āviśya ca bhūtāni dhārayāmy aham ojasā
puṣṇāmi cauṣadhīḥ sarvāḥ somo bhūtvā rasātmakaḥ

God takes care of all

Penetrating the earth, I support all beings with My vital energy and becoming the Moon (Sapful *Soma*), I nourish all the plants. (15.13)

Q What are the prayers for food and digestion and how is food digested in the body?

अहं वैश्वानरो भूत्वा प्राणिनां देहमाश्रितः।
प्राणापानसमायुक्तः पचाम्यन्नं चतुर्विधम् ॥ 14 ॥

ahaṁ vaiśvānaro bhūtvā prāṇināṁ deham āśritaḥ
prāṇāpāna-samāyuktaḥ pacāmy annaṁ catur-vidham

I am the fire of digestion (*Vaiswanara*) seated in the body of all living beings, and by uniting with vital breaths (*Prana* and *Apana*, incoming and outgoing), I digest the four kinds of food (masticated, sucked, licked, and drunk). (15.14)

Q Where does God reside and what does He do?

सर्वस्य चाहं हृदि संनिविष्टो मत्तः स्मृतिर्ज्ञानमपोहनं च।
वेदैश्च सर्वैरहमेव वेद्यो वेदान्तकृद्वेदविदेव चाहम् ॥ 15 ॥

sarvasya cāhaṁ hṛdi sanniviṣṭo
mattaḥ smṛtir jñānam apohanaṁ ca
vedaiś ca sarvair aham eva vedyo
vedānta-kṛd veda-vid eva cāham

God knows all

I alone reside in the heart (Inner psyche, as inner witness, Consciousness) of all beings and from Me emanate memory, wisdom (Self-Knowledge) and discrimination (removal of doubts and wrong notions). I am that Truth which is to be known by the study of all the Vedas. Indeed, I am the author of the *Vedanta* as well as the Knower of the Vedas. (15.15)

Who is *jivatma*-individual soul, *Atma*-Spirit and the *Paramatma*-Supreme-Soul

Q How many types of entities exist in the world?

द्वाविमौ पुरुषौ लोके क्षरश्चाक्षर एव च।
क्षरः सर्वाणि भूतानि कूटस्थोऽक्षर उच्यते ।। 16 ।।

dvāv imau puruṣau loke kṣaraś cākṣara eva ca
kṣaraḥ sarvāṇi bhūtāni kūṭa-stho 'kṣara ucyate

Body is temporary but Spirit is eternal

In the world, there are two types of entities: perishable (changeable, *Kshara*) and imperishable (Unchangeable, *Akshara*, *Brahman*). The bodies of all beings are perishable and the Soul within is imperishable. (15.16)

Q Who is the Supreme *Purusha* (*Purushottama*, Higher Self) and how is He known?

उत्तमः पुरुषस्त्वन्यः परमात्मेत्युदाहृतः।
यो लोकत्रयमाविश्य बिभर्त्यव्यय ईश्वरः ।। 17 ।।

uttamaḥ puruṣas tv anyaḥ paramātmety udāhṛtaḥ
yo loka-trayam āviśya bibharty avyaya īśvaraḥ

यस्मात्क्षरतीतोऽहमक्षरादपि चोत्तमः।
अतोऽस्मि लोके वेदे च प्रथितः पुरुषोत्तमः ।। 18 ।।

yasmāt kṣaram atīto 'ham akṣarād api cottamaḥ
ato 'smi loke vede ca prathitaḥ puruṣottamaḥ

But, besides these two (Eternal and Temporal), yet there is another Supreme Personality called the Higher Self (Supreme *Purusha*, Supreme-Soul, Absolute Reality, Godhead) and this Imperishable Lord enters the three worlds and sustains them (maintain, nourish, support). (15.17)

Because I am above and beyond the perishable and even the Imperishable (Eternal, Akshara), therefore, I am known in this world and also in scriptures as the Supreme Being (*Purushottama*, *Para-Brahman*, *Parmatma*, Absolute, Truth, *Sat*, Supreme-Soul, Supreme *Purusha*, etc.). (15.18)

Q Who worships God?

यो मामेवमसंमूढो जानाति पुरुषोत्तमम्।
स सर्वविद्भजति मां सर्वभावेन भारत ।। 19 ।।

yo mām evam asammūḍho jānāti puruṣottamam
sa sarva-vid bhajati māṁ sarva-bhāvena bhārata

O Arjuna, the wise one who truly understands Me as the Supreme Being knows all and worships Me wholeheartedly. (15.19)

Q How does this mysterious science help one attain enlightenment?

इति गुह्यतमं शास्त्रमिदमुक्तं मयानघ।
एतद्बुद्ध्वा बुद्धिमान्स्यात्कृतकृत्यश्च भारत ।। 20 ।।
iti guhyatamaṁ śāstram idam uktaṁ mayānagha
etad buddhvā buddhimān syāt kṛta-kṛtyaś ca bhārata

Once you know your true nature, you will know all

Thus, this most secret science of Transcendental Knowledge has been revealed by Me, O pious Arjuna by understanding this, one becomes Enlightened (Wise) and attains the purpose of his life, Self-Realization (*Moksha*). (15.20)

Non-attachment → self-satisfaction → self-contentment → Self-Realization (Nirvana, Higher Self)

Lessons to learn and practice in daily life

The entire existence is the tree of sanskaras (cause and effect)

1. We should try to live without being obsessed and without being attached to the material world.
2. We should set the Supreme goal of life to attain Higher Self (Oneness with God)
3. Seek to transcend from lower self to Higher Self (*Purshottama*)
4. Follow His Teachings that will help us to move toward complete contentment and the Supreme goal of life, Self-Realization—Oneness with Self/God, Higher Self.

Non-attachment → self-satisfaction → self-contentment → Self-Realization, Oneness with Self/ God (Higher Self, Purshottama)

ॐ तत्सदिति श्रीमद्भगवद्गीतासूपनिषत्सु ब्रह्मविद्यायां योगशास्त्रे
श्रीकृष्णार्जुनसंवादे पुरुषोत्तमयोगो नाम पञ्चदशोऽध्यायः ।।

AUM TAT SAT

Thus ends the fifteenth chapter named "*Purushottama Yoga*"
The Path of the Supreme Person
in the *Upanishad* of the glorious Bhagavad Gita, the scripture of Yoga,
the science of the Absolute (*Brahman*), in the form of the dialogue
between Lord Krishna and Arjuna.

Aum Shanti, Shanti, Shantihi

Union with God—Self-Realization

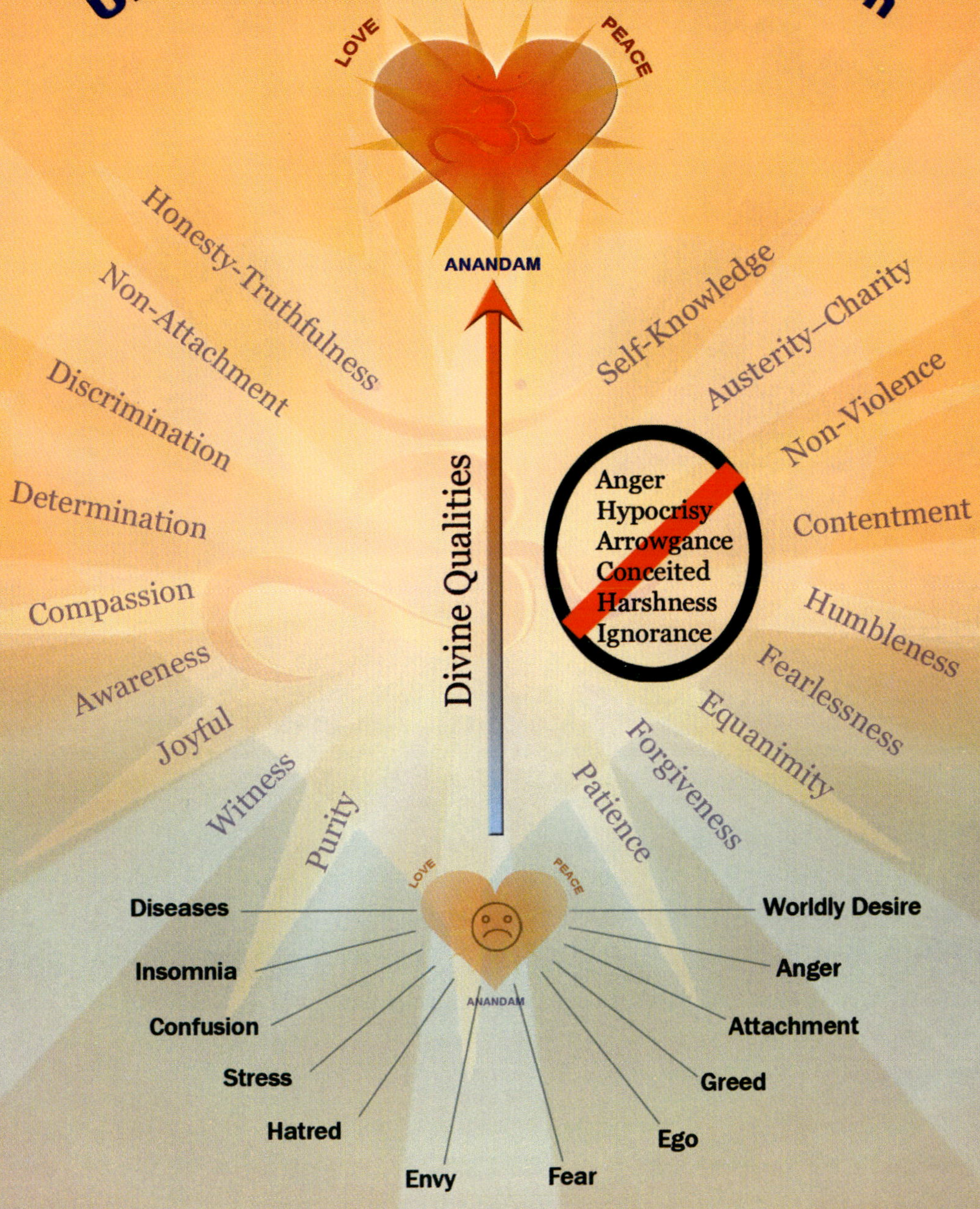

Self-Purification and Transformation through developing Divine Qualities

DEVA-ASURA SAMPAD VIBHAGA YOGA

The Path of Divine vs. Demonic Qualities

Union with God (Self-Realization) through the path of knowing the difference between divine and demonic qualities

The Gita is a Character Builder

In this chapter, Lord Krishna enlightens Arjuna with the knowledge of the distinction between divine (positive forces/attitude) and demonic qualities (negative forces/attitude); their conduct and actions. He explains which qualities are righteous in nature and conducive to divinity and how these can help one attain Self-Realization (Supreme Bliss).

This is the path of developing divine qualities and eliminating demonic qualities (virtues *vs.* vices). On this path one develops self-awareness, focused on self-improvment and self-transformation. One becomes aware of his own virtues and vices and works toward developing noble qualities (virtues) and substituting or eliminating bad qualites (vices). It may not be easy to eliminate old habits but it is easier to substitute them, just as if you want to become a vegetarian, first, you have to start adding vegetable and salad to your meals. Gradually increase the quantity of vegetable and reduce the quantity of meat. Eventually your body and mind will get used to it and you will have less craving for the meat. You will start enjoying vegetarian meals more and more and stop eating meat completely.

Main Message

The Gita is a Mirror that shows our true attributes

- Divine qualities(virtues) lead to Liberation/Salvation.They are the qualities/ virtues of God. By cultivating these, one will be self-purified and self-transformed and will attain the Higher Self with ease.
- *Sattvic Gunas* (Goodness, purity)—those who possess them lead a disciplined life. He or she lives according to the guidelines of scriptures and gradually

attains Higher Self (Liberation, *Moksha*, freedom from bondage of life and death).

- Demonic qualities (vices, egoistic) lead to bondage—these are the vices of the *Rajasic* and *Tamasic Gunas* (passion and ignorance). Those who possess them are very impulsive, do not follow the guidelines of scriptures, descend to the lower self and thus go to the cycle of birth and death (suffering is their destiny).
- There are two types of forces (impulses) in the world, divine and demonic. Therefore, there are two types of people in this world, divine and demonic in nature based on the qualities they possess. The battle between these two forces keeps going on all the time. They can uplift or damage/ruin families, societies, nations and even the entire world. Their impact could bring enormous turmoil or establish peace in the world, e.g. Mahatma Gandhi, Martin Luther King Jr., Mother Teresa, extremist or terrorist, etc.

Daivi sampad vimoksaya, nibandhayasuri mata
(Divine qualities/Virtues lead to Liberation and demonic qualities/vices lead to bondage)

—The Choice is ours

Divine Qualities (Virtues) → Liberation

Evil Qualities (Vices) → Bondage (Birth and death)

The choice is ours

Chapter Overview

01–05 The Twenty-six Virtues and six Vices

06–18 The mark of one who possess demonic qualities

19–20 The future for the ignorant is very gloomy

21–22 The Triple gates to hell

23–24 Follow the guidelines of scriptures-Vedas

The Twenty-six Virtues and six Vices

Q What are the divine qualities (signs of spirituality) of the person who possesses them?

श्रीभगवानुवाच
अभयं सत्त्वसंशुद्धिर्ज्ञानयोगव्यवस्थितिः ।
दानं दमश्च यज्ञश्च स्वाध्यायस्तप आर्जवम् ।। 1 ।।

śrī-bhagavān uvāca
abhayaṁ sattva-saṁśuddhir jñāna-yoga-vyavasthitiḥ
dānaṁ damaś ca yajñaś ca svādhyāyas tapa ārjavam

अहिंसा सत्यमक्रोधस्त्यागः शान्तिरपैशुनम् ।
दयाभूतेष्वलोलुप्त्वं मार्दवं ह्रीरचापलम् ।। 2 ।।

ahiṁsā satyam akrodhas tyāgaḥ śāntir apaiśunam
dayā bhūteṣv aloluptvaṁ mārdavaṁ hrīr acāpalam

तेजः क्षमा धृतिः शौचमद्रोहो नातिमानिता ।
भवन्ति संपदं दैवीमभिजातस्य भारत ।। 3 ।।

tejaḥ kṣamā dhṛtiḥ śaucam adroho nāti-mānitā
bhavanti sampadaṁ daivīm abhijātasya bhārata

The Supreme Lord said:

1. Fearlessness
2. Purity of mind
3. Firm resolution for Self-Knowledge (Self-Realization)
4. *Sattvic* form of charity
5. Control of senses
6. Sacrifice (performance of *Yajna*)
7. Study of the scriptures

8. Austerity
9. Honesty (straightforwardness)
10. Non-violence (in thought, action and speech)
11. Truthfulness
12. Absence of anger (even on provocation)
13. Renunciation (of doership)
14. Equanimity in all circumstances (tranquility, serenity, balanced self)
15. Abstinence from malicious talk (blaming, backbiting, gossip, slandering, fault-finding)
16. Compassion for all creatures
17. Freedom from greed
18. Gentleness
19. Modesty
20. Absence of fickle-mindness
21. Brilliance, patience, forgiveness
22. Fortitude
23. Courage
24. Purity (cleanliness)
25. Absence of hatred and envy
26. Absence of arrogance

Divine qualities are qualities of divinity and purity

These are the (twenty-six) divine qualities/virtues of divine people (Righteous, Noble, Pious), O Arjuna. (16.01–03)

Q What are the evil/demon qualities (vices—signs of a spiritual fall)?

दम्भो दर्पोऽतिमानश्च क्रोधः पारुष्यमेव च।
अज्ञानं चाभिजातस्य पार्थ संपदमासुरीम् ॥4॥
dambho darpo 'bhimānaś ca krodhaḥ pāruṣyam eva ca
ajñānaṁ cābhijātasya pārtha sampadam āsurīm

O Arjuna, the marks of one who is born with demonic qualities are:

1. Hypocrisy
2. Arrogance
3. Conceit (Ego)
4. Anger
5. Harshness (rudeness)
6. Ignorance (16.04)

Vices are signs of impurity and ignorance

Q Where do divine qualities and demonic qualities lead to?

दैवी संपद्विमोक्षाय निबन्धायासुरी मता।
मा शुचः संपदं दैवीमभिजातोऽसि पाण्डव ॥5॥

daivī sampad vimokṣāya nibandhāyāsurī matā
mā śucaḥ sampadaṁ daivīm abhijāto 'si pāṇḍava

Divine qualities (Virtues) lead to Liberation and demonic qualities (vices) lead to bondage. O Arjuna, do not grieve and worry, you are born with divine qualities. (16.05)

The mark of one who possess demonic qualities

Q How many types of persons are in this world?

द्वौ भूतसर्गौ लोकेऽस्मिन्दैव आसुर एव च।
दैवो विस्तरशः प्रोक्त आसुरं पार्थ मेंश्रृणु ॥6॥

dvau bhūta-sargau loke 'smin daiva āsura eva ca
daivo vistaraśaḥ prokta āsuraṁ pārtha me śṛṇu

What type of person are you?

There are only two types of beings in this world, the divine and the demonic. The divine has been described in detail; now hear about the demonic from Me, O Arjuna. (16.06)

Q What are the characteristics of a person of demonic qualities (vices)?

प्रवृत्तिं च निवृत्तिं च जना न विदुरासुराः।
न शौचं नापि चाचारो न सत्यं तेषु विद्यते ॥7॥

pravṛttiṁ ca nivṛttiṁ ca janā na vidur āsurāḥ
na śaucaṁ nāpi cācāro na satyaṁ teṣu vidyate

The people with a demonic nature do not know what should be done and what should be avoided. They have neither purity nor good conduct nor truthfulness. (16.07)

Q What do demonic, egoistic, imbalanced people think of the universe?

असत्यमप्रतिष्ठं ते जगदाहुरनीश्वरम्।
अपरस्परसंभूतं किमन्यत्कामहैतुकम् ॥8॥

asatyam apratiṣṭhaṁ te jagad āhur anīśvaram
aparaspara-sambhūtaṁ kim anyat kāma-haitukam

They say that the Cosmic manifestation (universe) is without truth, without any basis, without a God (not created by God), without an order (has no controller) and is caused and produced only by sexual union of man and woman (lust, desires) and nothing else. (16.08)

Q What kind of work do demonic people do and how do they damage the world?

एतां दृष्टिमवष्टभ्य नष्टात्मानोऽल्पबुद्धयः।
प्रभवन्त्युग्रकर्माणः क्षयाय जगतोऽहिताः ।।9।।

etāṁ dṛṣṭim avaṣṭabhya naṣṭātmāno 'lpa-buddhayaḥ
prabhavanty ugra-karmāṇaḥ kṣayāya jagato 'hitāḥ

काममाश्रित्य दुष्पूरं दम्भमानमदान्विताः।
मोहाद्गृहीत्वासद्ग्राहान्प्रवर्तन्तेऽशुचिव्रताः ।।10।।

kāmam āśritya duṣpūraṁ dambha-māna-madānvitāḥ
mohād gṛhītvāsad-grāhān pravartante 'śuci-vratāḥ

Having such views, these lost souls with very little understanding engage in unbeneficial violent work and are born as enemies of the world to destroy it. (16.09)

Filled with insatiable desires, absorbed in hypocrisy, conceit, pride and arrogance; adopting vain ideas due to delusion, they engage in actions with impure motives and vows (their own unholy interest and objectives, selfishness). (16.10)

Q What do demonic people believe in?

चिन्तामपरिमेयां च प्रलयान्तामुपाश्रिताः।
कामोपभोगपरमा एतावदिति निश्चिताः ।।11।।

cintām aparimeyāṁ ca pralayāntām upāśritāḥ
kāmopabhoga-paramā etāvad iti niścitāḥ

Obssessed with endless fears and anxieties which end only with their death, they consider that gratifying the senses is their highest goal of life and they are convinced that sense pleasure is everything. (16.11)

Q What are the expectations of demonic people and how do they fulfill them?

आशापाशशतैर्बद्धाः कामक्रोधपरायणाः।
ईहन्ते कामभोगार्थमन्यायेनार्थसञ्चयान् ।।12।।

āśā-pāśa-śatair baddhāḥ kāma-krodha-parāyaṇāḥ
īhante kāma-bhogārtham anyāyenārtha-sañcayān

Selfish desires create demonicity

इदमद्य मया लब्धमिदं प्राप्स्ये मनोरथम्।
इदमस्तीदमपि मे भविष्यति पुनर्धनम्॥13॥

idam adya mayā labdham imaṁ prāpsye manoratham
idam astīdam api me bhaviṣyati punar dhanam

असौ मया हतः शत्रुर्हनिष्ये चापरानपि।
ईश्वरोऽहमहं भोगी सिद्धोऽहं बलवान्सुखी॥14॥

asau mayā hataḥ śatrur haniṣye cāparān api
īśvaro 'ham ahaṁ bhogī siddho 'haṁ balavān sukhī

आढ्योऽभिजनवानस्मि कोऽन्योऽस्ति सदृशो मया।
यक्ष्ये दास्यामि मोदिष्य इत्यज्ञानविमोहिताः॥15॥

āḍhyo 'bhijanavān asmi ko 'nyo 'sti sadṛśo mayā
yakṣye dāsyāmi modiṣya ity ajñāna-vimohitāḥ

Bound by an unlimited number of expectations and hopes, absorbed in lust and anger, they strive to get wealth by illegal and unholy means to fulfill their desires. (16.12)

The deluded think this has been obtained by me today; I must fulfill the next desire soon. I have this much wealth now and will have more wealth in the future. (16.13)

I have already slain this enemy and I will slay others also. I am the master of everything. I am the enjoyer. I am successful, powerful and very prosperous. (16.14)

I am wealthy and born into a noble family. Who else is equal to me? (I am the only perfect one) I perform sacrifices, give charity, and enjoy as I please, thus he is deluded by ignorance. (16.15)

Q What is the destiny of demonic people?

अनेकचित्तविभ्रान्ता मोहजालसमावृताः।
प्रसक्ताः कामभोगेषु पतन्ति नरकेऽशुचौ॥16॥

aneka-citta-vibhrāntā moha-jāla-samāvṛtāḥ
prasaktāḥ kāma-bhogeṣu patanti narake 'śucau

Hell and heaven are our own creations

Thus, perplexed by many fantasies, entangled in the web of delusion, addicted to the gratification of desires and lustful pleasures, they fall into the foulest hell. (16.16)

Q How do demonic people lead their lives?

आत्मसंभाविताः स्तब्धा धनमानमदान्विताः।
यजन्ते नामयज्ञैस्ते दम्भेनाविधिपूर्वकम् ।। 17 ।।

ātma-sambhāvitāḥ stabdhā dhana-māna-madānvitāḥ
yajante nāma-yajñais te dambhenāvidhi-pūrvakam

Self-conceited, stubborn, and intoxicated with arrogance of their wealth, they perform sacrifices for their name and to show off their wealth and not according to scriptural ordinance (not for their spiritual progress) (16.17)

Q Do demonic people love God?

अहंकारं बलं दर्पं कामं क्रोधं च संश्रिताः।
मामात्मपरदेहेषु प्रद्विषन्तोऽभ्यसूयकाः ।। 18 ।।

ahaṅkāraṁ balaṁ darpaṁ kāmaṁ krodhaṁ ca saṁśritāḥ
māṁ ātma-para-deheṣu pradviṣanto 'bhyasūyakāḥ

These malicious people, chained to egoism, power, arrogance, lust and anger, despise Me in their own body and in the bodies of others. (16.18)

The future for the ignorant is very gloomy

Q What is the future of demonic people?

तानहं द्विषतः क्रूरान्संसारेषु नराधमान्।
क्षिपाम्यजस्रमशुभानासुरीष्वेव योनिषु ।। 19 ।।

tān ahaṁ dviṣataḥ krūrān saṁsāreṣu narādhamān
kṣipāmy ajasram aśubhān āsurīṣv eva yoniṣu

Everyone pays the price of their own action/deeds

I throw these haters, cruel, sinful and most degraded among men (lowest) into the wombs of demons (cycles of rebirth) over and over again. (16.19)

आसुरीं योनिमापन्ना मूढा जन्मनि जन्मनि।
मामप्राप्यैव कौन्तेय ततो यान्त्यधमां गतिम् ।। 20 ।।

āsurīṁ yonim āpannā mūḍhā janmani janmani
māṁ aprāpyaiva kaunteya tato yānty adhamāṁ gatim

Suffering is the destiny of malicious people

Born into demonical wombs, birth after birth, these devilish ones (foolish) sink to the lowest hell without ever attaining Me, O Arjuna. (16.20)

Demonic People/Ignorant → Miseries in Life → Hell

Triple Gates to Hell

Q What are the three gates (root causes) to hell and barriers to Eternal Peace and Self-Realization?

त्रिविधं नरकस्येदं द्वारं नाशनमात्मनः।
कामः क्रोधस्तथा लोभस्तस्मादेतत्त्रयं त्यजेत् ॥ 21 ॥

tri-vidhaṁ narakasyedaṁ dvāraṁ nāśanam ātmanaḥ
kāmaḥ krodhas tathā lobhas tasmād etat trayaṁ tyajet

Lust, anger, and greed are the triple gates to hell

Lust, anger and greed are the triple gates of hell that lead to the destruction (bondage) of the embodied self. Therefore, one should abandon these three. (16.21)

Q What are the benefits of giving up the triple gates of hell?

एतैर्विमुक्तः कौन्तेय तमोद्वारैस्त्रिभिर्नरः।
आचरत्यात्मनः श्रेयस्ततो याति परां गतिम् ॥ 22 ॥

etair vimuktaḥ kaunteya tamo-dvārais tribhir naraḥ
ācaraty ātmanaḥ śreyas tato yāti parāṁ gatim

O Arjuna, he who has abandoned these three gates of hell (darkness), works for his own Salvation (Self-Realization) and gradually attains the Supreme Abode (Supreme goal of his life). (16.22)

Follow the guidelines of scriptures–the Vedas

Q What is the future of one who disobeys the scriptures and acts under the influence of his selfish desires?

यः शास्त्रविधिमुत्सृज्य वर्तते कामकारतः।
न स सिद्धिमवाप्नोति न सुखं न परां गतिम् ॥ 23 ॥

yaḥ śāstra-vidhim utsṛjya vartate kāma-kārataḥ
na sa siddhim avāpnoti na sukhaṁ na parāṁ gatim

Scriptures are the road maps to navigate our life

One who acts merely under the impulses of his desires and disobeys the ordinances of the scriptures does not attain perfection or happiness or the Supreme Goal. (16.23)

Q Why should one follow the scriptures?

तस्माच्छास्त्रं प्रमाणं ते कार्याकार्यव्यवस्थितौ।
ज्ञात्वा शास्त्रविधानोक्तं कर्म कर्तुमिहार्हसि ॥ 24 ॥

tasmāc chāstraṁ pramāṇaṁ te kāryākārya-vyavasthitau
jñātvā śāstra-vidhānoktaṁ karma kartum ihārhasi

Therefore, let the scriptures be your authority in determining what should be done and what should not be done. Knowing this, you should perform your work only according to the guidelines of the scriptures then you will be gradually elevated. (16.24)

Lessons to learn and practice in daily life

Once the vices are removed, virtues are born automatically

1. We must know the difference between divine and demonic endowments and be aware of our own qualities.
2. We must work toward eliminating vices and put full efforts towards manifesting and developing divine qualities. Unless we develop divine qualities, we cannot proceed to a higher goal.
3. We must not waste all of our valuable time chasing worldly desires, living under stress and continue working to accumulate possessions, but work toward developing contentment and compassion. Thus we can be united with our inner-self and with God—Union with God and Self (Higher Self).
4. We must follow the teachings of the scriptures and live accordingly.

Everyone has the potential to be divine
—Swami Vivekananda

ॐ तत्सदिति श्रीमद्भगवद्गीतासूपनिषत्सु ब्रह्मविद्यायां योगशास्त्रे
श्रीकृष्णार्जुनसंवादे दैवासुरसंपद्विभागयोगो नाम षोडशोऽध्यायः ॥

AUM TAT SAT

Thus ends the sixteenth chapter named "*Deva-Asura Sampad Vibhaga Yoga*"
The Path of Divine vs. Demonic Qualities
in the *Upanishad* of the glorious Bhagavad Gita, the scripture of Yoga,
the science of the Absolute (*Brahman*), in the form of the dialogue
between Lord Krishna and Arjuna.

Aum Shanti, Shanti, Shantihi

Self-Purification and Transformation through Faith

SRADDHATRIYA-VIBHAG YOGA

The Path of Threefold Division of Faith

Union with God (Self-Realization) through the path of faith

The Gita is a self-purifier and self-transformer

A man consists of his faith; as is a man's faith, so is he

Lord Krishna enlightens Arjuna with the knowledge of three different types of faith which determine one's Consciousness in this world. Based upon people's inherent nature (material nature, *Gunas*) and their attributes (Conscious level) that dominate them, one can easily determine the kind of faith they possess. People also act according to their faith. The faith of a person with passion and ignorance will lead him to imperfect actions/bondage. However, the one with the faith of goodness will act according to the teaching of scriptures, leading to pure faith in God and self-purification. One who knows the difference among these faiths tries to transcend from *Tamasic* and *Rajasic* to *Sattvic* faith and finally to Higher Self God/Self-Realization (Supreme Bliss).

Main Message

One is always guided by one's faith

One can become whatever one believes in and wants to be

One is always guided by his faith

- There are three types of faith: People possess their faith according to their innate nature (*Gunas*), an individual of *Sattvic* (Goodness) nature will have pure faith but that faith will be clouded by worldly intentions in *Rajasic* nature (passion), and the *Tamasic* nature (ignorant) individual will have selfish and impure faith.
- There are also three types of food, sacrifices (Austerities and *Tapas*), charities and activities based upon their qualities (*Gunas-Sattvic, Rajasic* and *Tamasic*).
- People make their choices based upon their own *Gunas* (*Sattvic, Rajasic* and *Tamasic*).
- '*AUM TAT SAT*' (*Vedic Mantra*) is the three-fold name (triple designation) of God and is uttered while performing spiritual activities.

Chapter Overview

01–06	Three types of faith and the fate of men
07–10	Three types of food
11–13	Three types of sacrifices and penance
14–16	Austerity of deed, speech and thoughts
17–19	Three types of austerity-penance-*tapa*
20–22	Three types of charity-gifts
23–28	Three-fold names of God, '*Aum, Tat, Sat*'

Three types of faith and the fate of men

Q What does Arjuna want to know about the individuals who perform the spiritual practices but not according to the teachings of scriptures?

अर्जुन उवाच
ये शास्त्रविधिमुत्सृज्य यजन्ते श्रद्धयान्विताः।
तेषां निष्ठा तु का कृष्ण सत्त्वमाहो रजस्तमः॥1॥

arjuna uvāca
ye śāstra-vidhim utsṛjya yajante śraddhayānvitāḥ
teṣāṁ niṣṭhā tu kā kṛṣṇa sattvam āho rajas tamaḥ

Arjuna said: O Krishna, those who perform spiritual practices and sacrifices with faith but do not conform to the principal of scripture, what is the state of their devotion? Is it mode of goodness (*Sattvic*), passion (*Rajasic*) or ignorance (*Tamasic*)? (17.01)

Q How many kinds of faith exist?

श्रीभगवानुवाच
त्रिविधा भवति श्रद्धा देहिनां सा स्वभावजा।
सात्त्विकी राजसी चैव तामसी चेति तांश्रृणु॥2॥

śrī-bhagavān uvāca
tri-vidhā bhavati śraddhā dehināṁ sā svabhāva-jā
sāttvikī rājasī caiva tāmasī ceti tāṁ śṛṇu

The Supreme Lord said: The innate faith of embodied beings (born from their intrinsic nature) is one of three kinds: Goodness/pure, passion and ignorance (*Sattva, Rajas, Tamas*). Now, hear about these. (17.02)

Q How can one become whatever one wants?

सत्त्वानुरूपा सर्वस्य श्रद्धा भवति भारत।
श्रद्धामयोऽयं पुरुषो यो यच्छ्रद्धः स एव सः॥3॥

sattvānurūpā sarvasya śraddhā bhavati bhārata
śraddhā-mayo 'yaṁ puruṣo yo yac-chraddhaḥ sa eva saḥ

Faith of a man makes his fate

Arjuna, the faith of everyone is in accordance with his innate natural disposition (mental constitution governed by *karmic* impressions). One is made of one's faith. As is his faith, so is he. One can become whatever one believes in and wants to be. (17.03)

Q How to recognize individuals with different types of faith?

यजन्ते सात्त्विका देवान्यक्षरक्षांसि राजसाः।
प्रेतान्भूतगणांश्चान्ये यजन्ते तामसा जनाः॥4॥

yajante sāttvikā devān yakṣa-rakṣāṁsi rājasāḥ
pretān bhūta-gaṇāṁś cānye yajante tāmasā janāḥ

A *Sattvic* person (pure, mode of goodness) worships demi-gods (*devas*); *Rajasic* (mode of passion) worships demi-gods and demons and *Tamasic* (mode of ignorance) worship ghosts and spirits. (17.04)

Q How do demonic people practice austerity?

अशास्त्रविहितं घोरं तप्यन्ते ये तपो जनाः।
दम्भाहंकारसंयुक्ताः कामरागबलान्विताः॥5॥

aśāstra-vihitaṁ ghoraṁ tapyante ye tapo janāḥ
dambhāhaṅkāra-saṁyuktāḥ kāma-rāga-balānvitāḥ

कर्शयन्तः शरीरस्थं भूतग्राममचेतसः।
मां चैवान्तःशरीरस्थं तान्विद्ध्यासुरनिश्चयान्॥6॥

karṣayantaḥ śarīra-sthaṁ bhūta-grāmam acetasaḥ
māṁ caivāntaḥ śarīra-sthaṁ tān viddhy āsura-niścayān

Ignorant hurts himself and others

Those persons who practice severe austerities which are not recommended by scriptures, who are full of hypocrisy and egotism (arrogance) are driven by the force of desires (lust) and attachment. They senselessly torture the elements that constitute their body (organs and senses) as well as Me (Supreme-Soul) who dwells within their body, consider these ignorant people to be of demonic nature. (17.05–06)

Three Types of Food

Q How many types of food, austerity and charity are there?

आहारस्त्वपि सर्वस्य त्रिविधो भवति प्रियः।
यज्ञस्तपस्तथा दानं तेषां भेदमिमंशृणु ॥7॥

āhāras tv api sarvasya tri-vidho bhavati priyaḥ
yajñas tapas tathā dānaṁ teṣāṁ bhedam imaṁ śṛṇu

The food, which is liked by everyone, is also of three kinds. So are the sacrifice (*Yajnas*), austerity, and charity. Now hear the distinction among them. (17.07)

Q What is *Sattvic* food and who likes them?

आयुः सत्त्वबलारोग्यसुखप्रीतिविवर्धनाः।
रस्याः स्निग्धाः स्थिरा हृद्या आहाराः सात्त्विकप्रियाः॥8॥

āyuḥ-sattva-balārogya-sukha-prīti-vivardhanāḥ
rasyāḥ snigdhāḥ sthirā hṛdyā āhārāḥ sāttvika-priyāḥ

The foods which increase longevity, purity, strength, health, happiness, and cheerfulness are juicy, oleaginous, wholesome and nutritious are enjoyed by *Sattvic* persons (pure, the mode of goodness). (17.08)

Q What is *Rajasic* foods and who likes them?

कट्वम्ललवणात्युष्णतीक्ष्णरूक्षविदाहिनः।
आहारा राजसस्येष्टा दुःखशोकामयप्रदाः॥9॥

kaṭv-amla-lavaṇāty-uṣṇa-tīkṣṇa-rūkṣa-vidāhinaḥ
āhārā rājasasyeṣṭā duḥkha-śokāmaya-pradāḥ

Foods that are bitter, sour (acid), salty, hot, pungent, dry, burning and give rise to pain (distress), grief and disease are enjoyed by *Rajasic* people (the mode of passion). (17.09)

Q What is *Tamasic* food and who likes them?

यातयामं गतरसं पूति पर्युषितं च यत्।
उच्छिष्टमपि चामेध्यं भोजनं तामसप्रियम्॥10॥

yāta-yāmaṁ gata-rasaṁ pūti paryuṣitaṁ ca yat
ucchiṣṭam api cāmedhyaṁ bhojanaṁ tāmasa-priyam

Foods that are half cooked, rotten, putrid (very little nutritional value), stale (decomposed), refuse (junk), and impure (such as meat and alcohol) are enjoyed by *Tamasic* people (the mode of ignorance, darkness). (17.10)

Three Types of Sacrifice and Penance

Q What is *Sattvic* sacrifice (*Yajna*)?

अफलाकाङ्क्षिभिर्यज्ञो विधिदृष्टो य इज्यते ।
यष्टव्यमेवेति मनः समाधाय स सात्त्विकः ।। 11 ।।

aphalākāṅkṣibhir yajño vidhi-diṣṭo ya ijyate
yaṣṭavyam eveti manaḥ samādhāya sa sāttvikaḥ

Selfless service (Sacrifice) enjoined by the scriptural ordinance and performed without the desire for the fruit, and with the firm belief and conviction that it is a duty, is *Sattvic* (mode of goodness, Pure). (17.11)

Q What is *Rajasic* sacrifice (*Yajna*)?

अभिसंधाय तु फलं दम्भार्थमपि चैव यत् ।
इज्यते भरतश्रेष्ठ तं यज्ञं विद्धि राजसम् ।। 12 ।।

abhisandhāya tu phalaṁ dambhārtham api caiva yat
ijyate bharata-śreṣṭha taṁ yajñaṁ viddhi rājasam

However, the selfless service (Sacrifice, *Yajna*) that is performed only for name and fame and aiming for fruit (material benefit), is *Rajasic* (mode of passion), O Arjuna. (17.12)

Q What is *Tamasic* sacrifice?

विधिहीनमसृष्टान्नं मन्त्रहीनमदक्षिणम् ।
श्रद्धाविरहितं यज्ञं तामसं परिचक्षते ।। 13 ।।

vidhi-hīnam asṛṣṭānnaṁ mantra-hīnam adakṣiṇam
śraddhā-virahitaṁ yajñaṁ tāmasaṁ paricakṣate

Any selfless service (Sacrifice, *Yajna*) that is performed without following the scriptural ordinance, without distribution of food (*Prasadam*, spiritual food), without chanting of the mantras (Vedic hymns), without faith and without remuneration to the performing priest, is considered to be *Tamasic* (mode of ignorance). (17.13)

Austerity of Deeds, Speech and Thoughts

Q What is the austerity of body and how to practice it?

देवद्विजगुरुप्राज्ञपूजनं शौचमार्जवम्।
ब्रह्मचर्यमहिंसा च शारीरं तप उच्यते ।। 14 ।।

deva-dvija-guru-prājña-pūjanaṁ śaucam ārjavam
brahmacaryam ahiṁsā ca śārīraṁ tapa ucyate

Worship of demi-gods (*devas*), learned men, the guru, and the wise (like elderly), purity (cleanliness), straightforwardness, celibacy, and non-violence are called the austerity (*Tapas*, penance) of the body. *It is the best use of the body*. (17.14)

Q What is the austerity of speech (words) and how to practice it?

अनुद्वेगकरं वाक्यं सत्यं प्रियहितं च यत्।
स्वाध्यायाभ्यसनं चैव वाङ्मयं तप उच्यते ।। 15 ।।

anudvega-karaṁ vākyaṁ satyaṁ priya-hitaṁ ca yat
svādhyāyābhyasanaṁ caiva vāṅ-mayaṁ tapa ucyate

Truth spoken softly is like a rose without thorns

Speech that is non-offensive (causes no hurt and agitation to others), truthful, pleasing, beneficial, used for the regular study of scriptures and recitation of His name is called the austerity of speech. It is the best use of speech. (17.15)

Q What is the austerity of thoughts (mind) and how to practice it?

मनःप्रसादः सौम्यत्वं मौनमात्मविनिग्रहः।
भावसंशुद्धिरित्येतत्तपो मानसमुच्यते ।। 16 ।।

manaḥ-prasādaḥ saumyatvaṁ
maunam ātma-vinigrahaḥ
bhāva-saṁśuddhir ity etat
tapo mānasam ucyate

Best use of the mind/ thoughts is called austerity of mind

Serenity of mind (self-satisfaction, cheerfulness), gentleness, silence, Equanimity, self-control and purity of mind (thoughts) are called the austerity of mind. It is the best use of thoughts. (17.16)

Three types of austerity-penance-*tapa*

Q What is *Sattvic* austerity (mode of goodness)?

श्रद्धया परया तप्तं तपस्तत्त्रिविधं नरैः।
अफलाकाङ्क्षिभिर्युक्तैः सात्त्विकं परिचक्षते ।। 17 ।।

śraddhayā parayā taptaṁ tapas tat tri-vidhaṁ naraiḥ
aphalākāṅkṣibhir yuktaiḥ sāttvikaṁ paricakṣate

Sattvic is Satya, Simplicity and Selflessness

These three fold austerities (thought, speech and deed) practiced with Supreme faith by wise men without any expectations of fruit (without any material gain and rewards, but only for the Supreme) is called *Sattvic* (mode of goodness). (17.17)

Q What is *Rajasic* austerity (mode of passion)?

सत्कारमानपूजार्थं तपो दम्भेन चैव यत्।
क्रियते तदिह प्रोक्तं राजसं चलमध्रुवम् ।। 18 ।।

satkāra-māna-pūjārthaṁ tapo dambhena caiva yat
kriyate tad iha proktaṁ rājasaṁ calam adhruvam

Rajasic is a Royal Lifestyle

Austerity (Penance, *Tapa*) that is performed for gaining respect, personal rewards, honor, recognition for the sake of name and fame, produces temporary results called *Rajasic* (mode of passion). (17.18)

Q What is *Tamasic* austerity (mode of ignorance)?

मूढग्राहेणात्मनो यत्पीडया क्रियते तपः।
परस्योत्सादनार्थं वा तत्तामसमुदाहृतम् ।। 19 ।।

mūḍha-grāheṇātmano yat pīḍayā kriyate tapaḥ
parasyotsādanārthaṁ vā tat tāmasam udāhṛtam

Tamasic nature is harmful to others

Austerity practiced with self-torture (body, mind and senses), foolishness for causing pain and harm to others, is called *Tamasic* (mode of ignorance). (17.19)

Three types of charity-gifts

Q What is *Sattvic* (mode of goodness) charity/gift?

दातव्यमिति यद्दानं दीयतेऽनुपकारिणे।
देशे काले च पात्रे च तद्दानं सात्त्विकं स्मृतम् ।। 20 ।।

dātavyam iti yad dānaṁ dīyate 'nupakāriṇe
deśe kāle ca pātre ca tad dānaṁ sāttvikaṁ smṛtam

Charity that is given with a sense of duty at the proper time and place to a deserving person from whom nothing is expected in return is called *Sattvic* (mode of goodness). (17.20)

Q What is *Rajasic* charity (mode of passion)?

यत्तु प्रत्युपकारार्थं फलमुद्दिश्य वा पुनः ।
दीयते च परिक्लिष्टं तद्दानं राजसं स्मृतम् ।। 21 ।।

yat tu pratyupakārārthaṁ phalam uddiśya vā punaḥ
dīyate ca parikliṣṭaṁ tad dānaṁ rājasaṁ smṛtam

However, the charity that is given to get something in return or with expectation of reward or favor, or given reluctantly is called *Rajasic* (mode of passion). (17.21)

Q What is *Tamasic* charity (mode of ignorance)?

अदेशकाले यद्दानमपात्रेभ्यश्च दीयते ।
असत्कृतमवज्ञातं तत्तामसमुदाहृतम् ।। 22 ।।

adeśa-kāle yad dānam apātrebhyaś ca dīyate
asat-kṛtam avajñātaṁ tat tāmasam udāhṛtam

The charity that is given at an inappropriate place or time to undeserving recipients without respect or with ridicule is called *Tamasic* (mode of ignorance). (17.22)

Three-fold names of God– *Aum, Tat, Sat*

Q What is the meaning of ॐ '*AUM TAT SAT*' and what was originated by chanting them?

ॐतत्सदिति निर्देशो ब्रह्मणस्त्रिविधः स्मृतः ।
ब्राह्मणास्तेन वेदाश्च यज्ञाश्च विहिताः पुरा ।। 23 ।।

oṁ tat sad iti nirdeśo brahmaṇas tri-vidhaḥ smṛtaḥ
brāhmaṇās tena vedāś ca yajñāś ca vihitāḥ purā

'ॐ TAT SAT' - triple designation of God, Vedic mantra

'ॐ *AUM TAT SAT*' is said to be the triple designation of the Supreme Absolute Truth (Spirit, Eternal Being). By chanting these worlds, the Vedas, *Brahmins*, (persons with good qualities) and Sacrifice (*Yajna*) were created at the time of creation. (17.23)

Q When is ॐ '*AUM*' chanted?

तस्मादोमित्युदाहृत्य यज्ञदानतप:क्रिया: ।
प्रवर्तन्ते विधानोक्ता: सततं ब्रह्मवादिनाम् ।। 24 ।।

tasmād oṁ ity udāhṛtya yajña-dāna-tapaḥ-kriyāḥ
pravartante vidhānoktāḥ satataṁ brahma-vādinām

Therefore, with the utterance of the holy word 'ॐ *AUM*' the act of sacrifice (*Yajna*), charity, and other austerities as enjoined in the scriptures are always commenced by the expounders of *Brahman*. (17.24)

Q Why is '*TAT*' chanted and by whom?

तदित्यनभिसंधाय फलं यज्ञतप:क्रिया: ।
दानक्रियाश्च विविधा: क्रियन्ते मोक्षकाङ्क्षिभि: ।। 25 ।।

tad ity anabhisandhāya phalaṁ yajña-tapaḥ-kriyāḥ
dāna-kriyāś ca vividhāḥ kriyante mokṣa-kāṅkṣibhiḥ

Uttering '*TAT*' (He is all) without seeking rewards, various types of sacrifice (*Yajnas*), charity, and austerity are performed by the seekers of salvation (*Moksha, Liberation*). (17.25)

Q Why is '*SAT*' chanted?

God has many names

सद्भावे साधुभावे च सदित्येतत्प्रयुज्यते ।
प्रशस्ते कर्मणि तथा सच्छब्द: पार्थ युज्यते ।। 26 ।।

sad-bhāve sādhu-bhāve ca sad ity etat prayujyate
praśaste karmaṇi tathā sac-chabdaḥ pārtha yujyate

The divine name '*SAT*' is used in the sense of Absolute Truth (Reality) and goodness. The word '*SAT*' is also used for an auspicious act, O Arjuna. (17.26)

Q What else is called '*SAT*'?

यज्ञे तपसि दाने च स्थिति: सदिति चोच्यते ।
कर्म चैव तदर्थीयं सदित्येवाभिधीयते ।। 27 ।।

yajñe tapasi dāne ca sthitiḥ sad iti cocyate
karma caiva tad-arthīyaṁ sad ity evābhidhīyate

Steadfastness in sacrifice (*Yajna*, Selfless service), penance (austerity) and charity is also called '*SAT* (Truth)' and also the action in connection with these (for the sake of the Supreme) is called '*SAT*.' (17.27)

Q What is '*ASAT*' (Non-existent)?

No faith, no future

अश्रद्धया हुतं दत्तं तपस्तप्तं कृतं च यत् ।
असदित्युच्यते पार्थ न च तत्प्रेत्य नो इह ।। 28 ।।

aśraddhayā hutaṁ dattaṁ tapas taptaṁ kṛtaṁ ca yat
asad ity ucyate pārtha na ca tat pretya no iha

Whatever is done without faith (sincere devotion), whether it is sacrifice, charity, austerity or any other act is called '*asat*'. It is temporary and worthless here or hereafter (after death), O Arjuna. (17.28)

Lessons to learn and practice in daily life

1. We must have full faith in God and ourselves
2. We should always strive to lead *Sattvic* life style
3. We must perform sacrifice, charity, austerity and other activities with full faith

A lifestyle that is led with purity (goodness) in thoughts, purity in food, purity in speech, purity in listening and purity in action leads to purity of heart and liberation

ॐ तत्सदिति श्रीमद्भगवद्गीतासूपनिषत्सु ब्रह्मविद्यायां योगशास्त्रे
श्रीकृष्णार्जुनसंवादे श्रद्धात्रयविभागयोगो नाम सप्तदशोऽध्याय ।।

AUM TAT SAT

Thus ends the seventeenth chapter "*Sraddhatriya-Vibhag Yoga*"
The Path of Threefold Division of Faith
in the *Upanishad* of the glorious Bhagavad Gita, the scripture of Yoga, the science of the Absolute (*Brahman*), in the form of the dialogue between Lord Krishna and Arjuna.

Aum Shanti, Shanti, Shantihi

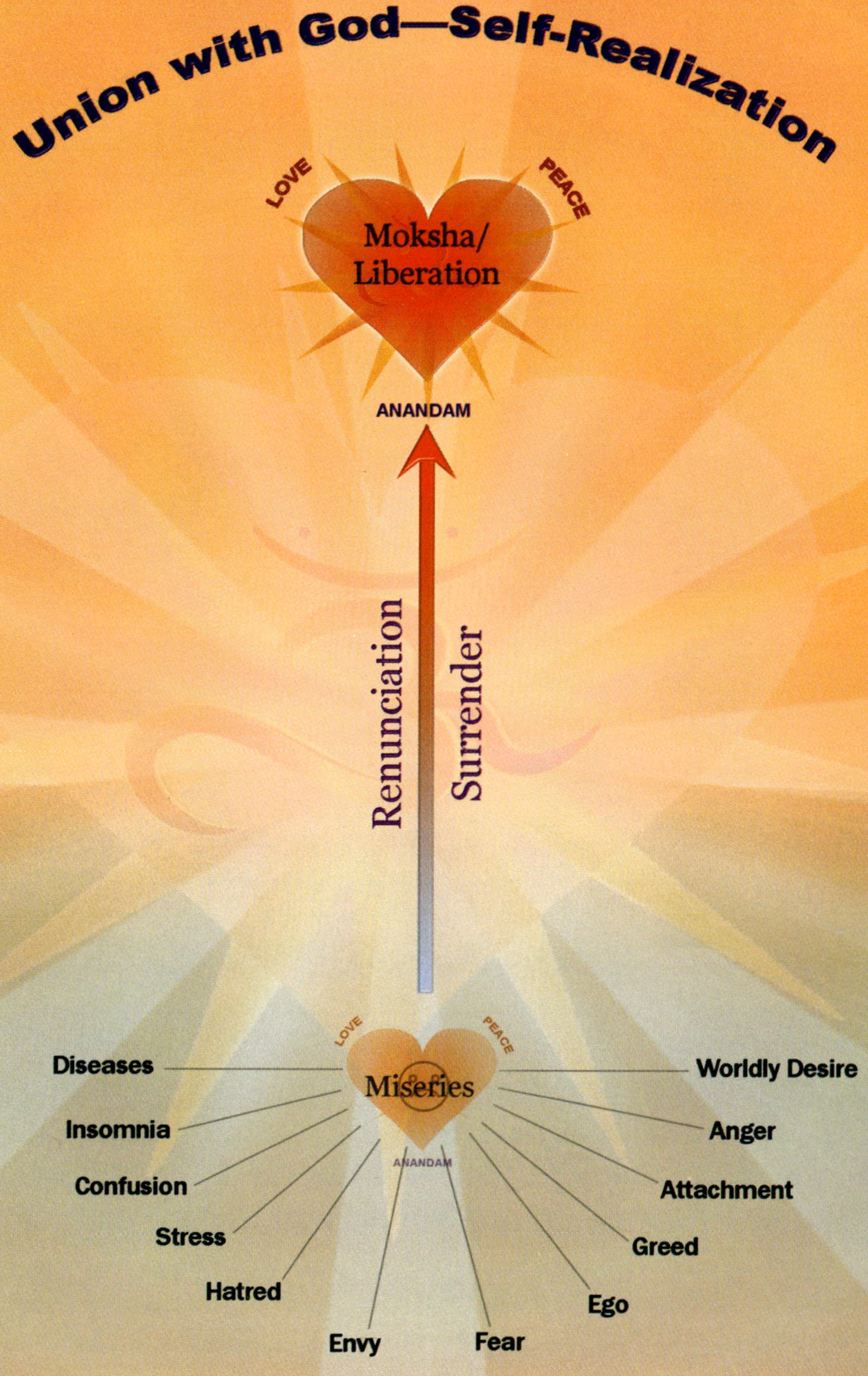

Self-Purification and Transformation through Total Renunciation

MOKSHA-SANYASA YOGA

The Path of Liberation through Renunciation

Union with God (Self-Realization) through the path of renunciation and surrender

The Gita is the Royal Road to Liberation

Ultimate Conclusion of the Gita

In the last chapter Lord Krishna concluded and emphasized His previous teachings of *Karma Yoga, Bhakti Yoga* and *Jnana Yoga*. He further enlightens Arjuna by explaining the distinction between *Sanyasa* (Physical Renunciation) and *Tyaga* (Mental Renunciation), the glories of Bhagavad Gita and how to practice its teachings in daily life. Thus living harmoniously and peacefully in this materialistic world and also attain the Supreme goal of life: Liberation/*Moksha*, Ultimate Bliss, *Sat Chit Ananda*.

The Gita is a call to action with renunciation of the fruits of all actions and attachment to their results, not the renunciation (abandonment) of the action itself.

Sanyasa is physical renunciation but Tyaga is mental-renunciation

Main Message

Miseries → Moksha

We can attain Liberation (from the cycle of birth and death) by doing our *svadharma* (one's prescribed duty) and not expecting anything in return (renoucing the fruit of action). The only requisite is to surrender all of our actions to God and give up attachment, desire, ego, and selfishness. By performing our duty with love and devotion as worship to God, we will receive His Grace and realize God/Self-Realization, Higher Self).

- *Sanyasa* is physical renunciation of all actions. *Sanyasi* (Renunciant) thinks all action is evil (full of fault) and his Yogic path is Meditation.
- *Tyaga* (Sacrifice, Relinquishment) is the mental renunciation of the fruits of all actions but not the action itself (desireless action). One who performs is called *Tyagi/Karma Yogi* and his Yogic path is selfless service.
- Based upon their material nature (*Gunas*) there are three types of Renunciation, Knowledge, Action, doers, intellect, firmness and happiness.
- One must perform his duty according to his innate aptitude and not only to mimic others.
- The glories of the Gita and the benefits of following its teachings are infinite.
- The Highest service to God is to propagate the message of the Gita, i.e. become a talking, walking, working Gita.
- After listening to the whole discourse of the Gita, Arjuna is fully transformed, his illusion disappeared, he recognized his duty as a warrior and then he said, "*I will do as you advice.*"
- Both Self-Knowledge and pure action are needed to achieve righteous results.

Chapter Overview

01–12	Definition and types of Renunciation and Sacrifices
13–18	Five causes of an action
19–40	Three types of Knowledge, Action, doer, intellect, determination and happiness
41–44	Division of the duty is based upon one's ability (Caste)
45–55	Self-Realization through *svadharma*, self-discipline and devotion
56–63	Living in God's Consciousness leads to His grace
64–66	Surrender is the ultimate path to Self-Realization
67–69	The best way to serve God
70–77	The grace of the Gita
78	Both righteousness and the protector of the righteousness are needed

Definition and Types of Renunciation and Sacrifice

Q What did Arjuna want to know more?

अर्जुन उवाच
संन्यासस्य महाबाहो तत्त्वमिच्छामि वेदितुम्।
त्यागस्य च हृषीकेश पृथक्केशिनिषूदन॥1॥

arjuna uvāca
sannyāsasya mahā-bāho tattvam icchāmi veditum
tyāgasya ca hṛṣīkeśa pṛthak keśi-niṣūdana

Arjuna said: I wish to know in detail the truth about renunciation (*Sanyasa*) and relinquishment – sacrifice (*Tyaga*), separately, O Krishna. (18.01)

Q What is the difference between the true nature of Renunciation (*Sanyasa*) and Sacrifice (*Tyaga*)?

श्रीभगवानुवाच
काम्यानां कर्मणां न्यासं संन्यासं कवयो विदुः।
सर्वकर्मफलत्यागं प्राहुस्त्यागं विचक्षणाः॥2॥

śrī-bhagavān uvāca
kāmyānāṁ karmaṇāṁ nyāsaṁ sannyāsaṁ kavayo viduḥ
sarva-karma-phala-tyāgaṁ prāhus tyāgaṁ vicakṣaṇāḥ

The Supreme Lord said: The sages classify renunciation (*Sanyasa, Sankhya-Yoga*), to be refraining from all actions prompted by selfish desire. The wise regard relinquishment (Sacrifice, *Tyaga, Karma Yoga*) to be the abandonment of the fruits of all actions. (18.02)

Q What activities should be abandoned and not abandoned?

त्याज्यं दोषवदित्येके कर्म प्राहुर्मनीषिणः।
यज्ञदानतपःकर्म न त्याज्यमिति चापरे ॥3॥

tyājyaṁ doṣa-vad ity eke karma prāhur manīṣiṇaḥ
yajña-dāna-tapaḥ-karma na tyājyam iti cāpare

Good conduct must be continued

Some wise men declare that all actions are evil and therefore should be given up, yet others say that acts of sacrifice (*Yajna*), charity and austerity should not be given up. (18.03)

Q How many types of sacrifice are there?

निश्चयंशृणु मे तत्र त्यागे भरतसत्तम।
त्यागो हि पुरुषव्याघ्र त्रिविधः संप्रकीर्तितः ॥4॥

niścayaṁ śṛṇu me tatra tyāge bharata-sattama
tyāgo hi puruṣa-vyāghra tri-vidhaḥ samprakīrtitaḥ

O Arjuna, listen to My final truth about Sacrifice (relinquishment of the fruit of action). Sacrifice is said to be of three kinds. (18.04)

Q What should not be abandoned and why?

यज्ञदानतपःकर्म न त्याज्यं कार्यमेव तत्।
यज्ञो दानं तपश्चैव पावनानि मनीषिणाम् ॥5॥

yajña-dāna-tapaḥ-karma na tyājyaṁ kāryam eva tat
yajño dānaṁ tapaś caiva pāvanāni manīṣiṇām

Good conduct is a purifier of our consciousness

Acts of sacrifice (*Yajna*), charity, and austerity should *not* be abandoned, but must be performed under all circumstances because service, charity, and austerity are purifiers of heart of the wise men. (18.05)

Q What action must be performed?

एतान्यपि तु कर्माणि सङ्गं त्यक्त्वा फलानि च।
कर्तव्यानीति मे पार्थ निश्चितं मतमुत्तमम् ॥6॥

etāny api tu karmāṇi saṅgaṁ tyaktvā phalāni ca
kartavyānīti me pārtha niścitaṁ matam uttamam

Therefore, all these actions (sacrifice, charity, and austerity) and other obligatory duties must be performed without any attachment to the fruit (any expectation of results and hope of rewards). This is indeed My final opinion, O Arjuna. (18.06)

Q What is *Tamasic* Renunciation (mode of ignorance)?

नियतस्य तु संन्यासः कर्मणो नोपपद्यते।
मोहात्तस्य परित्यागस्तामसः परिकीर्तितः॥7॥

niyatasya tu sannyāsaḥ karmaṇo nopapadyate
mohāt tasya parityāgas tāmasaḥ parikīrtitaḥ

Abandoning one's obligatory and prescribed duty is not proper and its abandonment due to delusion is considered to be *Tamasic* (mode of ignorance). (18.07)

Q What is *Rajasic* Renunciation (mode of passion)?

दुःखमित्येव यत्कर्म कायक्लेशभयात्त्यजेत्।
स कृत्वा राजसं त्यागं नैव त्यागफलं लभेत्॥8॥

duḥkham ity eva yat karma kāya-kleśa-bhayāt tyajet
sa kṛtvā rājasaṁ tyāgaṁ naiva tyāga-phalaṁ labhet

One who abandons his prescribed duty because it is painful or because of the fear of physical suffering, such giving up (Renunciation) is called *Rajasic* (mode of passion). Such renunciation does not bear any fruits so one does not get any benefits of the sacrifice (does not attain Self-Realization). (18.08)

Q What is *Sattvic* Renunciation (mode of goodness)?

कार्यमित्येव यत्कर्म नियतं क्रियतेऽर्जुन।
सङ्गंत्यक्त्वा फलं चैव स त्यागः सात्त्विको मतः॥9॥

kāryam ity eva yat karma niyataṁ kriyate 'rjuna
saṅgaṁ tyaktvā phalaṁ caiva sa tyāgaḥ sāttviko mataḥ

Selfless action is Sattvic Renunciation

Obligatory work that is done as a duty without selfish attachment and desire for fruit (*Tyaga*), in my view, is regarded as a *Sattvic* Renunciation (mode of goodness), O Arjuna. (18.09)

Q Who is a true Renunciant (*Tyagi*)?

न द्वेष्ट्यकुशलं कर्म कुशले नानुषज्जते।
त्यागी सत्त्वसमाविष्टो मेधावी छिन्नसंशयः॥10॥

na dveṣṭy akuśalaṁ karma kuśale nānuṣajjate
tyāgī sattva-samāviṣṭo medhāvī chinna-saṁśayaḥ

न हि देहभृता शक्यं त्यक्तुं कर्माण्यशेषतः।
यस्तु कर्मफलत्यागी स त्यागीत्यभिधीयते ॥ 11 ॥

na hi deha-bhṛtā śakyaṁ tyaktuṁ karmāṇy aśeṣataḥ
yas tu karma-phala-tyāgī sa tyāgīty abhidhīyate

A true Renunciant (*Tyagi*) is one who is imbued with the purity of *Sattva* (mode of goodness), whose doubts are fully dispelled and who neither hates the disagreeable work nor is attached to an agreeable one. (18.10)

It is indeed impossible for an embodied person (human being) to give up all activities completely. But he who renounces the selfish attachment to the fruits of all action is called a true Renunciant (*Tyagi*, a man of renunciation who has truly renounced). (18.11)

Q What are the three-fold results of these actions and what does a true Renunciant (*Tyagi*) get?

अनिष्टमिष्टं मिश्रं च त्रिविधं कर्मणः फलम्।
भवत्यत्यागिनां प्रेत्य न तु संन्यासिनां क्वचित् ॥ 12 ॥

aniṣṭam iṣṭaṁ miśraṁ ca tri-vidhaṁ karmaṇaḥ phalam
bhavaty atyāginām pretya na tu sannyāsinām kvacit

The three-fold fruit of action-good, bad and mixed, is reaped after death by those who have not renounced selfish attachment to the fruit of action. There is none whatsoever for those who have renounced the fruit of action (*Tyagi*). (18.12)

Five Causes of Action

Q What are the five factors required to complete an action (project) successfully?

पञ्चेमानि महाबाहो कारणानि निबोध मे।
सांख्ये कृतान्ते प्रोक्तानि सिद्धये सर्वकर्मणाम् ॥ 13 ॥

pañcaitāni mahā-bāho kāraṇāni nibodha me
sāṅkhye kṛtānte proktāni siddhaye sarva-karmaṇām

O Arjuna, according to the *Vedanta* (*Sankhya*) there are five factors for the accomplishment of all action, learn from Me. (18.13)

अधिष्ठानं तथा कर्ता करणं च पृथग्विधम्।
विविधाश्च पृथक्चेष्टा दैवं चैवात्र पञ्चमम् ॥ 14 ॥

adhiṣṭhānaṁ tathā kartā karaṇaṁ ca pṛthag-vidham
vividhāś ca pṛthak ceṣṭā daivaṁ caivātra pañcamam

शरीरवाङ्मनोभिर्यत्कर्म प्रारभत नरः ।
न्याय्यं वा विपरीतं वा पञ्चैते तस्य हेतवः ।। 15 ।।

śarīra-vāṅ-manobhir yat karma prārabhate naraḥ
nyāyyaṁ vā viparītaṁ vā pañcaite tasya hetavaḥ

Ultimate success comes only with God's Grace

There are five factors to complete every action:

1. The place of action
2. The doer (physical body)
3. The instrument of various kinds (sense organs and mind)
4. Diverse activities (the many different kinds of efforts)
5. The fifth is the Supreme-Soul (Destiny, God and His Grace). (18.14)

Whatever action one performs by one's body, mind (thought) and speech whether it is right or wrong, these five are its contributory causes (factors). (18.15)

Q Who considers oneself the doer?

Poor knowledge leads to poor judgment

तत्रैवं सति कर्तारमात्मानं केवलं तु यः ।
पश्यत्यकृतबुद्धित्वान्न स पश्यति दुर्मतिः ।। 16 ।।

tatraivaṁ sati kartāram ātmānaṁ kevalaṁ tu yaḥ
paśyaty akṛta-buddhitvān na sa paśyati durmatiḥ

This being so, the ignorant one (stubborn and foolish) who considers his body or the soul as the doer and not the five factors, has imperfect judgment due to his imperfect knowledge and does not understands the reality. (18.16)

Q Who is not considered a killer (a sense of doership)?

A soldier is not a killer. He is a patriot (Desh-Bhakt)

यस्य नाहंकृतो भावो बुद्धिर्यस्य न लिप्यते ।
हत्वापि स इमाँल्लोकान्न हन्ति न निबध्यते ।। 17 ।।

yasya nāhaṅkṛto bhāvo buddhir yasya na lipyate
hatvāpi sa imāl̐ lokān na hanti na nibadhyate

One who is free from the sense of doer ship (egoism, I-ness) and whose intellect is not tarnished by selfish desires and its fruit, even though he may kill these people, he does not kill and is not bound by the consequences of his action of killing—he is not considered a killer. (18.17)

Q How many types of motivators and constituents are there to do any action?

ज्ञानं ज्ञेयं परिज्ञाता त्रिविधा कर्मचोदना।
करणं कर्म कर्तेति त्रिविधः कर्मसंग्रहः ॥ 18 ॥

jñānaṁ jñeyaṁ parijñātā tri-vidhā karma-codanā
karaṇaṁ karma karteti tri-vidhaḥ karma-saṅgrahaḥ

The three-fold motivators (forces, incentive) to any action are knower, knowledge and object of knowledge. The three-fold bases (constituents) of any action are the doer/actor, the action itself and the sense (the instrument). (18.18)

Three Types of Knowledge

Q How many types of knowledge, action and doers are there?

ज्ञानं कर्म च कर्ता च त्रिधैव गुणभेदतः।
प्रोच्यते गुणसंख्याने यथावच्छृणु तान्यपि ॥ 19 ॥

jñānaṁ karma ca kartā ca tridhaiva guṇa-bhedataḥ
procyate guṇa-saṅkhyāne yathāvac chṛṇu tāny api

Everything in the universe is according to the three gunas

Knowledge, action (*karma*) and doer/actor are also three types, according to the three different qualities of *Gunas* of Mother Nature (*Sattvic*, *Rajas* and *Tamas*). Now hear about these also. (18.19)

Q What is *Sattvic* knowledge (mode of goodness)?

सर्वभूतेषु येनैकं भावमव्ययमीक्षते।
अविभक्तं विभक्तेषु तज्ज्ञानं विद्धि सात्त्विकम् ॥ 20 ॥

sarva-bhūteṣu yenaikaṁ bhāvam avyayam īkṣate
avibhaktaṁ vibhakteṣu taj jñānaṁ viddhi sāttvikam

One is all and all is One

The knowledge by which one sees *One* Imperishable Being in all beings though they are divided into innumerable forms, such Knowledge is *Sattvic* (mode of goodness). (18.20)

Q What is *Rajasic* knowledge (mode of passion)?

पृथक्त्वेन तु यज्ज्ञानं नानाभावान्पृथग्विधान्।
वेत्ति सर्वेषु भूतेषु तज्ज्ञानं विद्धि राजसम् ॥ 21 ॥

pṛthaktvena tu yaj jñānaṁ nānā-bhāvān pṛthag-vidhān
vetti sarveṣu bhūteṣu taj jñānaṁ viddhi rajas am

The knowledge by which one sees that in everybody there is a different type of living entity (each individual is separate from one another), such knowledge is *Rajasic* (mode of passion). (18.21)

Q What is *Tamasic* knowledge (mode of ignorance)?

यत्तु कृत्स्नवदेकस्मिन्कार्ये सक्तमहैतुकम् ।
अतत्त्वार्थवदल्पं च तत्तामसमुदाहृतम् ।। 22 ।।

yat tu kṛtsna-vad ekasmin kārye saktam ahaitukam
atattvārtha-vad alpaṁ ca tat tāmasam udāhṛtam

But that knowledge by which one holds to one, single, superficial perception as if it is everything without reason, and without recognizing the truth, such knowledge is worthless and considered to be *Tamasic* (mode of darkness, ignorance). (18.22)

Three Types of Action

Q What is a *Sattvic* action (mode of goodness)?

नियतं सङ्गरहितमरागद्वेषतः कृतम् ।
अफलप्रेप्सुना कर्म यत्तत्सात्त्विकमुच्यते ।। 23 ।।

niyataṁ saṅga-rahitam arāga-dveṣataḥ kṛtam
aphala-prepsunā karma yat tat sāttvikam ucyate

My duty is my Dharma (Svadharma)

The obligatory duty that is performed according to ordinances of scriptures, without attachment to the fruit and selfish motives (expects no return), without any partiality and prejudice, and without likes and dislikes (love and hate) is called *Sattvic* (mode of goodness). (18.23)

Q What is a *Rajasic* action (mode of passion)?

यत्तु कामेप्सुना कर्म साहंकारेण वा पुनः ।
क्रियते बहुलायासं तद्राजसमुदाहृतम् ।। 24 ।।

yat tu kāmepsunā karma sāhaṅkāreṇa vā punaḥ
kriyate bahulāyāsaṁ tad rājasam udāhṛtam

But the action that is performed by one to gratify one's selfish desire and selfish motive or is prompted by his egoism and is carried out further, with too much effort and pressure, is called *Rajasic* (mode of passion). (18.24)

Q What is a *Tamasic* action (mode of ignorance)?

अनुबन्धं क्षयं हिंसामनपेक्ष्य च पौरुषम्।
मोहादारभ्यते कर्म यत्तत्तामसमुच्यते ।। 25 ।।

anubandhaṁ kṣayaṁ hiṁsām anapekṣya ca pauruṣam
mohād ārabhyate karma yat tat tāmasam ucyate

Action that is blindly undertaken out of ignorance regardless of one's own ability, capacity and the consequences including loss to him and injury to others is called *Tamasic* (mode of ignorance). (18.25)

Three Types of Doer

Q Who is a *Sattvic* doer (mode of goodness)?

मुक्तसङ्गोऽनहंवादी धृत्युत्साहसमन्वितः।
सिद्ध्यसिद्ध्योर्निर्विकारः कर्ता सात्त्विक उच्यते ।। 26 ।।

mukta-saṅgo 'nahaṁ-vādī dhṛty-utsāha-samanvitaḥ
siddhy-asiddhyor nirvikāraḥ kartā sāttvika ucyate

The doer/actor is called a *Sattvic* doer (mode of goodness), who performs his prescribed duty:

1. Without attachment
2. Without egoistic speech (does not beat his own drum)
3. With great determination (steadfastness)
4. With enthusiasm and
5. With balance in both success and failure (18.26)

Q Who is a *Rajasic* doer (mode of passion)?

रागी कर्मफलप्रेप्सुर्लुब्धो हिंसात्मकोऽशुचिः।
हर्षशोकान्वितः कर्ता राजसः परिकीर्तितः ।। 27 ।।

rāgī karma-phala-prepsur lubdho hiṁsātmako 'śuciḥ
harṣa-śokānvitaḥ kartā rājasaḥ parikīrtitaḥ

The doer/actor is called a *Rajasic* doer (mode of passion) who is:

1. Full of attachment
2. Driven by the desires for the fruits of action
3. Greedy
4. Violent
5. Impure in thoughts and in conduct
6. Affected by the pair of opposites (joy and sorrow) (18.27)

Q Who is a *Tamasic* doer (mode of ignorance)?

अयुक्तः प्राकृतः स्तब्धः शठो नैष्कृतिकोऽलसः।
विषादी दीर्घसूत्री च कर्ता तामस उच्यते ॥ 28 ॥

ayuktaḥ prākṛtaḥ stabdhaḥ śaṭho naiṣkṛtiko 'lasaḥ
viṣādī dīrgha-sūtrī ca kartā tāmasa ucyate

The doer/actor is called a *Tamasic* doer (mode of ignorance), who is:

1. Undisciplined
2. Imbalanced
3. Vulgar
4. Stubborn
5. Deceitful
6. Malicious (dishonest, cheats and insults others)
7. Lazy
8. Depressed
9. Procrastinator (18.28)

Three Types of Intellect

Q What is the three-fold nature of intellect and determination?

बुद्धेर्भेदं धृतेश्चैव गुणतस्त्रिविधंश्रृणु।
प्रोच्यमानमशेषेण पृथक्त्वेन धनंजय ॥ 29 ॥

buddher bhedaṁ dhṛteś caiva guṇatas tri-vidhaṁ śṛṇu
procyamānam aśeṣeṇa pṛthaktvena dhanañjaya

O Arjuna, now hear, the three-fold nature of intellect (*Buddhi*) and determination (Firmness), according to the qualities of the *Gunas* (modes of material Nature). (18.29)

Q What is a *Sattvic Buddhi* (mode of goodness)?

Discrimination is the key to success

प्रवृत्तिं च निवृत्तिं च कार्याकार्ये भयाभये।
बन्धं मोक्षं च या वेत्ति बुद्धिः सा पार्थ सात्त्विकी ॥ 30 ॥

pravṛttiṁ ca nivṛttiṁ ca kāryākārye bhayābhaye
bandhaṁ mokṣaṁ ca yā vetti buddhiḥ sā pārtha sāttvikī

O Arjuna, that intellect (*Buddhi*) is *Sattvic* (mode of goodness) which can discriminate between action and inaction (path of work and path of renunciation), what ought to be done and what not ought to be done, what is to be feared and what is not to be feared and what binds and what liberates the soul (bondage). (18.30)

Q What is *Rajasic Buddhi* (mode of passion)?

यया धर्ममधर्मं च कार्यं चाकार्यमेव च।
अयथावत्प्रजानाति बुद्धिः सा पार्थ राजसी ॥31॥

yayā dharmam adharmaṁ ca kāryaṁ cākāryam eva ca
ayathāvat prajānāti buddhiḥ sā pārtha rājasī

O Arjuna, that intellect is *Rajasic* (mode of passion) which cannot correctly distinguish between righteousness (*Dharma*) and unrighteousness (*adharma*) and also what ought to be done and what not ought to be done (right and wrong action). (18.31)

Q What is *Tamasic Buddhi* (mode of ignorance)?

अधर्मं धर्ममिति या मन्यते तमसावृता।
सर्वार्थान्विपरीतांश्च बुद्धिः सा पार्थ तामसी ॥32॥

adharmaṁ dharmam iti yā manyate tamasāvṛtā
sarvārthān viparītāṁś ca buddhiḥ sā pārtha tāmasī

That intellect is *Tamasic* (mode of ignorance) which, due to being wrapped in darkness and illusion, perceives even unrighteousness (*adharma*) to be righteousness (*Dharma*) and vice-versa, sees all other things upside down and always strives in the wrong direction, O Arjuna. (18.32)

Three Types of Determination

Q What is *Sattvic* firmness (mode of goodness)?

धृत्या यया धारयते मनःप्राणेन्द्रियक्रियाः।
योगेनाव्यभिचारिण्या धृतिः सा पार्थ सात्त्विकी ॥33॥

dhṛtyā yayā dhārayate manaḥ-prāṇendriya-kriyāḥ
yogenāvyabhicāriṇyā dhṛtiḥ sā pārtha sāttvikī

That unwavering firmness (steadfastness, determination) by which one controls the functions of the mind, *Prana* (breath, life force) and senses through Yoga for God and Self-Realization, only that firmness-steadfastness is *Sattvic* (mode/nature of goodness), O Arjuna. (18.33)

Q What is *Rajasic* firmness (mode of passion)?

यया तु धर्मकामार्थान्धृत्या धारयतेऽर्जुन।
प्रसङ्गेन फलाकाङ्क्षी धृतिः सा पार्थ राजसी ॥ 34 ॥

yayā tu dharma-kāmārthān dhṛtyā dhārayate 'rjuna
prasaṅgena phalākāṅkṣī dhṛtiḥ sā pārtha rājasī

But the firmness by which one clings to duty, virtues, pleasure and wealth, with great attachment and desires for the fruits of action, that firmness is *Rajasic* firmness-steadfastness (mode of passion), O Arjuna. (18.34)

Q What is *Tamasic* firmness (mode of ignorance)?

यया स्वप्नं भयं शोकं विषादं मदमेव च।
न विमुञ्चति दुर्मेधा धृतिः सा पार्थ तामसी मता ॥ 35 ॥

yayā svapnaṁ bhayaṁ śokaṁ viṣādaṁ madam eva ca
na vimuñcati durmedhā dhṛtiḥ sā pārtha tāmasī

That firmness by which an ignorant person does not give up sleep (dreaming), fear, anxiety, grief, despair and arrogance, that firmness is *Tamasic* in nature (mode of ignorance), O Arjuna. (18.35)

Three Types of Happiness

Q How many types of pleasure are there?

Spirituality leads to Eternal happiness

सुखं त्विदानीं त्रिविधंशृणु मे भरतर्षभ।
अभ्यासाद्रमते यत्र दुःखान्तं च निगच्छति ॥ 36 ॥

sukhaṁ tv idānīṁ tri-vidhaṁ śṛṇu me bharatarṣabha
abhyāsād ramate yatra duḥkhāntaṁ ca nigacchati

O Arjuna, now please hear from Me about the three kinds of happiness (pleasure). The happiness one comes to enjoy by spiritual practices (Selflessness, Meditation, Adoration, Surrender, etc.) and in which he reaches the end of his miseries and pain. (18.36)

Q What is *Sattvic* pleasure (mode of goodness, the best kind)?

यत्तदग्रे विषमिव परिणामेऽमृतोपमम्।
तत्सुखं सात्त्विकं प्रोक्तमात्मबुद्धिप्रसादजम् ॥ 37 ॥

yat tad agre viṣam iva pariṇāme 'mṛtopamam
tat sukhaṁ sāttvikaṁ proktam ātma-buddhi-prasāda-jam

Happiness that appears as poison in the beginning but is just like nectar in the end, such happiness (*Anandam*) is born though Self-Knowledge and awakens one to God/Self-Realization. That happiness is called *Sattvic* in nature (mode of goodness). (18.37)

Spiritual practices → God's Grace → Eternal Happiness and Peace, Sat Chit Ananda, Self-Realization

Q What is *Rajasic* pleasure (mode of passion)?

विषयेन्द्रियसंयोगाद्यत्तदग्रेऽमृतोपमम् ।
परिणामे विषमिव तत्सुखं राजसं स्मृतम् ।। 38 ।।

viṣayendriya-saṁyogād yat tad agre 'mṛtopamam
pariṇāme viṣam iva tat sukhaṁ rājasaṁ smṛtam

Worldly happiness is always attached to miseries

The happiness which is driven from the contact of the senses with their objects and which is just like nectar in the beginning but in the end is like poison, that happiness is *Rajasic* in nature (mode of passion). (18.38)

Q What is *Tamasic* pleasure (mode of ignorance)?

यदग्रे चानुबन्धे च सुखं मोहनमात्मनः ।
निद्रालस्यप्रमादोत्थं तत्तामसमुदाहृतम् ।। 39 ।।

yad agre cānubandhe ca sukhaṁ mohanam ātmanaḥ
nidrālasya-pramādotthaṁ tat tāmasam udāhṛtam

Laziness causes lousiness

The happiness which deludes the embodied soul from the very beginning to the end, born from sleep (living in a dream world), laziness and carelessness that happiness is *Tamasic* in nature (mode of ignorance, darkness). (18.39)

Q Is there anyone in the entire universe who is free from the laws of nature (*Gunas*)?

न तदस्ति पृथिव्यां वा दिवि देवेषु वा पुनः ।
सत्त्वं प्रकृतिजैर्मुक्तं यदेभिः स्यात्त्रिभिर्गुणैः ।। 40 ।।

na tad asti pṛthivyāṁ vā divi deveṣu vā punaḥ
sattvaṁ prakṛti-jair muktaṁ yad ebhiḥ syāt tribhir guṇaiḥ

Everyone is made of mother nature

There is no living being either on earth or in heaven among the demi-gods or anywhere else in the creation who is free from the influence of these three *Gunas* (qualities, attributes) born of *Prakriti* (Material Nature). (18.40)

Division of the duty is based upon one's ability (Caste)

Q How does the Gita support the theory of division of labor?

ब्राह्मणक्षत्रियविशां शूद्राणां च परंतप।
कर्माणि प्रविभक्तानि स्वभावप्रभवैर्गुणैः ॥ 41 ॥
brāhmaṇa-kṣatriya-viśāṁ śūdrāṇāṁ ca parantapa
karmāṇi pravibhaktāni svabhāva-prabhavair guṇaiḥ

Formula to build a strong team

The duties (activities) of *Brahmanas, Kshatriyas, Vaishyas* and *Sudras* are divided into four categories/castes based upon their inherent qualities-*Svabhava* (Aptitude, and not necessarily as one's birth right). O Arjuna. (18.41)

Q What are the natural duties and hallmarks of *Brahmanas*?

शमो दमस्तपः शौचं क्षान्तिरार्जवमेव च।
ज्ञानं विज्ञानमास्तिक्यं ब्रह्मकर्म स्वभावजम् ॥ 42 ॥
śamo damas tapaḥ śaucaṁ kṣāntir ārjavam eva ca
jñānaṁ vijñānam āstikyaṁ brahma-karma svabhāva-jam

Wise are Brahmanas

1. Serenity
2. Self-control
3. Austerity
4. Purity—honesty
5. Patience
6. Forgiveness
7. Straightforwardness (honesty)
8. Wisdom in theory and practice (Transcendental Knowledge and experience)
9. Faith in God and the scriptures

These are the inherent duties (based upon their nature) and hallmarks of *Brahmanas* (Wise ones who have knowledge of the scriptures). (18.42)

Q What are the natural duties and hallmarks of *Kshatriyas* or Protectors?

शौर्यं तेजो धृतिर्दाक्ष्यं युद्धे चाप्यपलायनम्।
दानमीश्वरभावश्च क्षात्रं कर्म स्वभावजम् ॥ 43 ॥
śauryaṁ tejo dhṛtir dākṣyaṁ yuddhe cāpy apalāyanam
dānam īśvara-bhāvaś ca kṣātraṁ karma svabhāva-jam

Kshatriyas are leaders

1. Heroism
2. Vigor
3. Firmness
4. Bravery
5. Resourcefulness
6. Steadfastness in battle (not running away from the battle)
7. Charity
8. Leadership skills

These are the natural duties of *Kshatriyas* (Protectors of righteousness, true man of action) based upon their natural qualities. (18.43)

Q What are the natural duties and hallmarks of the *Vaishyas* and *Sudras*?

कृषिगौरक्ष्यवाणिज्यं वैश्यकर्म स्वभावजम् ।
परिचर्यात्मकं कर्म शूद्रस्यापि स्वभावजम् ।। 44 ।।

kṛṣi-go-rakṣya-vāṇijyaṁ vaiśya-karma svabhāva-jam
paricaryātmakaṁ karma śūdrasyāpi svabhāva-jam

Vaisyas are businessmen

1. Agriculture
2. Cattle rearing
3. Business, trade, and industry

These are the natural duties of the *Vaishyas* (traders) while the labor and service are the natural duty of the *Sudras* (labor and service class) based upon their inborn qualities. (18.44)

Self-Realization through *svadharma*, self-discipline and devotion

Q Can one attain the Highest perfection through fulfilling the responsibilities of life and how?

स्वे स्वे कर्मण्यभिरतः संसिद्धिं लभते नरः ।
स्वकर्मनिरतः सिद्धिं यथा विन्दति तच्छृणु ।। 45 ।।

sve sve karmaṇy abhirataḥ saṁsiddhiṁ labhate naraḥ
sva-karma-nirataḥ siddhiṁ yathā vindati tac chṛṇu

Performing one's own duty leads to Perfection, Liberation

यतः प्रवृत्तिर्भूतानां येन सर्वमिदं ततम् ।
स्वकर्मणा तमभ्यर्च्य सिद्धिं विन्दति मानवः ।। 46 ।।

yataḥ pravṛttir bhūtānāṁ yena sarvam idaṁ tatam
sva-karmaṇā tam abhyarcya siddhiṁ vindati mānavaḥ

One can attain the highest perfection (regardless of his caste and type of work) by sincerely being devoted to one's own natural born duty. Listen to Me now, how he attains the highest perfection while performing his own duty. (18.45)

One can attain the highest perfection by worshipping the Supreme Lord who has created all beings and pervaded this entire universe, through performance of one's own natural duty (prescribed duty). (18.46)

Q Why is it better to do one's own duty?

> *If one works according to his apptitute, he will get the best out of himself*

श्रेयान्स्वधर्मो विगुणः परधर्मात्स्वनुष्ठितात् ।
स्वभावनियतं कर्म कुर्वन्नाप्नोति किल्बिषम् ।। 47 ।।

śreyān sva-dharmo viguṇaḥ para-dharmāt sv-anuṣṭhitāt
svabhāva-niyataṁ karma kurvan nāpnoti kilbiṣam

Better is one's own duty (occupation, according to own nature, personality, *Gunas*), though performed imperfectly, than the duty of another performed perfectly (another's occupation, unnatural work, does not fit in own personality). One who does the duty ordained by one's own nature (without selfish motives) does not incur sins. (18.47)

Q Is there any activity that is free from defects?

सहजं कर्म कौन्तेय सदोषमपि न त्यजेत् ।
सर्वारम्भा हि दोषेण धूमेनाग्निरिवावृताः ।। 48 ।।

saha-jaṁ karma kaunteya sa-doṣam api na tyajet
sarvārambhā hi doṣeṇa dhūmenāgnir ivāvṛtāḥ

O Arjuna, therefore, one should not give up one's own natural work even though it might seem to have defects because every activity (undertakings, endeavors,) has some defects, as fire is covered by smoke. (18.48)

Q Who attains the Supreme state of freedom (Highest Perfection) and how?

असक्तबुद्धिः सर्वत्र जितात्मा विगतस्पृहः ।
नैष्कर्म्यसिद्धिं परमां संन्यासेनाधिगच्छति ।। 49 ।।

asakta-buddhiḥ sarvatra jitātmā vigata-spṛhaḥ
naiṣkarmya-siddhiṁ paramāṁ sannyāsenādhigacchati

One whose mind and intellect are always detached from everywhere, is self-controlled, is free from selfish and material desires to the fruits of work, attains the Supreme state of freedom (Highest Perfection) by continuous practice of renunciation. (18.49)

Q Who is qualified to attain the Supreme State of Knowledge?

सिद्धिं प्राप्तो यथा ब्रह्म तथाप्नोति निबोध मे।
समासेनैव कौन्तेय निष्ठा ज्ञानस्य या परा ।। 50 ।।

siddhiṁ prāpto yathā brahma tathāpnoti nibodha me
samāsenaiva kaunteya niṣṭhā jñānasya yā parā

O Arjuna, learn from Me briefly how one who has attained this perfection, and reaches Brahman (Supreme Being, the Eternal), the Supreme State of Knowledge (Transcendental Knowledge-Supreme goal of our life—*Sat Chit Ananda*). (18.50)

Q Who is qualified to become One with God (*Brahman*)?

बुद्ध्या विशुद्धया युक्तो धृत्यात्मानं नियम्य च।
शब्दादीन्विषयांस्त्यक्त्वा रागद्वेषौ व्युदस्य च ।। 51 ।।

buddhyā viśuddhayā yukto dhṛtyātmānaṁ niyamya ca
śabdādīn viṣayāṁs tyaktvā rāga-dveṣau vyudasya ca

विविक्तसेवी लघ्वाशी यतवाक्कायमानसः।
ध्यानयोगपरो नित्यं वैराग्यं समुपाश्रितः ।। 52 ।।

vivikta-sevī laghv-āśī yata-vāk-kāya-mānasaḥ
dhyāna-yoga-paro nityaṁ vairāgyaṁ samupāśritaḥ

अहंकारं बलं दर्पं कामं क्रोधं परिग्रहम्।
विमुच्य निर्ममः शान्तो ब्रह्मभूयाय कल्पते ।। 53 ।।

ahaṅkāraṁ balaṁ darpaṁ kāmaṁ krodhaṁ parigraham
vimucya nirmamaḥ śānto brahma-bhūyāya kalpate

Any deciplined person has potential to merge with God

One who is possessed with:

1. Purified intellect
2. Subdued mind with firm determination (*Sattvic*)
3. Turning away from sound and other objects of the senses (self-controlled, giving up the objects of sense gratification)
4. Giving up likes and dislikes (free from attachment and hatred)
5. Living in solitude
6. Controlled in diet (eating only sufficient and *Sattvic* food)
7. Controlled body, mind and speech (austerity)
8. Always absorbed in meditation and Yoga
9. Taking shelter in detachment or non-attachment (*vairagya*)
10. Free from false ego
11. Free from violence

12. Free from arrogance (egoism)
13. Free from lust, anger and greed for worldly possessions
14. Free from possessions (proprietorship), free from the notion of mine, "My-ness" (possessiveness)
15. Peaceful and Serenity (Liberation)

Such a person is fit and qualified to become One with the Supreme-Soul (*Brahman*, Supreme Being, Supreme Consciousness, God). (18.51–53)

Q Who attains Supreme devotion to God?

ब्रह्मभूतः प्रसन्नात्मा न शोचति न काङ्क्षति।
समः सर्वेषु भूतेषु मद्भक्तिं लभते पराम्॥ 54॥

brahma-bhūtaḥ prasannātmā na śocati na kāṅkṣati
samaḥ sarveṣu bhūteṣu mad-bhaktiṁ labhate parām

One who is fully joyful (happy, cheerful), never grieves nor has any selfish or materialistic desires, is impartial to all beings and in peace with himself, achieves Supreme devotion to Me. (18.54)

Q What does the Self-realized person get in return?

भक्त्या मामभिजानाति यावान्यश्चास्मि तत्त्वतः।
ततो मां तत्त्वतो ज्ञात्वा विशते तदनन्तरम्॥ 55॥

bhaktyā mām abhijānāti yāvān yaś cāsmi tattvataḥ
tato māṁ tattvato jñātvā viśate tad-anantaram

Through devotion, one realizes Me in Essence, what and who I am. Then, having known Me in My Essence, he immediately merges with Me. (18.55)

Living in God's Consciousness leads to His grace

Q How does one realize God and receive His Grace?

सर्वकर्माण्यपि सदा कुर्वाणो मद्व्यपाश्रयः।
मत्प्रसादादवाप्नोति शाश्वतं पदमव्ययम्॥ 56॥

sarva-karmāṇy api sadā kurvāṇo mad-vyapāśrayaḥ
mat-prasādād avāpnoti śāśvataṁ padam avyayam

God's grace takes one to the ultimate destination

One who takes refuge in Me (surrenders all action to Me) while performing all of his activities/duties, by My grace, attains the Eternal and Imperishable Abode (Supreme Abode, *Moksha*). (18.56)

Q O Krishna, what should I do and why?

चेतसा सर्वकर्माणि मयि संन्यस्य मत्परः।
बुद्धियोगमुपाश्रित्य मच्चितः सततं भव ।। 57 ।।

cetasā sarva-karmāṇi mayi sannyasya mat-paraḥ
buddhi-yogam upāśritya mac-cittaḥ satatam̐ bhava

मच्चितः सर्वदुर्गाणि मत्प्रसादात्तरिष्यसि।
अथ चेत्त्वमहंकारान्न श्रोष्यसि विनङ्क्ष्यसि ।। 58 ।।

mac-cittaḥ sarva-durgāṇi mat-prasādāt tariṣyasi
atha cet tvam ahaṅkārān na śroṣyasi vinaṅkṣyasi

If we live in His consciousness then all our obstacles will be removed by His Grace

Sincerely surrender all actions to Me, regard Me as your Supreme Goal, adhere to Yoga of Equanimity (Yoga of integral Wisdom, *Buddhi-Yoga* always focus your mind on Me (live in my Consciousness) and completely depend on Me). (18.57)

Thus focusing your mind on Me, you will overcome all difficulties and obstacles by My grace. But if you will not listen to Me due to your false ego (arrogance), you shall perish. (18.58)

Q What would happen if we do not listen to God?

यदहंकारमाश्रित्य न योत्स्य इति मन्यसे।
मिथ्यैष व्यवसायस्ते प्रकृतिस्त्वां नियोक्ष्यति ।। 59 ।।

yad ahaṅkāram āśritya na yotsya iti manyase
mithyaiṣa vyavasāyas te prakṛtis tvām̐ niyokṣyati

स्वभावजेन कौन्तेय निबद्धः स्वेन कर्मणा।
कर्तुं नेच्छसि यन्मोहात्करिष्यस्यवशोऽपि तत् ।। 60 ।।

svabhāva-jena kaunteya nibaddhaḥ svena karmaṇā
kartum̐ necchasi yan mohāt kariṣyasy avaśo 'pi tat

Svabhava makes everyone act

Because of your ego, if you think "I will not fight," your determination is wrong because your own nature (*svabhava*, *Gunas*, inner drive) will compel you to fight. (18.59)

O Arjuna, what you do not wish to do out of your delusion, you will be forced to do helplessly even against your will by your own natural-born *karmic* impressions (*Sanskaras*, inner dispositions) because you are controlled by them. (18.60)

Q Where does God live and how does His mystical power (Maya) work?

ईश्वरः सर्वभूतानां हृद्देशेऽर्जुन तिष्ठति।
भ्रामयन्सर्वभूतानि यन्त्रारूढानि मायया ॥61॥

īśvaraḥ sarva-bhūtānāṁ hṛd-deśe 'rjuna tiṣṭhati
bhrāmayan sarva-bhūtāni yantrārūḍhāni māyayā

Maya drives everyone crazy in the universe

O Arjuna, the Supreme Lord resides in the causal heart (the inner psyche) of all living beings causing them to revolve according to their *karmas* by His mystical power (*Maya*, illusive power), as if they were mounted on a machine. (18.61)

Q How does one get the Grace of God and attain Supreme Peace?

तमेव शरणं गच्छ सर्वभावेन भारत।
तत्प्रसादात्परां शान्तिं स्थानं प्राप्स्यसि शाश्वतम् ॥62॥

tam eva śaraṇaṁ gaccha sarva-bhāvena bhārata
tat-prasādāt parāṁ śāntiṁ sthānaṁ prāpsyasi śāśvatam

Surrender leads to the Eternal Abode

O Arjuna, whole-heartedly surrender unto Him with love and devotion; by His grace only you will attain Supreme Peace and Eternal Abode (*Parama-dhama*). (18.62)

Unconditional Surrender → Supreme Peace & Eternal Abode

Q Did Lord Krishna force Arjuna to act?

इति ते ज्ञानमाख्यातं गुह्याद्गुह्यतरं मया।
विमृश्यैतदशेषेण यथेच्छसि तथा कुरु ॥63॥

iti te jñānam ākhyātaṁ guhyād guhyataraṁ mayā
vimṛśyaitad aśeṣeṇa yathecchasi tathā kuru

Thus, the Supreme Knowledge that is most mysterious of all mysteries (most secret of all secrets), I have revealed to you. After fully reflecting on this, do as you like. (18.63)

Surrender is the ultimate path to Self-Realization

Q Why did Lord Krishna want to reinforce His teachings again?

सर्वगुह्यतमं भूयःश्रृणु मे परमं वचः।
इष्टोऽसि मे दृढमिति ततो वक्ष्यामि ते हितम् ॥64॥

sarva-guhyatamaṁ bhūyaḥ śṛṇu me paramaṁ vacaḥ
iṣṭo 'si me dṛḍham iti tato vakṣyāmi te hitam

Hear once again My Supreme word, the most confidential of all. Since you are extremely dear to Me, therefore, I will tell this for your benefit. (18.64)

Q What is God's promise to all of us?

मन्मना भव मद्भक्तो मद्याजी मां नमस्कुरु।
मामेवैष्यसि सत्यं ते प्रतिजाने प्रियोऽसि मे ।।65।।

man-manā bhava mad-bhakto mad-yājī māṁ namaskuru
mām evaiṣyasi satyaṁ te pratijāne priyo 'si me

Focus your mind on Me (always think of me, live in My Consciousness), be My devotee, worship Me, offer your homage and services to Me and you will undoubtedly come to Me. This is My promise to you because you are My very dear friend. (18.65)

Q Why should one surrender to God?

सर्वधर्मान्परित्यज्य मामेकं शरणं व्रज।
अहं त्वा सर्वपापेभ्यो मोक्षयिष्यामि मा शुचः ।।66।।

sarva-dharmān parityajya mām ekaṁ śaraṇaṁ vraja
ahaṁ tvāṁ sarva-pāpebhyo mokṣayiṣyāmi mā śucaḥ

Just come to me, I will take care of you

Abandon all the duties (Meritorious deeds, Rituals, *Dharma*), just totally surrender to Me (unconditionally with firm faith and loving devotion). I will liberate you from all sins (the bonds of *karma*). Do not fear (worry, grieve). (18.66)

The best way to serve God

Q Who should this Supreme message not be spoken to?

इदं ते नातपस्काय नाभक्ताय कदाचन।
न चाशुश्रूषवे वाच्यं न च मां योऽभ्यसूयति ।।67।।

idaṁ te nātapaskāya nābhaktāya kadācana
na cāśuśrūṣave vācyaṁ na ca māṁ yo 'bhyasūyati

Share the teachings of Gita (advice) with only those, who ask for it

These secret teachings of the Gita (Supreme knowledge) should never be told by you to anyone who is devoid of austerity, who lacks devotion, who is unwilling to listen and also who speaks ill of Me (finds fault in me, envies Me). (18.67)

Q Why should one teach this secret Knowledge to others?

> *The most dearest service to God is to propogate His message of Gita*

य इमं परमं गुह्यं मद्भक्तेष्वभिधास्यति।
भक्तिं मयि परां कृत्वा मामेवैष्यत्यसंशयः ।। 68 ।।

ya idaṁ paramaṁ guhyaṁ mad-bhakteṣv abhidhāsyati
bhaktiṁ mayi parāṁ kṛtvā mām evaiṣyaty asaṁśayaḥ

न च तस्मान्मनुष्येषु कश्चिन्मे प्रियकृत्तमः।
भविता न च मे तस्मादन्यः प्रियतरो भुवि ।। 69 ।।

na ca tasmān manuṣyeṣu kaścin me priya-kṛttamaḥ
bhavitā na ca me tasmād anyaḥ priyataro bhuvi

One, who with Supreme devotion to Me, preaches this most Supreme Secret (Transcendental Knowledge of the Gita) to My devotees will definitely come to Me. There is no doubt about it. (18.68)

No other service is dearest to me than this, nor will there be anyone on earth dearer to Me than he. (18.69)

Grace of the Gita

Q How can one worship God through sharing (Sacrifice, *Yajna*) of Wisdom (*Jnana Yajna*)?

अध्येष्यते च य इमं धर्म्यं संवादमावयोः।
ज्ञानयज्ञेन तेनाहमिष्टः स्यामिति मे मतिः ।। 70 ।।

adhyeṣyate ca ya imaṁ dharmyaṁ saṁvādam āvayoḥ
jñāna-yajñena tenāham iṣṭaḥ syām iti me matiḥ

One who studies this sacred dialogue of ours, will be worshipping me by Knowledge-sacrifice (*Yajna* of Knowledge-Wisdom, *Jnana Yajna*). Such is My conviction. (18.70)

Q Can one benefit just by listening to the Gita's teachings?

> *Good listening is as rewarding as good doing*

श्रद्धावाननसूयश्च शृणुयादपि यो नरः।
सोऽपि मुक्तः शुभाँल्लोकान्प्राप्नुयात्पुण्यकर्मणाम् ।। 71 ।।

śraddhāvān anasūyaś ca śṛṇuyād api yo naraḥ
so 'pi muktaḥ śubhāl lokān prāpnuyāt puṇya-karmaṇām

One who even just listens to this sacred dialogue of ours (the Gita) with faith and without an attitude of finding faults becomes free from sins and will attain higher worlds of the Virtuous (Righteous, pious). (18.71)

Q What did Lord Krishna ask Arjuna to confirm if he understood His teachings?

कच्चिदेतच्छ्रुतं पार्थ त्वयैकाग्रेण चेतसा ।
कच्चिदज्ञानसंमोहः प्रनष्टस्ते धनंजय ॥ 72 ॥

kaccid etac chrutaṁ pārtha tvayaikāgreṇa cetasā
kaccid ajñāna-sammohaḥ praṇaṣṭas te dhanañjaya

O Arjuna, have you listened to this with a focused mind? Has your delusion caused by ignorance been completely destroyed? (18.72)

Q What happens to one when he receives God's Grace?

I will do as you advice

अर्जुन उवाच
नष्टो मोहः स्मृतिर्लब्धा त्वत्प्रसादान्मयाच्युत ।
स्थितोऽस्मि गतसन्देहः करिष्ये वचनं तव ॥ 73 ॥

arjuna uvāca
naṣṭo mohaḥ smṛtir labdhā tvat-prasādān mayācyuta
sthito 'smi gata-sandehaḥ kariṣye vacanaṁ tava

Arjuna said: By Your grace My Dear Lord, my delusion is destroyed. I have regained my memory (Knowledge of Self). Now, I am determined and free from all doubts (regarding body and spirit). I shall act according to Your Word. (18.73)

Arjuna is fully transformed by the blessing of the Supreme

Ask for Advice → Listen → Follow → God's Grace

Q How did Sanjaya enjoy listening to this Supreme dialogue between Lord Krishna and Arjuna?

संजय उवाच
इत्यहं वासुदेवस्य पार्थस्य च महात्मनः ।
संवादमिममश्रौषमद्भुतं रोमहर्षणम् ॥ 74 ॥

sañjaya uvāca
ity ahaṁ vāsudevasya pārthasya ca mahātmanaḥ
saṁvādam imam aśrauṣam adbhutaṁ roma-harṣaṇam

व्यासप्रसादाच्छ्रुतवानेतद्गुह्यमहं परम् ।
योगं योगेश्वरात्कृष्णात्साक्षात्कथयतः स्वयम् ॥ 75 ॥

vyāsa-prasādāc chrutavān etad guhyam ahaṁ param
yogaṁ yogeśvarāt kṛṣṇāt sākṣāt kathayataḥ svayam

राजन्संस्मृत्य संस्मृत्य संवादमिममद्भुतम्।
केशवार्जुनयोः पुण्यं हृष्यामि च मुहुर्मुहुः ॥76॥

rājan saṁsmṛtya saṁsmṛtya saṁvādam imam adbhutam
keśavārjunayoḥ puṇyaṁ hṛṣyāmi ca muhur muhuḥ

Sanjaya said: Thus, I heard this marvelous and mystical dialogue between Lord Krishna and Great soul—Arjuna (*Mahatma*, Enlightened) which fills me with ecstasy and makes my hair stand on end. (18.74)

By the grace of sage Vyasa (Guru), who provided me with clairvoyance, I heard this most secret and Supreme Yoga directly from the Lord of Yoga, Krishna, Himself speaking to Arjuna). (18.75)

O King, as I recollect repeatedly this most wondrous, beneficial and holy dialogue between Lord Krishna and Arjuna; I enjoy over and over again. (18.76)

Q Did Sanjay (king's minister) enjoy seeing Lord Krishna's glorious form?

तच्च संस्मृत्य संस्मृत्य रूपमत्यद्भुतं हरेः।
विस्मयो मे महान्राजन्हृष्यामि च पुनः पुनः ॥77॥

tac ca saṁsmṛtya saṁsmṛtya rūpam aty-adbhutaṁ hareḥ
vismayo me mahān rājan hṛṣyāmi ca punaḥ punaḥ

O King, remembering, again and again that most magnificent Cosmic Form of *Hari* (Lord Krishna), I am greatly amazed and I am thrilled with joy and bliss over and over again. (18.77)

Both righteousness and the protector of the righteousness are needed

Q How to establish the everlasting prosperity, victory, glory, and morality (Sound Policy)?

Formula for gaining everlasting Prosperity, Victory and Glory

यत्र योगेश्वरः कृष्णो यत्र पार्थो धनुर्धरः।
तत्र श्रीर्विजयो भूतिर्ध्रुवा नीतिर्मतिर्मम ॥78॥

yatra yogeśvaraḥ kṛṣṇo yatra pārtho dhanur-dharaḥ
tatra śrīr vijayo bhūtir dhruvā nītir matir mama

Wherever there is Krishna the Lord of Yoga (Righteousness/*Dharma*, Gita) and wherever there is Arjuna, the supreme archer (Protector of righteousness with the weapons of duty), there will always be Everlasting Prosperity, Victory, Glory, and Sound policy; such is my firm conviction. (18.78)

Oneness of body, mind (Arjuna, Action) and Spirit (Lord Krishna) are needed to achieve anything in life

Righteousness/Dharma (Lord Krishna)
+
Protector of Dharma with weapon of Duty (Arjuna)
= Prosperity + Victory + Glory + Sound Policy

Lessons to learn and practice in daily life

The Gita is a step-by-step spiritual guide to attain the Ultimate goal of life—Peace and Anandam (Ultimate Bliss, Liberation)

1. Make Self-Realization the Supreme goal of life to fulfill the purpose of our life
2. Study the Gita and practice its teachings in daily life
3. Lead a spiritual and self-disciplined life
4. Keep divine (*Sattvic*) company (guru, the Gita)
5. Develop self-awareness
6. Perform your own duty selflessly with love, devotion and without any expectation of the fruit of action
7. Maintain a healthy body, healthy mind and connect with the Supreme-Soul
8. Do regularly Yoga, *Pranayam*, mantra, meditation and prayers
9. Transcend from the three *Gunas* (attributes)
10. Develop divine qualities and eliminate evil qualities

Be a living and working Gita not just talking Gita

11. Always live in God's Consciousness
12. Always communicate with Him (like your friend)
13. Have full faith in God and yourself
14. Surrender to Him unconditionally
15. Do your best and leave the rest to God
16. Have patience, do not be so hard on yourself. He will take care of us.
17. Relax, relax … let go …
18. Keep practicing: "Self-Realization is not an activity but a lifestyle and a lifetime commitment."

Live in peace and let others live in peace, this is the only way to God

ॐ तत्सदिति श्रीमद्भगवद्गीतासूपनिषत्सु ब्रह्मविद्यायां योगशास्त्रे
श्रीकृष्णार्जुनसंवादे मोक्षसंन्यासयोगो नामाष्टादशोऽध्यायः ॥

AUM TAT SAT

Thus ends the eighteenth chapter named "*Moksha-Sanyasa Yoga*"
The Path of Liberation through Renunciation
in the *Upanishad* of the glorious Bhagavad Gita, the scripture of Yoga, the science of the Absolute (*Brahman*), in the form of the dialogue between Lord Krishna and Arjuna.

Aum Shanti, Shanti, Shantihi

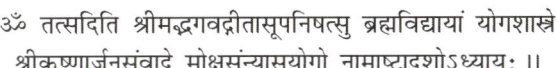

Time to Cogitate

Liberation/Moksha

Liberation/Moksha means:

Freedom from miseries and pain

Freedom from depression and delusion

Freedom from anger, fear and guilt

Freedom from vices and negative emotions

Freedom from attachment and selfish desires

Freedom from ego/arrogance

Freedom from stress and worry

Freedom from cycle of birth and death

Oneness

Oneness of Body, Mind & Spirit

Oneness of Head, Heart & Hand

Oneness of Thought, Speech & Action

Oneness of Karma, Bhakti & Jnana Yoga

Oneness of External and Internal world

Oneness of Guru, Geeta and Gopal

Oneness of Love, Peace and Anandam

Ultimate Summary of Gita

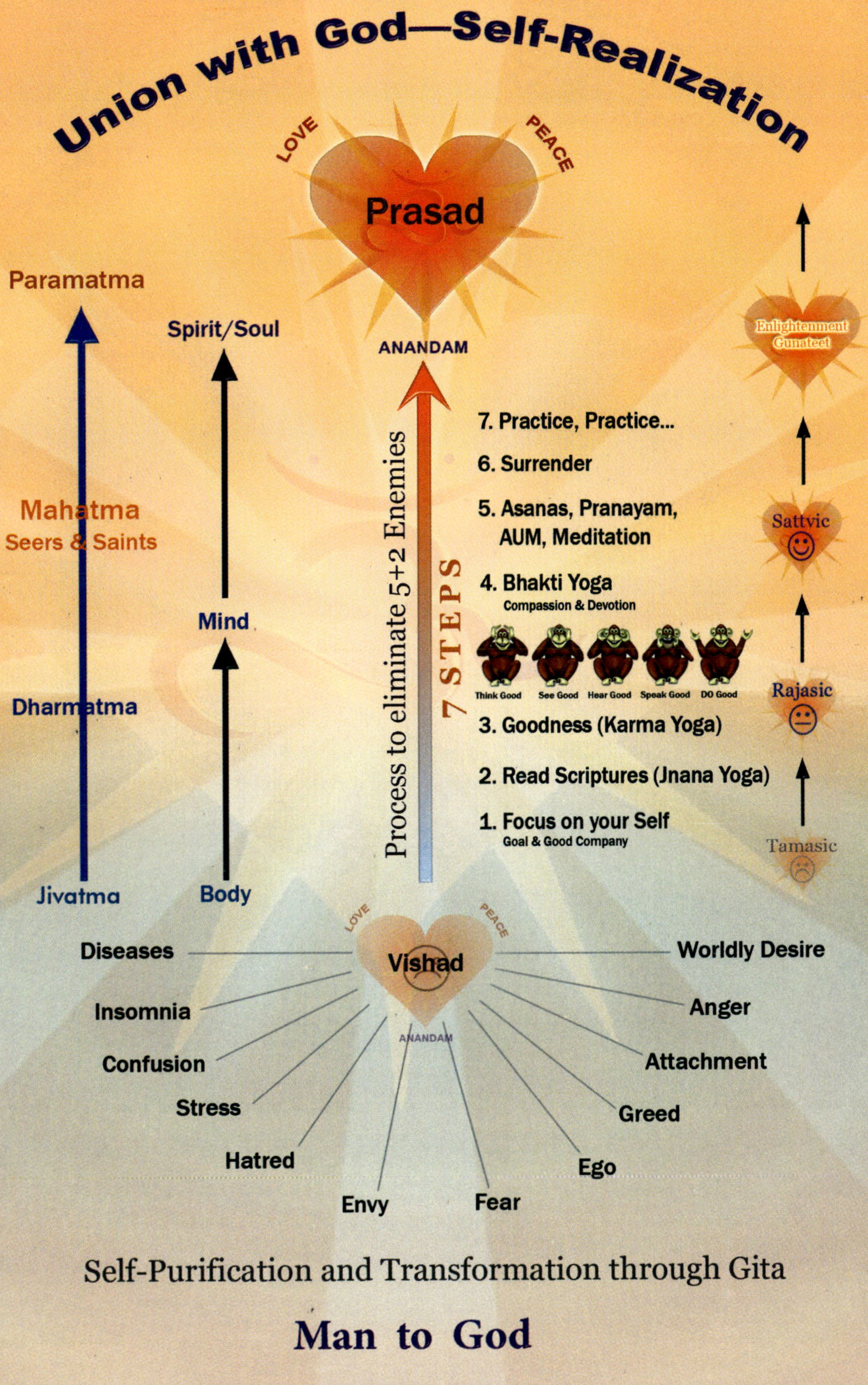

Ultimate Summary of the Gita's Teachings

Most of the time, many of us live in misery and pain, sorrow, dejection and dilemma (*vishad*). The Gita, source of unlimited Wisdom (Universal Knowledge, Self-Knowledge) is more than a book. It is all about how to remove pains and miseries from life, fulfill own *Dharma*, (duty, prescribed responsibilities) and attain Eternal Happiness, Peace and live in *Anandam* (Blissful life). It teaches us how to liberate our self from *vishad* and experience our true nature (*Prasad*, Nectar), '*Sat Chit Ananda*.'

The Gita answers All

It is a divine dialogue between the mind (lower self) and Supreme-Spirit (Higher Self) that answers all of our day-to-day queries and five basic universal questions:

1. **Who am I (What is my True Nature)?**

   I am Spirit, Soul, *Atma* (Chapter two)

2. **Where did I come from?**

   Every one originated from God (Chapter 13)

3. **Where will I go from here (after death)?**

   One could attain Self-Realization and merge with God or could keep going from one life to another depending one's own actions (2.13, 2.16, 2.22, Chapter 13)

4. **What is the purpose of my life?**

   God/Self-Realization, Liberation, *Moksha*, *Nirvana* (Attain Peace and *Anandam* (5.17, 15.04, 9.34, 11.55, 12.20,15.20)

5. **How can I fulfill the purpose of my life and still lead a happy and peaceful life in this materialistic world? (Chapter 2–18)**

The Gita is a step by step Anandam and spiritual guide for self-awareness, self-purification, self-transformation and Self-Realization

Gita teaches self-awareness, self-purification, self-transformation and self-unfoldment so one becomes a better person, fulfills one's responsibilities, contributes to the society, enjoys life to the fullest and attains Liberation (God-Realization and Self-Realization).

The Gita's teachings transformed Arjuna from, "I will not fight the battle" to, "I will do as you advise," (2.09, 18.73). It took Arjuna, very gradually, from *vishad*, confusion and dejection to Liberation. He became aware of his *Dharma*, duty as a warrior that his responsibility as a *Kshatriya* is to protect the society and then he fought the war. The teachings of Lord Krishna fully transformed him and finally he said, "My doubts are dispelled, I have regained the memory of Self-Knowledge and will do as you advised."

The Gita teaches us to overcome our limitations to reach highest potential.

- Gita removes doubts and leads to decision.
- It helps us to transform our negative attitude to positive attitude – lower self to Higher Self.
- It guides us to transcend from selfish to selfless and become more sharing and caring by performing our work/duty with love and devotion, and without expecting the fruit of action.
- It teaches us to develop the contentment and calmness (serenity of mind, *Equanimity*) that is a pre-requisite for success in life.
- The Gita is a mirror and a character builder that makes us aware of our short comings/vices and shows us how to remove them and develop noble qualities (virtues). It makes us a better person and leads us to divinity and attain Self-Knowledge (Wisdom) as well. (10.4, 12.13–20, 16.1–20)
- It guides us to transcend the three *Gunas* (*Sattvic, Rajasic, Tamasic*) (2.45.14.26), thus helps us to proceed from a *jivatma* → *Dharmatma* → *Mahatma* → *Parmatma.*
- The Gita guide us to have a healthy body, healthy mind and maintain good health by doing Yoga, *Pranayam* and other spiritual practices (*Sadhana*). (Chapter 6)
- It also details the varieties of food and urges us to eat good food and practice meditation. (Chapter17)
- It explains the value of having proper company of people and reading good books to feed our mind.
- It emphasises the importance of maintaining the balance in daily activities such as sleep, entertainment and work and explains how the balance in life

helps to attain healthy mind and body and also the Oneness of body, mind and Spirit. (Chapter 6)

- It teaches how our faith shapes our future and how to develop more faith within ourselves.
- It teaches how to live and how to die happily and peacefully.
- It teaches us surrender and let go—Do your best and leave the rest to God.
- It motivates us to practice its teachings by showing the benefit of applying its teaching—Get rid off your unwanted behavior and habits, develop divine qualities, free ourselves from miseries, live happy and peaceful life in the material world and beyond. It teaches us to how to spread Peace and *Anandam* to others though selfless action, love and devotion.
- Therefore, keep practicing and propagating its message because attaining Eternal Happiness and Peace and *Anandam* (God-Realization and Self-Realization) is not an activity but a lifetime goal.

Therefore, the Gita is called a Self-Transformer and the Royal Road to Liberation.

Every single chapter of the Gita guides us attain Eternal, Happiness, Peace and *Anandam* and enjoy our life to the fullest as well. The eighteen chapters are divided into three main Yogas/paths. One can attain Liberation through any path:

1. *Karma/Action Yoga* (Chapter 1–6): Path of Selfless action (For active and extroverted people)
2. *Bhakti Yoga* (Chapter 7–12): Path of Love, Devotion and Compassion (For emotional people)
3. *Jnana Yoga* (Chapter 13–18): Path of Knowledge (For introverted people)

All the three Yogas lead to the same goal of living peacefully and happily in the world and also attain the Supreme Goal of life — Self-Realization, Liberation, Union with God, Oneness with God. Based upon our aptitude, it also gives us freedom to choose any path of our choice.

Main Message of chapters

Chap 1—Attain Union with God/Self through the path of dejection, despondency, depression, deep sorrow and dilemma (*vishad*)—Do not give up, but learn to handle the difficult situations in life. Divine help is always there for you.

Chap 2—The contents of the entire Gita have been summarized in this chapter. This chapter not only focuses on the Knowledge of Self, (answers who am I) but also spells out the major barriers to our happiness and peace (5+2 Enemies: Desires, anger, greed, attachment, ego, hatred and envy). How to remove these barriers and attain the purpose of our life, live happily and peacefully in the material world, realize our true nature (*Sat Chit Ananda*).

Chap 3—In this chapter, the Path of Action spells out the art of action, how to master it and fulfill your duty through right action (*Karma Yoga*). This is one of the main paths to attain Eternal Happiness, Peace and *Anandam*. (Bliss)

Chap 4—Know your *Dharma*, goal, mission and act upon it.

Chap 5—Do your action with renunciation of the fruits of action, fulfill your responsibilities without any expectations in return—from selfish to selfless.

Chap 6—Self-discipline and meditation is the best yoga for self-transformation, self-purification and Union with Self. It teaches us how to take care of ourself and maintain a balance, doing too little or too much leads to miseries and pain in life.

Chap 7—Supreme Spirit (Supreme Power) is the sustaining force of everything in the universe. Witness His play and play your role well.

Chap 8—Recitation of 'ॐ *AUM*' mantra is the simplest way to live in God's Consciousness. Therefore it is called the simplest yoga.

Chap 9—Supreme Knowledge is the king of all knowledge and also the most confidential Knowledge. It is the *Royal Path to Liberation*. Everything is God's manifestation. He always takes care of his devotees. If build a partnership with Him and work just for Him, He will always take care of all of our needs (I said needs not necessarily wants) of the spiritual and material world).

Chap 10—God is the best of the best and He is the cause of all the causes in the Universe.

Chap 11—Purity leads to divinity and divinity leads to unity (Union with God). One can experience Him, feel Him and see Him if one has a pure heart.

Chap 12—*Bhakti Yoga* is the easiest, the highest and the most expedient method to attain God. Love all, Serve all.

Chap 13—Everyone is made up of matter and energy, body and Soul. We are only a fraction of His Supreme Yogic Power.

Chap 14—Everything in this universe is bound by the law of Material Nature (three *Gunas*: *Sattva*/Goodness, *Rajas*/Passion, *Tamas*/Ignorance). In order to realize God/Self, one must transcend these qualities of nature and reach beyond one's limitations.

Chap 15—The human body and the entire universe is a tree of *sanskaras*. It can only be cut down with the weapons of non attachment which is the main stumbling block experiencing eternal happiness and Peace—*Anandam* and to realize one's own true Self/God.

Chap 16—*The Gita is a Mirror that shows our true attributes.* Noble qualities (Virtues) lead to Eternal Happiness, Peace and Liberation, but demonic qualities (vices) lead to sorrow and miseries. The Gita helps substitute vices with virtues.

Chap 17—One can become whatever one believes in and wants to be. Have faith in yourself and God.

Chap 18—Liberation, Moksha from miseries through *svadharma* (Duty), self-discipline and devotion. Gita is a call to action with renunciation of the fruits of all actions and unconditional surrender.

Aum Shanti, Shanti, Shantihi

Summary of Karma Yoga, Bhakti Yoga and Jnana Yoga

Karma-Yoga	Bhakti-Yoga	Jnana-Yoga
Action Yoga	Love and Devotion Yoga	Knowledge Yoga
Chapter 1–6 (Main verses—2.47, 2.48, 2.50, 12.4)	Chapter 7–12 (Heart of the Bhakti Yoga—Chapter 12)	Chapter 13–18 (Summary of Gita—Chapter 18)
Union with God (Self-Realization) through the path of Right action	Union with God (Self-Realization) through the path of Love and Devotion	Union with Self (Self-Realization) through Self-Knowledge—Liberation through Renunciation
God-Realization (purity) through Selfless action/Body (austerity of body and speech) (17.14–15)	God-Realization (purity) through Feelings/Heart/spirit	Self/God-Realization (purity) through thoughts/Mind (austerity of mind—17.16)
Self-Transformation/ Purification through action (5.11)	Self-Transformation/ Purification through love and devotion	Self-Transformation/ Purification through Self-Realized Knowledge
Action based	Feelings based	Based upon self-experienced and realized Knowledge
Main activities, Selfless-action, Service, Seva	Selfless-action, Service, Devotional songs and Prayers	Spiritual practices: Asanas, Meditation, Pranayam, prayers etc.
Do every thing to please Him	Always live in God-Consciousness as Meera	Always live in God/Self-Consciousness
Practice the path of Goodness: • Think good • Speak good • Hear good • See good • Do good (5 Monkeys)	Worshiping God with form and shape (*Saguna*)	Focus on Contemplation and Meditation on Self Practice all the eight limbs of Patanjali Yoga*— 1. Yama 2. Niyama, 3. Asanas 4. Pranayam, 5. Pratyahara 6. Dharana, 7. Dhyana 8. Samadhi
For active people and extroverted, A type personality	Emotional people	For introverted people

Karma-Yoga	Bhakti-Yoga	Jnana-Yoga
Develop divine qualities: Selflessness, detachment contentment, *Tyaga*	Develop divine qualities: 12.13–20	Develop divine qualities: Equanimity, Calmness, awareness, self-analysis, self-disciplining, become witness and observer (13.9–11, 16.1–3)
Need Guru, Geeta, scriptures	Devotion	Need a Guru
Easier to practice	Easiest	Most difficult to practice
Action that is done skillfully with knowledge (Wisdom, *Jnana*), love and devotion and to the best of one's ability without any expectation in return (renunciation of the fruit of action), for the benefit of others is called *Karma Yoga-Art of action*	**Work + compassion/love/ devotion = *Bhakti Yoga*** *Bhakti yoga is The Heart of Gita.* —Swami H. H. Hari Harji Maharaj	Self-Knowledge: self-experienced and realized knowledge of the Absolute, God, Self
Serve God through His creation—**Duality**	Worship God externally—**Duality**	**Non-duality (advaita), Oneness:** Realize God within, own true nature of *Sat Chit Ananda* (Self-Realization) 'I am God and so is every one else'
Karma Yogi, who practice *Karma Yoga* and is free from bondages, cause and effect of law of *karma* e.g. Arjuna, Mahatma Gandhi, Mother Teresa	True Devotee/Bhakta e.g. Meera, Gopies	Sadhaka who does spiritual practices and become Wise, Equanimous, Enlightened Person e.g. Buddha
Help Ever, Hurt Never	Love All, Serve All	See God in all
Purity →	→ Divinity	→ Unity
God-Realization	God-Realization	Self-Realization

All three, *Karma Yoga*, *Bhakti Yoga* and *Jnana Yoga* are interconnected and must be practiced together.

Karma Yoga + *Bhakti Yoga* + *Jnana Yoga* → Self-Purification → Self-Transformation → God/Self-Realization

*Ashtanaga Yoga: The Eight Parts of Yoga

1. **Yama:** Universal morality
2. **Niyama:** Personal observances
3. **Asanas:** Body postures
4. **Pranayama:** Breathing exercises and control of prana
5. **Pratyahara:** Control of the senses
6. **Dharana:** Contemplation and cultivating of inner awareness
7. **Dhyana:** Devotion, Meditation on the Self/Divine, AUM (Formless/Nirguna)
8. **Samadhi:** Union with Self/God

Aum Shanti, Shanti, Shantihi

Summary of Gunas: Tamasic, Rajasic and Sattvic

No	Type of	Tamasic	Rajasic	Sattvic
1	**Mode of Nature**	Mode of Ignorance Ignorance/Inertia/ Darkness	Mode of Passion Passion/Activity	Mode of Goodness Goodness/Purity/ Luminous
2	**Qualities-Attributes (14.06–08)**	*Tamas* is born of ignorance and the delusion of all embodied beings (*jiva*). It binds *jiva* by negligence, laziness, and excessive sleep (14.08)	*Rajas* is born by intense craving and therefore is the source of desire and attachment. It binds the embodied beings (*jiva*) by attachment to the fruit of action (14.07)	*Sattva* being pure, is luminous and free from sickness and yet in its own way binds the soul to the body (*jiva*, embodied beings, individuals) by creating attachment to happiness and wisdom (14.06)
		Leads to negligence, delusion, and slowness of mind	Leads to greed, desires (Lust, Kama, 5+2 Enemies)	Leads to Self-Knowledge (Wisdom), Equanimity and Self-Realization
		Tamas obscures Self-Knowledge, clouds discrimination, creates negligence and triggers wrong action (14.09) When inertia (*Tamas*) predominates, ignorance, darkness, lack of effort, carelessness and delusion arise (14.13)	When *Rajas* (passion) predominates followings arise: 1. Greed 2. Overexertion 3. Undertaking of action with selfish motives 4. Restlessness and uncontrollable desire (14.12)	When *Sattva* increases the light of Self-Knowledge (Wisdom) radiates through every gate of the body (all the senses) (14.11)
		Ignorance <	**Passion <**	**Goodness**

No	Type of	Tamasic	Rajasic	Sattvic
		Fruit of action is ignorance (14.16)	Fruit of passionate action is pain is misery, pain and sorrow (14.16)	The fruit of good/ virtuous action is purity (14.16)
3	**Work and Action (Karma) (18.23–25)**	Action that is blindly undertaken out of ignorance regardless of one's own ability, capacity and the consequences including loss to him and injury to others (18.25)	The action that is performed by one to gratify one's selfish desire and selfish motive or is prompted by his egoism and is carried out further, with too much effort and pressure (18.24)	The obligatory duty that is performed according to ordinances of scriptures, without attachment to the fruit and selfish motives (expects no return), without any partiality and prejudice, and without likes and dislikes (love and hate) (18.23) Spiritual Activities
4	**Worship (17.04)**	Worships ghosts and spirits	Worships Yaksas and Demons	Worships demi-gods and God
5	**Food (7.08–10)**	• Enjoy unhealthy food: stale, rotten, impure (meat) • Consume alcohol	Like food that is extreme in taste (overly spicy, sour, salty or sweet); and cause pain, grief, and disease (17.09)	Like healthy juicy foods Eat only vegetarian food
6	**Yajna-sacrifice (17.11–13)**	Sacrifice, *Yajna* (any selfless service) that is performed without following the scriptural ordinance, without distribution of food, without chanting of the mantras (Vedic hymns), without faith and without remuneration to the performing priest	However, the selfless service (Sacrifice, *Yajna*) that is performed only for name and fame and aiming for fruit (material benefit)	Selfless service (Sacrifice) enjoined by the scriptural ordinance and performed without the desire for the fruit, and with the firm belief and conviction that it is a duty

No	Type of	Tamasic	Rajasic	Sattvic
7	**Austerity-Tapas (of body/deed, mind/thought and speech) (17.17–17.19)**	Gives charity at wrong place and time to unworthy person, with no respect or insult	Gives charity with expectation of something in return (17.21)	Gives charity as a matter of duty to deserving candidates without any expectation
8	**Renunciation-Tyaga (Abandonment) (18.7–10)**	Abandons obligatory work/duty due to delusions (18.07)	Abandons duty merely because it is difficult or because of fear of bodily trouble (18.08)	Obligatory work as his duties without any selfish attachment and desire for fruit (18.09)
9	**Jnana-Knowledge (18.20–22)**	The knowledge by which one holds to one, single, superficial perception as if it is everything without reason, and without recognizing the truth, such knowledge is worthless (18.22)	The knowledge by which one sees that each individual is separate from one another (18.21)	The knowledge by which one sees *One* Imperishable Being in all beings though they are divided into innumerable forms (18.20)
10	**The doer/ actor (Karta) (18.26–28)**	The doer/actor who is: 1. Undisciplined 2. Imbalanced 3. Vulgar 4. Stubborn 5. Deceitful 6. Malicious (dishonest, cheats and insults others) 7. Lazy 8. Depressed and 9. Procrastinates (18.28) e.g. extremist, terrorist	The doer/actor who is: 1. Full of attachment 2. Driven by the desires for the fruits of action 3. Greedy 4. Violent 5. Impure in thoughts and in conduct 6. Affected by the pair of opposites (joy and sorrow) (18.27) Do lot of efforts and get good results. They are achievers e.g. Business tycoons, Politicians, Bill Gates	The doer/actor who performs his prescribed duty: 1. Without attachment 2. Without egoistic speech (does not beat his own drum) 3. With great determination (steadfastness) 4. With enthusiasm and 5. With balance in both success and failure (18.26)

No	Type of	Tamasic	Rajasic	Sattvic
11	**Intellect-Buddhi (18.30–32)**	That intellect which perceives even unrighteousness (*adharma*) to be righteousness (*Dharma*) and vice-versa, sees all other things upside-down, and always strives in the wrong direction due to darkness and illusion (18.32)	Intellect which cannot correctly distinguish between righteousness (*Dharma*) and unrighteousness (*adharma*), and also what ought to be done and what not ought to be done (right and wrong action) (18.31)	Intellect which can discriminate between action and inaction (the path of work and the path of renunciation), what ought to be done and what not ought to be done (right and wrong action), what is to be feared and what is not to be feared (fear and fearlessness), and what binds and what liberates the soul (bondage and liberation) (18.30)
12	**Determination-Firmness (18.33–35)**	The firmness by which an ignorant person does not give up sleep (dreaming), fear, anxiety, grief, despair and arrogance (18.35)	The firmness by which one clings to duty, virtues, pleasure and wealth, with great attachment and desires for the fruits of action, that firmness (18.34)	The unwavering firmness (steadfastness, determination) by which one controls the functions of the mind, *Prana* (breath, life force) and senses through Yoga for God and Self-Realization, only that firmness-steadfastness (18.33)
13	**Happiness-Pleasure (18.36–39)**	The happiness which deludes the embodied - soul from very beginning to the end, born from sleep (living in a dream world), laziness, and carelessness (18.39)	The happiness which is driven by the contact of the senses with their objects and which is just like nectar in the beginning but in the end is like poison (18.38)	The happiness that appears as poison in the beginning, but is just like nectar in the end; such happiness is born by the grace of Self-Knowledge (through spiritual practices and meditation) and awakens one to Self-Realization (God-Realization) (18.36–37)

No	Type of	Tamasic	Rajasic	Sattvic
14	**Lifestyle**	• Leads unethical life, untruthful to themselves and to other • Unhealthy body and mind • Hide from law in, live in secret places, may be in prisons Becomes liability to the society	Leads very stressful life When directed properly, one could help the society e.g. Bill Gates	Leads very simple, calm happy and peaceful life Performs selfless services, guide and nurture individuals, and the communities e.g. saints, Pujya Swami Chidanandaji, Ammachi, Mother Teresa, Mahatma Gandhi etc.
15	**Goal of Life**	Due to their ignorance, do not even understand the purpose of their life and thus waste 'The most precious gift of God, Human Life'	The goal of their life is to fulfill their sensual pleasures, worldly gains, needs of body and mind and thus waste 'The most precious gift of God, Human Life'	The Supreme goal of their life is to establish Righteousness, and attain God-Realization and Self-Realization
16	**Future**	Born in the animal kingdom as a lower creature (14.15, 14.18)	Born among those engaged in fruit-oriented activities (14.15, 14.18)	Go to heaven or born in the world of those who are pure and wise (Noble ones) (14.14, 14.18)

Everyone is slave of *Gunas*: There is no living being, either on earth or in heaven among the celestials (*devas*) or anywhere else in the creation, who is free from the influence of these three *Gunas* (qualities, attributes) born of *Prakriti* (Material Nature). (18.40)

However, one can transcend from *Tamas* to *Rajas* to *Sattva* with his awareness, commitment, and efforts. Therefore Lord Krishna asked Arjuna to transcend *Gunas.* (2.45, 14.20, 14.26)

Ignorance/*Tamas* → Passion/*Rajas* → Goodness/*Sattva* → Supreme Peace/*Nirvana*

Most of the people fall in the category of Rajasic nature. One has to put the conscious effort not to fall to Tamasic level but transcend to Sattvic level.

Assessment Guide

Q How to distinguish and recognize individuals based upon their Gunas and characteristics?

Type of	Tamas	Rajas	Sattva
Characteristics of individuals	• Lazy • Selfish • Poor discrimination • Lie most of the time • Full of conflict (crimes) • Negative attitude • Depressed • Dependent • Confused • Careless • Sleeps too much • Not trustworthy • Full of miseries and pain • Causes hurt-miseries and pains to others • Eats unhealthy food • Unhealthy body and mind • Leads unethical life e.g. criminals, murderers, terrorist…	• Passionate • Focus on body and external world • Extremely self-centered (Selfish) • Could be unethical • Very Ambitious • Enthusiastic • Somewhat trustworthy • Very active • Restless • Possess intense craving and full of 5+2 Enemies • Never ever satisfied • Full of uncontrollable desires • Attachment to their causes • Greedy • Egoistic, Arrogant • Tensed and tempered (become angry easily) • Enjoyments • Full of conflict • Very critical • Aggressive • Very impatience • Jealous and resentful • Eats unhealthy food • A type personality • Hypocrite-Show off • Hypertension, stressful • Controller • Manipulators	• Focus on God/Self and the purpose of life • Selfless, Sharing • Spiritual • Good Discrimination • Positive Attitude • Honest and truthful • Very trustworthy • Contented • Peaceful • Calm and serene • Enlightenment • Even minded (control their senses and mind) • Detachment • No attachment to fruit of their action • Humble • Happy • Caring and Compassionate • Forgiving • Patience • Righteous • Full of divine qualities/virtues • Soft spoken • Has healthy body and mind • Let go, surrender • Leads simple lifestyle e.g. Gandhiji, Mother Teresa, Former President Jimmy Carter, Saints and Yogis etc.

Type of	Tamas	Rajas	Sattva
		• Doers and get the job done • Hopeful • Intelligent and street smart • Good planner, goal oriented • Achievers- business tycoons, entrepreneurs, politicians etc. • Like to live a fancy life style (like a king-raja)	

This guide can be used for self-assessment and self-analysis.

Where do you stand?

Aum Shanti, Shanti, Shantihi

Glossary

A

Abhyasa	Practice
Acharya	A spiritual master, one who teaches by his own example
Adhyatma	The self, the embodied soul
Agni	Fire
Ahankara	Arrogance, false pride
Ahimsa, Ahinsa	Non-violence, non-hurting, non-killing
Ahuti	Offering
Akarma	The action that does not have any consequences
Akarta	One who has renounced selfish attachment to the fruits of action and remains ever content and dependent on no one but God. Such a person does not do anything (Akarta) though fully engaged in all kind of actions.
Akshara	Indestructible, Imperishable, Unchangeable, Brahman, Supreme-Soul, Parmatma, Absolute Reality, Supreme-Purusha, Godhead
Anandam	Eternal happiness, Joy, Blissful
Arjuna	Main character of the Bhagavad Gita along with Lord Krishna. *See* Pandavas
Aryan	Fully civilized of Vedic culture, whose only goal is spiritual advancement. *See* Vedic
Asana	Physical posture and poses referred as asanas in Sanskrit
Asat	Non-existent
Ashram	A place where a group of spiritual aspirants study, practice and reside
Ashramas	There are four stages of life according to the Vedic social system. In ancient times, the life span of people was about 100 years

and it was divided into four parts. 1. Bhrahmacharya (student life, first stage), which covers the first 25 years of life, is devoted to study, self-discipline, and self-transformation. 2. The next 25 years (second stage) is grihastha (householder life), which is spent performing one's responsibilities and duty selflessly, skillfully toward family and society. 3. The next 25 years (third stage) is Vanaprastha (retirement), during which one trying to work toward attaining the Supreme goal of life. 4. During the fourth and final 25 years, (Sanyasa or Renunciation) one totally focuses on the Supreme goal of life through self-purification, spiritual practices and leaving the external world behind.

Asura Antagonist of goodness and God

Asvattha Banyan tree which roots grow downward from branches.

Atma individual soul (the self with small "s" NOT big S of the Self that means Higher-Self)

AUM OM, ॐ The scared syllable and the eternal sound, that represents the Ultimate reality. All the mantras originate from Aum, therefore they always start with Aum. *See* OM

Austerity Severity of discipline. *See* Tapa

Avatara Manifestation of God in human form for re-establishment of Righteousness (Dharma)

Avidya Ignorance

B

Bhagavad Gita The Song of God

Bhagavan Almighty, Creator, God, Absolute, Supreme Power, Supreme Spirit, Super-Conscious, Higher Self, Supreme Being, Brahman, Ultimate Truth. *See* Purushottama

Bhakta Devotee

Bhakti Yoga Union with God through love and devotion. Unconditional Love for God without any expectations

Bharata An ancient king of India from whom the Pandavas descended. India is also referred as Bharata.

Bhrahmacharya	Student life, which covers the first 25 years of life, is devoted to study, self-discipline, and self- transformation. During this period, students must practice celibacy.
Bhishma	The great grandfather of Kuru dynasty
Brahma	The Lord of creation, One of the gods of Hindu trinity.
Brahman	Almighty, Creator, God, Absolute, Supreme-Power, Supreme-Spirit, Super-Conscious, Higher Self, Purushottama, Supreme-Being, Ultimate Truth.
Brahmanas	Knower of Brahma-Knowledge, Knowledge of Self, Wise, scholarly and Sattvic in nature (Goodness, highest caste), according to the four Vedic occupational division of the society. *See* Caste
Brahma-Nirvana	Liberation, Spiritual Kingdom of God, Oneness with God, Self-Realization, Supreme Peace, Eternal Bliss. *See* Moksha
Brahma-Vidya	Knowledge of God, Self-Knowledge, Transcendental Knowledge
Brahmic State, Brahmi sthitih	Pure Super-Conscious State, Blissful-State, State of Love, Peace and Anandam.
Buddhi	Intellect, Decisive faculty.
Buddhi Yoga	(Yoga of Equanimity) Union with God through Meditation on Self and one atains Equanimity, Transcendental Knowledge, Self-Knowledge. This is also called Yoga of integral Wisdom. *See* Jnana Yoga

C

Celibacy	Control of the senses, abstaining from sex
Creation	Cosmos, universe, body, field
Creator	*See* God
Caste	Four Vedic occupational divisions of society: Brahmans, Kshatriya, Vaisyas, and Sudras.

D

Danam	Charity
Darshan	Seeing the presence of divine
Daya	Compassion
Devas	Godly person or demigod such as Hanuman, Ganesha
Devotion Yoga	*See* Bhakti Yoga
Dharma	Duty, Righteousness
Dharmaksetra	Field of dharma, Field of righteousness
Dhritarashtra	The blind king and father of Duryodhana. The leader of the Kauravas (a mind that is blind to the truth and leader of evils and negative tendencies)
Dhrit	Firmness
Dhyana	Contemplation, Meditation
Dhyana Yoga	Union with God/Self through the path of meditation
Divine manifestations	Glories of God (Attributes)
Divine qualities	Virtues, according to the Gita there are twenty six virtues (*See* 16.01–03)
Divya chakshu	Divine vision
Drupadi	Wife of the Pandavas
Duryodhana	The eldest son of Dhritarashtra, who is believed to be the cause of the war, Mahabharata
Duty	Righteousness, Dharma
Dvesha	Jealousy

E

5+2 Enemies	1. Selfish desire 2. Anger 3. Greed 4. Attachment 5. Ego/ Arrogance 6. Hatred or Resentment 7. Envy/Jealousy
Equanimity	Serenity of mind, calmness, evenness, stability of mind

G

Gandiva Bow of Arjuna

Gayatri Mantra The mantra (hymn) of Goddess Gayatri

Gita Same as Srimad Bhagavad Gita, "the Song of God." *See Gita*

God *See* Brahman and Ishvara, Supreme Being

God-Realization Experiences of divinty/God. One thinks that God is separate from him (duality) and one tries to attain God-Realization through external means such as rituals, selfless services with love and devotion, sacrifices, yajnas without expecting the fruit of his actions (Karma Yoga). He does every activity to please God. He lives in God's Consciousness and attains God.

Grace The highest spiritual achievement. *See* Kripa

Greed Insatiable appetite, wants more and more

Grihastha *See* Ashramas

Gunas Three modes of Material Nature (attitude of mind): *Sattva*-Goodness, *Rajas*-Passion, *Tamas*-Ignorance

Gunateet One who has been self-transformed and has risen above the Gunas and Gunatriya—Three modes of Material Nature/ Gunas (*Sattva*-Goodness, *Rajas*-Passion, *Tamas*-Ignorance)

Guru Spiritual Master who teaches the spiritual path to students

H

Hanuman Devotee of Lord Rama, the monkey god. Also *see* devas

Higher Self Free from negative emotions and 5+2 enemies:—1. Selfish desire 2. Anger 3. Greed 4. Attachment 5. Ego/Arrogance 6. Hatred or Resentment 7. Envy/Jealousy

I

Indra God of rain. Demigod, celestial ruler and the king of heaven.

Indriyas Senses

Ishvara God, The almighty God resides in everyone's heart and directs every activity. Also *see* Brahman, God

J

Japa	Recitation of mantra
Jiva and Jivatma (interchangeable)	Embodied soul, embodied beings, individual soul, individual being
Jnana	Transcendental Knowledge
Jnana Yoga (Yoga of Knowledge)	It is one of the path to realize God/Self/Truth and attain Self-Realization through experienced and realized knowledge.
Jnani	One who is adhering to Jnana Yoga, the path of Transcendental Knowledge (Wisdom).
Jyoti	Divine light

K

Kala	Time
Kalpa	Time cycle, a day and night of Brahma. A set of four Yugas is called Mahayuga. One thousand Mahayuga comprise the period of creation (one day of Brahma: 4,326,000 years) and another thousand comprise the period of dissolution (one night of Brahma: 4,326,000 years). These two thousand such Mahayugas are called Kalpa, which is 8,652000,000 years). Also *see* Yugas
Kama	Selfish desire that gives birth to 5+2 enemies:-1. Selfish desire 2. Anger 3. Greed 4. Attachment 5. Ego/Arrogance 6. Hatred or Resentment 7. Envy/Jealousy
Karma	Action that is performed with self-interest, therefore, bears the subsequent consequences
Karma Yoga	Yoga of action-one of the paths of God and Self-Realization, in which one performs one's action selflessly and skillfully as a duty with love and devotion, and dedicates the fruit of one's work to God.
Karma	Action Yoga, perform every action selflessly as a service to God
Karta	Doer
Kauravas	One hundred wicked sons of the blind king, Dhritarashtra, represent negative tendencies in human beings

Kripa	Grace-the highest spiritual achievement
Krishna	Lord Krishna—God, Pure Consciousness who enlighten Arjuna
Krishna	Descending solar energy.15 days in each month, black, darkphase. Waning moon. An inauspicious time to die
Ksetra	Creation, body, field
Ksetrajana	Creator, Knower of the field, Supreme Being, Super-Soul, Supreme Spirit, God
Kshara	Perishables, changeable. Everything in the world including the physical body of all beings is perishable
Kurukshetra	The battlefield of Mahabharata. A small town located in the northern part of India

L

Liberation	*Moksha*. Nirvana, Self-Realization
Lobha	Greed. One of the 5+2 Enemies-cause of miseries and pain in life
Lord Krishna	*See* Krishna
Lower self	Slave of 5+2 enemies: 1. Selfish desire 2. Anger 3. Greed 4. Attachment 5. Ego/Arrogance 6. Hatred or Resentment 7. Envy/Jealousy
Lust	Selfish desires. One of the 5+2 Enemies, cause of anger, miseries and pain in life

M

Mahabharata	An Indian epic consisting of 100,000 verses in Sanskrit that describe the story of two kings, knowledge of codes of ethics, morality, social laws, metaphysics, philosophy and spirituality.
Mahatma	A Sattvic and spiritually evolved person whose focus is to attain union with God, Liberation, Moksha.
Mahayuga	A set of four yugas: (4,326,000 years). Also *see* kalpa and yuga.
Mamakah	Mine, My-ness, possesiveness, undue attachment to possessions

Mantra Vedic hymn, sacred sound, syllable, word, or group of words which are considered capable of creating transformation.

Maun Silent

Maya Illusion (External world)—The energy of God that deludes individuals into forgetfulness of their real spiritual nature and their origin from God. Thus one projects unreal in place of Real.

Meditation (Dhyana) Meditation is a mental discipline by which one attempts to go beyond the thinking mind into a deeper state of relaxation and awareness

manifest Can be perceived by five sense organs

Meta-Physics Science of energy and matter. Also *see* Purusha and Prakriti.

Metaphysical Knowledge Knowledge of both material and energy

Moksha Liberation, Nirvana, Self-Realization

Moksha Sastra Scripture of Liberation

Mukti Liberation from material existence. Also *see* Liberation and Moksha

Muni A sage who practices silence both mentally and verbally

N

Nasa Nose

Nasagre Tip of the nose

Nirguna God without any form

Nirvana Liberation from material existence. *See* Liberation, Moksha and Mukti

Non-violence Non-hurting, non-killing. *See* Ahimsa

O

OM	AUM, ॐ the scared syllable and the eternal sound, that represents the Ultimate reality. The Vedic Mantra that designates the three states of waking, dreaming, and sleeping.
OM TAT SAT	The triple designation of the Supreme Absolute Truth-Vedic mantra.

P

Pandu	Father of Arjuna. King Pandu had five pious sons called Pandavas
Pandavas	Five sons of King Pandus (represent divine qualities in human beings. *See* Arjuna
Pandit	A learned man, wise, a person who is well versed in scriptures and follows the path of spirituality
Parmatma	*See* God, Super-Conscious
Pathan	Study
Prakriti	Energy, Nature
Prana	Life force
Pranava	ॐ the eternal sound, also *see* Aum and OM
Pranayama	Control/discipline of breath, breathing exercise. One of the yogic practices
Prasad	Blessings, blessed food or other objects
Prasadam	Sanctified food, first offered to God and then distributed to others
Prithvi	Mother earth
Pure Thought	A thought devoid of 5 + 2 Enemies
Puranas	18 supplements to the Vedas
Purusha	Individual soul. *See* Jivatma
Purushottama	Supreme Being. *See* God

R

Raja Yoga	Integral Yoga of body, mind and Spirit. Royal Union is the cultivation of the mind through meditation to attain Self-Knowledge and Liberation
Rajas	The activity mode of passion
Rajasic	The characteristics of the mode of passion
Rajo-Guna	The mode of passion
Raksasas	Demons
Rama	Incarnation of Krishna and the main character (Righteous King) of another Indian epic-Ramayana written by sage Valmiki
Ratri	Night
Real	Everlasting exists in past, present and future—permanent
Reincarnation	Rebirth
Righteousness	Dharma
Rig-Veda	*See* Vedas

S

Sadhaka	One who follows the spiritual path
Sadhana	Spiritual practice
Saguna	God with form and qualities (Attributes) e.g. LORD KRISHNA and Rama
Sama-Veda	*See* Vedas
Samadhi	Trance, complete absorption in God's Consciousness
Sansara	The materialistic world
Samskaras (Sanskaras)	Subtle impressions of past action
Samvad	Discussion between two calm and wise people (Heart to heart). Opposite of Vivad. *See* vivad
Sanatan	Eternal

Sanjay	Dhritrashtra's intuitive minister. The narrator of Bhagavad Gita, who was given extra ordinary power to see and hear the events of Mahabharata's war. He explains to his master, Dhritrashtra, the details of the war and the celestial song of Lord Krishna, the Gita.
Sankhya	Science of body, mind and spirit. Matter and spirit (Energy)
Sanyasa	Renunciation
Sanyasi	A renunciant, who is not attached to fruit of his action and also to any materialistic things in the world
Sanskrit	An ancient Vedic language (Epics, Puranas and Upanishads) that is very elegant and euphonious
Sat	Eternal
Sat Chit Ananda	Eternal, full of knowledge and blissful
Sato-guna	Mode of Goodness
Sattva	The mode of Goodness, Purity, Light. One of the Gunas
Sattvic	The characteristics of the mode of Sattva
Satyam	Truth, honesty
Self-Purification	The process of eliminating one's vices and developing virtues by dwelling on pure thoughts
Self-Realization	One realizes that the Self with One is Supreme, so One is Atma (Sprit, Self, God). However, due to his vices and 5+2 enemies (impurities), he cannot experience Oneness. Hence, he is separated from Self (God). Therefore, he focuses on his self-purification through self-improvement, self-transformation (path of non-duality, Jnana Yoga, Knowledge Yoga). He attains Self-Realization through spiritual practices, such as transcending from Gunas, developing divine qualities, going within through contemplation and meditation. He goes through many transcendental experiences and finally realizes his true nature, *Sat Chit Ananda*, He is no longer separated from God–He is God.
Shastra	Vedic literature
Shatriya	Protector (Arjuna)

Shlokas	Verses
Shravan	Listening to the divine knowledge
Shukla	Ascending solar energy. Fifteen days in each month. White, lightphase
Shiva	Demigod who supervises the Tamo guna, mode of ignorance and who annihilates the material universe
sin	Misdeed, mistake made due to ignorance
Smriti	Memory
Soma	Plant that gives the nectar for long life
Spirit	Soul/Atma
Sradha	Faith-one of the divine qualities
Sri	Prosperity. A title of respect
Sthith-prajna	Equanimity of mind. Steady mind
Sudra	The working class of people. lowest class according to the four Vedic occupational divisions of society. *See* Caste
Svabhava	Innate quality. Habitual tendencies that make one act unconsciously
Svadharma	One's prescribed duty
Swami	One who has renounced the mundane world and also has full control on his senses especially on his mind (Master of all the senses).

T

Tamas	Mode of ignorance/darkness/inertia (Guna)
Tamasic	The characteristics of the mode of ignorance. *See* Gunas, Tamas
Tamo guna	Mode of ignorance
Tapas	Power of self-discipline (*See* Austerity)
Tyaga	Sacrifice, Relinquishment
Tyagi	One who is adhering to tyaga

U

Upanishad	The books of wisdom that appear within the Vedas. These are the foundation of Vedanta philosophy and offer practical instructions for wholesome life.
Unmanifest	The Divinity that cannot be perceived by 5 sense organs but can only be felt and realized
Unreal	Only in the present not in the past or future, temporary
Uttama-Purusa	Supreme Being (*See* God)

V

Vairagya	Dispassion or non-attachment
Vaisya	The business class and land-owners, according to the four Vedic occupational divisions of society. *See* Caste
Vasana	Subtle traces of one's desires and thoughts
Vasudeva	The biological father of Lord Krishna. Lord Krishna is also referred to as Vasudeva.
Vedanta	The system of Indian philosophy that explains the theory of non-duality, Advaita for Self-Realization
Vedas	The four scriptures of the original knowledge (Rig, Sama, Atharva, and Yajur). The realized knowledge was attained during the deep meditation by sages. The sages imparted this knowledge to their disciples for many centuries. All the assimilated knowledge was organized based on subjects and their application by great sage Vyasaji into four Vedas (Rig, Sama, Atharva, and Yajur).
Vibhaga	Division
Vibhuti	The glorious manifestation of God
Vidya	Knowledge
Vijnana	Science or higher knowledge. It mainly refers to the spiritual knowledge instead of mundane, worldly knowledge
Vikalpa	Confused, unsettled, and doubtful state of mind

Vikarma Unrighteous action, not in accordance with the codes of scriptures

Virat-Rupa The Cosmic Form of Lord Krishna

Vishad Dejection, low spirit, deep sorrow, dilemma, confusion

Vishnu Supreme Being. Lord Krishna and Rama are incarnations of Vishnu.

Visva-Rupa Cosmic Form of Lord Krishna

Vivad Argument between two egoistic people, opposite of Samvad. *See* samvad

Vyasaji A great sage who assimilated all the knowledge from sages and organized it based on subjects and their application, into four Vedas: Rig, Sama, Atharva, and Yajur.

Y

Yajna Sacrifice or ritual ceremony

Yaksha Nature spirit, care taker of all natural things

Yama The lord of death

Yoga Union with God, Self-Realization. The term yoga in the West is primarily associated with stretches and postures, asanas, however yoga is much more. Originated in ancient India, Yoga means 'Union with Self,' (oneness of the body, mind, and spirit. The purpose of practicing Yoga is to create a balance between the body and the mind and to attain self-enlightenment. In order to accomplish it, Yoga makes use of different movements, breathing exercises, relaxation technique, meditation and other spiritual practices for self-purification and self-transfromation.

Yoga Sastra Scripture of Yogas

Yoga-Maya Spiritual Power of God

Yoga-Nidra Sleep that unites one with Higher Self. In this type of sleep, one does not go through a regular dream and sleep state but goes into complete rest and alignment of body, mind, all the chakras and resides restfully in seventh chakra. A yogi practices this type of sleep – called yogic-sleep. This is the most powerful meditation that is recommended by Lord Krishna to attain Liberation at the time of death. (8.12–13)

Yogi One who practices Yoga (Sadhana, spiritual practices for attaining Union with God)

Yuga Age. Time. Mahayuga: There are four yugas or time periods: Satya-yuga (1,728,000 years), Treta-yuga (1,296,000 years), Dvapara-yuga (864,000 years), and Kali-yuga (432,000 years). As the time proceeds from Satya to Kali, the goodness and righteousness in people gradually declines. A yuga consist of thousands of years. A set of four yugas is called Mahayugas (4.326, 000 years).

Two thousand Mahayuga are called Kalpa, which is 8,652000,000 years (single day of Brahma/Creator). Three hundreds and sixty Kalpas make one year of Brahma, who lives for one hundred such years.

Aum Shanti, Shanti, Shantihi

Index

A

Abandoning selfish attachments, 56
Abandonment, 109, 309, 312–313, 351
Abhyasa, 15, 357
Abode, 178, 216, 220, 222
Abode of Imperishable Brahman, 267
Absence of
  anger, 286
  arrogance, 245, 286
  ego, 246
  fickle-mindness, 286
Absolute
  Reality, 278, 357
  Truth, 131, 167, 195, 304
Action
  bondage of, 53, 72, 80, 181
  consequences of, 74, 181
  desireless, 104, 310
  detached, 97
  five causes, 311, 314
  forbidden, 92, 96–97
  fruit of, 17, 21, 69, 85, 110, 114, 120, 123, 202, 241, 261, 309, 312, 314, 334, 340
  futile, 176
  good/virtuous, 263
  ignorant, 263
  passionate, 263, 350
  righteous, 53, 71, 77
Acts of sacrifice, 312
Adharma, 32, 61, 89–90, 94, 104, 320, 352
Adhibhuta, 153, 159–160
Adhidaiva, 153
Adhiyajna, 153, 159–160
Adhyatma, 159, 357
Agni, 221, 357
Ahankara, 357
Ahimsa, 357, 364
Ahuti, 178, 357
Akarma, 97, 357
Akarta, 98, 357
Aksara-Brahma Yoga, 155–168
Akshara, 278, 357
Aksaya Kala, 200
Ambrosial fruit, 241
Anandam, 13
Anantavijaya, 27
Ancestors, 33, 180, 200
Anger, 21–22, 40–41, 59–61, 71, 83, 90, 95, 109, 118–119, 186, 268, 286, 289–291, 327, 336, 362–363
Annihilation, 173, 175
Anxiety, 21–22, 40–41, 59–61, 71, 83, 90, 95, 109, 118–119, 186, 268, 286, 289–291, 327, 336, 362–363
Arjuna Vishad Yoga, 19–36
Arjuna's
  confusion, 109, 209, 213
  dejection, 8, 45
  Despondency, 21, 36
  dilemma, 23–24, 30
  divine vision, 209–210
  duty, 209–210
Arrogance, 41, 245, 272, 275, 286, 288, 290, 298, 321, 327–328, 352, 357
Aryan, 357
Asanas, 15, 138, 345, 347, 357, 370
Asat, 47, 178, 220, 246, 305, 357
Ashanti, 22
Ashrams, 357, 361
Asuras, 215, 358
Asvattama, 26
Atma, 39–40, 46–49, 214, 251–252, 257, 260, 273, 275, 339, 358, 367
Atmadarshini, 40

Atma/Spirit, 84
Attachment to Unrighteousness, 352
Attributes/qualities/Gunas, 257
Aum, 147, 156–159, 161–163, 167, 178, 199, 297, 303–304, 342, 347, 358, 364–365
AUM TAT SAT, 303
Austerity, 119, 148, 167, 181, 192, 208, 223, 225, 286, 296–299, 301–302, 304–305, 312–313, 323, 326, 330
Austerity
  of body, 301, 345
  of mind, 301, 345
  of thoughts, 301
  speech, 301
Avatara, 94, 358
Avidya, 358

B

Balanced lifestyle, 129–130
Battlefield of Righteousness, 24
Beings
  celestial, 199
  embodied, 232, 261, 297, 349, 362
Benefits of Bhakti Yoga, 230
Bhagavan, 358
Bhagavad Gita, 8, 13–14, 41, 309, 357–358, 361, 367
Bhakti Yoga, 227–238
Bhakti Yoga and Jnana Yoga, 5, 309, 345–346
Bhakti/Devotion Yoga, 172, 230
Bhisma, 7, 359
Birth, cycle of, 164, 180, 284, 309, 336
Blissful Divine State, 57
Body
  Consciousness, 242
  relationship of, 40, 83
  transcendental, 212
Bondage of action, 53, 72, 80, 181
Bondage karmic, 71, 274
Bonds
  emotional, 229
Brahma, 156, 163–164, 220–221, 359, 362, 371
Brahma-Jnana, 83
Brahman, 36, 64–65, 76, 86, 99, 105, 113, 116, 153–154, 159–160, 166–167, 267, 304–305, 326–327, 357–359, 361
Brahma-Nirvana, 64, 118, 266, 359
Brahma's day, 164, 175
Brahma-vidya, 10, 272, 359
Brahmic State, 40, 64, 267, 359
Brahmisthiti, 64
Breath control, see Pranayama, 100, 347, 365
Buddhi, 244, 319, 359
Buddhi-Yoga, 328

C

Calamities, 23, 45
Calmness/Equanimity, 62
Caste, 33, 311, 323, 325, 359, 368–369
Causes of adharma, 90
Celestial
  controllers, 45, 199
  elephants, 200
  horse Uccaihsravas, 200
Celibacy, 129, 162, 301, 359
Charity, 100, 167, 181, 192, 223, 225, 285, 289, 296, 299, 303–305, 312–313, 324, 351, 360
Chief Brihaspati, 199
Clairvoyance, 8, 333
Codes of righteous living, 89–90
Company
  wise/divine, 36
Conches
  celestial, 27
  mighty, 27
Consciousness
  of Brahman, 99
  of Self, 76
Contemplation, 117, 124, 229, 345, 347, 360, 367
Contentment, 192, 340
Cosmic
  Being, 222
  body, 213, 216, 219
  creation, 222, 244

cycle, 259
dissolution, 216
evolution, 164
Manifestation, 220, 288
Tree, 273
Counselor and Divine Teacher, 41
Creation, 10, 15, 74, 76, 93–94, 138, 144, 173–176, 183–184, 202, 241–244, 248, 252, 273–274, 359, 362–363
Creator, 163–164, 175, 241–244, 247–248, 252, 358–359, 363
Cycle of destruction of human values, 34

D

Dada Vaswani, 124
Danam, 360
Darshan, 360
Daya, 360
Death
all-devouring, 200
time of, 63, 135, 153, 157, 159–162, 370
Deeds, 27, 43, 115, 136, 179, 330
Deities, minor, 99
Delusion
adopted, 176
Demi-gods
worshippers of, 152, 180
Demolisher, 247
Demonic Qualities, 283–287, 292, 343
Depression, 8, 21–23, 38, 336, 341
Desirous, 29, 179
Despondency, 8, 21, 23, 341
Destination, 6, 62, 125, 135
Destiny, 124, 135–136, 264, 284, 289–290, 315
Destroy, 33, 47, 194, 218, 288
Destruction, 32, 34, 60, 78, 94, 104, 136, 199, 217, 291
Detachment, 38, 110, 162, 246, 273–4, 326, 355
Deva-Asura Sampad Vibhaga Yoga, 281–292
Devas, 45, 75, 95, 99, 151–152, 160, 166, 180, 191, 195, 199, 216, 224, 298, 301, 360–361
Devotees, 57, 94, 144–145, 150–152, 172, 179–180, 182, 194, 230–231, 233, 235–237, 248, 330–331, 342, 358
Devotion Yoga, 4, 191, 193, 230, 237, 360
Devotion
constant, 246
loving, 330
single minded, 233
steadfast, 231
undivided, 165, 180, 182, 224–225, 233
unwavering, 258, 267
Dharma, 8, 10, 23, 44, 89–90, 94, 104, 148, 174, 214, 267, 317, 320, 339–340, 352, 360
Dharma/Duty, 23
Dharma/righteousness, 89
Dharmakshetra, 23
Dharana, 345, 347
Dhritarashtra, 7–8, 24, 29, 34, 45, 360, 362
Dhritih, 200
Dhyana, 345, 347, 360, 364
Dhyana Yoga, 121–140
Dialogue
holy, 8, 333
mystical, 333
sacred, 331
unique spiritual, 41
Dilemma, 8–9, 21, 23, 36, 38, 41, 339, 341, 370
Divine Company, 15, 35–36, 41, 64
Disasters/Miseries, 110
Disciplined life, 283
Discus/Chakra, 213, 222
Disgrace, 52, 236, 266
Dishonor, 52, 127
Dispassion, 246, 369
Dissolution, 94, 147, 164, 192, 209, 362
Distressing, 52
Divine
Attributes, 201
beings, 160
birth, 94
company, 15, 35–6, 41, 64
energy, 175
Form, 222

friend, 23
Glories, 189, 195, 197, 203
illusion, 144–145, 149
Manifestations, 189, 196, 201
mystery, 171, 173
Nature, 177, 264, 271
Power, 152, 195, 202, 271
qualities, 10, 70, 176, 229–230, 237, 242, 252–253, 283–287, 292, 334, 341, 346, 365, 368
Teacher, 8, 41
vision, 207–208, 211, 226, 360
weapons, 212
Yoga, 174
Draupadi, 183
Dr. Radhakrishna, 184, 190, 241
Duty, 8, 10, 17, 39–41, 51–53, 71–72, 76–80, 82, 85, 87, 96, 218, 309–311, 323–325, 333–334, 350–352
Duryodhana, 7, 26, 29, 360
Dvesha, 360

E

5+2 Enemies, 40, 90, 127, 208, 341, 349, 355, 360–363, 367
Ego, 9, 64, 71, 90, 146, 244, 246, 272, 274, 286, 309, 328, 341
Eight Limbs of yoga, 345
Embodied soul, 48, 83, 160, 241, 257–258, 271, 275, 322, 357, 362
Endurance, 46
Enemies 40, 43, 52, 71, 83, 90, 110, 124, 126–128, 184, 200–201, 208, 219, 236, 288–289, 360–363
Energy, 10, 36, 79, 147, 180, 190, 241–242, 273, 277, 342, 364–365, 367
Enlighten, 157, 193, 363
Enlightenment, 8, 10, 116, 119, 279, 355
Enmity, 32, 225
Epic War, 7
Equanimity, 12, 38, 42, 56–57, 59–60, 62, 64, 104, 116, 122–123, 126, 135, 192, 234, 246, 286
Essential Nature, 160
Eternal and Imperishable Abode, 327
Eternal
Being, 62, 153, 160, 165, 214, 246, 267, 303
Bliss, 118, 359
Brahman, 157, 167
Divine, 194–195
Goal, 162, 275
Happiness, 10, 13, 16–17, 64, 321, 339, 342–343, 357
Knowledge, 171
Mantra, 157
Peace and Self-Realization, 291
Spirit, 47, 49
Supreme Peace, 129
Unmanifest, 165
Ethical behavior, 89
Everlasting Peace and Anandam, 23
Exhalation, 100
Experience God, 143, 157

F

Faith
impure, 296
innate, 297
man's, 295
steadfast, 151
Fearlessness, 192, 285, 352
Fearsome form, 215
Five basic elements, 244
Five monkeys, 70
Five objects, 244
Flowery speeches, 55
Food, 33, 75, 189, 277, 296–297, 299–300, 305, 340, 350
Forgiveness, 192, 200, 221, 245, 286, 323
Formless God-Nirguna, 231
Formula for Devotion Yoga, 230
Fortitude, 286
Fruit of Self-Realization, 70

G

Gandharvas, 200, 215
Gandiva, 30, 361
Garuda, 200
Gayatri, 201, 361

Generator, 247
Gita, 5–17, 21, 23, 35–36, 38–41, 89, 92, 207–208, 229, 283, 309–311, 330–331, 333–334, 339–341, 343, 360–361
Glories of selfless devotion, 173, 183
Glories, immortal, 209
Glory and Sound policy, 333
Goal of Self-Realization, 232
God and Prakriti work, 175
God Consciousness, 138, 233
God manifestation, 184, 358
God of Sacrifice, 153
God
  glory of, 145, 152
  knowing, 143
  manifested, 229, 241
  people approach, 95
  real nature of, 195
  vision of, 209, 224
  worshiping, 230
God-Realization, 54, 114, 136, 159, 162, 208, 229–231, 233, 248, 253, 345, 352, 361
God's
  Cosmic Form, 209–210
  creation, 85
  glories, 191, 194, 197
  Grace, 7, 182, 208, 315, 322, 327, 332
  incarnation, 92–93
  manifestation, 172–173, 177, 184, 195–197, 202, 342
Grace, 16, 64, 208, 221–223, 309, 311, 315, 327–329, 331–333, 352, 361
Greed, 22, 32, 40–41, 90, 262, 264, 349, 360–363
Greedy, 318, 351, 355
Guide to
  Higher Self, 271
  Eternal Happiness, 13
Gunas
  modes of, 55, 79, 148–149, 248, 264
  transcended, 257
Gunas-Sattva, 149
Gunateet, 361
Guna-Traya Vibhaga Yoga, 255–268
Guru, 6, 11, 15, 21, 24, 36, 89, 301, 333–334, 336, 346, 361

H

Habits, 122, 124, 283, 341
Hallmarks, 58, 125, 229–231, 235, 257, 259, 265, 323–324
Happiness 10, 13, 16–17, 35, 59, 62, 64, 85, 87, 101, 104, 110, 117–18, 120, 257, 261, 310–11, 321–2, 339, 341–3, 352, 357
Hanuman, 360–361
Hatred, See 5+2 enemies
Heart of Gita, 229, 346
Heaven, attainment of, 54, 179
Hell, 33, 71, 78, 124, 264, 285, 289–291
Higher
  Nature, 146
  Self, 9, 23, 90–91, 124, 127, 241–242, 267, 271–272, 274, 278–279, 283–284, 292, 309, 339–340, 358–359, 361
  Self and Peace, 124
  Self/Supreme Consciousness, 91
  vision, 110
Himalaya, 13, 99
Hindu scriptures, 114, 201
Hindu trinity, 213, 359
Holy Ganga, 200
Human
  existence, 208
  life, 10, 271, 353
  psychology, 9
  society, divisions of, 95–96
Humiliation, public, 183
Hypocrites, 73

I

Ignorance
  darkness of, 162, 248
  mode of, 261, 264, 298, 300, 302–303, 313, 317–322, 368
  utter, 153
Illusion, 273, 310, 320, 352, 364
Immorality, 46, 178, 246, 265
Impartiality, 116
Imperfections, 118

Imperishable
nature, 152
Seed, 178
Supreme State, 272, 274
Supreme-Soul, 250–251
Infinite Bliss of Oneness, 133
Infinite Form, 213, 216, 220
Inhalation, 100
Indra, 199, 361
Indriyas, 244, 361
Innumerable forms, 316, 351
Integral Knowledge, 242
Integral Wisdom, 328, 359
Intellect
three-fold nature of, 319
Intelligence, 146, 148
Intuitions, 9, 11, 143, 202
Inter-relationship, 249
Invisible
forces, 137
Spirit, 47
Ishvara, 361

J

Japa, 362
Jayadayal Goyandka, 15
Jiva, 242, 257, 260–261, 349, 362
Jivatma, 8, 12, 46, 115, 232, 241, 247, 251, 257–258, 260, 266, 271, 273, 275–276, 340, 362, 365
Jnana, 69, 103, 143, 246–247, 346, 351, 362
Jnana Yogi, 116
Jnana-Karma-Sanyasa Yoga, 87–106
Jnana Vijnana Yoga, 141–154
Jnana Yajna, 331
Joy, 9, 12, 192, 236, 318, 333, 351, 357
Jyoti, 362

K

Kala, 218, 362
Kalpa, 175, 362, 371
Kama, 71, 83, 349, 362
Kamadhenu, wish-granting cow, 200
Karma, 42, 53, 74, 80, 96–98, 101, 104, 109, 113, 153, 159–160, 175, 273–274, 316, 329–330, 336, 350, 362
Karma Sanyasa, 110–111
Karma Yoga and Bhakti Yoga, 241
Karma Yogi, 54, 57, 71, 85, 98, 110–114, 125, 346
Karma Yoga,
knowledge of, 69, 123
path of, 39, 69
performing, 110
practices, 71
Karmic impressions, 151, 298
Karta, 351, 362
Kartavya, 71
Karna, 26, 217, 219
Kauravas, 7, 28, 183, 360, 362
Knowing God-Divinity in Essence, 145
Knowledge of
scriptures, 234
Spirit, 39
Knowledge,
bookish, 137
experiential, 143, 145, 272
imperfect, 315
secret, 171, 173
spiritual, 105, 200, 369
Kripa, 361, 363
Krishna, 32–33, 58, 72, 82, 111, 134–136, 159, 209, 215–217, 219, 221–222, 224, 229, 311, 328, 333, 363
Kshetra, 243–244, 252
Kshetrajna, 243–244, 252
Ksetra-Ksetrajna Vibhaga Yoga, 239–254
Kurukshetra, 7, 13, 18, 23, 363

L

Law of karma, 97
Leadership skills, 324
Liberation/Moksha, 266, 309, 336
Liberation 3, 10, 12, 41, 46, 57, 63, 69–70, 77, 89, 96, 101, 109–110, 112–3, 119, 122, 153, 162, 166, 172, 183, 186, 233, 249, 252, 257–9, 266–7, 274, 276, 283–4, 287, 304–5, 309, 324, 327, 334–6, 339–43, 345, 352, 359, 363–4, 366, 370
Life cycle, 46
Life style, 16, 138, 305

Lord Brahma, 213
Lord Hanuman, 28
Lord Krishna, 7–9, 11, 13, 15, 27–29, 32, 35–36, 38–45, 48, 58, 69, 85, 89, 93, 104, 109, 123, 125, 127, 135, 143, 157–158, 171, 183, 189, 191, 196, 201, 207, 209, 211–212, 214, 216–224, 229, 241, 243, 248, 257–259, 265, 271, 283, 295, 309, 329, 332–334, 340, 353, 357, 363, 367, 369–370
Lord of creation, 213, 359
Lord of demi-gods, 216
Lord of infinite prowess, 221
Lord of Sacrifice, 160
Lord of universe, 180
Lord of wealth, 199
Lord of Yoga, 333
Lord Rama, 200, 361
Lord Shiva, 199, 213
Lord Vishnu, 200
Love, 6, 8, 10, 12, 17, 69, 89, 91, 116, 156, 173, 176, 181–184, 186, 189, 193–194, 200, 202, 208, 226, 229–230, 237–238, 241, 266, 268, 309, 317, 329, 334, 336, 340–342, 345–346, 350, 358–359, 361–362
Love & Devotion, 70
Lower self, 271, 279
Lust, 71, 83–84, 288–291, 298, 327, 349, 363

M

Macrocosm, 193, 242
Mahabharata, 7–8, 18, 183, 201, 360, 363
Mahatma Gandhi, 14, 69, 284, 346, 353
Mahayuga, 362–363, 371
Mamakah, 22–23, 363
Manifestations of the Lord, 215
Manifestations
    elements-material, 160
    partial, 190
Mantras, 99, 162, 178, 273, 300, 334, 342, 350, 358, 361–362, 364
Martin Luther King Jr., 284
Master of Yoga, 196
Material Nature
    modes of, 147, 257–258, 265–266, 361
    primary, 244
Materialistic, 327, 367
Maya, 12, 144–145, 149, 175, 242, 273, 329, 364
Medha, 200
Medicinal herb, 178
Meditation
    practicing, 131, 161
Meera, 230, 345–346
Manifestation, 99, 160, 177, 189, 193, 195–196, 203, 207, 211, 215, 360
Matter, 10, 144, 146–147, 178, 189, 241–243, 248, 250, 260, 342, 351, 364, 367
Mental-Renunciation, 310
Mentor, 77–78, 85, 102
Metaphysical Knowledge, 143, 242–243
Microcosm, 193, 242
Milch cow, 74, 86
Mind
    analytical, 14, 73
    conquered, 131
    healthy, 62, 334, 340–341
    serenity of, 61–62, 301, 340, 360
    tranquil, 62
    uncontrolled, 135
Modesty, 246, 286
Moksha Sastra, 3, 364
Moksha-Sanyasa Yoga, 307–336
Moment of Reckoning, 8
Mother Teresa, 69, 284, 346, 353, 355
Mukti, 265, 364
Maun, 364
Muni, 126, 364
Multifarious divine forms, 211
Mundane world, 259, 368
Mystic Power, 210

N

Natural
    disposition, 298
    duties, 323–324
    tendencies, 81

Nature
demonic, 149
innate, 71, 115, 296
intrinsic, 297
modes of, 257, 259–260, 262
Negative attitude, 22, 340, 355
Niyama, 345, 347
Nirguna, 231–232, 364
Nirvana, 64, 70, 95, 101, 113, 118, 122, 129, 166, 259, 263–266, 272
Non-attachment, 12, 110, 124, 135, 162, 167, 246, 271, 274, 279, 326, 369
Non-delusion, 192
Non-violence, 286, 357, 364

O

Objects
luminous, 248
material, 102
Obstacles on the path of Self-Realization, 41, 81
Ocean of
Anandam, 157
Eternal Knowledge, 171
Knowledge, 2
Life, 2, 21
Offerings, ceremonial, 33
OM (AUM), 347, 358
OM TAT SAT, 365
Omnipotent, 143, 189, 198
Omniscient, 143, 162, 189, 198, 200
Omnipresent, 115, 143, 189, 195, 198, 232, 246–247
Oneness of
body, 39, 334, 336
Self, 177
Origin of Universe, 259

P

Pandavas, 7, 24, 183, 201, 357–358, 359, 360, 365
Pandit, 97, 365
Pandu, 7, 28, 365
Parama-dhama, 165, 167, 247
Parmatma, 258, 273
Patanjali, 345
Patanjali yoga, 345
Path of
Action, 72, 342
Action and Renunciation, 109, 120
Dejection, 23, 341
Devotion, 229–230
Divine, 283, 292
Divine Vision of God, 208
Faith, 295
Karma Yoga, 71
Knowledge, 89, 105, 341
Liberation/Moksha, 266, 309, 336
Love and Devotion, 229–230, 238, 345
Meditation and Devotion, 111, 119
Most Secret and Most Sacred Knowledge, 171
Renunciation, 17, 69, 89, 91, 105, 109–112, 120, 125, 181, 230, 234, 286, 309–314, 319, 325, 335, 342–343, 345–346, 352, 358, 367
Renunciation and Surrender, 309
Right Action, 69, 86, 345
Sankhya Yoga, 39, 69
Self-discipline, 123
Self-Discipline and Meditation, 123, 139
Self-Knowledge, 39–40, 65, 72–73, 111–112, 115
Self-Realization, 5–6, 10–12, 14–15, 23, 39–41, 69–72, 74–75, 81, 85, 89–91, 100–102, 104, 109–111, 119, 123, 126, 131, 135, 137, 143, 157, 159, 161–163, 166–167, 171–172, 184, 186, 189, 207–208, 226, 229–230, 232, 234, 241, 248, 252, 263–264, 271–272, 274, 279, 283, 285, 291, 295, 309, 311, 313, 320, 322, 324, 329, 334–335, 339, 341, 345–346, 349, 352, 359, 362–364, 367, 369–370
Threefold Division of Faith, 295, 305
Peace
everlasting, 11, 71, 85, 110, 127, 157
inner, 35, 62, 124
Penance, 297, 300–302, 304

Perennial Knowledge, 91
Perfection
attained, 77
highest, 77, 135, 163, 259, 267, 324–325
Person
balanced, 127
philanthropic, 98
self-controlled, 63, 115
self-disciplined, 127
Pleasure
worldly, 54, 276
Poem, xviii, 2, 38, 87, 122, 156, 186, 268, 336
Pompousness, 54
Possessions
worldly, 327
Possessiveness, 22, 90, 128, 208, 272, 327
Potency
internal, 195
Power
creative, 153
discriminating, 149, 176
illusive, 149, 329
infinite, 215
majestic, 209, 218
mystical, 329
Practice
deceitful
Devotion Yoga, 238
Equanimity, 64
Gita's teachings, 14
meditation, 120, 340
ritualistic, 234
Spirituality, 16
yogic, 100, 103, 137, 365
Pranayam, 15, 138, 334, 340, 345
Prana into Apana, 100
Prakriti, 55, 79, 94, 146, 149, 164, 175, 241, 243–244, 246, 248–251, 257, 260, 275, 322, 353, 364–365
Prasad, 38, 184, 339, 365
Pratyahara, 345, 347
Prithvi, 365
Protector, 201, 214, 311, 323, 333, 367
Purity of
Heart, 230
Mind, 102
Purusha, 220, 241, 243, 246, 249–250, 259, 364–365
Purushottama, 160, 195, 242, 271, 278, 358–359, 365
Purushottama Yoga, 269–280

Q

Qualities
demonic, 283–287, 292, 343
everlasting, 33
evil/demon, 286
intrinsic, 73

R

Raja Yoga, 366
Rajas, 83
Rajasic
action, 317
Buddhi, 320
charity, 303
doer, 318
firmness, 321
knowledge, 316
mode of nature, 261
pleasure, 322
Renunciation, 313
Rajavidya-Rajaguhya Yoga, 169–186
Raga and Dvesa, 81
Rajo-Guna, 366
Raksasas, 366
Rama, 366
Real, 102, 143, 156, 195, 250, 274, 364, 366
Relationship of Body, 84
Relationship of Karma Yoga, 5
Reincarnation, 366
Renunciation
Resentment, 40, 268, 360–363
Rig-Veda, 366
Right Action, 69, 86, 342, 345
Righteous
Living, 14, 89
Path, 42, 60, 109

Righteousness, 10, 23–24, 89, 91, 94, 104–105, 148, 171, 174, 201, 214, 267, 311, 320, 324, 333, 352–353, 360, 366, 371
Royal Path to Liberation, 172, 342
Royal Road to Liberation, 309, 341
Rudras, 199, 211, 215

S

Sacred knowledge, 171, 174, 178, 185
Sacrifice, 21, 71–74, 91–92, 98–102, 119, 153, 160, 167, 178, 199, 223, 285, 289–290, 296–297, 299–300, 303–305, 310–313, 331, 350, 361, 368, 370
Sadhana, 73, 85, 208, 226, 340, 366, 371
Sadhaka, 85, 346, 366
Saguna, 229, 231, 233, 241, 345, 366
Salvation, 101, 158, 166–167, 265, 291, 304
Sama-Veda, 366
Samadhi, 58, 100, 124, 144, 345, 347, 366
Sansakaras, 137
Samvad, 11, 64, 366, 370
Sankhya, 39, 314, 367
Sankhya Yoga, 37–66
Sanjaya, 8, 17, 24, 25, 29, 35, 42, 45, 211, 219, 224, 332–333
Sansara, 366
Sanskrit, 7, 13, 357, 363, 367
Sanyasa, 109, 309–312, 358, 367
Sanyasa Yoga, 109–111
Sanyasi, 111–113, 125, 310, 367
Sarathi, 36
Scriptures, 11, 23, 36, 57, 100, 120, 138, 143, 234, 250, 278, 285, 291–292, 295, 297–298, 301, 304, 323, 365, 369–370
Sat, 47, 303–305
Sat Chit Ananda, 11–12, 14, 23, 85, 111, 117, 119, 131, 171, 185, 230. 268, 272, 275–6, 309, 322, 326, 339, 342, 367
Sathya Sai Baba, 89, 143, 237–238
Satya-yuga, 371
Sato-guna, 367
Satyam, 367
Sattvic
    action, 317
    austerity, 302
    Buddhi, 319
    form of charity, 285
    Gunas, 283
    knowledge, 316
    life style, 305
    Renunciation, 313
Self, 9, 15, 58, 71, 125–127, 160, 250, 339, 357–358, 367
Self Knowledge, 59, 102
Self-analysis, 12, 241, 346, 356
Self-awareness, 12, 36, 64, 241, 283, 334, 339–340
Self-contentment, 10, 279
Self-control, 42, 61–62, 64, 91, 110, 162, 246, 301, 323
Self-destruction, 90
Self-Discipline, 131
Self-Purification, 5, 91, 186, 230, 258, 346, 367
Self–Realized 12, 55–6, 77, 89, 96, 102, 116, 127, 132, 173, 327
Self–Realizer, 40
Self–Realization 5–6, 10–2, 14–5, 23, 39–41, 69–72, 74–5, 81, 85, 89–91, 100–2, 104, 109–1, 119, 123, 126, 131, 135, 137, 143, 157, 159, 161–3, 166–7, 171–2, 184, 186, 189, 207–8, 226, 229–30, 232, 234, 241, 248, 252, 263–4, 271–2, 274, 279, 283, 285, 291, 295, 309, 311, 313, 320, 322, 324, 329, 334–5, 339, 341, 345–6, 349, 352, 359, 362–4, 367, 369–70
Self-salvation, 273–274
Self-transformation, 5, 10, 12, 15, 69, 91, 109, 123–124, 130, 230, 241, 257–258, 283, 339–340, 342, 345–346, 358
Self-unfoldment, 340
Sense control, 69
Serenity, 61–62, 126, 132, 286, 301, 323, 327, 340, 360
Shanti, 36, 65, 86, 105, 120, 139, 154, 167, 185, 203, 226, 238, 253, 267, 280, 292, 305, 335, 343, 347, 356, 371
Shiva, 215, 247, 368

Shukla, 368
Shlokas, 8, 368
Siddhas, 215, 220
Signs of spirituality, 285
Sin, 21, 32, 42, 52–53, 71–72, 75–76, 82, 94, 98, 100, 102, 114, 116, 118, 132–133, 137, 153, 179, 192, 325, 330–331, 368
Six vices, 285
Sthith-Prajna, 368
Soul/Spirit, 242, 249
Source of
- Anandam, 167
- Self-Knowledge and Wisdom, 39

Sovereign Science, 174
Spiritual
- disciplines, 72–73, 101, 229, 246
- growth, 13, 81
- instruction manual, 11, 69
- truth, 16
- progress, 290
- Spirit, 249
- World, 190

Sraddha, 368
Srimad Bhagavad Gita, 7, 21
Sri Shankarachaya, 208
State of freedom, 9, 131, 325
Sudra, 96, 183, 323–324, 359, 368
Sun, 92–93, 147, 162, 166, 212–213, 215, 252, 275–277
Surrender, 15, 149, 153–154, 183–184, 233, 236, 252, 271, 274, 309, 311, 321, 327–330, 335, 341, 355
Super Concious, 63–64
Supreme
- Abode, 250
- Bliss, 109, 111–112, 117, 119, 131, 171, 229, 246, 257, 265, 267, 271, 283, 295
- Bliss and Immortality, 246
- Brahman, 166, 194, 246
- Consciousness, 8–9, 40, 58, 64, 91, 101, 115–117, 124, 133, 160, 242, 248, 260, 272, 327
- Devotion, 327, 331
- Divine, 161–162, 165
- Energy, 191
- Eternal Abode, 167
- Happiness, 132
- Peace, 64, 103, 110, 114, 118, 234, 329, 359
- Self, 55, 58, 76, 127, 249, 271, 275

Svabhava, 328
Svadharma, 10, 14, 21, 40, 51, 87, 89, 257, 309, 311, 317, 324, 343, 368
Swami Chidanand Saraswatiji, 23
Swami Hariharji Maharaj, 10
Swami Prabhupada, 13
Swami Vivekananda, 292
Sraddhatriya-Vibhag Yoga, 293–306
Symbolic, 9

T

Tamas, 55, 148–149, 259–265, 297, 316, 349, 353, 368
Tamasic
- action, 318
- austerity, 302
- Buddhi, 320
- charity, 303
- knowledge, 317
- nature, 296, 302
- pleasure, 322
- Renunciation, 313

Tamo guna, 368
Tat, 303–304
Therapists, modern, 41
Three types of
- action, 317
- austerity – penance, 297, 302
- charity, 297, 302
- determination, 320
- doer, 318
- faith and the fate of men, 297
- food, 297, 299
- happiness, 321
- intellect, 319
- knowledge, 316
- sacrifices and penance, 297, 300

Three-fold names of god, 297, 300
Timeless Wisdom, 3, 89
Tranquility, 61, 124, 132, 192, 286

Transcend, 55, 144, 149, 258, 265, 267, 271, 279, 295, 334, 340, 342, 353
Transcendental
experience, 173, 368
Happiness, 131
Knowledge, 39, 53, 71, 84, 100, 102–104, 110, 116, 173, 177, 194, 242, 259, 279, 323, 331, 359, 362
Meditation, 58
Transitory, 46–47, 239
Treta Yuga, 371
Truthfulness, 192, 266–267
True Nature, 11, 16, 40, 97, 152–153, 186, 196, 268, 279, 311, 339, 342, 346, 367
True knowledge, 241–243, 245
Tyaga, 69, 120, 230, 234, 309–313, 346, 368
Tyagi, 313–314, 368
Twenty four elements, 244
Twenty six virtues, 285, 360

U

Undesirable progeny, 33
Ultimate
Bliss, 11, 40, 64, 132, 167, 309, 334
Conclusion, 309
Knowledge, 145, 245
Peace, 230, 233–234
Peace/Liberation, 110
Soul, 241
Truth, 10, 99, 358–360
Union of Matter and Spirit, 260
Union of Spirit, 250
Unlimited Universal Form, 207
Unlawful Exile, 7
Un-manifest, 49–50, 165, 369
Unreal, 47, 364, 369
Upanishad, 36, 65, 86, 105, 120, 139, 154, 167, 185, 203, 226, 238, 253, 267, 280, 292, 305, 335, 367, 369
Uttama-Purusa, 369
Uttarayana, 166

V

Vairagya, 110, 246, 326, 369
Vaisya, 96, 183, 324, 359, 369
Values, 33, 127, 340
Varnas, 33, 96
Vasana, 369
Vasudeva, 151, 201, 369
Vedas, 54–56, 58, 76, 100–101, 152, 162, 167, 178–179, 199, 201, 223, 225, 273, 277, 303, 364–366, 369–370
Vedanta, 277, 314, 369
Vibhuti, 369
Vikarma, 97, 370
Vijnana, 143, 154, 369
Veda Vyas, 7
Vedic
hymns, 215, 244, 273, 300, 350, 364
Mantra, 298, 365
rituals, 137, 178
scholars, 137
Vibhuties, 196, 201
Vibhuti Yoga, 187–204
Vidya, 369
Vijnana, 143, 145, 369
Vikarma, 97, 370
Viratrupa, 370
Vishad, 6–9, 12, 21–23, 30, 39, 41, 370
Vishad Yoga, see Arjuna Vishad Yoga
Visvarupa-Darsana Yoga, 205–226
Vivad, 11, 64, 366, 370
Vyasaji, 370
Vishnu, 156, 199, 247, 370

W

War, 7–9, 13, 16–17, 22, 24, 26, 28–29, 31–32, 34, 42, 52–53, 72, 104, 218, 340, 360, 367
Warrior
royal, 7
skillful, 8
Wealth, 31, 44, 100, 150, 199, 289–290, 321, 352
Wilkins, Charles, 13
Wisdom
experiential, 127
psychological, 3
spiritual, 3, 209
timeless, 3, 89

Work
- disagreeable, 314
- fruits of, 10, 54, 56–57, 114, 126, 234, 325
- selfless, 78

Worry, 64, 287, 330
Worship demi-gods, 151
Worship ghosts, 298
Worship God, 95, 149, 184, 193, 331, 346
Worshipping formless, 231
Worshipping idols, 229

Y

Yajna, 71–72, 74–75, 85, 91, 99, 101, 178–181, 199, 223, 285, 299–300, 303–304, 312, 331, 350, 361, 370
Yajna of Knowledge-Wisdom, 331
Yajur Vedas, 178
Yama, 200, 221, 345, 347, 370
Yoga of
- action, 111, 125, 250, 362
- integral Wisdom, 328, 359
- practice, 234
- Realization, 143
- renunciation, 181
- selfless action, 53
- Surrender, 153
- theoretical knowledge, 144
- understanding-integral wisdom, 194
- Wisdom, 39

Yoga-Maya, 94, 152, 189, 202, 370
Yoga Sastra, 3, 370
Yoga-Nidra, 370
Yogas of Bhagavad Gita, 4
Yogi, 63, 97, 99, 118, 125–129, 131–133, 136–138, 165–167, 276, 355, 371
Yogic Power, 190–191, 193–194, 223
Yudhisthira, King, 27
Yugas, 164, 362–363, 371